The Art of Voice Acting

The Art of Voice Acting

third edition

The Craft and Business
of Performing for Voice-over

James R. Alburger

ELSEVIER

AMSTERDAM • BOSTON • HEIDELBERG • LONDON
NEW YORK • OXFORD • PARIS • SAN DIEGO
SAN FRANCISCO • SINGAPORE • SYDNEY • TOKYO
Focal Press is an imprint of Elsevier

Focal
Press

Commissioning Editor: Catharine Steers
Editorial Assistant: David Bowers
Publishing Services Manager: George Morrison
Project Manager: Marilyn E. Rash
Marketing Manager: Christine Degon
Cover and Interior Design: James R. Alburger
Interior Printer: Maple-Vail Book Manufacturing
Cover Printer: Phoenix Color Corp.

Focal Press is an imprint of Elsevier
30 Corporate Drive, Suite 400, Burlington, MA 01803, USA
Linacre House, Jordan Hill, Oxford OX2 8DP, UK

∞ Recognizing the importance of preserving what has been written, Elsevier prints its books on acid-free paper whenever possible.

Library of Congress Cataloging-in-Publication Data
Alburger, James R., 1950-
The art of voice acting : the craft and business of performing for voice-over / James R. Alburger. — 3rd ed.
   p. cm.
Includes index.
ISBN-13: 978-0-240-80892-5 (alk. paper)
ISBN-10: 0-240-80892-4 (alk. paper)
1. Television announcing — Vocational guidance. 2. Radio announcing — Vocational guidance. 3. Voice-overs. 4. Television advertising — Vocational guidance. 5. Radio advertising — Vocational guidance. I. Title.
PN1992.8.A6A42 2007
791.4502'8023—dc   222006028865

British Library Cataloguing-in-Publication Data
A catalogue record for this book is available from the British Library.

For information on all Focal Press publications,
visit our website at *www.books.elsevier.com,*

06 07 08 09 10   10 9 8 7 6 5 4 3 2 1

Printed in the United States of America

This book is first dedicated to my many friends in the world of voice-over, both full-time professionals, teachers, and students. You are all very talented performers, producers, and performance coaches.

This book is also dedicated to the other half of The Voiceover Team, my coaching and business partner Penny Abshire. Your direction and coaching is truly inspirational.

Thank you all for maintaining high standards of performance and ethics for our craft of voice acting.

And for your willingness to share your wisdom and skills with those who are hungry to learn the craft and business of voice-over.

Welcome to the Workshop

This is where you pound it out,
Grind until you're smooth
Life will give you what you need
Situations are your tools
Can't you hear the hammers pounding?
Listen closely now
Take a look and you can feel
Walls goin' up and comin' down

Welcome!
Welcome to the Workshop!

I'm talking about
Love – Anger – Hate – Greed
It's all sandpaper – hammers – nails and grease

In all these things I'm sayin' to you
Situations, they are your tools
Any game you need to play
Mother Earth will lead the way

Welcome
Welcome to the Workshop!

Partial lyrics from the song "Welcome to the Workshop"
from the CD, *Spiritually Wet*
by Christina Fasano © 1999
Used by permission.
www.cdbaby.com/cd/funkywhitegirl
www.ceeceejames.com

Contents

THE BUSINESS OF VOICE-OVER: PART 2

Acting is about letting yourself feel like an idiot.
Most people feel like idiots most of the time . . .
But they don't get paid for it!
Michael J. Fox as Mikey — *Life With Mikey*
(Touchstone Pictures, 1993)

CD Index

Foreword

For all the wonderful silliness that James Alburger brings to his characters, he takes the discipline of voice-over seriously. After all, the title of his excellent book is the *Art of Voice **Acting**: The **Craft** and Business of **Performing** for Voice-Over*. Art? Acting? Craft? Performing? Although these are important words to James' teaching style, they aren't words that the book publishing world likes to hear. They like words such as *Fun*, and *For Dummies*, and *Profit*. When I was creating a title for a recorded set of teaching tapes on character voice, I came up with, *Creating Character Voices*. My publisher insisted on adding, . . . *for fun and profit*.

James is always happy to share his knowledge with others, which is evident in this book. He also takes the field of voice-over seriously, and he believes in being very thorough. Within the covers of this book, you can be assured that you'll get more information than you can possibly retain. Why is this book so comprehensive? Because James Alburger is motivated by generosity. I've taught James, I've taught alongside him, and I've occasionally taught his students for him. I can tell you that he is a breathing portrait of generosity. Generosity is a fundamental quality shared by all really stellar teachers — he has it in spades.

James is hugely successful (poke your head inside his incredible home studio and you'll be dazzled by the gold rays reflecting off his many Emmy Awards . . . ouch!), but he's also fearless in his truthfulness — he's not afraid to share his failures. "Don't do what I did," he tells his students, and he means it. We professional voice-over actors all fail many more times than we succeed. The real pros eat failure for breakfast. James uses his own failures as examples in teaching his students what to avoid. In this way, his students progress and learn by leaning on his wisdom. This is a true, fearless generosity.

Please enjoy this book, and may your journey in advancing your talents be blessed. If you read *The Art of Voice Acting* into the night as I did, don't worry about a reading lamp. The generous light of James Alburger might very well illuminate the pages!

Patrick Fraley
www.patfraley.com

Tell me, and I'll forget.
Show me, and I may remember.
Involve me, and I'll understand.
Chinese Proverb

People will forget what you
said, people will forget what you
did, but people will never forget
how you made them feel.
Maya Angelou, poet
From an interview by Oprah Winfrey

Foreword

Congratulations!

You've stopped dreaming about becoming a successful voice-over artist and finally decided to do something about it. Maybe you've picked up this book because people always comment on the sound of your voice. Maybe you feel a pull, a calling to express yourself behind the microphone. Or maybe you're just looking for a fun, creative way to make some extra cash in a home-based business, acting with your voice.

No matter the reason, there's never been a better time to get into voice-over. Why? Because the barrier to entry has never been lower. If you already have a computer, a few hundred dollars will buy everything you need to audition from home or from your laptop anywhere in the world. I've even tested MP3 recorders that are fine for auditions and are about the size of a pack of gum. Just add a mic, and voila! You've got a tiny little studio in your purse or pocket!.

The Internet and broadband communications have brought major changes to our business. There are more voices needed in more types of media than ever before. Advertising is in no danger of diminishing and web audio is spreading rapidly.

New York, Los Angeles, Toronto, and Chicago are still major production centers, but you don't need to live there to get in on the action. You can gain access to casting opportunities by signing up with one of the online casting services, or submit your demo to one of the many "virtual" talent agencies who, if they accept you, will allow you to email them MP3 auditions you record from home.

When I first started in voice-over, you had to sound like Richard Burton or God to get work. Now there are many more opportunities for everyone: women, people of color, and fluent speakers of Spanish and other languages.

But . . . and this is a huge *but*, you still need two vitally important things that neither money nor technology can buy. The first is acting "chops" and the second is business know-how. Fortunately, you've come to the right place, because James Alburger is the "go-to" guy to get these crucial skills.

I first met James when I invited him to be a guest in my Inner Circle teleconference series. These are classes where I invite voice-over experts to speak to my coaching group members. I'm very picky about who I invite and I wasn't disappointed. James gave a class on his ABC's of Voice

Acting and I was blown away by his focused and practical approach to character development for the voice actor. I took so many notes during that class that my hand got a cramp! James and I have since become friends and affiliate partners and I continue to be impressed by his integrity, know-how, and genuine respect for his students. In fact, he is one of the few teachers whose classes I whole-heartedly recommend.

You're in good hands. Read this book carefully and enjoy it. Beginners will find it to be a valuable blueprint for a successful voice-over career. Working pros will find, as I did, some important tweaks and key distinctions that will help take your career to the next level, whatever that happens to be.

Susan Berkley
www.greatvoice.com

~ ~ ~

Patrick Fraley is one of Hollywood's busiest and most creative voice actors. He has voiced thousands of commercials, created voices for more than 4,000 animated characters, and recorded dozens of audio books. He is also one of the best voice-over coaches you'll find anywhere. Patrick's teaching style is generous, precise, and to the point, bringing any student to a new level of performance.

~ ~ ~

Susan Berkley is a top professional voice-over artist. She is one of the voices who says "Thank You for Using AT&T," and is the telephone voice of Citibank. She is the author of *Speak to Influence: How to Unlock the Hidden Power of Your Voice* and president of The Great Voice Company, which provides well-known and highly respected training and home study programs for voice talent.

He who does not risk
will never drink champagne.
Russian Proverb

Preface

      Who would have dreamed that what began as a set of workshop notes in 1997 would evolve into the most popular book on the craft and business of voice-over?

      Certainly not I!

      I never imagined that this book would be as well received as it has been. And the thought of writing a third edition never crossed my mind! Yet, here it is — with more content than either of its two predecessors.

      This book is written as an effort of love. A love for a performing craft that is unique in the world of show business. A love for teaching something I know well. A love for wanting to help others starting out in this business to become the best they can be. And a love for living life to its fullest by doing something that I truly enjoy doing.

      The business of voice-over is one that is in a constant state of flux. Although the fundamental performing techniques may be consistent, there are trends and performing styles that are constantly changing. As a voice talent, we must keep up with the trends and maintain our performing skills in order to keep the work coming in. There's actually a lot more to it than that, and this book will go into the details of not only what you need to know to become a successful voice-over artist, but also how to do what is necessary to become successful.

      What you hold in your hands is a manual for working in the business of voice-over that will take you from the fundamentals of performing to the essentials of marketing . . . and everything in between.

      Most books on voice-over talk about interpretation — how to deliver phrases or analyze a script — and some actually teach "announcing." The authors of these books are generally very talented and skilled voice-over artists in their own right, and I recommend you purchase their books and learn from them. But I strongly recommend you read this book first.

      This book is different! This book was written with the intention of giving you a solid foundation in both the craft *and* business of voice-over. Within these pages you'll find dozens of tools and techniques that are essential for success in this area of show business. With this book, you will learn exactly how to use these tools, not just in voice-over, but in everything you do. Unlike some other books on voice-over, I don't focus on how "I" did it, or go into boring stories of my voice-over career — I show you how *you* can do it! Every story and every technique you'll read in this book is here for a reason — to teach you exactly how some aspect of this craft and business works, and how you can make it work for you.

The tools and techniques are just that — tools and techniques. Without understanding how to use them, they are little more than words on the page. But once you learn how to use a few of these tools, you'll discover that they can be used to improve relationships, get more customers, resolve problems, close more sales, make you a better actor, improve your public speaking skills, and so on, and so on. You won't use every performance tool all the time, and some of the tools may not work for you. That's fine. Find the tools and techniques that work for you, take them, and make them your own. Create your own unique style.

This is a book about how you can bring your personal life experience to every message you present and, by using a few simple voice and acting techniques, communicate more effectively than you can imagine. Christina Fasano, one of our workshop graduates — and an amazing singer/song writer, summed up the essence of this craft in her song "Welcome to the Workshop!" The wisdom of her lyrics is profound in its simplicity, yet the basic premise is one that is often missed by voice-over performers: "Life will give you what you need . . . Situations are your tools."

This is one of the hidden secrets for great voice acting: The situations of your life are your key. When you apply voice-acting techniques, you are communicating on an emotional level with your audience. Your message has power and impact that would not be there otherwise. Everything you experience in life holds an emotion that can be used to make you more effective as a voice actor. And even if you never intend to stand in front of a microphone in a recording studio, you can still use what you learn here to become a more effective communicator. You'll learn how in this book!

You may have noticed the conductor on the cover. If I hadn't brought it to your attention, you may have never given it a second thought. Doesn't it seem a bit odd that an orchestra conductor appears as the logo for a book on voice-over? Now why would that be?

I use the conductor and the phrase "orchestrate your message" because performing voice-over is much like performing music: There are only a limited number of musical notes, yet there are specific techniques and an almost unlimited variety of possibilities for performing those notes. The same is true with a voice-over script. Words and phrases can be delivered with infinite variety. A voice-over performance is, indeed, very similar to the way a conductor blends and balances the instruments of the orchestra. Your voice is your instrument, and this book will give you the tools to create a musical performance.

My goal with this book, as it is with my workshops, seminars, and other products, is to provide you with the best possible training in this craft that I possibly can. If I help you on your journey, please let me know.

Acknowledgments

This third edition of my book would not have been possible without generous support and help from so many people and companies who work in the world of voice-over every day. As you read through the pages of this edition, you will see names, website links, and other references to the many individuals who have supported my efforts with their contributions.

I am truly honored that two of the top voice-over coaches in the United States, Susan Berkley and Patrick Fraley, have written the Forwords for this book.

A very special thank you goes to my coaching, creative, and business partner, Penny Abshire. As a skilled coach and brilliant copy writer, you're the best! Thank you for your contributions and keen editing eye.

I would like to personally thank the following individuals for their inspiration, support, and for allowing me to share their thoughts and ideas with you.

Penny Abshire, Don Barrett, Susan Berkley, Jon Beaupré, Bob Bergen, Marc Cashman, Joyce Castellanos, Joe Cipriano, Tom Clark (UK), Terri Douglas, Peter Drew, Pat Fraley, Kathy Garver, Hillary Huber, Bob Jump, "Shotgun" Tom Kelly, Stefan Kinell, Don LaFontaine, MJ Lallo, Lani Minella, Michael Minetree, Debbie Munro, CW Powers, Rodney Saulsberry, Connie Terwilliger, Jennifer Vaughn, Joni Wilson, Wally Wingert, and Bettye Pierce Zoller.

The following companies have graciously allowed me to include scripts or other materials so that you might benefit from their work:

Penny Abshire, The Commercial Clinic, DPAnimations (Dustin Parr), Peter Drew, Christina Fasano (Cee Cee James), GlaxoSmithKlein, JumpWorldwide.com, MJ Productions, Marshall Marketing & Communications, Inc., Minewurx Studios, No Fish Today Restaurant, Science Media, Sylver Enterprises (Marshal Sylver), TeleMinder, Jennifer Vaughn Voice Imaging, Roy Williams Wizard of Ads, Joni Wilson Voice (Joni Wilson), and 42nd Street Productions (Connie Terwilliger).

What would you attempt
if you knew you could not fail?
Dr. Robert Schuller

A Wealth of Additional Voice Acting Resources

My goal in writing this book, and with my workshops and coaching, is to provide the best and most comprehensive training and resources available anywhere for this fascinating area of the entertainment and communication industries. In addition, I've created **www.voiceacting.com** as a place where those interested in the craft and business of voice-over can learn more, find resources in their local area, purchase products, and learn about training to develop their skills.

As a reader of this book, you'll have access to a special web page at **www.voiceacting.com/aovaextras** with lots of additional information and special offers not available anywhere else. I've also created a Yahoo Group for our workshop graduates to stay in touch and help each other through their growth in this business. The group is free and open for anyone to join. You don't have to be a graduate of our workshop — all you need is an interest in the craft and business of voice-over. You can join at **www.groups.yahoo.com/group/aovagraduates**.

My personal philosophy is that a student will have many teachers, and each teacher will give the student something not obtainable from any other teacher. With that in mind, the Resources area of **www.voiceacting.com** includes thousands of references and links, including coaches, on-line listing services, articles from the *Art of Voice Acting* newsletter (subscribe for free at **www.voiceacting.com**) and much, much more.

I invite you to visit our website. It's very large, so give yourself some time to browse around, read the articles, and learn about what it takes to be part of this business. And don't forget to visit the extras page. Should you choose to attend one of our workshops, I look forward to meeting you in person.

Voice acting is the performing craft
of creating believable characters,
in interesting situations, telling compelling stories,
using only the spoken word.

Mastering and applying the skills of voice acting
will take your personal and professional
communication to an entirely new
level of effectiveness.

James R. Alburger
www.jamesalburger.com

Introduction

"You should be doing commercials!"

"You've got a great voice!"

"You should be doing cartoons!"

If anyone has ever said any of these things to you — and you have, even for an instant, considered his or her suggestions — this may be just the book you need! If you simply enjoy making up funny character voices or sounds, or enjoy telling stories and jokes, this book will show you how to do it better and more effectively. If you need to make presentations as part of your job, this book will definitely give you a new insight into reaching your audience. If you are involved in any line of work for which you need to communicate any sort of message verbally to one or more individuals, this book will help you make your presentation more powerful and more memorable.

This book is about acting and performing, but it's about a kind of acting that is not on a stage in front of thousands of people. In fact, with this kind of acting you rarely, if ever, see your audience or receive any applause. This is a kind of acting in which you will create illusions and believable images in the mind of the audience — a listening audience who might never see you, but who may remember your performance for many years.

This is a book about acting and performing for voice-over. Even though the focus here is on developing your talent for working in the world of voice-over, the skills and techniques you will learn can be applied to any situation in which you want to reach and motivate an audience on an emotional level.

Voice-over!

The term can be inspiring or intimidating. It can conjure up visions of a world of celebrity and big money. True, that can happen, but as you will learn in the pages that follow, the business of voice-over is just that — a business. It is a business that can be lots of fun and it can be a business that is, at times, very challenging work. And it can be both at the same time!

Voice-over is also an art! It is a highly specialized craft with skills that must be developed. The voice-over performer is an actor who uses his or her voice to create a believable character. The business of voice-over might, more accurately, be called the business of *voice acting*. It is most definitely a part of show business.

I'll be perfectly honest with you right from the beginning. Working as a voice actor is not for everyone. It requires an investment of time, energy, persistence, and money to get started. And, perhaps, just a bit of luck. As the saying goes in show business: An overnight success is the result of 20 years of study and paying dues.

However — if you love to play, have the desire to learn some acting skills, can speak clearly, read well, don't mind the occasional odd working hours, don't take things too seriously, have a good attitude, can motivate yourself to be in the right place at the right time, and are willing to do what is necessary to develop your skills and build your business — this type of work may be just right for you. In addition, as I mentioned earlier, the skills and techniques of voice acting can be applied to any situation in which you want your audience to connect emotionally with the message you are delivering. These skills are not limited to radio and TV commercials.

This book shows you the steps to take to learn the performing skills necessary to be successful as a voice talent. It also has the information you need to get your demo produced and into the hands of those who will hire you. Study these pages and you will get a solid foundation that you can build on to achieve lasting success in the business of voice-over.

You *don't* have to be in Los Angeles, New York, or Chicago to find voice-over work. Work is available everywhere. You *do* need to have the right attitude, the right skills, and a high-quality and professional presentation of your talents, or the casting people won't even give you a second look (or listen). If you master the techniques explained in this book, you will be able to present yourself like a pro — even if you have never done anything like this before.

Notice that I refer to the voice-over artist as voice talent, voice-over performer, or voice actor — never as "announcer." This is because that's exactly what you are — a performer (or actor) telling a story to communicate a message to an audience on an emotional level.

"Voice-over" is the standard phrase used to refer to all areas of performing in which the actor is not seen. This term is, however, somewhat misrepresentative of what the work actually entails. It tends to place the focus on the voice, when the real emphasis needs to be on the performance. *Announcers* read and often focus their energy on the sound of their voice, striving to achieve a certain "magical" resonance. Effective voice acting shifts the focus from the voice to the emotional content of the message. This requires knowledge, skill, and a love of performing. Focusing on your performance, instead of on the sound of your voice, helps you become more conversational, more real and more believable. In other words, this type of work is not about your voice . . . it's about what you can *do* with your voice.

This is why acting is such an important aspect of good voice-over work. Talking *to* your audience conversationally is much better than talking *at* them as an uninterested, detached speaker. The best communication closes the gap between the audience and the performer and frames the performance with a mood that the audience can connect with emotionally. Many people have "great pipes" or wonderfully resonant voices. But it takes much more than a good voice to be an effective communicator or voice actor. In fact, a good voice isn't even necessary — most people have a voice that is perfectly suitable for voice acting. What is necessary are the knowledge and skill to use your voice dramatically and effectively as part of a voice-over performance.

As with most businesses today, the business of voice-over is constantly evolving. The applications for voice-over work are growing every day and changing trends may require new or modified performing techniques. This revised, third edition has been expanded to include more techniques, new scripts, more "tricks of the trade," and lots of Internet resources. Even more information and resources can be found at **www.voiceacting.com** and **www.voiceacting.com/aovaextras**.

I began my adventure through the world of sound and voice acting when I taught myself to edit music at the age of 12. I worked for several radio stations creating dozens of commercials as engineer, performer, writer, and director. I have also performed professionally for more than four decades as a stage and close-up magician. I put my ideas about performing magic to music in my first book, *Get Your Act Together — Producing an Effective Magic Act to Music*, which became a standard in the magic community. However, it was when I worked as a recording engineer in Hollywood that I began to realize what voice acting was all about.

In the nearly four decades since then, I have directed some of the top voice talent in the country, I have been honored as a recipient of eleven Emmy Awards[1] for sound design, and my production company, The Commercial Clinic (**www.commercialclinic.com**), has received numerous awards for creative commercial production. I teach voice-acting workshops and seminars; speak professionally on how to improve performing skills and the effective use of radio advertising; and operate my own business as a voice actor, sound designer, and performance coach.

As you read the pages that follow, I promise to be straightforward and honest with you. You will find techniques and tricks of the trade that you cannot find anywhere else. For those of you considering a move into the business of voice-over, you will learn what it takes to be successful. If you simply want to learn new ways to use your voice to communicate effectively, you will find a wealth of information within these pages.

I wish you much success — and please let me know when you land your first national commercial, or land that big contract as a result of using the techniques in this book.

---

[1] National Academy of Television Arts and Sciences, Southwestern Regional Emmy awarded for outstanding sound design for television promos and programs.

The Art of Voice Acting

**James R. Alburger
and Penny Abshire**

For your continued training in the craft and business of voice-over, we invite you to consider The Art of Voice Acting workshops, seminars, and personalized coaching. For more information, please visit **www.voiceacting.com**.

A special web page has been created just for readers of this book at **www.voiceacting.com/aovaextras**. This website contains bonus material that couldn't be included here. It's valuable information you can use immediately, and that you won't find anywhere else — not even on the main website at **www.voiceacting.com**.

- Additional information on the craft and business of voice-over
- More articles, tips, and "tricks-of-the-trade" from top voice-over professionals
- More exercises and scripts
- More audio
- Demos from professional voice talent
- Links to resources
- Special discount offers on workshops and selected products

1

What Is Voice Acting?

We live in an age of information and communication. We are bombarded with messages of all types 24 hours a day. From 30-second commercials to hour-long infomercials; from documentary films, to video games; from telemarketing sales messages to corporate presentations; and thousands of others. Much of our time is spent assimilating and choosing to act or not act on the information we receive.

It is well known among marketing and communications specialists that there are only two ways to communicate to an audience: intellectually and emotionally. Of these, the most effective way to reach an audience is to connect on an emotional, often unconscious level. This frequently involves drawing the listener (or viewer) into a story or creating a dramatic or emotional scene that the listener can relate to. In short, effective voice-over performing is storytelling and requires acting skills. The voice-over (VO) performer, in fact, can be more accurately referred to as a voice actor.

The Many Roles of the Voice Actor

Voice actors play a very important role in sales, marketing, and delivery of information. It is the voice actor's job to play a role that has been written into the script. To effectively play the role and thus sell the message, the performer must, among other things, be able to quickly determine how to best communicate the message using nothing more than the spoken word. Chapters 5 through 10 cover these subjects in detail. For the moment, you only need to know that this type of work requires more from you than simply reading words off a page.

The purpose of voice acting is to get "off the page" with your message. Make it real — connect with your audience emotionally — and make the message memorable in the mind of the listener.

Types of Voice-Over Work

When most people think of voice-over, they think of radio and TV commercials. These are only a small part of the business of voice-over. There is actually much more to it.

Let's begin with a simplified definition of voice-over. *Voice-over* can be defined as *any recording or performance of one or more unseen voices for the purpose of communicating a message.* The voice-over is the spoken part of a commercial, program, or other announcement that you hear, but do not see the person speaking. It could be anything from a phone message to a television commercial, sales presentation, instructional video, movie trailer, feature film, or documentary narration. It may be nothing more than a single voice heard on the radio or over a public address system. The production may include music, sound effects, video, animation, or multiple voices. In most cases, the message is selling something, providing information, or asking the listener to take some sort of action.

You hear voice-over messages many times every day, and you are probably not even aware of it. Here are just some of the many types of voice-over work that require talented performers, like you.

RADIO — On-air, Commercials, Promo

There are three basic categories of radio voice-over work:

- **The radio DJ** — This is a specialized job that requires a unique set of skills. Most radio DJs are not considered to be voice actors.
- **Promo & Imaging** — Most radio promos are produced in-house, using station staff. Outside talent will be used for station imaging.
- **Commercials** — Most commercials are produced outside the station by advertising agencies. However, many radio stations do produce local commercials for their clients, usually with station staff.

TELEVISION — On-air, News, Commercial, Promo, Programs

Television stations use voice talent in three ways:

- **Promotions Department** — Handles the station's on-air promotion, including VOCs (voice over credits), promos, and marketing videos. Voice talent may be on staff, on contract, or booked through an agent.
- **Production Department** — This department is responsible for production of commercials, programs, sales presentations and other productions. Voice talent may be on staff or hired per project.
- **News and Sales Departments** — News reporters handle their own voice-over for news stories. Sales will usually use on-staff VO talent or work through the Production Department.

Most TV stations have an established pool of voice-over talent on staff or readily available. Staff announcers may come to the station to record on a daily basis, or the copy may be emailed or faxed to the talent a few days before it is needed. The voice actor records it in their home studio and delivers the track to the station for production, or it may be recorded at a local recording studio. Some TV stations are equipped with *ISDN* telephone technology that allows for a live, high-quality recording of a voice-over performer in another city, or across the country.

CORPORATE/INDUSTRIAL — Training, Web-learning, Marketing

There are literally thousands of locally produced audio and video presentations recorded each year for the business community. Here are just a few examples of corporate and/or industrial voice-over work:

- **Telephony** — Messages-on-hold are what you hear while on hold. Also includes voice prompts (IVR) and outgoing messages.
- **In-store Offers** — Usually these are part of the background music program played over a store's speaker system while you shop.
- **Sales and Marketing Presentations** — Video presentations that are designed to attract clients and promote vendors or products. Talent could be either on-camera or voice-over. You will often find these videos as ongoing product demos in department stores or shopping mall kiosks.
- **Convention and/or Trade Show Presentations** — These are similar to sales and marketing presentations, but usually target potential buyers at a convention or trade show. Usually a video presentation.
- **Training and Instructional** — As the name implies, these projects are designed to train personnel on anything from company policies and procedures, to the proper use of equipment. Most corporate presentations are rarely seen by the general public.
- **Web-learning** — The Internet has opened up an entirely new world of voice-over opportunities for online training and education.

ANIMATION — Cartoons, Anime, Video Games

This is a very specialized area of voice-over work. It's definitely not for everyone, and it can be difficult to break into. Good animation voice actors usually can do a wide range of character voices and have years of acting experience. Most animation voice-over work is done in Los Angeles, while Anime and Video Game work is done in many cities.

CD-ROM AND MULTIMEDIA — Games, Training, Marketing

This market for voice-over talent developed as a result of the explosion of computer-based CD-ROM games and instructional software. Some software manufacturers produce audio tracks for these products entirely in-house, while others are produced by outside production companies.

FILM — Looping, ADR, Narration

Looping and ADR (Automated Dialog Replacement) are specialized areas of voice-over work that require a high level of acting ability and a often a talent for mimicking other voices. Film narration is common for documentaries, instructional, and marketing programs.

AUDIO BOOKS — Entertainment

Recordings of books and magazines, fall into two basic categories: commercial audio books for sale and recorded books or magazines for the visually impaired. Audio books of best-selling novels are often read by a celebrity to make the recording more marketable. However, there is a growing market for audio book projects that use unknown voice talent. Recorded books and magazines for the visually impaired may be produced locally by any number of service organizations or radio stations. The pay is usually minimal or nonexistent (you volunteer).

Most reading services prefer their "readers" to deliver their copy in a somewhat flat tone. There may be several people reading chapters from a book over a period of days. To maintain a degree of continuity in the "reading," the readers are generally asked to avoid putting any emotional spin or dramatic characterization into their reading. This type of work is excellent for improving reading skills and acquiring the stamina to speak for long periods of time, but it limits your opportunities to develop characterization and emotional or dramatic delivery skills. Check your local white pages under Blind Aids and Services or contact your local PBS radio station and ask about any reading services they might provide.

INTERNET STREAMING AUDIO — RSS, MP3, Web Learning

The introduction of the iPod® by Apple Computer created opportunities for streaming audio Podcasts on the Internet. Basically, a Podcast is an RSS (Really Simple Syndication) streaming audio program that is designed to synchronize with subscriber's computers. It is commonly used to provide news feeds and other audio content that is automatically downloaded to a computer for listening at a convenient time. Many Podcasts are also available online in the form of downloadable MP3 files.

Podcasting gives anyone with the ability to record audio on their computer an opportunity to record their opinions and original creations or performances for the world to hear. Many Podcast programs are recorded by people who are not trained in the craft and performance of voice-over.

Web learning, or Internet-based, online training, is becoming very popular with many business that need to efficiently train a large number of people.

THE ESSENTIALS

Regardless of the type of voice-over work you do, there are several basic requirements:

- **A decent speaking voice:** The days "Golden Pipes" are over. Voice acting is <u>not</u> about your voice — it's about what you can <u>do</u> with your voice.
- **Excellent reading skills:** All voiceover work requires excellent reading skills. There is no memorization in voiceover work.
- **An ability to act and take direction:** You must be able to change your delivery and interpretation at the whim of the director.
- **Passion:** You must be willing to spend the time, energy, and money necessary to develop your acting and business skills, and market and promote your talent.

The Difference between "Voice-over" and "Voice Acting"

If you accept the definition of voice-over as being anything in which you hear the voice but don't see the performer, then, in the strictest sense, anyone who can speak can do voice-over. But that doesn't mean that anyone who can speak has the ability or skill to work professionally as a voice talent. If you've ever recorded an outgoing message on your answering machine, you've done a form of "voice-over." But just because you can record your voice doesn't mean you have the talent or ability to deliver someone else's sales message or create a believable performance. Every month I receive demos from "voice-over artists" who have recently completed a class and rushed into the production of a demo in an attempt to break into the business. Many of these individuals have some talent, but unfortunately, many more have not polished their skills or honed their craft to a point where they can effectively compete as voice talent. Occasionally, I'll receive a demo that demonstrates skill, versatility, variety, and a level of professionalism that tells me the individual has made the transition from "doing voice-over" to performing as a "voice actor."

"So," I hear you ask, "what's the difference?"

There are several factors that differentiate simple voice-over and professional voice acting. Among them are: competent training, acting ability, interpretive skill, dedication, business acumen, and computer skills.

But the real difference can be summed up in a single word:

Believability

You can listen to the radio or watch TV any hour of any day and hear commercials that literally make you cringe. If you analyze the performance, most of these "bad" commercials have several things in common: they sound flat and lifeless, with every sentence sounding the same; they sound like the script is being read; the performers sound like they are shouting with no clear focus as to who they are speaking to; the performer is talking "at" and not "to" the listener, or they are trying to talk to everyone listening at the same time; there is absolutely nothing compelling about the delivery or the message. In short, the performance lacks "believability."

Here's a simple way to determine if it's "voice-over" or "voice acting." A "voice-over" performance has <u>one</u> or more of the following:

- Often "read-y" or "Announcer-y" (sounds like reading the script.)
- Content is information-heavy, primarily intellectual, often with many featured items, and with little or no emotional content.
- The goal of the message is to "sell" the listener on something, and this attitude of "selling" comes through in the performance.
- The overall effect of the message is to create "listener tune-out."
- Delivery of the message may, in some way, actually damage or reduce credibility of the advertiser.

A "voice acting" performance has ALL of the following characteristics:

- The performer creates a believable and real character in conversation with the listener.
- The message content is primarily emotional, with a single clearly defined focus.
- The goal of the message is to "tell a story" that the listener can relate to on an emotional level — often coming from a place of helping the listener in some way, rather than "selling."
- The overall effect of the message is one of keeping the listener's attention and creating a memorable moment.

Using the preceding definition, there is certainly a place for "voice-over," and if done properly it can be quite effective. But good "voice-over" is done within the context of a larger performance or is designed for a very specific purpose, and presented by a very specific character. The best "voice-over" is performed from a foundation of "voice acting."

Voice acting is about creating real and believable characters in real and believable situations that listeners can relate to and be motivated by. To do this, the performer must be able to reach the audience on an emotional level.

Voice acting is about creating compelling characters
in interesting situations telling interesting stories

We communicate on an emotional level every day in a completely natural manner. But when we work from a script, we suddenly flounder: the words are not ours and the life behind those words is not ours. It's not as easy as it may appear to get "off the page" and speak from a written script in a manner that is natural, real, and conversational. In order for us to speak those words from the point of view of a real and believable character, we must momentarily forget who we are and become that character. That's why it is important to master basic acting techniques.

Learning basic "voice-over" techniques for reading and interpreting a script is a good start. But don't stop there. If this is what you love to do, keep studying: take acting and improvisation classes; study commercials and analyze what the professionals are doing to create character and make their scripted words sound real; learn how to take direction; read every book on this craft you can get your hands on; visit talent websites and listen to the demos to learn what works and what doesn't; watch television programs about acting and theater, and finally . . . never stop learning.

Even if you are an experienced actor, you need to know that the disciplines of "voice acting" are different from stage, film, or TV. In all other forms of acting, your lines are committed to memory and you have time to understand and develop your character. In voice acting, you have only a few minutes to create a believable character, find the voice, and perfect your delivery as you read from a script.

Voice acting is creative, fun and potentially lucrative — if you know what you are doing! In some circles, the term "voice acting" is used to refer to the niche area of voice-over work for anime. However, if you look closely at what anime voice actors are doing, you will discover that they are creating (or in some cases attempting to create) what will ideally be perceived as real and believable characters. And that is exactly what we need to be doing as we voice a radio commercial or corporate narration.

To be a successful voice actor, learn how to be natural, confident, real, and most of . . . believable.

Breaking into the Business of Voice-over

For the balance of this book, the terms "voice-over" and "voice acting" will be used interchangeably." This book is about the acting craft behind voice-over work, so although "voice acting" is a more accurate term, I'll often resort to the term most commonly used to refer to this kind of work:

"voice-over." I'll refer to the performer as either a voice actor, voice-over performer, or voice talent.

Most people think voice-over work is easy. You have probably even said to yourself after listening to a commercial, "I can do that!" For some people, it is easy. For most, though, voice-over work — just like theatrical acting — is an ongoing learning process. In our Art of Voice Acting Workshops, it is not uncommon for someone, after only the first or second class, to say "Oh, my! I had no idea there was this much to voice-over! This really isn't about just reading a script!"

Even experienced professionals will tell you that voice-over work can be potentially more difficult than on-camera or on-stage work. After all, the advantages of props, scenery, and lighting are not available to the voice actor. The drama, comedy, or emotions of a message must be communicated solely through the spoken word. This often requires a tremendous amount of focus and concentration, plus an ability to make quick changes in mid-stream. Prior acting experience is an advantage, but these are skills you can pick up as you go, so don't let a lack of experience stop you. As long as you can use your imagination, you can do voice-over.

One of the greatest misconceptions is that you need a certain type of voice to do voice-over. You do not need a "good" voice, or "announcer" voice. You do need a voice that is easily understood. If your voice has a unique quality or sound, you can use that to your advantage, especially for animation work. But a unique voice quality can also become a limitation if that is the only thing you do. You may find you are better suited to one particular type of voice-over work — corporate/industrial, for example. If that's the case, you can focus on marketing yourself for that type of work. Still, you should consider other types of voice work when the call comes.

Variety is an important aspect of voice-over performing. By variety I mean being able to use your voice to convey a wide range of attitudes, personality, delivery, and emotions (that's why acting is so important). These are the characteristics of your voice presentation that will sell the message. And selling a message is what voice-over is all about.

Many people think that because they can do lots of impersonations or make up crazy character voices, they can do voice-over work. Vocal versatility is certainly valuable; however, success in the world of voice-over also takes focus, discipline, and an ability to act.

So, just how do you learn voice-over performing skills, break in, and get yourself known as a voice actor? The simple answer is: Get your voice recorded and get yourself known. The more complex answer is: Learn everything you can about acting, communication, and marketing. In this business, an old adage, "It's not what you know, but who you know," is very true. Getting voice-over work is largely a numbers game — a game of networking and making yourself known in the right circles. To be successful you cannot be shy. Let every person you meet know what you do! But you must also possess the skills that qualify you as a professional, and that is what this book is really about!

2

The Best-Kept Secret

Let's face it — if everyone were equally good at every job, there would be no need for résumés or auditions. Fortunately, in this world, every person has uniquely different talents, abilities, and levels of skill. It is this variety that makes the voice-over business a potentially profitable career for anyone willing to invest the time and effort.

For years, voice-over was one of the best-kept secrets around. The job can be loads of fun and very profitable, but it is not an easy business to break into. Today, there are roughly 5 times as many people who claim to be voice-over talent as there are actors trying to break into TV and movies. Add to that the major film stars who have discovered that voice-over work is more fun than spending many hours in makeup each day. The simple truth is that competition is tough, and it is easy to become frustrated when just beginning.

Voice-over work is part of "Show Business." As such it has all the potential excitement, celebrity status, and opportunities as the other areas of Show Business, as well as the long periods of waiting, frustrations in getting "booked," and problems dealing with agents and producers.

The Realities of Voice Acting

You have probably heard most of the pros of voice-over work: big money, short hours, celebrity status (fame and fortune without anyone actually knowing who you are), and more. For some voice-over performers, these things are true but it takes a long time, and constantly being in the right place, to get there. In other words, they had to work at it. Most overnight successes are the result of many years of hard work, constant study, dedication to the craft, and a mastery of business skills. One voice-over coach I know suggests that it takes 15 years to become successful in voice-over. I disagree with that! Everyone defines "success" differently.

Sure, if you define success as being in high demand and making the "big bucks," it might take 15 years or longer to get there. But if you are doing voice-over because you really love it, and you wonder why you're not paying them to let you get in front of the mic, then success can be as soon as next week.

Like most of the performing arts, voice acting is a hurry-up-and-wait kind of business. By that I mean you will spend a lot of time waiting: waiting at auditions, waiting for a callback, waiting in the lobby of a recording studio, waiting for the email with your script, and waiting to get paid. Once a voice-over recording session begins, things tend to happen very fast. But you may still find yourself waiting in the studio as the producer works on copy changes, or while the engineer deals with a technical problem.

If you are recording in your home studio, which is rapidly becoming a standard practice for voice-over work, you will be expected to deliver studio-quality recordings. You'll also be expected to know how to do some limited production and editing — even though you are not a recording engineer. That means you need to be computer-literate and you'll need to invest in the training, equipment, software, and acoustic improvements necessary to build a functional recording facility in your home.

From a performance standpoint, producers assume that you know what you are doing and expect you to deliver your lines professionally. You are expected to be able to deliver a masterful interpretation of a script after only a short read-through — usually within the first two or three takes. Direction (coaching) from the producer or director often comes very fast, so you must listen and pay attention. Sometimes, the producer or director completely changes the concept or makes major copy changes in the middle of an audition or session — and you need to be able to adapt quickly. If you're recording in your home studio, the session may be a director-less and producer-less session, meaning you are on your own! You need to develop excellent interpretive skills and be a versatile performer with the ability to provide what your client is asking for, even when you're not certain exactly what that is.

Your job as a voice-over performer is to perform to the best of your abilities. When you are hired, either from your demo or after an audition, your voice has been chosen over many others as the one most desirable for the job. Unless there is a serious technical problem that requires your being called back, or revisions that are made after the session has ended, you will not get a second chance after leaving the studio.

Full-Time or Part-Time

If you think voice-over work is for you, you may have some decisions to make. Not right this minute, but soon. Do you want to do voice-over work as a full-time career, or as a part-time avocation? What niche area of voice-over do you want to focus on? Should you move to a different city in search of work in your niche area? The choices may not be easy!

Doing voice-over work on a full-time basis is unlike just about any other job you can imagine. You must be available on a moment's notice when you are called for an audition. In addition, you must constantly market yourself, even if you have an agent.

Full-time voice-over work may also mean joining a union, and even moving to a larger city — if that's where your destiny leads you. Los Angeles, Chicago, New York, and many major cities are strong union towns for voice-over work, and you must be in the union to get well-paying jobs in these cities. Although the possibility for nonunion work does exist in larger cities, it may require some additional effort to find it.

In smaller cities, the union for voice-over, AFTRA (the American Federation of Television and Radio Artists), is not as powerful, and there is a much greater opportunity for freelance voice-over work than in bigger cities. You'll find more about unions in Chapter 18.

OK — you have decided eating is still a pleasurable pastime, and you would rather not quit your day job just yet. So, how about doing voice-over work on a part-time basis? Good question!

Doing voice-over work part-time is quite possible, although you probably won't be doing the same kind of work as you would if you devoted more time to it. You will most likely do some corporate/industrial work, telephone messages, and smaller projects for clients who have a minimal or nonexistent budget. Some of your work may be voluntary, barter, or you will do it just because you want the experience. The pay for nonunion freelance work is usually not terrific — but freelance work is a very good way of getting experience doing voice-over. You can gradually build up a client list and get copies of your work that you can use later on when, or if, you decide to go full-time.

The biggest problem with doing voice-over work part-time is that you may find it difficult to deal with last-minute auditions or session calls. If you have a regular full-time job, you usually will need to arrange your voice-over work around it, unless you have a very understanding employer. With the advent of Internet audition services and advanced computer technology, it has become very convenient to record auditions in a home studio and submit them as MP3 files via the Internet. Part-time voice-over work can be an ideal opportunity for the homemaker or self-employed individual with a flexible schedule.

Doing voice-over work can be very satisfying, even if you only do an occasional session. Yet, the day may come when you decide to go for the "big money" in LA, Chicago, New York. In the meantime, don't be in a hurry. Make the best of every opportunity that comes along and create your own opportunities whenever possible. Networking — telling people you meet what you do — is extremely important. You never know when you might be in just the right place to land that important national spot that changes your entire life!

7 Things You Must Know About Voice-over Work

Of all the areas of show business, voice-over is unique. Although the basic acting and performing techniques may be the same, the disciplines are radically different from other types of acting. Here's a list of some essential things you need to know about voice-over before you take the leap:

1. You can't learn how to perform for voice-over on your own. You need the guidance of a qualified coach who knows the business.

2. You can't learn how to perform for voice-over by reading a book. Any VO book (yes, even this one!) is only as good as the information it contains. The purpose of a book is to provide you with the information you need so you can more effectively learn the skills. You need talent, dedication, passion, and training that goes beyond the information contained in a book.

3. You can't learn how to perform for voice-over from a tele-class. A tele-class will give you lots of information, but by its very nature, will be limited in the effectiveness of any performance coaching. You may get the general idea of how to use a technique from a tele-class, but it won't qualify you to compete in this business. Personal coaching and experience are your best training.

4. You can't learn this craft from a single workshop. Some workshops are excellent — and some are, well . . . not. Any workshop (yes, even ours!) will only be good enough to get you started on the path. You need to take the next steps with additional training. Professional film, stage, and television actors are constantly taking classes between projects. Continued training is essential in the voice-over business.

5. If you produce your demo immediately following a workshop, you will be wasting your money. Your demo must be great — it cannot be merely "good." Even more than that, your performance must be of a caliber comparable to the best voice talent out there. Do not even think about spending money on producing your demo until you <u>know</u> you are ready. See Chapter 16, Your Voice-over Demo, to learn more about how to prepare for your demo.

6. Be wary of workshops and coaches who promise success and a substantial income from taking their course. No one can promise you success, and no one can promise your demo will be heard.

7. If a demo is included as part of a course, find a different course. No one is ready for a demo after 8, 10, or even 20 weeks of training, unless they already have a substantial acting and performing background.

Throughout this book, I'll be encouraging you to take classes, visit web sites, and learn from other authors and coaches. Many people consider this book "The Bible of Voice-over," but you will learn something from each book you read and every class you attend.

3

Where to Start:
Voice-over Basics

The Voice-over Performer as Actor and Salesperson

When you stand in front of a microphone as voice talent, your job is to effectively communicate the message contained in the words written on the paper in front of you. You are a storyteller. You are an actor! The words, by themselves, are nothing but ink on a page. As a voice actor, your job is to interpret the words in such a way as to effectively tell the story, bring the character to life, and meet the perceived needs of the producer or director. I use the words "perceived needs" because many producers or writers only have an idea in their head. The producer may think he knows what he wants, when, in reality, he hasn't got a clue as to the best way to deliver the message. You may find yourself in the enviable position of solving many of your producer's problems simply by performing the copy in a way that you feel effectively communicates the message. In other words, your acting abilities are the vital link between the writer and the audience.

YOUR ROLE AS A VOICE ACTOR

You are the actor playing the role of the character written in the script. Unlike stage performers, who may have several days, or weeks, to define and develop their characters, you may have only a few minutes. You must use your best acting skills to deliver your best interpretation of the copy— and you must do it quickly. Your job is to breathe life into the script, making the thoughts of the writer become real. You need to be able to quickly grasp the important elements of the script, figure out who you are talking to, understand your character, find the key elements of the copy, and choose what you believe to be the most effective delivery for your lines.

Every script is written for a purpose and you must be able to find and give meaning to that purpose, regardless of how or where the voice track will be recorded. In most cases, especially in studio sessions, the producer or director will be coaching you into the read that gets you as close as possible to his or her vision. However, with the increasing prevalence of high quality home studios, more and more voice talent are being asked to provide self-directed, unsupervised, sessions.

One mistake made by many beginning voice-over performers is that they get nervous when they approach the microphone. They are focused on their voice, not their performance. They fidget, stand stiff as a board, cross their arms, or put their hands behind their backs or in their pockets. It is impossible to perform effectively under those conditions.

What is needed is to get into the flow of the copy, breathe properly, relax, have fun, and let the performance take you where it needs to go. Discover your character and let that character come into you so that you can "become the character."

UNDERSTAND YOUR AUDIENCE

Every message (script) has an intended (or target) audience. Once you understand who the audience is and your role in the copy, you will be on your way to knowing how to perform the copy for the most effective delivery. Figure out who you are talking to. Narrow it down to a single individual and relate to that person on an emotional level. This is the first step to creating an effective performance and a believable character.

Chapter 10, The Character in the Copy, goes into greater detail about analyzing the various kinds of copy and creating characters.

WHAT TO LOOK FOR IN A SCRIPT — CD/8

Now that you know some of the basics for creating an effective voice-over delivery, here's a script for you to work with. This is copy for a single voice :20 TV promo. Read it through once to get a feel for the copy. You'll instinctively make some choices as to how you will deliver the copy. Deliver the script using the choices you make. Then listen to track 8 on the CD.

It happens everyday . . . in hotels, restaurants and other public buildings . . . without warning. It's responsible for 20,000 fatalities – and its the 2nd leading cause of death and disability. Slip and fall accidents – learn how to protect your rights if it happens to you. Tonight at 11 on Eye Witness News.

Do you think your delivery achieved the objective of communicating the message effectively? An effective delivery is often the result of looking beyond the words of a script to dig out the details and subtlety hidden in the message. Now, read it a second and third time, looking for the following points. Finally, read it out loud for time, to see how close you can come to 15 seconds.

- Who is the audience this copy is trying to reach?
- How can you create interest within the first few words?
- How can you create an emotional response to keep the audience listening?
- What is the single primary message in the copy?
- What are the supporting statements for the primary message?
- What is your role (your character) in the story?
- Why is your character telling this story?
- What does your character want or need from telling this story?
- What is the primary emotion, if any?
- What sort of delivery do you think would be the most effective to create the strongest memory of the message — strong, hard-sell, happy, smiling, mellow, soft-sell, fast, slow?
- What is your attitude as the character in this spot — serious, comfortable, happy, sad, and so on?
- In what way can you make the audience feel safe, comfortable, and in control of their decision to keep listening?
- What visual images come into your mind as you read the copy?

OK, how did you answer the questions? By the way, there are no wrong answers! This spot is a TV promo for a news feature series, so there are visuals that go with the copy. You would normally know that at the session and would most likely have access to a storyboard that would describe the visual action your words would play against. Sometimes, however, you will not have anything more than the words on the page. Here's an interpretation of this copy:

- The target audience is men and women who spend time in public places, and who are concerned about safety issues. The focus is primarily on adults who travel or work in large buildings. To effectively reach this audience, you need to be speak to one person.
- The message does not answer any questions, but instead, creates awareness of a potential problem. Your delivery of the first line of copy should instantly grab the listener's attention and you should deliver the remaining copy in a way that hints at solutions, but reveals that solutions to the problem can only be resolved by the viewer watching the program.

- There are several very visual and emotional references that can be used to help create a mood or tone for the message: "hotels," "restaurants," and "other public places," are words that can conjure up powerful images in both your mind as a performer, and in the mind of the listener. By the same token, the phrases "it happens every day," and "without warning" are phrases the listener can identify with. The words "death" and "disability" are emotionally charged words that are intended to illicit a response. Each viewer's response to these words will be unique, but the intent is to create an impact in the viewer's mind as to the potential for serious injury when least expected.

- The person, or character, speaking here is telling a story — a sort of mystery story about a serious problem. The telling of this story is done with a sense of drama and suspense, all of which is leading up to the revelation of exactly what the problem is and what the listener can do.

- The overall delivery is sincere, compassionate, and concerned, with a serious, almost foreboding tone. This attitude is retained throughout the delivery. Each element — almost every word — of the message is given value and importance. The end of the copy is delivered in a more matter-of-fact manner, but still keeping a tone of compassion about the story.

All these answers combine to provide the information you need to effectively deliver the copy. The visual image is important because it sets a solid framework for your character and helps establish the attitude of the spot. As an actor, you need to know these things. Otherwise, you are just reading words on a page — and that's boring!

With experience, you can analyze a script in a matter of seconds, just from a single read-through. You'll instantly know how to take AIM, Interrupt, Engage, and Educate to make your delivery compelling. Trust your instincts and use what you have learned from your interpretation to give depth to your character and life to the copy. Above all, bring your unique personality into the copy and everything else will come naturally.

THE VOICE ACTOR AS A SALESPERSON

The message — or sell — is the most important part of all copy, and virtually all voice-over copy is selling something. Commercials usually sell products or services, or try to get an emotional response from the audience and motivate action; instructional tapes sell procedures; books on tape sell entertainment; and so on. Acting is the means by which any of these messages can be effectively communicated, the story told, and the listener motivated to take action. So, you are not only a performer, but you are also a salesperson. For the time you are in the recording studio, you are an employee of your client's business. In fact, you are the advertiser's top salesperson and must present yourself as a qualified expert.

Your acting job may only last a few minutes in the studio, but that performance may be repeated thousands of times on radio or TV. Your voice may be heard by more people in a single minute than might walk through the front door of a business in an entire year. The credibility of the product or advertiser — and the success of an advertising campaign — may be directly related to the effectiveness and believability of your performance. Are you beginning to see there's more to this thing called voice-over than merely reading words on a page?

Getting the Skills You Need

The bottom line here is to get experience — as much as you can, wherever you can, any way you can! Take classes in acting, voice-over, improvisation, business, and marketing. Get as much experience as you can reading stories out loud. Read to your children. Read to your spouse. Practice telling stories with lots of variety in your voice.

Analyze the characters in the stories you read. Take more classes. Read the same copy in different ways, at different speeds, and with different feelings or emotional attitudes — loud, soft, slow, fast, happy, sad, compassionate, angry. If possible, record yourself and listen to what you did to see where you might improve. Take some more classes. Become a master of performing on a microphone. You can't take enough classes!

One of the best ways to acquire skills as a voice actor is to constantly be listening to what other voice-over performers are doing. Mimicking other performers can be a good start to learning some basic performing techniques. But to really get an understanding of communicating on an emotional level, listen to how they deliver the lines:

- How do they interpret the message?
- How do they reach you emotionally?
- How do they use inflection, intonation, pacing, and express feelings?
- Is their delivery conversational or screaming?
- What is your reaction?

In short, do they sound as if they are reading or do they sound natural and believable? Use what you learn from studying others and adapt that information to your own voice and style. Learn how to "make the copy your own." This simply means that you bring to the performance something of yourself to give the character and copy truth and believability. That's good acting! Chapters 5 through 10 will show you how to do it!

A TWIST OF A WORD

You will notice that the better commercials and voice-over work do not sound like someone doing voice-over work. They sound like your best friend talking to you — comfortable, friendly, and most of all, not "announcery." A good performer can make even bad copy sound reasonably good — and what they can do with good copy is truly amazing.

Create an emotional, visual image in the mind of the audience with a twist of a word. A slight change in the delivery of a word — a shift of the nuance — can change the entire meaning of a sentence. Speaking a word softly or with more intensity, or perhaps sustaining a vowel, making the delivery crisp, or taking the inflection up or down can all affect the meaning of a sentence and its emotional impact in the mind of the listener. These are skills that are acquired over time and are all basic acting techniques that help to create an emotional connection with the audience.

To be an effective voice performer you need to discover the qualities and characteristics of your voice that will make you different from all those other voices out there. Keep developing new techniques. Keep practicing and studying the work of others in the business. Find your unique qualities and perfect them. Learn how to make any piece of copy your own, and you will be in demand. Remember, it's not about your voice, but what you can do with it.

CLASSES

I've said it before and I'll say it again: You can never take enough classes! There is always something new to be learned. Even if you leave a class with only one small piece of useful information, that small piece may someday pay big dividends. The same is true of books and articles. You will be amazed at where you can find a tip or trick that will help you create a believable performance.

There are three types of classes that are most valuable for the voice-over performer: acting, voice-over, and improvisation. Acting classes will give you opportunities to learn about directing, dramatic structure, comedic timing, stage presence, emotional delivery, and innumerable other fine points of performing. Voice-over classes will give you opportunities to practice your skills on-mic and get some coaching. Improvisation in voice work is most common with dialogue or multiple voice copy. This type of training helps improve your spontaneity and ability to adapt quickly. You will also learn skills that can be applied to character development and copy interpretation. I truly encourage you to take some classes! They are an incredibly worthwhile investment in your performing career. I promise you will learn a lot, and you might actually have (lots of) fun. Here are some of the places you can find classes:

- Community theater groups are constantly in need of volunteers. Even if you are working on a crew, you will be able to study what goes on in the theater. Watch what the director does, and learn how the actors become their characters. Don't forget that voice acting is theater of the mind — without props, scenery, or lighting.

- Most community colleges offer continuing education classes, often in the evenings or on weekends. Tuition is usually reasonable and the skills you can learn will pay off later on. Suitable courses can also be found in most college theater arts curriculums.

- Many cities have adult education classes in voice-over, acting, comedy, improvisation, and other subjects that can give you opportunities to acquire the skills you need. Check your local adult or continuing education office, or local colleges and universities for classes offered in your area.

- Many cities have private acting and voice-over courses. They are usually not advertised in the phone book, so they may be somewhat difficult to locate. Check the classifieds of the local subscription and free newspapers in your area. You can also call the drama department at high schools and colleges for any referrals they might be able to make. Your local professional and community theater groups may also be able to give you some guidance. You'll find a comprehensive listing of voice-over coaches in the links area at **www.voiceacting.com**.

- For voice-over classes, try calling some of the recording studios in your area. Many recording studios work with voice-over performers every day and can offer some valuable insights or give you some good leads. Some studios offer classes or do the production work for a class offered by someone else. Or they might be able to simply point you in the right direction by suggesting local workshops or refer you to a local talent agent who might be able to give you some direction.

A WORD OF CAUTION

Larger cities, such as Los Angeles and New York, have many voice-over workshops and classes available. Most are reputable and valuable resources. Be careful, though, because some classes are little more than scams designed to take your money. Usually the scam classes will provide you with "teaser" information. They tell you just enough to get you excited — usually conveniently underplaying the negatives of the business. Then they tell you they will produce and market your demo for a fee — usually $500 to $1,500. You may even be required to take their class if you want them to produce your demo. Demo fees are usually in addition to the fees you pay for the class, although some will include a demo as part of their overpriced tuition. You may get a demo from these classes, but the quality may be poor, and their promises of marketing the tape or sending it out to agents are usually worthless.

Many legitimate classes will also offer their services to assist with your demo. The difference is that you will not be pressured into buying their services and the demo will not be a condition of taking the class. An honest and reputable voice-over instructor will not encourage you to do a demo until you are ready. When they do assist with your demo, the production quality is generally high. Regardless of who you hire to produce your demo, be sure to check them out. Get copies of some demos they have done and get a list of former clients. If they are legitimate, they will be happy to help you. Some will even give you a free consultation.

Be aware that no workshop coach or demo producer can guarantee your demo will be heard. No matter what they tell you, you will be much better off making the calls to the agents and other talent buyers yourself to get your demo out there. Do not rely on someone else to do it for you. For more about marketing your demo, see Chapter 17, Your Demo Is Done, Now What?

Excitement and reward exist only
outside your comfort zone. You'll experience
neither of them until you make yourself
do something you really don't want to do.

So what is it that scares the hell out of you?
Roy H. Williams, Wizard of Ads

4

The Business of Voice-over: Getting Paid to Play

It's Show-biz, Folks!

One thing many people seem to forget is that voice-over is part of Show Business — and the larger part of Show Business is Business! Before making the investment in time, energy, and money for workshops, training, and equipment to become a voice actor, it is important to have an understanding of what this business entails, how it works, and what is expected of you as an independent business owner.

This chapter will introduce you to the business of voice-over so you will be able to make an educated decision as to whether or not this type of work is right for you. Demos, marketing, auditions, and many other aspects of this business are discussed in detail later in this book.

Acting for voice-over may be one of the best-kept secrets around. You get to be serious, funny, and sometimes downright silly and your voice may be heard by thousands. Working hours can be relatively short, and you get paid for it! In short, you get paid to play!

To be perfectly honest, voice acting can be very challenging at times. There will be moments when you wish you were somewhere else. You will encounter producers and/or directors who do not seem to know what they are doing. You will be faced with cramming :40 of copy into :30 — and the producer will expect it to sound natural and believable. That's show-biz!

Fortunately, the uncomfortable moments are relatively rare, and the majority of voice-over work is enjoyable and often downright fun. If you really enjoy what you do, and become good at it, even challenging sessions can seem like play, although it may appear to be hard work to everyone else. To a large extent, your level of success as a voice actor will depend on your attitude and how you approach your work.

Many successful voice actors do much more than just perform as voice talent. It is not uncommon to find voice actors wearing many hats — ad-agency rep, copywriter, producer, and performer. Many voice actors also work as on-camera talent or in theatrical productions. As you master voice-acting skills, you may find yourself developing other talents as well. This diversification can provide income from several sources.

Making Money Doing Voice-over Work

There are only two ways to get paid for voice-over performing: union jobs and nonunion freelance jobs. If you are just starting out, it is a good idea to do as much nonunion work as possible before joining the union. It's sort of like "on-the-job training." You'll have the time and opportunities to get the experience you need and accumulate some recordings of your work.

If you pursue voice-over work as a career, you may eventually join a union, especially if you live in a large market. However, it is not necessary to join a union to become successful. There are many independent voice-over performers in major markets who are earning substantial incomes, even though they are not members of any union. The choice of whether or not to join a union is one that only you can make — and you don't need to make that decision now.

THE UNIONS

Nothing in this book is intended to either promote or discourage union membership. However, joining a performing union is an important decision for anyone pursuing the art of voice acting. If you are just beginning to venture into the world of voice acting, a basic knowledge of the unions is all you need. As you gain experience and do more session work, you may want to consider union membership. Much of the information in this section can be found in the information packet available from your local AFTRA or SAG office[1] or online at **www.aftra.com** or **www.sag.com**.

There are two unions that handle voice-over performers in the United States: AFTRA (American Federation of Television and Radio Artists) and SAG (Screen Actors Guild). In Canada, voice-over work is handled by ACTRA (the Alliance of Canadian Cinema, Television, and Radio Artists) — **www.actra.ca**. British Columbia has UBCP (the Union of BC Performers), **www.ubcp.com**, which is the BC branch of ACTRA. In the United Kingdom, the voice-over talent union is Equity **www.equity.org.uk**. Other countries with collective bargaining unions will also have one or more unions that work with voice talent. It may be necessary to contact a local talent agent to learn which union applies in your country.

The job of all unions is to ensure proper working conditions, to make sure you are paid a reasonable fee for your work, to help you get paid in a timely manner, and to provide health and retirement benefits. The degree to which these are accomplished may vary. Since the focus of this book is on the general craft and business of voice-over, I'll limit the discussion of performing unions to AFTRA and SAG. If you will be doing voice-over work outside of the United States, you should contact the performance union in the country where you will be working. Many performance unions have agreements or affiliations with unions in other countries, so your original union will be the best place to start.

In the US, the two major performing unions came into being in the early days of film, radio, and later, television. Unscrupulous producers were notorious for not paying performers a decent wage — some not even paying them at all. So, the unions were set up to make sure performers got paid and were treated fairly.

As the unions grew, it was decided that it was unfair for a person just working once or twice a year to have to join the union and pay dues every six months. The result was the Taft-Hartley Act, which made some major changes in US labor-management relations. In regards to voice-over, this law gives you (the actor) an opportunity to work under the jurisdiction of the union for 30 consecutive days without having to join AFTRA or SAG. You then become "Taft-Hartley'd" or "vouchered" and must join the union if you do another union job. What this means is that if you do a lot of freelance work, you can still do a union job without having to join the union or pay union dues. The trick is that the next union job you do, you must join the union, whether it is three days or three years after your first union job. Immediately after the 30-day grace period you have the option to join or not join the union. At the time of this writing, with AFTRA, you can immediately join after your first union job. With SAG, you can join after working one job as a principal performer. As a background player, you must work three union jobs (3 vouchers) before you can join. All membership details are explained at **www.aftra.com** and **www.sag.com**.

One of the advantages of being in the union is that you are more likely to be paid a higher fee, or scale, than if you did the same job as a freelancer — although, in some situations, you can actually negotiate a higher fee as a freelancer. Union *scale* is the fee set by the union for a specific type of work. By the time you reach the level of skill to have been hired for a union job, you will most likely be ready to join the union.

AFTRA is an *open union*. Anyone can join by simply paying the initiation fee and current dues. SAG works a little differently in that you must be hired for a union job in order to join the union, and you must join the union when you are hired for a union job. It used to be that you had to somehow get a union job to join SAG. However, today you can join SAG if you are a paid-up member of AFTRA or another affiliated union for one year, and have worked at least one job as a principal performer during that time in that union's jurisdiction.

AFTRA and SAG cover different types of performing artists and do not duplicate the types of performances covered. Certain types of voice-over work are covered by AFTRA (radio, television, and sound recordings), while other performances are covered by SAG (film and multimedia). For example, if you were hired to work voice-over for a CD-ROM interactive program, you probably would be working a SAG job (although some interactive work is covered by AFTRA). A radio commercial or corporate video would be covered by AFTRA.

Sound confusing? Well, it can be, and there are some gray areas. But if you are a member, the union office will help sort out the details, and if you're not a union member yet, you don't need to worry about it. Although separate unions, AFTRA and SAG work closely together and even share office space in many cities.

Both unions have a one-time initiation fee to join and semi-annual dues. Joining AFTRA and SAG requires payment in full of the initiation fee and current dues. Each union has a set Initiation Fee and charges semi-annual dues. Dues are set at a base fee until you reach a minimum income from union work. Above the minimum, dues are a calculation of the base plus a percentage of your union income. Visit the websites or call the AFTRA or SAG office in your area for current fees. New member information packets, which will answer most of your questions about the unions, can be purchased for a nominal fee. You can also ask the union what the current scale is for the type of work you are doing (commercials, industrial, etc.) and you can find current talent rates for most types of voice-over work online at **www.aftra.com**. The staff at the AFTRA and SAG offices are union members and will be happy to answer your questions.

One function of the unions is to protect your rights as a performer. A recording of your performance can be used for many different projects, and unless you are a union member, there is little you can do to protect yourself. A voice-over performance for a radio commercial can also be used in a TV spot or for an industrial video. There are some 400 different AFTRA and SAG agreements for different types of projects, each of which has a different pay scale. Radio and TV commercials are paid based on the market in which they air and how long they will be aired. Industrial videos and CD-ROMs are handled in other ways. Without the union you are potentially at the mercy of the person hiring you, and your voice may end up being used for projects you never agreed to.

AFTRA and SAG work under the principal of *Rule 1*, which simply means that union members agree not to work without a guild or union contract. A union member working in a nonunion production cannot be protected if the producer refuses to pay, pays late, makes unauthorized use of the performance, or in any other way takes advantage of the performer. Any legal action taken by a performer working outside of Rule 1 is at the performer's expense, and the union may actually discipline the member with fines, censure, suspension, or even expulsion.

As a member of AFTRA, you are free to audition for any job, including nonunion jobs. If you are hired for a nonunion job and the employer is not a signatory, the union may contact the producer and have him or her sign a signatory agreement before hiring you. If you are a union member, and are not sure about your employer's status with the union, call the union office in your area.

One way for a union member in the US to work a nonunion job is a waiver called a *One Production Only* (O.P.O.) *Limited Letter of Adherence*. This waiver is good for one job only, and the work you do on that job is considered union work. The advantage is that the nonunion producer agrees to the terms of the union agreement, but does not have to become a union signatory. The O.P.O. contract must be signed before any session work.

There are producers who, for one reason or another, will not work with union performers. Money is usually not the reason. It may be unrealistic demands from an agent, company policy to work only with nonunion talent, or simply a dislike of the paperwork. To get around the paperwork and other issues, some agents and production companies will work as a union signatory effectively separating a nonunion producer from the union. This is a win-win situation — because the producer does not have to deal directly with the union, the quality of the talent remains high, and union performers have the opportunity to work for a greater variety of clients at a fair level of compensation. Some voice-over performers operate their own independent production companies as signatories and essentially hire themselves. It is also possible for you, as a union member, to handle the paperwork, thus making it more attractive for a producer to hire you.

FINANCIAL CORE

Financial core, or *fi-core* is an aspect of union membership in the US that has been and remains very controversial. Fi-core is a level of union membership at which an actor can be a member of AFTRA or SAG and still be able to work nonunion jobs.

Since the beginning of labor unions, states would make their own laws about whether they would be a "union shop," or a "right-to-work" state. In a Union Shop state, laws were passed that required a person to be a union member and pay dues in order to do union work. Right to Work states allowed unions to exist, but membership was (and is) voluntary, and the union cannot require a person to pay anything as a condition of employment.[2]

Financial core came about as a result of union members who disagreed with the way their union was using a portion of their dues for political activities. They also disagreed with their union's control over work they could and could not accept. A series of US Supreme Court legal battles beginning in 1963[3] eventually culminated in a 1983[4] landmark decision that changed the way all unions work (not just AFTRA and SAG). In 2001, President George Bush signed an executive order that requires all unions to inform prospective members of their "financial core rights," or "Beck Rights," before they join the union.

The resulting legal decisions for Financial Core require that an individual must first be a union member, and then formally request a change to Financial Core membership status. Upon declaration of Fi-Core status, the union member loses specific membership rights: the right to vote, hold union office, receive the union newsletter, declare their union status, and participate in union-sponsored events, among others. Payment of semi-annual dues is still required, however at a slightly reduced rate. The union determines the portion of dues that are spent for political and other activities that do not directly apply to the union's collective bargaining efforts, and for those at Fi-Core status, that percentage of dues is deducted from the dues payment.

At its essence, Financial Core creates a nonmember, dues-paying status that allows a performer to work both union and nonunion jobs. Those who favor Fi-Core will mention that the performer regains control over the kind of work they do and their compensation. Those against Fi-Core claim that this membership status seriously disables the effectiveness of collective bargaining. Ultimately, as a voice-over talent, it is up to you to fully research Fi-Core so you completely understand it's ramifications when the time comes for you to join AFTRA or SAG.

A Google or Yahoo Internet search for "financial core" will bring up dozens of websites that discuss both sides of this controversial aspect of union membership.

WHEN SHOULD I JOIN THE UNION?

It is generally a good idea to put off joining AFTRA until you have mastered the skills necessary to compete with seasoned union talent. Producers expect a higher level of performance quality and versatility from union performers and it takes time and experience to master those skills. Joining AFTRA too soon not only may be an unwise financial expense, but could have the potential for adversely affecting your voice-acting career. Most voice talent need the seasoning of working lots of nonunion jobs before they will be at a level of skill that can be considered competitive with union talent.

Here are some reasons to consider union membership when you feel you are ready, or when you begin getting calls for union work:

- Union membership is considered an indicator of professionalism and quality. Producers know they will get what they want in 2 or 3 takes instead of 20.
- Your performance is protected. Union signatories pay residual fees for use of your work beyond the originally contracted period of time.
- You will also be paid for any time over one hour on first and second auditions, and paid a fee for any additional callbacks.

WORKING FREELANCE

Nonunion, freelance work is an excellent way to get started in the business, and there are lots of advertisers and producers who use nonunion performers. As a nonunion performer, you negotiate your own fee, or take what is offered — the fee will be a one-time-only *buyout* payment. There are no residuals for nonunion work, including work done at *financial core*. The going rate for freelance voice work can be anywhere from $50 to $250 or more depending on the project, the market, your skill level, and what you can negotiate. For nonunion work, or work booked without representation, the negotiated terms are between you and the producer.

If a nonunion producer should ask your fee, and you are not sure what to say, the safest thing to do is to quote the current minimum union scale for the type of project you are being asked to do. You can always negotiate a lower fee. If you have an agent, the correct thing to do is to ask the client to contact your agent. A complete discussion of setting rates, negotiating fees, and getting paid is in Chapter 18, How to Work the Business of Voice-over.

Talent Agencies, Casting Agents, Personal Managers, and Advertising Agencies

The jobs of talent agents, casting agents, and personal managers are often misunderstood by people not in the business or just starting out. They all have different functions in the world of voice-over.

THE TALENT AGENCY

Talent agents represent performers. Talent agencies are licensed by the state and must include the words "Talent Agent" or "Talent Agency" in any print advertising, along with their address and license number. The talent agent works with advertising agencies, producers, and casting directors to obtain work for the performers they represent.

A talent agent receives a commission of 10% to 25% based on the scale they negotiate for their performer and whether their performer is union or nonunion. For AFTRA/SAG work the commission is above and beyond the performer's fee (scale plus 10%). In some cases, the commission may be taken out of the talent fee, especially for nonunion freelance work obtained by an agent. For talent agencies to book union talent, they must be franchised by the local AFTRA and SAG unions. Contact the union office in your area for a list of franchised talent agents.

Unfortunately, this is not a perfect world, and there are many unscrupulous agents who will attempt to relieve you of your money. If anyone asks you for money up front to represent you or get you an audition, he or she is operating a scam. Period! The same is true for 1-900 numbers that charge a fee for information on auditions and casting. Most of the information is available elsewhere, either for free or a minimal charge. The best thing to do is find a reputable agent and stay in touch with him or her. Even if you are freelance and must pay your agent a 25% commission, the advantages of representation may well be worth it.

Do you need a talent agent to do voice-over work? No. Will a talent agent benefit you in your voice-over career? In most cases, yes. Chapter 18 includes a complete discussion on how to find and work with a talent agent.

THE CASTING AGENCY OR CASTING DIRECTOR

A casting agency is hired by an advertiser or production company to cast the talent for a particular project. They may also provide scriptwriting and some producing services, such as directing talent. They may even have a small studio where some of the production is done. Casting agent fees normally are charged directly to the client and are in addition to any fees paid for the talent they cast.

Most voice casting agencies work with talent agents and have a pool of talent that covers all the various character styles they use. Talent from this pool are used for all projects they work on and they will rarely add a new voice to their pool unless there is an opening or special need. The talent in their pool may be represented by several talent agents. Casting agencies may occasionally hold open auditions to cast for their projects.

THE PERSONAL MANAGER

A personal manager is hired to manage a performer's career. The personal manager attempts to get the talent agent to send the performer out on auditions, and encourages the agent to go for a higher talent fee. Managers usually work on a commission of up to 20% of the performer's fee, which is taken out before payment to the performer and in addition to the agent's commission. Some managers may work on a retainer. Either way, a manager can be expensive, especially if you are not getting work. Personal managers are fairly rare in the world of voice-over.

HOW ADVERTISING AGENCIES WORK

Advertising agencies work for the companies doing the advertising, coordinating every aspect of an advertising or marketing campaign. They write the scripts, arrange for auditions, arrange for the production, supervise the sessions, handle distribution of tapes to radio and TV stations, purchase air time, and pay all the fees involved in a project.

Ad agencies are reimbursed by their clients (advertisers) for production costs and talent fees. They book airtime at the station's posted rate and receive an agency discount (usually about 15%). They bill their client the station rate and get their commission from the station as a discount. If the advertising agency is an AFTRA or SAG signatory, they will also handle the union fees according to their signatory agreement. Since the ad agency books all airtime, they also handle residual payments, passing these fees on to their clients.

Most advertising agencies work through production companies that subcontract everything needed for the production of a project. Sometimes the production company is actually a radio or TV station that handles the production. In some cases a casting agent might be brought in to handle casting, writing, and production. Some larger ad agencies, with in-house facilities, may work directly with talent agents for casting performers.

Ad agencies can be a good source of work. Your agent should know which agencies use voice-over and will send out your demo accordingly. You can also contact ad agencies directly, especially if you are nonunion. Phone ad agencies and let them know who you are and what you do. You will find many ad agencies work only in print or use only union talent. When you call, ask to speak to the person who books voice-over talent.

The ad agency assigns an account executive (AE) or on-staff agency producer (AP) to handle the account. Sometimes both an AE and AP are involved, but it is usually the AP who knows more about the production than the AE. The AE is more involved with arranging the schedules for airtime purchases. The AP is the person who is generally in charge of selecting talent. The AE is less involved, but often approves the AP's talent choices.

Either the AE or AP may be present during auditions and one or both is almost always present at the session. If the ad agency is producing the spot, they will want to make sure everything goes as planned. If the spot is being produced by a casting agency, someone from that company may also be at the session. Casting agencies are more common for television on-camera productions than for voice-over, but a casting agency rep may be present at an audition or session if their agency is handling the production. And, of course, advertisers are very likely to be at the audition and session to provide their input.

HOW PRODUCTION COMPANIES WORK

As their name implies, production companies are where the work of creating the radio commercial, TV spot, industrial video, video game, or other production is done. They come in all shapes and sizes, from the one-man shop to the large studio with 100's of people on staff. Most production companies have a small staff of 2 to 10 people, many of whom may be freelancers.

Production companies generally work directly for a client, or as a production resource for an ad agency or a corporation's on-staff producer. Many large corporations have their own in-house production facility.

Although some production companies can be a good source of voiceover work, most work primarily with talent booked by the producer or ad agency. Learn which production companies do the kind of voiceover work you want to do, and get to know the producers and directors. You can find production companies in your area by checking your phone book under "Recording Services—sound and video," through an Internet search for "production company your city," or by contacting your city's Chamber of Commerce. Many cities have a film bureau that maintains a list of local production companies.

*All the world is a stage
and all the men and women
merely players. They each have
their exits and their entrances.
And one man in his life
plays many roles.*
William Shakespeare
As You Like It

---

[1] AFTRA-SAG Information Packet, 1997.
[2] Source: *http://www.bizparentz.com/coreTruth.html*
[3] US Supreme Court, *NLRB v. General Motors*, 373 U.S. 734, 1963.
[4] US Supreme Court, *Communications Workers vs. Beck*, 487 U.S. 385, 1988.

5

Using Your Instrument

As a voice actor, the tool of your trade — the instrument for your performance — is your voice. Just as any other craftsperson must know how to care for the tools of his or her trade, before you can begin to learn the craft of performing for voice-over, it is vital that you first learn how to properly use, and care for, the most important tool you have... your voice! So, with that in mind, this chapter includes some essential information about how your voice works, how to deal with common vocal problems, simple warm-up exercises, and tips for keeping your voice healthy. You'll also find some resources for further research if you feel that necessary. If you've never thought much about your voice, you'll probably find most of the exercises and tips helpful, some merely interesting, and a few perhaps totally weird.

All About Breathing

Your voice is a wind instrument. To do any voice-over work, it is essential that you know how to play your instrument properly. In other words, you need to know how to breathe. Proper breathing provides support for your voice and allows for emotional expression. It allows you to speak softly or with power, and to switch between the two styles instantly. Proper breathing is what makes possible the subtleties of communicating a broad range of information and emotion through the spoken word.

Breathing comes naturally, and it is something you should not be thinking about while performing. From the moment we are born, we are breathing. However, during our formative years, many of us were either taught to breathe incorrectly, or experienced something in our environment that left us with an improper breathing pattern. It may be that we learned to breathe from our chest, using only our lungs. Or perhaps, we adapted to our insecurities and created a mental block that inhibits our ability to breathe properly.

31

YOUR VOCAL PRESENTATION

Arthur Joseph, a voice specialist and creator of Vocal Awareness, describes vocal presentation as the way in which others hear and respond to you. The way you are perceived by others is directly related to your perception of yourself. If you perceive yourself to be outgoing, strong, forceful, and intelligent, your voice reflects these attitudes and perceptions with a certain loudness and assertiveness. By the same token, if you perceive yourself to be weak, helpless, and always making mistakes, your voice reflects your internal beliefs with qualities of softness and insecurity. How you breathe is an important factor in your individual vocal presentation because breath control is directly related to the loudness, tonality, and power behind your voice.

Your perception is your reality. So, if you want to change how you are perceived by others, you must first change how you perceive yourself — and that requires awareness. In most cases, a problem with vocal presentation is a habit directly related to a lack of vocal awareness — and habits can be changed. Changing a habit requires an extreme technique — discipline, conscious diligence, and constant awareness. A number of vocal presentation problems, and exercises for correcting them, are discussed later in this chapter.

Many of the exercises in this book will help you discover things about yourself and your voice, of which you might not have been aware. They will also help you improve or change your breathing technique and vocal presentation, and maintain the new qualities you acquire. The lessons you learn about your voice from this and other books will help give you awareness of your voice and will be of tremendous value as you proceed on your voice-acting journey.

Joni Wilson has written an excellent series of books for improving and maintaining the sound of your voice. The first book of the series, *The 3-Dimensional Voice* is the much-needed owner's manual for the human voice and introduces her ideas and techniques. You can learn more about Joni and her books by visiting her website at **www.joniwilsonvoice.com**. On Track 2 of the CD, Joni describes 20 facts you should know about your voice (CD/2).

BREATH CONTROL FOR THE VOICE ACTOR

The first lesson you must learn before you can begin mastering the skills of voice acting is how to breathe properly. Take a moment to observe yourself breathing. Is your breathing rapid and shallow? Or do you inhale with long, slow, deep breaths? Observe how you breathe when you are under stress or in a hurry, and listen to your voice under these conditions. Does the pitch of your voice rise? When you are comfortable and relaxed, is the pitch of your voice lower and softer? Feel what your body is doing as you breathe. Do your shoulders rise when you take a deep breath? Does your chest expand? Do you feel tension in your shoulders, body, or face? Your observations will give you an idea of how you handle the physical process of breathing that we all take for granted.

Of course, the lungs are the organ we use for breathing, but in and of themselves, they cannot provide adequate support for the column of air that passes across your vocal cords. The diaphragm, a muscle situated below the rib cage and lungs, is the real source of support for proper breathing.

Allowing your diaphragm to expand when inhaling allows your lungs to expand more completely and fill with a larger quantity of air than if a breath is taken by simply expanding your chest. When you relax your mind and body, and allow a slow, deep, cleansing breath, your diaphragm expands automatically. Contracting your diaphragm, by pulling your lower abdominal muscles up and through your voice as you speak, gives a constant means of support for a column of air across your vocal cords. For a performer, correct breathing is from the diaphragm, not from the chest.

Good breath control for a performance begins with a relaxed body. Tense muscles in the neck, tongue, jaw and throat, usually caused by stress, constrict your vocal cords and cause the pitch of your voice to rise. Tension in other parts of your body also has an effect on the quality of your voice and your ability to perform. Relaxation exercises reduce tension throughout your body and have the additional benefit of improving your mental focus and acuity by providing increased oxygen to your brain. Later in this chapter, you'll find several exercises for relaxing your body and improving your breathing.

Good breath control and support can make the difference between a voice actor successfully transcending an especially unruly piece of copy or ending up exhausted on the studio floor. A voice actor must be able to deal with complex copy and sentences that seem to never end, and to make it all sound natural and comfortable. The only way to do it is with good breath control and support.

The following piece of copy must be read in a single breath in order to come in at :10, or "on-time." Even though the words will go by quickly, it should not sound rushed. It should sound effortless and comfortable, not strained or forced. It should be delivered in a conversational manner, as though you are speaking to a good friend. Allow a good supporting breath and read the following copy out loud (CD/10).

Come in today for special savings on all patio furniture, lighting fixtures, door bells, and buzzers, including big discounts on hammers, saws, shovels, rakes, and power tools, plus super savings on everything you need to keep your garden green and beautiful.

How did you do? If you made it all the way through without running out of air, congratulations! If you had to take a breath, or ran out of air near the end, you need to increase your lung capacity and breath support. Long lists and wordy copy are commonplace and performing them requires a relaxed body, focus, concentration, and breath support. You need to start with a good breath that fills the lungs with fresh air.

Check your breathing technique by standing in front of a mirror. Place your fingers just below your rib cage, with thumbs toward the back and watch as you take a slow, deep breath. You should see and feel your stomach expand and your shoulders should not move. If your hands don't move and your shoulders rise, you are breathing from your chest.

As the diaphragm expands, it opens the body cavity, allowing the rib cage to open and the lungs to expand downward as they fill with air. If you breathe with your chest, you will only partially fill your lungs. It is not necessary for the shoulders to rise in order to obtain a good breath. In fact, rising shoulders indicates that the breath is getting caught in the chest or throat. Tension, fear, stress, and anxiety can all result in the breath getting caught in the chest or throat, causing the voice to appear weak and shaky and words to sound unnatural.

Breathing from your diaphragm gives you greater power behind your voice and can allow you to read longer before taking another breath. This is important when you have to read a lot of copy in a short period of time, or when the copy is written in long, complicated sentences.

Do the following exercise and then go back and read the copy again. You should find it easier to get through the entire piece in one breath.

- Begin by inhaling a very slow, deep, cleansing breath. Allow your diaphragm to expand and your lungs to completely fill with air. Now exhale completely, making sure not to let your breath get caught in your chest or throat. Rid your body of any remaining stale air by tightening your abdominal muscles after you have exhaled. You may be surprised at how much air is left in your lungs.

- Place your hands below your rib cage, lower your jaw, and allow two very slow preparatory breaths, exhaling completely after each one. Feel your diaphragm and rib cage expand as you breathe in and contract as you exhale. Your shoulders should not move. If they do, you are breathing from your chest for only a "shallow" breath.

- Allow a third deep breath and hold it for just a second or two before beginning to read. Holding your breath before starting allows you to get a solid start with the first word of your copy and gives stability to your performance.

A slow, deep, cleansing breath is a terrific way to relax and prepare for a voice-acting performance (see Exercise 1 on page 43). It will help center you and give you focus and balance. However, working from a script requires a somewhat different sort of breathing. You will need to find places in the copy where you can take a breath. For some scripts you may need to take a silent catch breath. At other times you might choose to vocalize a breath for dramatic impact, or take a completely silent breath so as not to not create an audible distraction.

If you breathe primarily from your chest, you will find that breathing from your diaphragm makes a difference in the sound of your voice. Your diaphragm is a muscle and, just as you tone other muscles in your body, you may need to tone your diaphragm.

Here's a quick exercise from Joni Wilson that will help you develop strong diaphragmatic breathing. You'll find other exercises in her book *The 3-Dimensional Voice*[1]:

- Put the fingers of both hands on the abdominal diaphragm and open the mouth in a yawn position. Inhale the air, then say as you exhale the air, "haaaaaaaaaaaaaaa," manually pushing the diaphragm with your fingers in toward the spine for as long as air comes out of the mouth.

- When there is no more air, and what comes out begins to resemble a "death rattle," slowly relax the pushing and allow the diaphragm to drop back down and suck the air back into the lungs. You may experience some dizziness. Stop for a moment, and let it pass before you do the exercise again. You can do this throughout the day to strengthen the diaphragm.

BREATHE CONVERSATIONALLY

One of the secrets for proper breathing with a voice-over performance is to only take in enough air for what you need to say. We do this instinctively in normal conversation. If you only need to say a few words, there's no point in taking a deep breath. Inhaling too much air may result in a sudden and unnatural exhale at the end of your line.

Listen to how you and others speak in conversation. You'll notice that no one takes a deep breath before they speak. You'll also notice that no one waits until someone else finishes talking before they take a breath. In conversation, we breath in a natural and comfortable manner. When we speak, we only take in enough air for the words we say, and we breath at natural breaks in our delivery without thinking about what we are doing. When you understand how to properly use your diaphragm to provide breath support you will eliminate the need for frequent deep breaths and rapid catch breaths.

You need to breathe, and you will sometimes be working a script with extremely long, complicated sentences. Breath points in most copy usually occur after a portion of a thought has been stated. Listings provide natural break points between each item. You probably won't want to breathe between each item, but there usually is an opportunity if you need it. To make lists more effective, try to make each item in a list unique by altering your delivery or inflection.

Of course, when we are performing from a script, the words aren't ours, but as voice actors we must make the words sound conversational and believable as if they are ours. We can achieve this by breathing naturally as we speak. In order to find the natural breath points in a script, you need to understand the story, your character, and the myriad other details in the script. A few run-throughs out loud will prove tremendously valuable.

Be Easy on Yourself

My first recommendation as you begin studying the craft of voice-over is for you to record yourself reading copy every chance you get. I guarantee that you will most likely not care for the way you sound, and what you hear may surprise you. There is a good reason why most people are uncomfortable listening to their recorded voice. When you speak, you are not actually hearing your own voice in the same way others do. Much of what you hear is actually resonance of vibrations from your vocal cords traveling through your body and bones to your inner ear. When other people hear you, they don't get the advantage of that nice resonance. The way your voice sounds to other people is what you hear when your voice is played back from a recording.

I suggest you find a way to record your voice. In this age of digital audio, there are new devices coming out every day for recording audio. Some offer extremely high-quality recordings, while others are marginal. What you need, at least to start, is a way to record a reasonably high quality voice recording so you can play it back to study what you are doing. For the purpose of rehearsal and mastering your technique, you don't need to spend a lot of money on building a home studio. The time for that will come when you start marketing yourself as a professional voice talent. For now, an old tape recorder or some simple recording software for your computer will do the job.

Practice reading out loud — the newspaper, magazine ads, pages from a novel — anything that tells a story. Record yourself reading a few short paragraphs with different styles of delivery and different emotions. Create different characters and read the copy with their attitudes. Change the pitch of your voice — make your voice louder or softer — and vary the dynamics of pacing, rhythm, and emotion. Practice looking for, and giving value to, the key elements of the copy. Now, go back and read the same copy again — this time, read with an entirely different attitude, emotion, and character. All of these techniques are explained in detail later in this book.

One of the best ways to learn this craft is to listen to voice-over work at every opportunity. How do you compare? Adapt your style to imitate the delivery of someone you have heard on a national radio or TV commercial. Don't try to be that other performer, but rather imitate the techniques and adapt them to your style. If you are still looking for your style, the exercises in this chapter will help you find it.

Listen to your recordings to evaluate what you are doing, but don't be too hard on yourself. Don't be concerned about what your voice sounds like. Focus on what it feels like as you work on your reading. Listen to where you are breathing and if your delivery conveys an understanding of the story. Listen for your pace, rhythm, and overall believability. Be as objective as you can and make notes about the things you hear that you would like to correct. Practice the exercises and techniques in this book that apply. Recording and listening to yourself can be an enjoyable process and a great learning experience that helps give you an awareness of what you are doing with your voice. Remember, it's not about your voice, it's about what you can do with your voice — and it might take some time before you really discover what you can do, especially if you're doing it on your own.

One other tip: You might want to videotape yourself as you work on your vocal delivery. It may sound odd, but studying your physical movement will make a big difference in the way you sound.

Exercising Your Voice

Two things are essential when exercising your voice: (1) a deep breath with good breath control and (2) making a sound. Your vocal cords are muscles, and as with all other muscles in your body, proper exercise and maintenance will provide greater endurance and stronger performance. The vocal cord muscles are little more than flaps that vibrate as air passes over them. Sound is created by a conscious thought that tightens the vocal folds, enabling them to resonate as air passes by. Overexertion and stress can cause the vocal cords to tighten too much, resulting in hoarseness and an impaired speaking ability. A sore throat, cold, flu, or other illness can also injure these muscles. If injured, your vocal cords will heal more rapidly if they are allowed to stay relaxed. However, if you don't correct the source of the vocal injury, the problem will reoccur.

The manner in which we speak, breathe, and use our vocal and facial muscles, can often be traced to our childhood. Cultural and regional speech patterns influence the way we speak, as do family attitudes and speaking habits. From the time we first began to talk, we developed speaking habits and attitudes that remain with us today. We became comfortable with these habits because they worked for us as we learned to communicate with others. Some of these habits might include a regional accent, rapid speech, slurred speech, not thinking thoughts through before speaking, a lack of confidence in our ability to communicate, and poor breathing. These and many other speech habits can be corrected through exercise and technique.

Changing a habit will take approximately 21 days and at least 200 or more repetitions. For most people, it takes about seven days of repetition of a new behavior pattern before the subconscious mind begins to accept the change. It takes another 14 days, more or less, for a new habit pattern to become established in the mind. This time frame is true for changing just about any habit and will vary from person to person. As much as we might wish otherwise, it does take a concentrated effort and constant awareness to achieve the desired results.

Discover which of the exercises in this chapter are most helpful and do them on a regular basis, setting aside a specific time each day for your voice exercises. A daily workout is especially important if you are correcting breath control or a specific speaking habit.

Correcting Speech Problems and Habits

As you exercise your voice, awareness of what is happening physically is vital to improving your ability to experience yourself as you work on changing a habit. Observe what is happening with your voice, diaphragm, body, and facial muscles. Self-awareness helps you discover and correct problems with your speech. Without it, you will not be able to recognize the characteristics you need to work on. As you develop self-awareness skills, you will also be developing instincts for delivery and interpretation that will be of tremendous benefit during a performance.

It is often helpful to have another set of ears listening to you as you work on correcting a problem or speaking habit. A speech therapist, voice coach, or a local voice-over professional can be invaluable to improving your speaking voice. You can also get constructive criticism designed to improve your communication skills from acting classes and workshops.

There are many common speech problems that can be corrected by simple exercise and technique. However, all these problems have an underlying cause that requires self-awareness to correct them. In her book *Voice and the Actor* (1973),[1] Cicely Berry discusses the human voice and methods to improve a vocal performance in great detail. She also explains some of the following common speech problems and how to correct them.

UNCLEAR DICTION OR LACK OF SPEECH CLARITY

Usually, unclear diction or lack of speech clarity is the result of not carrying a thought through into words. A lack of focus on the part of the performer or an incomplete character development can affect diction. This problem can be heard in the voice as a lack of clarity or understanding, often communicated through inappropriate inflection or attitude.

To correct this, you'll need a clear understanding of each thought before you speak. Then, speak more slowly than what might feel comfortable to you. Speaking slowly forces you to focus on what you are saying.

Stuttering can be classified in this problem area. Although the actual cause of stuttering is still not known, research has shown that it may have different causes in different people and is generally a developmental disorder. Even though research has found three genes that appear to cause stuttering, there is no evidence that all stutterers have these genes or that stuttering is an inherited trait.

There are two traditional therapies to correct stuttering. The first is *stuttering modification therapy,* focusing on reducing fears and anxieties about talking. It can be done with a self-therapy book or with a speech pathologist. The second is *fluency shaping.* This therapy teaches the stutterer to talk all over again by beginning with extremely slow, fluent speech and gradually increasing the speaking rate until speech sounds normal. This therapy is normally done at a speech clinic.[2]

OVEREMPHASIS, EXPLOSIVE CONSONANTS, AND OVERENUNCIATION

The source of overemphasis or overenunciation usually derives from the actor's insecurity or lack of trust in his or her ability to communicate. As a result, the tendency is to push too hard to make sense and start to explain. The moment you begin to overemphasize, you lose the sense.

To correct this problem, don't worry about the listener understanding what you are saying. Stay focused on your thought and just tell the story. Don't explain it, just tell it. It may help to soften the tone of your voice and slow down, or simply to focus on talking to a single person. If you find yourself overemphasizing, you may be trying too hard to achieve good articulation.

Sibilance, the overemphasis of the "s" sound, is often caused by not differentiating between the "s," "sh," and "z" sounds. It can also be the result of dental problems, loose dentures, or missing teeth. Minor sibilance problems can be corrected in the studio with a "de-esser," but serious problems can only be corrected with the help of a speech therapist or perhaps a good dentist.

LOSING, OR DROPPING, THE ENDS OF WORDS

A habit common to many people who are just starting in voice-over and acting is to simply not pronounce the ends of words. Words ending in "b," "d," "g," "p," "t," and "ing" are especially vulnerable.

One cause of this problem is simply not thinking through to the end of a thought. The brain is rushing from one thought to another without giving any thought an opportunity to be completed. This is usually due to a lack of trust in one's abilities, but can also be the result of a lack of focus or concentration. Another cause of this problem is a condition known as "lazy mouth," which is simply another way of saying poor articulation.

This problem can be corrected by forcing yourself to slow down — speaking each word clearly and concisely as you talk. Think each thought through completely before speaking, then speak slowly and clearly, making sure that the end of each word is spoken clearly. You may find this difficult at first, but stick with it and results will come. Awareness of this problem is critical to being able to correct it. Exercise #9, *The Cork*, on page 46 addresses this problem.

LACK OF MOBILITY IN THE FACE, JAW, AND LIPS

A person speaking with lack of mobility is one who speaks with only minimal movement of the mouth and face. This can be useful for certain types of characterizations, but is generally viewed as a performance problem. Lack of mobility can be due in part to insecurity or a reluctance to communicate; however, it can also be a habit.

To correct this problem, work on the facial stretching exercises described later. Practice reading out loud in front of a mirror. Watch your face as you speak and notice how much movement there is in your jaw, lips, forehead, and face. Work on exaggerating facial expressions as you speak. Raise your eyebrows, furrow your brow, put a smile on your face, or frown. Stretch your facial muscles. Go beyond what feels comfortable.

CLIPPED VOWELS

Many people think in a very logical sequence. Logical thinking can result in a speech pattern in which all parts of a word are treated equally. This often results in a monotone delivery with vowels being dropped or clipped. There is little emotion attached to the words being spoken even though an emotional concept may be the subject.

Vowels add character, emotion, and life to words. To correct the problem of monotony, search for the emotion in the words being spoken and commit to the feeling you get. Find the place in your body where you feel that emotion and speak from that center. Listen to your voice as you speak and strive to include emotional content and a variety of inflections in every sentence. For someone who is in the habit of speaking rapidly or in a monotone, this problem can be a challenge to overcome, but the rewards are well worth the effort. Once again, slowing down as you speak can help you overcome this problem.

BREATHINESS AND DEVOICING CONSONANTS

Breathiness is the result of exhaling too quickly, or exhaling before starting to speak. Improper breath control, resulting from nervousness or an anxiety to please, is the ultimate cause. Consonants and ends of words are often dropped, or unspoken, and breaths are taken at awkward or inappropriate places within a sentence.

To correct this problem, work on breathing from your diaphragm. Take a good breath before speaking and maintain a supporting column of air as you speak. Also, be careful not to rush, and think each thought through completely.

EXCESSIVE RESONANCE OR AN OVEREMOTIONAL QUALITY

This problem arises from an internal involvement with an emotion. It is usually the result of becoming more wrapped up in the emotion than understanding the reason for the emotion.

To correct this, you may need to learn how to look at things a bit more objectively. People who exhibit this problem are generally reactive and live life from an emotional center. For them life is drama. Work on looking at situations from a different angle. Try to be more objective and less reactive. When you feel yourself beginning to react, acknowledge the feeling and remind yourself to step back a bit from your emotional response.

ACCENT REDUCTION OR MINIMIZATION

Many people feel their natural accent or dialect is a problem when doing voice-over. This can certainly be true if you are unable to adapt your style of vocal delivery. In some cases, an accent or dialect can be used to your advantage to create a distinctive style for your performance, when you create a character, or when you are working in only a certain region. However, if you want to be well received on a broad geographic level, you will need to develop the skill to modify your delivery style to one that is expected, and accepted, by the general population. In the United States, most people have come to expect a certain "sound" for a voice-over performance, commonly referred to as "non-accented American English." However, different regions of a country may respond better when hearing a message in their regional accent. If you want to do voice-over, and have a foreign, or thick regional accent, you have two choices: 1) develop your acting skills to a high degree and create a niche for the sound of your voice, or 2) learn how to adapt your voice to create characters with an accent different from yours, and that includes the "expected" generic accent.

Many famous actors have learned how to either use their accent to enhance their performance image, or have learned how to adapt their voice to create uniquely believable characters: Sean Connery, Mel Gibson, Patrick Stewart, Nicole Kidman, Meryl Streep, and Tracy Ullman to mention only a few. Mel Gibson has a thick native Australian accent, yet he can play a very believable American. Tracy Ullman has a native British accent, yet she creates dozens of characters from around the world. And Meryl Streep has developed a reputation for creating incredibly authentic and believable foreign accents, even though she is American.

When we first learn to speak, we imitate and mimic those around us as we develop our speaking skills. The mannerisms and vocal stylings that we adopt become the habit pattern for our speaking. Over the years, we become very comfortable with our speaking patterns to the point where it can be difficult to modify them. However, if you have lived in different regions or countries, you may have noticed that your speaking patterns begin to take on the characteristics of that region.

Accent reduction or minimization is, in essence, a process of learning new habit patterns for speaking. For most adults, it is impossible to eliminate completely their native accent. However, reducing the accent or modifying the way words are formed is certainly possible. There are many good books and audio programs designed to help people speak with a more "natural" American, regional, or foreign accent. An Internet search for "accent reduction" will result in a wealth of resources.

The process of re-training your speaking habits can be lengthy, and may involve working with a dialect coach or speech pathologist. Contact your local University's speech department for recommendations of a licensed speech pathologist, or look into an English as a Second Language (ESL) program in your area. The time and energy required can be more than most people are willing to invest. But a basic level of accent reduction or modification can be achieved if you simply listen to someone with the desired accent, study the sound of their speech, mimic the sound of their words, and practice the speaking pattern until it feels comfortable. This is essentially how actors do it.

In the United States, most voice-over talent perform with the standard non-accented American English. Regional inflections, dialects, and other tonalities are, for the most part, absent unless required for a character in the script. Although this has become the generally accepted sound for American voice-over, it does not mean that someone who speaks with an accent or dialect cannot be successful. The most successful voice actors are those who are versatile with their speaking voice and who possess the ability to create a variety of believable characters. If you have an accent (foreign or domestic) there are several things you can do to make yourself more marketable as a voice actor:

1. Refine your accent and learn how to use it to your advantage. Although you may be able to create a unique performing style, you may find that you are limited in the types of projects you can do if you focus only on improving your native accent.

2. Learn how to adapt your speaking voice to mimic other accents for the purpose of creating believable characters. Learn to do this well and you can develop the ability to create any character on demand.

3. Work with a diction coach or study methods of modifying your speech patterns. All of these will require some time and effort on your part, but the results will be well worth it.

Voice and Body Exercises — CD/3

A variety of methods to use to care for your voice are covered later in this chapter. But first, let's begin with some ways to create a relaxed body and mind. That will be followed by a variety of exercises designed to tune your voice and exercise the muscles of your face. When doing breathing or relaxation exercises, it is important for you to breathe correctly. Most of us were never taught how to breathe as children — we just did it. As a result, many of us have developed poor breathing habits. See the *All About Breathing* section starting on page 31 for breathing techniques and exercises to help you become comfortable breathing from your diaphragm.

You will find it much easier to get into the flow of a script and concentrate on your performance if you are in a relaxed and alert state of mind. The exercises that follow will help you relax and serve to redirect your nervous energy to productive energy that you can use effectively as you perform. Breathe slowly and deeply, and take your time as you allow yourself to feel and experience the changes that take place within your body. Try to spend at least a few minutes a day with each of these exercises.

EXERCISE 1: RELAX YOUR MIND

This exercise is a basic meditation technique best done while sitting in a quiet place. Begin by allowing a very slow, deep breath through your nose. Expand your diaphragm to bring in as much air as you can, then expand your chest to completely fill your lungs. Hold your breath for a few seconds, then slowly exhale through your mouth — breathe out all the air. As you do this, think calm thoughts, or simply repeat the word "relax" silently to yourself. Take your time. Do this about ten times and you will find that your body becomes quite relaxed, and your mind will be much sharper and focused. You may even find yourself becoming slightly dizzy. This is normal and is a result of the increased oxygen going to your brain.

This exercise is an excellent way to convert nervous energy into productive energy. Do this in your car before an audition or session.

EXERCISE 2: RELAX YOUR BODY

The deep breathing exercise for relaxing your mind will also help to relax your body. But you may still experience some tension in certain parts of your body. An excellent way to release tension is to combine breathing with stretching. There are several steps to this stretching exercise, so take it slow and if you feel any pain, stop immediately.

Stand with your feet about shoulder width. Close your eyes and breathe deeply from your diaphragm, inhaling and exhaling through your nose. Extend your arms over your head, stretching to reach the ceiling. Stretch all the way through the fingers. Now, slowly bend forward at the waist, lowering your arms as you stretch your back. Try to touch the floor if you can. If you need to bend you knees, go ahead. The idea here is to stretch the muscles in your arms, shoulders, back, and legs. When you feel a good stretch, begin to slowly straighten your body, allowing each vertebra to straighten one at a time as you go. Don't forget to keep breathing.

Now that you are once again standing, with your arms still over your head, slowly bend at the waist, leaning to the left, reaching for a distant object with both arms. You should feel a stretch along the right side of your body. Slowly straighten and repeat with a lean to the right, then straighten.

Next, lower your arms so they are directly in front of you. Rotate your body to the left, turning at the waist and keeping your feet pointing forward. Allow your hips to follow. Slowly bend at the waist as you stretch your arms out in front of you. Keep your head up and your back as straight as you can. Now, rotate forward and repeat the stretch as you reach in front of you. Finally, repeat to the other side before returning to an upright position.

EXERCISE 3: RELAX YOUR NECK

A relaxed neck helps keep the vocal cords and throat relaxed. Begin by relaxing your entire body with the technique described in Exercise 1. If you want to close your eyes for this one, feel free — unless you're driving.

This exercise should be done very slowly and it can be done sitting or standing. If, at any time, you feel any pain in your neck, stop immediately. There may be a neck injury present that your doctor should know about. Begin by sitting or standing up straight. Slowly tilt your head forward until your chin is almost resting on your chest. Allow your head to fall forward, slightly stretching your neck muscles. Slowly rotate your head to the left until your left ear is over your left shoulder; then move your head back and to the right. Continue to breathe slowly as you move your head around until your chin returns to its starting point. Now rotate your head in the opposite direction. This exercise will help release tension in your neck and throat.

EXERCISE 4: RELAX YOUR ARMS

This exercise helps remind you to keep your body moving and converts locked-up nervous energy into productive energy you can use. When you are in a session, it often can be helpful to simply loosen up your body, especially if you have been standing in front of the mic for a long time. Remember that moving your body is a very important part of getting into the flow of the script. Loosen your arms and upper body by letting your arms hang loosely at your side and gently shake them out. This relaxation technique works quickly and can be done inconspicuously. You can also expand your shake out to include your entire upper body.

EXERCISE 5: RELAX YOUR FACE

A relaxed face allows you to be more flexible in creating a character. You can use your facial muscles to add sparkle and depth to your delivery. Your face is one of the best tools you have as a voice actor.

Begin by relaxing your body. Then, scrunch up your face as tight as you can and hold it that way for a count of ten. Relax and stretch your face by opening your eyes as wide as you can. Open your mouth wide and stretch your cheeks and lips by moving them while opening and closing your jaw. The process of stretching increases blood flow to your face and gives a feeling of invigoration.

EXERCISE 6: HORSE LIPS

Take a long deep breath and slowly release air through your lips to relax them. Let your lips "flutter" as your breath passes over them. This is a good exercise to do alone in your car on your way to a session. By forcing the air out of one side of your mouth or the other, you can also include your cheeks as part of this exercise.

EXERCISE 7: RELAX YOUR TONGUE

This may sound odd, but your tongue can get tense too. A simple stretching exercise can relax your tongue, and also helps relax the muscles at the back of your mouth. You may want to do this exercise in private.

Begin by sticking out your tongue as far as you can, stretching it toward your chin. Hold for a count of five, then stretch toward your right cheek. Do the same toward your left cheek and finally up toward your nose.

Another tongue stretch that also helps open up the throat is to gently grasp your extended tongue with your fingers. You might want to use a tissue or towel to keep your fingers dry. Begin with a deep breath and gently stretch your tongue forward as you slowly exhale and vocalize a "HAAA" sound, much like the sigh you make when yawning. In fact, this exercise may very well make you feel like yawning. If so, good. Yawning helps open your throat.

EXERCISE 8: YAWNING

As you do these exercises, you may feel like yawning. If that happens, enjoy it. Yawning is a good thing. It stretches your throat, relaxing it and opening it up. More important, yawning helps you take in more air, increasing the flow of oxygen to your brain, improving your mental acuity. It also helps lower the pitch of your voice and improves resonance.

To increase the feeling of relaxation, vocalize your yawn with a low pitch "HAAA" sound, concentrating on opening the back of your throat. It is also important that you allow yourself to experience what happens to your body as you yawn.

EXERCISE 9: THE CORK EXERCISE — CD/4

You may find this exercise a little odd at first, but the results will most likely amaze you. Although a pencil is a suitable substitute, using a cork will give you quicker results simply because it forces you to work your muscles harder.

Get a wine bottle cork — save the wine for later, or have it first (your choice). Now, find a few good paragraphs in a book or newspaper. Before doing anything with the cork, begin by recording yourself reading the copy out loud. Stop the recorder. Now place the cork in your mouth horizontally so that it is about one-quarter inch behind your front teeth — as though  biting on a stubby cigar. If you use a pencil, place it lengthwise between your teeth so you are gently biting it in two places. Don't bite hard enough to break the pencil, and don't place the pencil too far back — it should be positioned near the front of your mouth. Now read the same paragraphs out loud several times. Speak very slowly and distinctly, emphasizing every vowel, consonant, and syllable of each word. Don't cheat and be careful not to drop the ends of words. In a very short time your jaw and tongue will begin to get tired.

After you have spent a few minutes exercising your mouth, remove the cork, turn the recorder back on, and read the copy one more time. Now, play back both recordings. You will notice a remarkable difference in the sound of your voice. The *after* version will be much clearer and easier to listen to.

The cork is an excellent warm-up exercise for any time you feel the need to work on your articulation or enunciation. You can even do this in your car, singing to the radio, or reading street signs aloud as you drive to an audition or session.

EXERCISE 10: THE SWEEP

Vocal range is important for achieving emotional attitudes and dynamics in your performance. By vocal range, I am referring to the range from your lowest note to your highest note. Start this exercise by taking a deep breath, holding it in, and releasing slowly with a vocalized yawn. This will help to relax you. Now fill your lungs with another deep breath and release it slowly, this time making the lowest note you can with a

"HAAAA" sound. Gradually increase the pitch of your voice, sweeping from low to high. It may help to start by holding your hands near your stomach and gradually raise your hands as you raise the pitch of your voice.

Probably, you will find one or two spots where your voice breaks or "cracks." This is normal and simply reveals those parts of your voice range that are not often used. Over time, as you practice this exercise, your vocal range will improve. This is also a good breathing exercise to help you with breath control. If your recordings reveal that you take breaths in mid-sentence or that the volume (overall loudness) of your voice fluctuates, this exercise will help. Practicing this regularly will improve your lung capacity and speaking power, as well as vocal range.

EXERCISE 11: ENUNCIATION EXERCISES

The following phrases are from a small but excellent book titled *Broadcast Voice Exercises* by Jon Beaupré (1994).[3]

To improve diction and enunciation, repeat the phrases that follow. Do this exercise slowly and deliberately making sure that each consonant and vowel is spoken clearly and distinctly, stretching your lips and cheeks as you read. Don't cheat on the ends of words. Watch yourself in a mirror, listen to yourself carefully, and be aware of what you are feeling physically and emotionally. Remember that consistent repetition is necessary to achieve any lasting change. For an extra challenge, try these with the cork.

Specific Letter Sounds — do each four times, then reverse for four more. Make a clear distinction between the sounds of each letter.

Gudda-Budda (Budda-Gudda)
    [Emphasize the "B" and "G" sounds.]
Peachy-Weachy (Weachy-Peachy)
    [Emphasize the "P" and "W" sounds.]
Peachy-Neachy (Neachy-Peachy)
    [Emphasize the "P" and "N" sounds.]
Peachy-Leachy (Leachy-Peachy)
    [Emphasize the "P" and "L" sounds.]
Fea-Sma (Sma-Fea) [pronounce as FEH-SMA]
    [Emphasize the difference between the "EH" and "AH" sounds.]
Lip-Sips (Sip-Lips)
    [Make the "P" sound clear and don't drop the "S" after lips or sips.]
TTT-DDD (Tee Tee Tee, Dee Dee Dee)
    [Emphasize the difference between the "T" sound and the "D" sound.]
PPP-BBB (Puh Puh Puh, Buh Buh Buh)
    [The "PUH" sound should be more breathy and have less vocalizing than the "BUH" sound.]
KKK-GGG (Kuh Kuh Kuh, Guh Guh Guh)
    [Emphasize the difference between the "K" and "G." Notice where the sounds originate in your mouth and throat.]

Short Phrases — make sure every syllable is spoken clearly and that the ends of words are crisp and clear.

Flippantly simpering statistics, the specifically Spartan
strategic spatial statistics of incalculable value

[This one works on "SP" and "ST" combinations. Make sure
each letter is clear.]

She stood on the steps
Of Burgess's Fish Sauce Shop
Inexplicably mimicking him hiccuping
And amicably welcoming him in.

[Make each word clear — "Fish Sauce Shop" should be three
distinctly different words and should not be run together. Once
you've mastered this, try speeding up your pace.]

TONGUE TWISTERS — CD/3

Tongue twisters are a great way to loosen up the muscles in your face and mouth. Go for proper enunciation first, making sure all letters are heard and each word is clear. Speak each tongue twister slowly at first, then pick up speed. Don't cheat on the end of words. For an extra challenge, practice these using your cork. You will find that after working these with your cork, they will be a bit easier to do.

I slit a sheet; a sheet I slit, upon the slitted sheet I sit.
A proper cup of coffee in a copper coffee pot.
A big black bug bit a big black bear, and the big black bear bled blood.
The sixth sick sheik's sixth sheep's sick.
Better buy the bigger rubber baby buggy bumpers.
Licorice Swiss wrist watch.
Tom told Ted today to take two tablets tomorrow.
The bloke's back brake block broke.

Most Dr. Seuss books can provide additional tongue twisters, and can be lots of fun to read out loud in a variety of styles. Some excellent tongue twisters can be found in *Fox in Sox* and *Oh, Say Can You Say* (1979). Another good book of tongue twisters is *You Said a Mouthful* by Roger Karshner (1993). Most retail and online booksellers can help you find a variety of other tongue twister books.

In 1984, while at a dinner party with people from 12 countries representing more than 15 languages, Michael Reck, of Germany, began collecting tongue twisters. Since then, he has compiled the largest collection of tongue twisters to be found anywhere — "The 1st International Collection of Tongue Twisters" at **www.uebersetzung.at/twister/en.htm** and at **www.voiceacting.com/freestuff**. You'll find more than 2,000 tongue twisters in 87 different languages. If you think the English tongue twisters are challenging, try some of the other languages (assuming, of course, you can read them!).

Tips and Suggestions for Maintaining Your Voice

Keeping your voice in good condition is vital to keeping your performing abilities at their peak. Some of the following tips may seem obvious, and you may already be aware of others. Some of the tips here were taken from the private files of some top professional voice actors. None of them is intended to be a recommendation or endorsement of any product, and as with any remedy, if you are unsure please consult your doctor.

TIP 1: SEEK GOOD TRAINING

A good performer never stops learning. Take classes in acting, improvisation, and voice-over. Even singing classes can be helpful. Learn the skills you need to become the best you can be. Study other performers. Watch, listen, and learn from television and radio commercials. Observe the trends. Practice what you learn to become an expert on the techniques. Rehearse regularly to polish your performing skills. Take more classes.

TIP 2: DEALING WITH MOUTH NOISE (aka DRY MOUTH)

Every voice actor dreads the inevitable *dry mouth*. There can actually be many causes of mouth noise, but it is most often the result of saliva bubbles popping because the mouth is not hydrated. The next several tips in this section can help minimize mouth noise or reduce the possibility of it happening — but eventually it will.

Here are a few of the many solutions voice actors have come up with to deal with the symptoms of dry mouth: distilled water with Emergen-C (1 packet per quart), no dairy for two days prior to a VO session, or a swish of carbonated water (flavored or not).

Allowing a throat lozenge or cough drop to slowly dissolve in your mouth can help keep your throat and mouth moist. However, most lozenges are like hard candy and contain sugar that can actually dry your mouth. Exceptions to this are Ricola Pearls natural mountain herbal sugar-free throat lozenges and breath mints, Fisherman's Friend, and Grether's Red Current or Black Current Pastiles lozenges. Some throat sprays such as Oasis, Entertainer's Secret, and Singer's Relief can help keep your throat lubricated. The best time to use a lozenge is about 30 minutes before a session. Lubricating sprays can be used at any time.

TIP 3: NO COFFEE, SOFT DRINKS, SMOKING, ALCOHOL, OR DRUGS

Coffee contains ingredients that tend to impair voice performance. Although the heat from the coffee might feel good, the caffeine can cause constriction of your sinuses or throat. Coffee is also a diuretic. The same is true for some soft drinks. Soft drinks also contain sugar that can cause your mouth to dry out.

Smoking is a sure-fire way to dry out your mouth quickly. Smoking over a long period of time will have the effect of lowering your voice by damaging your vocal cords, and presents potentially serious health risks.

Alcohol and drugs both can have a serious effect on your performance. You cannot present yourself as a professional if you are under their influence. Using alcohol and drugs can have a serious negative influence on your career as a voice actor. Word can spread quickly among talent agents, studios, and producers affecting your future bookings. I have seen sessions cancelled because the talent arrived at the studio "under the influence."

TIP 4: KEEP WATER NEARBY

Keep a bottle of room temperature water with you whenever you are doing voice work. Water is great for keeping the mouth moist and keeping you hydrated.

As your mouth dries out, tiny saliva bubbles begin to form, and as you speak, the bubbles are popping. Well known voice coach Bettye Pierce Zoller recommends keeping a bottle of water handy — the type with a squirt top. When *dry mouth* is noticed, squirt all areas of the mouth wetting the cheeks, teeth, and tongue — even underneath it. Then, do not swallow right away, but instead swish for about 5 seconds or more. The idea is to get all mouth tissues wet. Swishing water in your mouth will help reduce dry mouth temporarily, but only hydration will correct the cause.

Your water should be at room temperature because cold liquids may constrict your throat. Here are some interesting statistics about water, hydration, and the human body:

- It is estimated that up to 50% of the world population is chronically dehydrated.
- It is estimated that in 37% of Americans, the thirst mechanism is so weak that it is often mistaken for hunger.
- Mild dehydration can slow down the human metabolism up to 3%.
- One glass of water shuts down midnight hunger pangs for almost 100% of dieters studied in a University of Washington study.
- Lack of water is the #1 trigger of daytime fatigue.

- Research indicates that drinking 8-10 glasses of water a day could significantly ease back and joint pain for up to 80% of sufferers.

- A drop of 2% in body water can trigger fuzzy short-term memory, trouble with basic math, and difficulty focusing on a computer screen or a printed page.

- Drinking 5 or more glasses of water daily may decrease the risk of colon cancer by 45%, plus it may slash the risk of breast cancer by 79% and reduce the likelihood of bladder cancer by up to 50%.

- It takes about 45 minutes for a drink of water to achieve proper hydration. You may want to start drinking water well before you leave for a session.

TIP 5: SWISH VIRGIN OLIVE OIL

Swish a small amount of virgin olive oil to reduce or kill mouth noise and clicks. The olive oil has a mild taste and leaves a coating on the inside of the mouth that holds moisture in. Since learning about this little trick, I've used it on several occasions with good results.

TIP 6: EAT GREASY POTATO CHIPS

I warned you that some of these tips might sound a bit weird. Well this insider secret and the next are two that fit that category. During a session a singer asked if I had any potato chips handy. This, of course, raised my curiosity. She then explained that a trick singers will use is to eat greasy food, like potato chips, before a session to lubricate their mouth and throat. Odd as it may sound, it does seem to work.

TIP 7: HAVE SOME JUICE

Some juices can be helpful in keeping your mouth moist and your throat clear. Any of the Ocean Spray brand juices do a good job of cleansing your mouth. A slice of lemon in a glass of water can also help. Grapefruit juice, without pulp, can help strip away mucus and cleanse the mouth. Any juice you use to help clear your mouth and throat should be a clear juice that contains no pulp. Be careful of fruit juices that leave your throat "cloudy" or that leave a residue in your mouth. Orange juice, grape juice, carrot juice, and others can be a problem for many people.

TIP 8: THE GREEN APPLE THEORY

This is a good trick for helping reduce "dry mouth." Taking a bite of a Granny Smith or Pippin green apple tends to help cut through mucous buildup in the mouth and clear the throat. Lip smacks and mouth noise are the nemesis of the voice actor, and a green apple can help with this problem. This only works with green apples. Red apples may taste good, but they don't produce the same effect.

TIP 9: AVOID DAIRY PRODUCTS

Dairy products, such as milk and cheese, can cause the sinuses to congest. Milk will also coat the inside of the mouth, affecting your ability to speak clearly. Stay away from milk and cheese products when you know you are going to be doing voice-over work.

TIP 10: CLEARING YOUR THROAT

When you need to clear your throat, do it gently with a mild cough rather than a hard, raspy throat clearing, which can actually hurt your vocal cords. Try humming from your throat, gradually progressing into a cough. The vibration from humming often helps break up phlegm in your throat. Always be sure to vocalize and put air across your vocal cords whenever you cough. Building up saliva in your mouth and swallowing before a mild cough is also beneficial. Be careful of loud yelling or screaming and even speaking in a harsh, throaty whisper. These can also hurt your vocal cords.

TIP 11: AVOID EATING BEFORE A SESSION

Eating a full meal before a session can leave you feeling sluggish and may leave your mouth in a less-than-ideal condition for performing. If you do need to eat, have something light and rinse your mouth with water before performing. Avoid foods that you know will cause digestive problems. I know of one voice actor who had to avoid eating anything for several hours before a session. Even the smallest amount of food resulted in her saliva glands working overtime, causing her speaking to be very "slurpy."

TIP 12: BE AWARE OF YOURSELF AND YOUR ENVIRONMENT

Get plenty of rest and stay in good physical condition. If you are on medication (especially antihistamines), be sure to increase your intake of fluids. If you suspect any problems with your voice, see your doctor immediately. Be aware of dust, smoke, fumes, pollen, and anything in your environment that may affect your voice. You can also have reactions to food that will affect your voice. If you have allergies, you need to know how they will affect your performance, and what you can do about them. An Internet search for "allergies" will reveal resources with lots of information you can use.

TIP 13: AVOID ANYTHING THAT CAN DRY OUT YOUR THROAT

Air conditioning can be very drying for your throat. Be careful not to let cold, dry air be drawn directly over your vocal cords. Smoke and dust can also dry out your throat.

TIP 14: DON'T COVER UP THROAT PAIN

Covering up throat pain will not improve your performance and may result in serious damage to your vocal cords. If you feel you cannot perform effectively, the proper thing to do would be to advise your agent or client as soon as possible so that alternative plans can be made. The worst thing you can do is to go to a session when you are ill. If you must attend a session when your voice is not in top form, be careful not to overexert or do anything that might injure your vocal cords.

TIP 15: KEEP YOUR SINUSES CLEAR

Clogged or stuffy sinuses can seriously affect your performance. They can be appropriate at times, if they are consistent with a character, or if they are part of a style that becomes something identified with you. Usually, however, stuffy sinuses are a problem.

Many performers use a decongestant to clear their sinuses. Nasal sprays tend to work more quickly than tablets or capsules. Be careful when using medications to clear your sinuses. Although they will do the job, they can also dry your mouth and can have other side effects. Even over-the-counter decongestants are drugs and should be used in moderation.

When used over a period of time, the body can build up an immunity to the active ingredient in decongestants, making it necessary to use more to achieve the desired results. Once the medication is stopped, sinus congestion can return and may actually be worse than before. Some decongestants can make you drowsy, which can create other problems.

An alternative to decongestants is a saline nasal rinse, technically known as Buffered Hypertonic Saline Nasal Irrigation. Rinsing the nasal passage with a mixture of warm saline solution is a proven method for treating sinus problems, colds, allergies, post-nasal drip, and for counteracting the effects of environmental pollution.

There are a variety of ways to administer the nasal wash, including a syringe, bulb, and water pik. However, one of the easiest to use, and most effective, is a Neti™ Pot. This is a small lead-free ceramic porcelain pot with a spout on one end. Although the nasal wash can be done using only a saline solution, some studies have shown that the addition of baking soda (bicarbonate) helps move mucus out of the nose faster and helps the nose membrane work better. An Internet search for *nasal rinse* will bring up numerous resources and recipes. You'll find an assortment of Neti Pots at **www.thenetipot.com**.

TIP 16: IF YOU HAVE A COLD

You know what a cold can do to your voice and sinuses. If you feel a cold coming on, you should do whatever you can to minimize its effects. Different precautions work for different people. For some, taking Alka Seltzer changes their blood chemistry and helps to minimize the effects of a cold. For others, decongestants and nasal sprays at the first signs of a cold help ease its onset. Lozenges and cough drops can ease the symptoms of a cold or sore throat, but be aware that covering up the soreness may give you a false sense of security and that your vocal cords can be more easily injured in this condition.

The common cold is a viral infection characterized by inflammation of the mucous membranes lining the upper respiratory passages. Coughing, sneezing, headache, and a general feeling of "being drained" are often symptoms of the common cold. In theory, there are more than 200 strains of rhinovirus that can enter the nasal cavity through the nose, mouth, or eyes. Once in the nasal cavity, the virus replicates and attacks the body. Most cold remedies rely on treating the symptoms of a cold to help you "feel better" while your body's immune system attempts to repair the damage.

Zicam® is a homeopathic cold remedy that has been shown in clinical studies to reduce the duration and severity of the common cold. According to the manufacturer, Gel Tech, LLC (**www.zicam.com**), Zicam's active ingredient is "Zincum Gluconicum contained in Zinullose™, a unique patented ionic emulsification formula." I'm not quite sure what that is, but I do know it works for me, and many people I've recommended Zicam® to have told me it has worked for them.

Other OTC remedies that claim to reduce a cold's severity and duration include Airborne® (**www.airbornehealth.com**), developed by second-grade teacher Victoria Knight-McDowell; Cold-Eeze®, manufactured by Quigley Pharma, Inc. (**www-coldeeze.com**); and Emergen-C®, manufactured by Alacer Corp. (**www.alacer.com**).

There are literally dozens of herbal remedies that reportedly reduce the symptoms of a cold. Health food and online specialty stores are a good source for herbal remedies. Many voice actors recommend special teas from online stores like **www.traditionalmedicinals** (Throat Coat products and

Breathe Easy Tea), **www.yogitea.com** (Breathe Deep Tea), and Chinese cold remedies from **www.yinchaio.com**, drinking at least 1/2 gallon of white grapefruit juice a day, Echinacea, and others. As with OTC remedies, some herbal remedies may work better for some people than others.

Yet another cold and sore throat remedy that seems to do the job for many people is this rather tasty recipe: 1 can of regular Dr. Pepper (not diet), 1 fresh lemon, 1 cinnamon stick. Pour Dr. Pepper into a mug and add 1 slice (circle) of lemon. Heat in microwave to preferred temperature. Remove and add one cinnamon stick. Relax and sip slowly.

For the more adventurous, here's a recipe for *Cold Killer Tea* given to us by one of our workshop students. To one cup of tea (Green Tea is an excellent choice) add 1 tsp lemon juice, 1 tsp honey, 1 tsp apple cider vinegar, and a dash of cayenne pepper. The key ingredients are the vinegar and the cayenne pepper. Ingredients can be adjusted for taste.

If you have a cold and need to perform, it will be up to you to decide if you are fit for the job. Many performers find that they can temporarily offset the effects of a cold by drinking hot tea with honey and lemon. The heat soothes the throat and helps loosen things up. Honey is a natural sweetener and does not tend to dry the mouth as sugar does. Lemon juice cuts through the mucus, thus helping clear the throat. The only problem with this is that tea contains caffeine, which may constrict or dry the throat.

You can't prevent a cold, but if you can find a way to minimize its affects, you will be able to perform better when you do have a cold.

TIP 17: LARYNGITIS

There can be many causes of laryngitis, but the end result is that you temporarily lose your voice. This may be the result of a cold or flu infection that has moved into the throat and settled in your larynx, or another cause.

When this happens to a voice actor, it usually means a few days out of work. The best thing to do with laryngitis is nothing. That is, *don't* talk and get lots of sleep! Your vocal cords have become inflamed and need to heal. They will heal faster if they are not used. Also, the remedy of drinking hot tea with honey and lemon juice will often make you feel better.

A classic bar remedy (I'll give the nonalcoholic version here) is a mix of hot water, Collins mix, and fine bar sugar. This is similar to hot tea, lemon juice, and honey with the benefit of no caffeine. The idea is to create a hot lemonade that can be sipped slowly. Many performers have reported this mixture actually helped to restore their voice.

Another remedy that is said to be effective is to create a mixture of honey, ground garlic cloves, and fresh lemon juice. This doesn't taste very good, but many have reported a quicker recovery from laryngitis after taking this remedy. Garlic is known to strengthen the immune system, which may be a factor in its effectiveness.

Similar to hot tea with honey and lemon is a remedy popular in the eastern United States. This was given to me by one of my voice students and seems to work quite well. Boil some water and pour the boiling water into a coffee cup. Add 1 teaspoon of honey and 1 teaspoon of apple cider vinegar. The mixture tastes like lemon tea, but with the benefit of having no caffeine. Slowly sip the drink allowing it to warm and soothe your throat.

TIP 18: ILLNESS

The best thing you can do if you have a cold or laryngitis or just feel ill is to rest and take care of yourself. If you become ill, you should let your agent, or whoever cast you, know immediately and try to reschedule. Talent agents and producers are generally very understanding in cases of illness. However, there are times when you must perform to the best of your abilities, even when ill. These can be difficult sessions, and the sound of your voice may not be up to your usual standards. In situations such as this, be careful not to force yourself to the point of causing pain or undue stress on your voice. Use your good judgment to decide if you are capable of performing. You may cause permanent damage to your vocal cords.

TIP 19: BE PREPARED

Sooner or later you may find yourself at a session where you are recording in a very strange environment, or the studio may be out of pencils or not have a pencil sharpener, the water may be turned off, or any number of other situations might occur. It's a good plan to arrive prepared.

Enter the Voice-over Survival Kit! You can purchase a small bag or pouch to hold the essential items and keep it with you whenever you go to an audition or session. You'll find the complete list of recommended items for your "survival kit" at the end of Chapter 20, Auditions.

TIP 20: HAVE FUN

Voice-over work is like getting paid to play. Your sessions will go more smoothly when you are relaxed, prepared, and ready to perform. Choose to not worry about any mistakes you might make. Use your mistakes as opportunities to learn more about your craft and to hone your skills.

---

[1] Berry, Cicely. *Voice and the Actor*. New York: Macmillan, 1973.
[2] Kehoe, Thomas David. *Stuttering: Science, Therapy and Practice*. Boulder: Casa Futura Technologies, 1997.
[3] Beaupré, Jon. *Broadcast Voice Exercises*. Los Angeles: Broadcast Voice Books, 1994.

6

The Seven Core Elements of an Effective Performance

(AKA: The A-B-C's of Voice Acting — CD/5)

Acting is an art! As with any art form, acting has some very specific processes, techniques, and component parts — or elements — that must be understood and properly applied in order to achieve the desired result of creating a sense of believability. If any element is overlooked or omitted from a performance, the audience will sense that something is missing.

During the course of teaching The Art of Voice Acting Workshops, we've boiled down the essence of acting for voice-over to Seven Core Elements that we refer to as *The A-B-C's of Voice Acting*. Traditional acting classes for stage, film, and television teach many of these concepts, but not quite the way you'll learn here.

Take a look at the title of this chapter again. I'll wait.

You'll notice that the title includes the words *Effective Performance*. Voice-over work is not about what most people think of as "acting" or performing. Any actor can deliver words from a script, but to be effective, an actor must be believable. To be effective, an actor must create a sense of drama. *Drama* can be defined as that which appears real. All drama contains elements of conflict, humor, mystery, emotion, and feelings. Drama also creates tension, suspense, and anticipation for what will happen next. In other words, an effective performance creates the illusion of real life.

As you learn how to apply the concepts in this chapter, you will be able to create compelling, believable, and real characters in the mind of your audience. That's what an effective performance is all about.

So now the question you should be asking is: "How do I create drama?" The answer is simple in concept but complex in execution. The answer is: "You must make choices and you must commit to those choices." The Seven Core Elements of a performance are all about making choices.

It Starts with Pretending

A voice-over performer is an actor — period. It doesn't matter what the copy or script is for. It doesn't matter if the copy is well written or poorly written. It doesn't matter if you are delivering the copy alone or with others. You are an actor when you stand in front of the microphone.

It is truly a rare individual who is born with natural acting ability. For most people, acting skills take time to learn and master. Acting is not difficult; it's just that as we've grown, we've simply forgotten how to play. As a child, you were acting whenever you pretended to be someone you were not. Pretending is where it starts. But there's a lot more to it than that.

Voice-over performing — or, more accurately, voice acting — is an opportunity to bring out your inner child. Regardless of the copy you are reading, there will always be some sort of character in the words. To be believable, that character must be brought to life. To do that effectively, you must start by becoming a master of pretending.

By definition, the word *pretend* means "to give a false appearance of being." If you are strictly pretending, you are not being real, and the objective of all acting is to create the illusion of reality. Learning how to pretend allows you to step outside of yourself and use what you know so you can move down the path of creating that illusion of reality. This is where the Seven Core Elements of an Effective Performance come in. By applying these seven elements, you will be able to take your acting from simple pretending to a level of creating a completely believable reality.

If you remember nothing else from this book, the following concepts will take you further in voice acting, or any other performing craft, than just about anything else. You can also apply these ideas in any area of your personal or professional life to achieve a high level of communication skill.

These techniques do not have to be done in sequence. In fact, most of the time one element will help define another. As you work on your performance, begin by making choices in whichever element seems to be a good place to start, but be sure that you include them all.

A = AUDIENCE: Core Element #1

Who are you (or, more accurately, who is your character) talking to? Decide on who will be hearing the message — the ideal person who needs to hear what you have to say. Different styles of delivery are appropriate for different audiences. In most cases, the copy will give you a good idea of who the ideal audience is. It may be helpful to ask the producer who he or she is trying to reach, or you may need to make a choice based on your gut instincts. By knowing your audience, you will be able to figure out the most effective way to speak to them.

The most important thing to remember about your audience is that no matter what the script or project may be, you are *always* talking to ONLY ONE PERSON. Attempting to *shotgun* your performance, by trying to connect with many people at once, will generally result in the listening audience losing their interest and becoming uneasy with you as a performer. There is a very subtle difference between focusing attention on an individual versus focusing on a mass of people. You've no doubt experienced seminars where the speaker just doesn't seem to reach the audience, and yet there are others where everyone is hanging on the speaker's every word. In the first instance, the speaker is most likely "shotgunning" the message in an attempt to reach everyone in the audience (or he's just incredibly boring). In the second, the speaker is getting eye contact with individuals in the audience — one at a time, and has a crystal clear idea of the ideal person who needs to hear the message. When you focus your attention on one person, and speak with honesty and sincerity, everyone listening will feel drawn in, as though you are speaking only to them. This is an incredibly powerful technique that many people who do conventional "voice-over" simply don't understand or apply.

For the following line of copy, make some choices as to who the one, ideal person who needs to hear the message might be:

Some people think they're a mistake! But most people think they're delicious! OK . . . so they've got a big seed and they're green . . . Avocado's are still my favorite fruit. Great in salads . . . or all by themselves. Get some today.

Focus your attention on speaking to just one person as though you were having a conversation with them. Describe the person you are speaking to in as much detail as possible and give him or her a name. Use a photograph to get the feeling of having eye contact with a real person. Doing this will make your delivery more conversational and believable. It's entirely possible that as you begin working on a voice-over performance, the original choice you make for your audience may not be the best choice. You may realize it yourself, or your producer may give you direction that reveals to you that your choice isn't working. When that happens, you will need to make an *adjustment* and make a new choice. The RISC AmeriScan process discussed in Chapter 10, The Character in the Copy, will give you additional tools you can use to define your one-person audience.

B = BACK STORY: Core Element #2

In voice-over, a *back story* is the specific event that takes place immediately before the first word of copy. It is what the character in the script is responding to. The back story is the reason why your character is saying the words in the script. If the back story is not clearly defined in the script — your job, as an actor, is to make one up! This is a very important aspect of performing from a written script because the back story sets your character's motivation, attitude, and purpose for speaking.

Acting coaches will often refer to a back story as "the moment before." Technically, a back story consists of the character's entire life experience that has brought them to the moment in time for the story in the script. For voice-over work, that's too much information, and we don't have the time to deal with a long, involved story leading up to the first word of the script. So, I suggest that you define a back story in specific terms that can be described in a single sentence. It must be something very immediate and powerful that has caused your character to speak. It can't be a vague description of a scene — it must elicit a specific response.

In some scripts, the back story is pretty obvious. In others, you'll have to make up something. Either way, the back story is essential to the development of your character. By knowing the specific event to which your character is responding, you will know how your character will respond to other characters or situations in the story being told.

For the following line of copy, make some choices as to the specific event that occurred, or words spoken immediately before this statement, and to which this statement is in response:

> Some people think they're a mistake! But most people
> think they're delicious! OK . . . so they've got a big seed
> and they're green . . . Avocado's are still my favorite fruit.
> Great in salads . . . or all by themselves. Get some today.

A back story can be found for any type of copy, and there can be more than one back story in a script. For example, a character might be responding to several different things during the course of the script. Each of those events can be viewed as a separate back story. To discover the back story, look for clues in the script that reveal specific details about what is taking place. Use these clues to create your own idea of what took place *before* the story in the script. This is the essence of your back story, and this is what brought your character to this moment in time. By understanding what brought your character to this moment, you will know how your character should respond. This, in turn will make it much easier for you to sustain your character and effectively communicate your character's feelings, attitudes, and emotions.

Learn how to find the back story and you will learn how to understand the motivation of your character.

One way to use a back story to your advantage is to create a *lead-in line*, or *pre-sentence*. This is simply a verbalization of the back story to assist you in creating a believable response.

C = CHARACTER: Core Element #3

Who are you as the speaker of those words on the paper? Define your character in as much detail as you like. How does your character dress? What does the voice sound like? Does the character exhibit any sort of attitude? How does the character move? What is the character's lifestyle? How does the character feel about the product, service, or subject of the script? The more details you can come up with, the more believable your character will be to you and to your audience. Every script has a character, regardless of how poorly the script may be written or what the content of the script may be. Find that character and give it life.

Just as in life, scripted characters have feelings and experience emotions about the stories they tell. And, just as in life, characters respond, evolve, and express emotions during the course of the story. Learn how to reveal those emotions and feelings through your voice and you will create believable characters. Chapter 10, The Character in the Copy, will explain many ways for you to do this, and you will find additional tools in Chapter 13, Character Copy.

For the following line of copy, make some choices that will clearly define and describe the person speaking:

> Some people think they're a mistake! But most people
> think they're delicious! OK . . . so they've got a big seed
> and they're green . . . Avocado's are still my favorite fruit.
> Great in salads . . . or all by themselves. Get some today.

D = DESIRES: Core Element #4

All characters have wants and needs! This can also be thought of as a character's objectives, intentions, or *desires*. There is always something very specific the character wants from speaking the words. It may be simply to enlighten the listener with a valuable piece of information, it may be to entertain, or it may be to instruct the listener in the fine points of operating a complex piece of machinery. Whatever it may be, your character wants, needs, and *desires* to accomplish something from speaking those words. If that desire is not clearly explained in the script — use whatever information is available to make it up.

Here's a quick test: What does the character in the following script want and need (desire) as a result of speaking these words? Come up with some choices of your own before reading further. No fair cheating.

> Some people think they're a mistake! But most people
> think they're delicious! OK . . . so they've got a big seed
> and they're green . . . Avocado's are still my favorite fruit.
> Great in salads . . . or all by themselves. Get some today.

Here are some possibilities for the character's desires and the words that might be clues to the ultimate desire:

- *Establish curiosity (Some people think they're a mistake!)*
- *Tease to create interest (...they're delicious...)*
- *Add a touch of humor (...so they've got a big seed...)*
- *Intrigue the listener (...they're green...)*
- *Provide important information (they're a fruit and good in salad)*
- *Create urgency* (Get some today.)

As you can see, there are many possibilities. There is really no single, correct way to interpret or deliver any piece of copy. As an actor, you need to make a choice as to what might be the most appropriate message that your character wants to communicate. And there may be more than one.

There are no wrong choices. But there *are* choices that may be more effective than others in terms of communicating the message.

Theatrical actors will refer to this aspect of character development as the character's *objectives* or *intentions*. Desires, *objectives*, and *intentions* all refer to what your character ultimately wants as a result of his or her words and actions. Use whichever term works best for you, but for the purpose of this alphabetical mnemonic, "D" for *desires* works best. A-B-C-O, just doesn't seem right!

E = ENERGY: Core Element #5

Voice acting comes from your entire body.
If only your mouth is moving, that's all anyone will hear.[1]
Cory Burton

There are three levels of energy in every performance: psychological energy, physical energy, and emotional energy. All three must be present. Leave one of these out and your character will lack a sense of truth and honesty.

PSYCHOLOGICAL ENERGY

Think back to a time when you said one thing, but what you really meant was something else entirely — and the person you were speaking to somehow knew exactly what you meant. We've all done this at one time or another. The thought you hold in your head can directly affect the way the words come out of your mouth.

Try this: Say the phrase "That's a really nice hat." You most likely just spoke the words without any objective, intention, or desire, so it probably sounded pretty flat and uninteresting. Now hold the thought in your head that the hat you're looking at is the most incredible hat you've ever seen, and on the person you're talking to, it looks amazing! You want them to know how excited and happy you are that they have found a "look" that works for them. Say the phrase again and notice how different it sounds.

"That's a really nice hat."

Now, change the thought in your imagination to be that you are very jealous to see the other person wearing a hat that is exactly like your favorite hat. Your desire is to outwardly compliment them on their hat, but on the inside you really don't think it looks very good (even if it does). You're not happy, and you want them to know it without really saying it.

"That's a really nice hat."

The words are exactly the same in both situations, but the thoughts you held in your mind were different. The result is that the perceived meaning of the words is different.

In theater, the term *subtext* is used to refer to the underlying personality, and unspoken thoughts of a character that define the character's behavior and reveal what they really believe. *Psychological energy* is simply another way to understand *subtext*.

Psychological energy is a powerful concept when applied to voice acting. In voice-over, the sound of our voice is all we have to communicate the message in a script, and we need to use every tool available to create a believable reality.

The trick to using psychological energy properly is to keep the true belief just under the surface and to not reveal it during the performance, except through subtle intonation and behavior. By keeping the true belief hidden behind the words, it allows other characters to respond more appropriately, and it keeps the audience curious. This is especially important if the true meaning is in direct opposition to the textual meaning.

PHYSICAL (KINETIC) ENERGY

Physicalize the moment . . . and your voice will follow.
Bob Bergen

I think it's pretty safe to say that when you are in conversation with someone, you are not standing or sitting perfectly still, without moving. OK, maybe some of you reading this don't move, but most people use much more than just their mouth when talking. Facial expressions, body language, and gestures are all part of the way we communicate when speaking to others. I'll bet you move your body even when you're talking on the phone.

Have you ever noticed that your physical movements are a big part of the way you speak? You use *physical energy* to give power to the thoughts and emotions that lay just under the surface of the words you speak.

Physical energy is absolutely essential in any voice-over performance. When you move your body with appropriate energy to support the emotions and thoughts of the words you speak, the result can be a totally believable performance.

A mistake many beginning voice actors make is that they will stand perfectly still and stiff-as-a-board when they are in front of a microphone. Their hands will hang at their sides and their faces will show no expression. Their performance will be flat and uninteresting, with often an almost monotone delivery. Once they start moving, everything changes. Words come to life, we can hear how the character feels, and we are actually drawn in to the drama of the story.

Unfortunately, for some, the idea of putting physical movement to words while reading from a script is much like walking and chewing gum at the same time — it can be a challenge to learn how to do it. Fortunately, it is an easily acquired skill. Usually, lack of movement is the result of nervousness or comes from a feeling of discomfort from being in an unfamiliar environment. But the simple truth in voice acting is that you <u>must</u> move. It is one element of a performance that is essential to creating compelling and believable characters.

EMOTIONAL ENERGY

Life will give you what you need.
Situations are your tools.[2]
Christina Fasano

Understanding how your character feels about an event, situation, thing, product, or person is an aspect of *subtext*. Your character's emotional energy is different from psychological energy in that psychological energy deals with the thoughts behind the words, whereas *emotional energy* is the expression of the feelings and emotions that underscore the thoughts. The two go hand in hand.

Using the hat example, consider how your character feels emotionally about the discovery that someone else has the exact same hat they have — and that they look great wearing it. Your character might feel devastated, frustrated, angry, happy, proud, or even excited. A full range of emotions is possible, but the most appropriate emotion will be determined by looking at the overall context of the story — understanding the big picture. Based on your choices as to how your character behaves and speaks within the context of the whole story, you will better understand the how and why of the character's feelings and emotional responses.

Keep in mind, that as actors, our job is to create a sense of reality, so any expression of emotion that is *over-the-top* might destroy any chance of believability. The best way to use emotional energy is to keep the emotions just under the surface. Start by allowing yourself to remember how you felt in a similar situation, and then base your performance from that feeling. By using a personal experience the emotional response will have truth and honesty, which will support the thoughts held in your imagination, which will result in an authentic and believable performance.

The essence of how the three levels of energy affect your performance can be summed up as:

- Change your thoughts — it will change the way you move
- Change your physical movement — it will change the way you feel
- Change your emotions — it will change the way you sound

For the following line of copy, make some choices as to how your character might think (psychological energy), how he/she might move and where tension is held in the body while talking (physical energy), and how he/she feels about the subject (emotional energy).

Some people think they're a mistake! But most people think they're delicious! OK . . . so they've got a big seed and they're green . . . Avocado's are still my favorite fruit. Great in salads . . . or all by themselves. Get some today.

F = FORGET WHO YOU ARE AND FOCUS: Core Element #6

Acting is all about listening and forgetting who you are.[4]
Shirley MacLaine

A key principal of acting is to "get out of your own way" so the character or role you are playing can emerge and appear real to your audience. It sounds simple on the surface, but this idea may be confusing to some people. After all, isn't it an actor's job to figure out how a particular role should be played? Doesn't the actor need to be present during a performance? Aren't there a whole bunch of techniques that an actor can use to make a role believable? And doesn't all this mean that an actor needs to put a lot of thought into their performance?

Although all of these things are true to some degree, they are all just part of the process of creating a performance. They are not the performance. The reality of all acting is that the role you are playing is not you. The secret to excellent acting is to do everything that needs to be done to understand the story, character, relationships, responses, moods, attitudes, dynamics, and energy; apply the appropriate acting techniques to give meaning to the story, breathe life into the character, and "take the words off the page;" then put all of that behind you as the real you steps aside to let the character come to life. If there is any part of the real you that is apparent in a performance, it is you "doing" the character — not the character being authentic. You're thinking too much about what you need to do, or you're giving too much importance to the techniques you are using. In other words, when you put too much effort into the process of creating a performance, the performance will suffer.

One of the most difficult things for any actor to learn is how to forget who they are so the character can become real. The reason this is often a difficult task is because, as human beings, we have an ego that can cause us to second guess ourselves or stand in the way of what we know needs to be done. We can be a master of performing techniques and still be in our own way on an unconscious level. Often the only way we know it's happening is when our director asks us to make an adjustment in our performance.

Learning how to get out of our own way is, for most of us, an acquired skill that can take years to master — or it can be achieved in an instant. This is one of the reasons acting is a craft and not a skill. A skill is a specific talent or ability, while a craft is the application of multiple skills to achieve a specific end result. Mastering any skill or craft takes time, patience, and dedication.

Listen to your director, listen to your instincts, listen to the unspoken words to which your character is responding, listen to the other actors in the studio, listen to everything. It is only through listening that you will be able to *focus* on doing what needs to be done to create the reality of the moment. When you are fully focused, you will discover that you no longer need to think about what you are doing. The characters you create will almost magically come to life. The second you allow yourself to drift off focus, or start to think about what you are doing, you will fall out of character.

If you don't fully grasp the idea of *forget who you are and focus*, don't be concerned. Many very successful actors and performers don't fully understand this concept and may never experience what it is like to truly forget who they are and get out of their way. For most actors, the experience is erratic at best, happening only occasionally. Achieving this state of performance on a consistent basis usually comes only with consistent work and study. The best I can say is that when you achieve this state of performance, you'll know it! It will feel as though you are outside of yourself observing your performance. Sort of like an "out-of-body" experience, except that you have complete control. This is the state of performance we strive for.

G = GAMBLE: Core Element #7

Be willing to gamble. Be willing to take a chance.

You must be willing to risk.

Every performance requires that the performer be willing to step outside of their comfort zone to do or be something that most people would feel uncomfortable doing or being. It could be as simple as making an announcement at a party, standing on stage in front of an audience of thousands, or standing all by yourself in front of a microphone in a voice-over booth.

All performing is about risk. You risk the chance of not being liked, you risk making inappropriate choices, you risk the chance of not being believable, you risk the chance of not being hired again, you risk many things on many levels.

All performing is about taking a chance on an uncertain outcome. You may never know exactly what the producer or director is looking for in your performance, if your performance truly meets their needs, or how your performance will ultimately be used. Even though you may not know, you must be willing to take a chance, based on experience and observation, that what you do will be best bet for a successful outcome.

All performing is a *gamble*. You are gambling that the choices you make for creating your character and delivering your lines will bring the character and the story to life.

If you are not willing to take a risk, performing as a voice actor is probably not something you should pursue any further. Just stop reading right now and give this book to someone who is willing to take the risk of doing something they have never done before. A simple truth of this business is that you cannot achieve any level of success if you insist on being only you as you read a script.

Voice-over is a craft based on creating compelling characters in interesting relationships. The only way you can create a character that is not you is to be willing to *gamble* that you can do what needs to be done for a believable performance.

Gambling on your performance is <u>not</u> about winning or losing. It <u>is</u> about using the tools of your trade, your experience, your training, and your many performing skills to create more certainty for an otherwise uncertain outcome. In other words, you can stack the deck to improve the odds for a masterful performance each time you stand in front of a microphone.

Fear is nothing more than a feeling . . .
You feel hot, you feel angry, you feel afraid.
Fear cannot kill you.
Joel Gray as Chiun
Remo Williams, The Adventure Begins (MGM—1985)

---

[1] Cory Burton, *Scenes for Actors and Voices by Daws Butler,* Bear Manor Media, 2003.
[2] Christina Fasano Lyrics from the song "Welcome to the Workshop," *Spiritually Wet,* published by FWG Music, 1999. www.ceeceejames.com
[3] Bob Bergen, Warner Bros. voice of Porky Pig and other characters.
[4] Shirley MacLaine in an interview by James Lipton, *Inside the Actor's Studio,* Bravo Television Network.

The A-B-C's of Voice Acting
the complete alphabet

A	**Audience**	Authentic in Attitude	Articulate (cork exercise)
B	**Back Story**	Be Real	Believe in Yourself
C	**Character**	Commit to Choices	Critical Thinking
D	**Desires**	Different Approach	Dynamics for Variety
E	**Energy**	Emotion	Environment
F	**Forget Who You Are**	**Focus**	Feelings
G	**Gamble**	Gestures	"Go for It!"
H	Hands (use your arms)	How Does Your Character . . . ?	Have Alternatives Ready
I	Intentions	"Into the White"	Imagination
J	Juxtapose (change words to find emotion)	Jargonize (when appropriate)	Journey (explore options)
K	Key Words & Phrases	"Keep It Real"	Kid (let yours come out)
L	Listen Carefully	"Less Is More"	Lose Yourself
M	Mouth Work	M.O.V.E.	"Moment Before"
N	No Guessing	Never Touch the Mic	Nuance
O	Objectives	"Out of the Black"	"Off the Page"
P	Pitch	Pitch Characteristics	Physicalize
Q	Quality (always do your best)	Question Everything	Quickly Find Your Character
R	Rhythm	Respond	Relax
S	Sense Memory (use your past experience)	Script Analysis (woodshed)	Suspension of Disbelief
T	Tempo	Think Out of the Box	Teamwork
U	Understand the Whole Story	Underplay	Use Tools & Techniques
V	Voice Act (not "voice-over")	Visualize the Scene	Vision (the big picture)
W	Warm-up	Water (to stay hydrated)	Woodshed Copy (the 6 W's)
X	X-periment	X-plore	X-citement
Y	Yawn to Open Throat	Yourself (Don't Be)	Yell (if appropriate to character)
Z	Zicam (homeopathic cold remedy)	Zeppo (a famous Marx brother)	Z end of Z list

7

Developing Technique

Think of *technique* as the tools of your trade. There are always new techniques to study and learn. The application or use of any technique is something that becomes very personal over a period of time as the process of the technique evolves into something uniquely yours.

A voice-over technique is really nothing more than a skill that allows you to become a better performer. Sure, you can do voice-over without mastering any skills, or you may already have an innate ability with many of them. However, having an understanding of basic acting and voice-over techniques gives you the knowledge necessary to work efficiently under the pressure of a recording session — and to make your performance more real and believable.

As a voice actor, your job is to give life to the words written by the copywriter. The writer had a vision — a sound in mind — when writing the script. You must make the words real and believable. Technique is the foundation for your performance. It is the structure on which your character, attitude, and delivery are built. Technique must be completely unconscious. The moment you begin thinking about technique, the illusion is broken and the moment is lost.

As you begin to study and learn the techniques in this book, you will find yourself at first thinking a lot about what you are doing. However, as you gain experience and become more comfortable, your technique will become automatic, and you will be able to adapt quickly to changes without having to think. Acting techniques are much like riding a bicycle or driving a car. Once you've mastered the process, it becomes automatic.

Voice exercises can help you develop and perfect your acting techniques. Chapter 5, Using Your Instrument, includes many exercises, tips, and suggestions for improving your voice and developing your skills.

Style

It is interesting to note that using the voice is the only art form in which an individual style may be developed out of an inability to do something. It may be an inability to form certain sounds, or it may be a cultural affectation (an accent or dialect) that results in a quality uniquely your own.

One person's vocal style might emphasize lower frequencies, creating an image of strength and power. Someone else may not be able to reach those low tones, and his or her style might be based on a somewhat warped sense of humor expressed through attitude as he or she speaks. Each of us has developed a unique vocal style for speaking in our everyday lives.

Your fundamental speaking style is a reflection of how you perceive yourself, and it may change from moment to moment as you move from one situation to another. When you are confident of what you are doing, you might speak with determination and solidarity. But when your insecurities take over, your voice might become weak, breathy, and filled with emotion.

Your style as a voice actor comes first from knowing who you are, and then expands on that by adding what you know about human nature, personality, character development, and acting.

Developing your vocal style is an ongoing process. You start with your voice as it is now, and as you master new acting and performing skills your style will begin to develop. Your vocal range will expand, as will your ability to express attitude, emotion, subtlety, and nuance in your delivery.

The Road to Proficiency

Acquiring a skill, and becoming good at that skill, is called *competency*. Becoming an expert with the skill is called *proficiency*. You must first be competent before you can become proficient. Sorry, but it just doesn't work the other way around.

BECOMING COMPETENT

Your degree of competency with any skill actually falls into the following four distinct levels. Each person works through these levels at his or her own pace and with varying degrees of success.

LEVEL #1: *Unconscious Incompetence.* At this level you are not even aware that you don't know how to do something. You have absolutely no skill for the task at hand.

LEVEL #2: *Conscious Incompetence.* You become aware that there is something you don't know or understand, and you begin to take steps to learn what you need to know.

LEVEL #3: *Conscious Competence.* You have acquired the basic skills necessary to accomplish the task. However, you must consciously think about what you are doing at each step of the process.

LEVEL #4: *Unconscious Competence.* When you reach this level, you have mastered the skills necessary to accomplish the task without thinking about what you are doing.

THREE STAGES TO PROFICIENCY

There are three stages to acquiring a proficient level of skill to become an expert that must be worked through regardless of the skill that is being learned. Playing the piano, building a table, or performing in a recording studio all require the same three stages of learning and perfecting the skills needed to achieve the end result.

STAGE #1: *Understand the underlying mechanics.* Every skill requires an understanding of certain basic mechanical techniques that must be learned before any level of expertise is possible. In the craft of voice acting, some of these mechanics include: breath control, pacing, timing, rhythm, inflection, acting, and effective use of the microphone.

STAGE #2: *Understand the theory and principles that are the foundation for using the skill effectively.* In voice acting, these principles include script analysis, character development, audience psychology, and marketing.

STAGE #3: *Apply the knowledge learned in the first two stages and continually improve on the level of skill being achieved (practice and rehearsal).* For the voice actor, this means constantly studying acting techniques, taking classes and workshops, studying performances by other voice actors (listening to commercials, etc.), following the trends of the business, and working with what you learn to find the techniques that work best for you.

Three Steps to Creating an Effective Performance

In all areas of performing, there are three steps to creating an effective performance; the end result of any task can be considered as a performance. For example, when building a table, you are performing a series of tasks required to result in a finished table. Your degree of proficiency (expertise) at performing the various tasks will determine how sturdy your table is and what it looks like when you are finished.

The following three basic steps to performing any task are necessary in the business of voice acting as well:

1. Practice — learning the skills and techniques
2. Rehearsal — perfecting and improving techniques and skills
3. Performance — the end result of learning and perfecting

The steps must be done in that order. You, no doubt, have heard the phrase "practice makes perfect." Well, guess what! It's a misnomer. Even *perfect* practice may not make perfect, because it is possible to practice mistakes without realizing it — only to discover too late that the end result is ineffective — and you may not understand why.

A voice-over performance will rarely be "perfect." So what we need to do as a voice actor is to practice with a mind-set of knowing that there may be dozens of ways to apply a certain technique or deliver a line of copy. Our mastery of a technique will come through testing and experimentation as we discover how it works when combined with other techniques.

PRACTICE

Practice is the process of learning what is needed to achieve the desired result — acquiring the skills and applying the underlying mechanics and techniques to achieve proficiency. In voice-over work, the practice phase begins with the initial read-through; having any questions answered by the producer; doing a character analysis; doing a script analysis; working on timing, pacing, and delivery; locking in the correct pronunciation of complicated words; and possibly even recording a few takes to determine how the performance is developing. To discover problems in the copy or character, and correct them, practice is an essential step in voice-over.

If problems are not corrected quickly, they will need to be addressed later during the rehearsal phase. In the real world of voice-over, there are two aspects to the practice phase. The first is when you are practicing on your own to learn basic skills and techniques, and the second is the initial practice read-through at a session while wood shedding. Personal practice should be a life-long quest of learning new skills and techniques. The practice phase at a recording session generally lasts only a few minutes.

REHEARSAL AND PERFORMANCE

Rehearsal begins once all the details of the performance are worked out. The character's attitude, voice, delivery, and timing are set during practice. You have committed to your choices of attitude, character, vocal texture, and so on. Rehearsal in voice-over work often begins as tracks are recorded. The choices you have committed to are polished, tweaked, tuned, and perfected with each take. Every rehearsal, or recorded take, has the potential of being used as the final performance, either in whole or in part.

The process of perfecting the performance progresses through a series of takes. Each take is subject to refinement by direction from the producer, director, or engineer. Once an aspect of the performance is set, it should be rehearsed in the same manner, as much as possible, until adjusted or modified by the director. When the delivery on a line is set, don't vary it too much in the takes that follow. Set the tone of the delivery in your mind so that you can duplicate it as you polish the rest of the copy.

Eventually, every line of copy will be set to the liking of the producer. In some cases, a producer may actually have the voice actor work line-by-line, getting just the right timing and delivery on one line before moving on to the next line. Later, the engineer will assemble each line's best take to create the final track.

Theatrical actors practice their lines as they work on their blocking and staging. The director gives them some instruction, but for the most part, actors are in the practice phase as long as they are working with a script. By the time they are ready to put down their scripts, they are at a point where they know what they are doing on stage — and rehearsal begins.

As they rehearse, the director makes adjustments and polishes the performance. Finally, there is a dress rehearsal where all the ingredients of the show — music, scenery, props, lighting, special effects, actors, and so on — are brought together. The dress rehearsal is normally the final rehearsal before opening night and usually is considered to be the first complete performance. There is no such thing as a dress practice! Some theatrical directors even consider the entire run of a show as a series of rehearsals with an audience present.

As voice talent, we're fortunate if we receive the script a day or so prior to recording. Quite often the time we have for practice and rehearsal is very limited, so it is essential that our use of technique be instinctive.

Never assume you have perfected a technique. There will always be something new, more, or different that you can learn to expand your knowledge. There will always be new techniques for you to try and use. There will always be a different way you can approach a character or piece of copy. There will always be new trends in performance style that require learning new techniques. To be an effective and versatile voice actor, you need to be aware of the trends and willing to learn new techniques.

The Elements of a Voice-Acting Performance

There are many aspects to voice-over performing, and as with any skill, a certain level of proficiency is needed before a person is considered to be working at a professional level. Working at a professional level means that a performer has a thorough understanding of the many intricacies of the craft and is a master of many skills and techniques. A voice actor working at this level can make any character believable by unconsciously bringing together the many elements of a performance.

LESS IS MORE

Just because you love what you do does not necessarily mean you are good at what you do. In voice acting, accuracy with pronunciation or an obvious presentation does not necessarily create the highest level of believability. You will find that you can often create a greater level of truth and honesty in a character by simply holding back a little (or a lot). It may be that speaking a bit slower, a bit softer, altering the phrasing, or being somewhat more relaxed might be just the thing to make that emotional connection with the listener. If your character has a specific regional sound or accent to his or her voice, you may find that softening the edge makes your performance more effective. If your character is intended to be an exaggeration, the *less is more* philosophy probably won't apply, and to be effective you may actually have to go overboard on the characterization.

Less is more is a technique often used by filmmakers to create tension and suspense or as a form of misdirection to set the audience up for a surprise. For example, in the Steven Spielberg film *Jurassic Park*, the initial appearance of the T-Rex was not accompanied by a huge roar. Instead, the tension of the moment was created by ripples in a simple cup of water, implying the approach of something huge and menacing.

The same technique of minimalizing in your voice-over performance can create a moment of dramatic tension, or wild laughter. It often has to do with the character's attitude, the twist of a word, the phrasing of a sentence, the pace of the delivery, or simply a carefully placed pause.

Understanding and applying the principle of *less is more* is an acquired skill, much like comedic timing. It requires a mastery of the craft of voice acting to a point where you are not thinking about what you are doing, and your delivery comes from someplace inside you. Although some people seem to have a natural instinct for interpretation and using the *less is more* concept to create a believable performance, most acquire this skill through experience.

PERFORMANCE DYNAMICS — PACING, VOLUME, RANGE

Performance dynamics are the fundamental elements of vocal variety and lay at the heart of any voice-over performance. It is the dynamics of your performance that makes *less is more* a powerful technique. When you understand and apply the dynamics of *pacing*, *volume*, and *range*, you will be able to make any vocal presentation interesting and captivating.

Pacing refers to the variations of speed in your delivery. It is closely related to the rhythm and timing of the copy and to the tempo of your delivery. *Pacing* is how fast or how slow you are speaking at any given moment. I'm sure you've heard commercials or other voice-over that is delivered at the same pace throughout. There is no phrasing, no pausing for impact, absolutely nothing that makes an emotional connection. Only intellectual information being delivered often at a rapid-fire pace. Or you've heard people who . . . seem . . . to . . . take . . . for . . . ever . . . to . . . say . . . what's . . . on . . . their . . . mind. Does either of these styles of delivery get and keep your interest? No! In most cases a steady pace is boring and uninteresting, if not downright hard to listen to. There are some exceptions in projects for which a steady or slow pace may be critical and necessary to the effective delivery of information, as in an educational or training program. However, in most cases, slowing down or speeding up your pacing to give importance to certain words, phrases, or ideas will make a big difference in your presentation. Create interesting phrasing by varying your pace or tempo. Within two or three read-throughs, you should be able to find the pace and phrasing that will allow you to read a script within the allotted time and in an interesting manner. Some directing cues that relate to pace are: "pick it up" (speed up), "stretch" (slow down), "fill" (you have extra time), and "tighten" (take out breaths or pauses between words).

Volume refers the loudness dynamics of your presentation, and is how soft or how loud you speak at any given moment. Just as volume changes in a piece of classical music keep things interesting, dynamic range in voice-over directly relates to the believability of a performance. Performing a script at the same volume throughout is very much like delivering at the same pace throughout. Both result in loss of credibility in the mind of the listener, because real people change how fast and how loud they speak depending on how they feel about what they are saying. The dynamic range of a performance is directly related to attitude and tone — from soft and intimate to loud and aggressive. Dynamic range is expressed as variations in the *volume* (loudness) of your voice as your speak.

Range refers to a performer's ability to put variety into the performance by adjusting the pitch and placement of the voice to maintain interest. You've, no doubt, experienced a seminar or lecture at which the speaker spoke in a monotone, resulting in the audience tuning out and losing interest. Vocal *range* covers the spectrum from your lowest pitch to your highest pitch. Voice actors for animation have developed a wide range from which to create many characters. You have a normal vocal range for speaking in everyday conversation, and you can speak at a lower or higher pitch when necessary. Practice speaking at a slightly lower or higher pitch and notice how a small change in vocal range can result in a big shift in interpretation.

Listen to the way people talk to each other and you will notice a wide range of speaking styles. Excitement, enthusiasm, awe, sarcasm, pity, wonder, sorrow, cynicism, and sadness are all expressed in different ways by different people. The variations in the way a person expresses herself or himself reflect that individual's *vocal range*.

Observe how you instinctively adjust your *pacing, volume,* and *range* in your everyday conversations. Practice altering your dynamics as you speak to your friends or at work, and notice how they pay more attention to what you have to say.

Be aware, however, that performance dynamics can be easily misused, forced, or overdone. The secret to understanding these dynamics is in the interpretation of a script. What is the writer's objective? Who is the intended audience? How should the words be spoken to achieve the maximum emotional and dramatic effect? How should the intellectual content be delivered so the listener can understand and use it?

When combined, the dynamics of voice acting serve to help create drama, humor, and tension in a performance. When effectively used, they go hand-in-hand to result in a performance that inspires, motivates, and is believable.

ARTICULATION

Complex sentences are an everyday occurrence that every voice actor must deal with. Words must be spoken clearly and concepts communicated in a way that can be understood. Voice acting, and effective communication in general, is a blend of intellectual and emotional information delivered in an interesting and understandable manner. Unless a specific speech affectation is called for in a script, it is generally unacceptable to stumble through words or slur through a piece of copy. *Articulation* refers to the clarity with which words are spoken. Most common problems with articulation are the result of *lazy mouth*, or the tendency to not fully use the muscles of the tongue, jaw, and mouth when speaking.

Good articulation, or enunciation, can be especially tricky when copy must be read quickly. The script on page 33 works well as an articulation warm-up exercise. Read the following copy, this time making sure that your articulation is crisp and clear. Don't worry about getting it in "on-time," just focus on making every word clear and distinct. For the purpose of the warm-up exercise, you'll want to force yourself to over-articulate — and don't forget to speak the ends of every word. (See "The Cork" exercise on page 46 and CD/3.) When delivered in a performance, the articulation will be conversational, but more clear because your vocal instrument is warmed-up.

> Come in today for special savings on all patio furniture, lighting fixtures, door bells, and buzzers, including big discounts on hammers, shovels, and power tools, plus super savings on everything you need to keep your garden green and beautiful.

When the same letter is back-to-back in adjacent words such as the "s" in "hammers, shovels" and "plus super," it's easy to slide through the words sounding the letter only once. In a conversational delivery, it's fine to tie those letters together, but for this exercise speak the end of each word clearly. It is also easy to drop the letter "d" from words like "and" and "need," especially when the next word begins with a "t," "d," "g," or "b."

The letter "g" on words, such as "big," can sometimes be swallowed resulting in the phrase "big discounts" sounding like "bih discounts." The suffix "ing" can often be modified when in a hurry, causing words, such as "lighting" and "everything," to sound like "lightin" and "everythin." With good articulation, the ends of words are clearly heard, but not overenunciated and suffixes are properly pronounced.

The "s" and "z" sounds should be clearly distinct. The "s" in "door bells" should have a different sound from the "z" in "buzzers." The consonant "s" should sound like the end of the word "yes," which is primarily a non-vocalized release of air over the tongue. To properly pronounce the more complex "z" sound, the tip of the tongue starts in the "es" position and a vocalization is added. Say the word "buzz" and hold the "z." You should feel a distinct vibration of your tongue and teeth.

Plosives are another articulation problem area. *Plosives* are caused by excessive air rushing out of the mouth when speaking letters such as "P," "B," "G," "K," and "T." When this sudden rush of air hits a microphone's diaphragm, the result is a loud "pop." Plosives can be corrected by turning slightly off-axis of the microphone or by using a foam windscreen or nylon "pop filter" in front of the mic. To feel the effect of plosives, place your hand directly in front of your mouth and say "Puh, Puh, Puh" several times. Turning your hand to the side will show you how the blast of air is reduced when turning off-mic.

To achieve a conversational and believable delivery, it is often necessary to violate some of the basic rules of crisp articulation. However, it is important to understand and to master the correct way to do something before you can effectively do that thing incorrectly and make it believable. In other words, you've got to be good before you can do bad, believably. When speaking in a conversational style, be careful NOT to over-articulate.

Singers use a technique called *linking* (see page 88) in which the end of a word is dropped and the sound of the dropped letter is spoken as part of the next word. For example the phrase "he was fast and foolish" might be spoken as "he was fas an' foolish." With linking, the "t" on "fast" is moved to the beginning of "and," and the "d" on "and" would be moved to the front of the word "foolish." The result would be spoken as "he was fas tan d'foolish." Another trick that works for vocalizing consonants is to replace "t" and "d," "b," and "p," "f" and "v," "s" and "z," and "c" and "g." So, for example, "next time" would sound like "nex dime," "a big zebra" might sound like "a big seebra," and "a grand vacation" could be spoken as "a grand faycation."

DICTION

Diction is defined as the accent, inflection, intonation, and speaking style dependent on the choice of words. Diction is directly related to articulation, the clarity of your delivery, the correct pronunciation of words, and the sound of a character's voice. Diction is important in all voice-over performances — you really do want to say the client's name correctly and clearly. One of the best ways to improve your diction is simply to slow down as you speak and focus on your enunciation and clarity.

If you are creating a character voice, your diction becomes even more important. A character voice may be a dialect or specific speaking style, and it is vital that your words be understood. Listen to yourself closely to make sure you are speaking clearly and at the correct pace for the character. Exercise 9: "The Cork" on page 46, can help with diction.

RHYTHM AND TIMING

All voice-over copy has a built-in rhythm. *Rhythm* is an aspect of phrasing, but it is not directly tied to anything. It is the flow of the words, the way the words are organized in sentences, and the placement of emphasis, or value, on certain words. Poetic copy has an obvious rhythm (or meter). The rhythm of narrative copy is a bit more challenging to find, but it is there. Finding the proper rhythm is critical to an effective delivery.

Dialogue copy has a definite rhythm, which often includes a sort of verbal syncopation, gradually, or quickly, building to a punch line. Dialogue copy also involves timing. *Timing* refers to the interaction between characters or pauses between lines of copy, and is directly related to rhythm. How quickly does one character speak after another finishes a line? Do the characters step on each other's lines? Is there a long silence before a character speaks? These are all aspects of timing.

If you have a natural sense of timing, you are ahead of the game. If not, the producer will direct you into the timing, and you will get a sense of what is needed as the session progresses. As you become comfortable with your character, timing becomes automatic.

Watch TV sitcoms to study timing. Study the interaction between characters and how they deliver their lines. Listen for the jokes, and how a joke is set up and delivered. Watch the physical characteristics of the actors as they work together. What are their gestures? What facial expressions do they use when they deliver a joke? What expressions do they have when they react to something? How do they express emotion? Use what you learn to help develop your rhythm and timing.

All performances have a rhythm. Theater has the slowest rhythm, then film, followed by television and finally, radio with the fastest rhythm. In some ways, radio can be performed at almost any rhythm, but generally *radio rhythm* is faster than *TV rhythm*. Because radio uses only one of the senses, the rhythm, timing, and pace are set a bit faster to create a more real and believable interaction between characters. The faster tempo of radio gives the copywriter and talent an opportunity to quickly establish and develop an interesting story that will grab the listener's attention and hold it while the message is delivered.

PHRASING

Phrasing in voice-over copy is very much like phrasing in music. It refers to the flow of your delivery, the variations in tempo, rhythm, and timing as you speak, and the subtle nuances of your tone of voice. More specifically, phrasing relates to the way you say certain words or sentences. For example, a short statement — "I don't want to go" — can be phrased in several different ways. The first word "I" can be emphasized as the sentence is spoken rapidly to give personal emphasis. By the same token, the word "don't" can receive the emphasis to give an entirely different meaning. Putting a bit of a whine in the voice, and a frown on your face will create a clear image that "going" is something you really do not want to do.

Try this exercise to discover different ways to express this simple phrase. Read each line, emphasizing the word in bold:

I don't want to go!
I **don't** want to go!
I don't **want** to go!
I don't want **to** go!
I don't want to **go!**

Another way of phrasing this sentence would be to stretch out the word "don't," sustaining the word and those that follow while adding natural vocal sounds and pauses as the phrase is spoken more slowly and deliberately. This technique, called *pulling lines*, adds realism and believability to the character. A pulled version of this line would read like this: "I . . . dooon't . . . waaant tooo goooo." Although pulling lines can help to create a sense of realism in the delivery, it takes up valuable time, and most voice-over projects don't have time to spare. So this technique is generally used in a shortened form, or only when necessary.

Phrasing is closely related to pacing, rhythm, and timing in that it refers to how quickly words are spoken within a sentence or paragraph. But, even more than that, phrasing allows you to make the words more real and believable by adding emotional content.

THEE AND THUH, AE AND UH

Few words in the English language are used improperly more often than the little words "the" and "a." When used correctly, these words can help add power and emotion to your delivery. Used improperly, your message may sound awkward, and might even create an impression of your being "uneducated." Here are a few quick rules to keep in mind when you see these words in a script. Keep in mind these rules are not set in stone, but are only guidelines. Ultimately, whatever sounds best in the context of your performance, or the way you are directed, is the way you should go:

Basic Rules for "the"

1. Pronounce stressed as "thee" (long ē):
   - When "the" precedes a vowel: *The English alphabet has 26 letters.*
     Exception: pronounce as "thuh" if the word starts with a long "U"
     as in "thuh university" or "thuh United States."
   - When "the" precedes a noun you wish to stress for emphasis (replacing
     "a" or "an"): *Yes, that is **the** book you gave me.*
   - When "the" precedes a word you wish to indicate as unique or special,
     or is part of a title: ***the** place to shop, **the** King of France.*
2. Pronounce conversationally and unstressed as "thuh":
   - When "the" precedes a word that begins with a consonant: *The kitchen
     cabinet is empty. The car ran out of gas. The dog chased the cat.*
   - When "the" modifies an adjective or adverb in the comparative degree:
     She's been exercising regularly and looks the better for it.

Basic Rules for "a" and "an"

1. Use "a" before words that begin with a consonant, "an" before words
   that begin with a vowel: *a lifetime of choices, an extreme sense of duty.*
   - Words that begin with a vowel but are pronounced with the consonant
     sound "y" or "w" are preceded with "a": *a European farmer, a united
     front, a one-room school.*
   - Words that begin with a consonant but are pronounced with a vowel
     sound are preceded with "an": *an SST (es es tee), an F (ef) in English.*
2. Pronounce stressed as "ae" (as in "hay") (long ā):
   - When "a" is intended to emphasize the next word in a singular sense or
     is referring to the letter "A": *That is **a** singular opportunity. The letter
     A is the first letter of the alphabet.*
   - The pronunciation of "a" in its stressed form (ae) will be relatively rare
     for most voice-over copy as it is not generally conversational.
     However some technical copy may require this pronunciation to
     properly convey the message or instructions for training purposes.
3. Pronounce unstressed as "uh" when:
   - "a" precedes a consonant: a *horse, a new car, a cat, a personal debt.*
   - Your character is speaking conversationally or casually.
   - This unstressed form of "a" (uh) is used in most situations.

ATTITUDE

What is it that you, as an actor, bring to the performance of voice-over
copy? Are you happy? Sad? Angry? What is the mood of the copy? How do
you visualize the scene? What is there — in your personal history — that
you can tap into to help make the words real and your performance
believable? Answer these questions and you will have your personal
attitude. Answer these questions in terms of your script, and you will have
your character's attitude.

Attitude is the mind-set of the character in the copy. It gives a reason for the words, and motivation for the character's existence. When you read through copy for the first time, find something in the words that you can relate to. Find an emotional hook. Bring something of yourself to the copy as you perform and you will create more effective characters, a strong suspension of disbelief and a believable illusion of reality.

SENSE MEMORY

Every moment of your life is stored in your memory. And every emotional experience has a physical tension associated with it. The tension might reside anywhere in your body. There is also a sensory experience associated with the emotional experience that is closely linked to the physical tension.

Your five senses are some of your most valuable tools as a voice actor. Constantin Stanislavski, founder of "method acting," developed this tool to help actors create believable characters, and most acting schools teach some variation of the technique. To truly master the technique of *sense memory* you may need to take some acting classes which involve creative exercises in which you tap into your senses of sight, touch, taste, sound, and smell.

It is said that all creativity originates in the sensory organs. So, to fully utilize your creative voice-acting abilities, you will need to develop skills for recalling and utilizing sensory memories. However, once the basic concept of *sense memory* is understood, anyone can apply this technique to become a better communicator and achieve some amazing results. Here's how you can use this powerful tool:

Close your eyes and think back through your life to a time, event, experience, sensation, or feeling that is similar to what your character is experiencing and hold that memory in your mind. Make the memory as visual as you possibly can. With that memory held in your mind, recall how your senses were affected by what took place. Was there a special smell? A certain sound? Did something taste odd, or especially good? Did you see something unusual? Do you recall touching something in your memory?

As your memory becomes more visual, observe where in your body the physical tension for that memory is being held: neck, shoulders, chest, stomach, legs, arms, etc. Recall the physical tension, body posture, facial expression, etc. and hold onto it. Keep that memory firmly fixed in your imagination. Now, open your eyes and allow your character to speak the words in the script, in a sense filtered through your experience.

Although it may take some time for you to master this technique, even doing just the basics will put you well on your way to becoming a successful voice actor. Many people who do voice-over either don't utilize this technique, or simply are not aware of it.

The exercise on page 143 (CD/7) takes the concept of *sense memory* to a higher level to help create a totally believable character.

SUBTEXT

All commercials have an attitude. In fact, all copy has an attitude. Your job is to find it and exploit it. One way to find the attitude is to uncover the thoughts or feelings behind the words. This is commonly known in theater as *subtext*. Subtext is what sets your attitude and establishes, or shades, the meaning of what you are saying. It is the inner motivation behind your words. Subtext allows you to breathe life into the words in a script and into the character you create.

Using your sense memory to unlock emotional hooks is a technique for setting attitude. Now take that process a step further and define the attitude in words to arrive at the subtext. For example, let's say you have this line: "What an interesting fragrance." If the thought behind your words is "What is that disgusting odor? You smell like something that's been dead for a week!" the perceived meaning will be quite different than if your thought and/or feeling is "Wow! You smell amazing! That perfume you're wearing makes me want to be close to you." Each of these subtexts results in a completely different mental and physical attitude that comes through in your voice.

What you are thinking and feeling as you deliver your lines makes a tremendous difference in the believability of your character. You have a subtext in your everyday conversations and interactions with others. The idea here is to include a subtext in your performance. Decide how you want the listener to feel or respond to your character — what emotional response do you want to produce? To get the desired response, all you have to do is internalize the appropriate thoughts and feelings as you perform.

For some copy, creating a believable character can be challenging, even with a well-understood subtext. The problem may lie in the subtext itself. If you have chosen a subtext that is weak or unclear, try changing the subtext to something completely different, using an entirely different set of emotional hooks. You may find that by shifting your subtext, your entire performance attitude will change.

TONE

Closely related to attitude and subtext, *tone* is the volume of your voice, and the overall delivery of your performance. It is the sum total of *pacing, volume, range, articulation, diction, rhythm, phrasing, attitude,* and *subtext.* It is important to be consistent throughout your performance. Do not change your tone in mid-copy. If you are doing a soft, intimate delivery with a friendly attitude, maintain that tone from beginning to end. If your copy is fast-paced, aggressive, and hard-sell, keep the attitude and tone throughout.

Tone can also refer to the quality of your performance. If you change tone as you read, you will fall out of character and your levels on the audio console will fluctuate, which will drive the engineer and producer crazy. To maintain a consistent tone, do not drift off-mic. Keep your head in the same position relative to the microphone from start to finish. Working close to the mic gives a warm, soft tone, while backing off as little as a few inches gives a cooler tone for straighter, more direct reads.

Occasionally a script is written that calls for a complete change of attitude and tone in mid-copy. If there is a logical motivation for your character to change attitude, then it would be out of character to maintain a consistent tone throughout the copy.

REMOVE OR CHANGE PUNCTUATION MARKS

Copy writers use *punctuation marks* because a script is originally written for the eye, to be read. However, we don't use punctuation marks when speaking in conversation. Part of our job as voice talent is to take the words "off the page" and make them real and believable. If you're working the punctuation marks, your delivery will sound like you're reading.

One of the best ways to create an illusion of reality in a performance is to remove or change the punctuation marks. Instead of instinctively pausing at a comma, or stopping at a period, try ignoring the punctuation to create a contiguous flow of words.

Removing the punctuation marks doesn't mean literally going through the script with white-out, although I do know of some voice-actors who actually do that. What it does mean is performing the copy in a real, believable, and conversational manner. A real-life conversation is punctuated with pauses, changes of inflection, dynamics (soft, loud), emotional attitude (excitement, sadness, and so on), vocalized sounds (uh-huh, hmmm, etc.), and many other subtleties. Voice-over copy should be delivered the same way. Let your delivery dictate the punctuation.

Just because there is a comma in the script, it doesn't mean you have to take a breath! Just because there is a period, doesn't mean you can't deliver the line as a question or as an exclamation. What would your delivery sound like if you changed a comma to a hyphen? What if you put a comma at a different place in the script? You have an almost infinite number of possibilities for delivering any line of copy.

Allow the scripted punctuation marks to guide you, but not to take them too literally. Sometimes, a simple change of punctuation can make a big difference in the interpretation, thus improving the performance. Allow the lines of a script to flow into one another as they would if you were telling the story to another person, not reading it. Take the punctuation marks out of your performance and your performance will be on its way to being more believable.

Occasionally, you'll get a piece of copy that just doesn't make sense because the grammar or punctuation is wrong. The writer may understand what she wants to say, and even how the words should be spoken, but because it isn't punctuated properly for the eye, the words are pretty much meaningless. It then becomes your job to figure out what the correct punctuation should be so you can give the words meaning. For example, punctuate the following phrase to give it meaning[1]:

that that is is that that is not is not is that it it is

There is only one correct way to punctuate this line of copy to give it meaning. Most copy will also have one punctuation that works best for the eye, but there may be multiple options from which to choose when those words are spoken. You'll find the correct punctuation for the above line of text at the end of this chapter.

Changing and removing punctuation marks as you perform is a way of making the words your own to truly take them "off the page." This tool can help you find the inflection, energy, and dynamics you are looking for as you begin to make the critical choices for delivering your copy.

PAUSE FOR IMPORTANCE

A *pause* is much more than just a beat of silence between words or phrases. It is an aspect of phrasing, and a powerful tool you can use to take a voice-over performance to an entirely new level. A pause in your delivery can be any length from a fraction of a second to a few seconds, depending on the context of a script. You pause instinctively in normal conversation whenever you are thinking about what you'll say next. It's almost possible to hear the thought or the intention of importance that takes place during even the shortest pause. A pause implies that something big is coming and builds tension and suspense in the mind of the listener. When you pause, whatever follows is automatically perceived as being more important. And that's exactly what we want to achieve by using this tool.

Learning how to use a *pause* effectively can take some time, but once understood, the concept can be used to help create humor, drama, tension, suspense, and emotional response.

Another way to look at a pause is in terms of *timing*. Comedic timing requires just the right amount of time — or beat — between the set-up of a joke and it's punch line. If the timing is off, the joke isn't funny. The same is true when using a pause in a voice-over performance. Timing is everything.

Improper use of a pause can result in an uneven or choppy delivery. If there is nothing happening in your mind during the pause, those beats of silence are little more than empty holes in the phrasing. To be effective, there must be something happening that fills those holes. There must be thoughts taking place that are in alignment with the *desires*, or wants and needs, of your character. Those thoughts won't be verbalized, but their mere existence will be heard in your tone of voice, attitude, and overall delivery.

The following phrase will give you an idea of how you can use a pause to create value and importance. Begin by just reading the line once to get an understanding of its meaning and to come up with an initial delivery. Now deliver the line out loud as one continuous thought — no pauses.

Everything in our store is on sale this week only at Ponds.

Since there are no commas or other punctuation to give you hints as to the delivery, you're on your own to find the most effective way to say the phrase. Delivering the line as one continuous stream of words is certainly a valid choice, but it may not be the strongest. Now, deliver the same phrase, this time experimenting with placing a pause or two in your delivery. Use each hyphen in the lines below as a cue for a beat or brief pause in your delivery. Notice that no matter where you place a pause, you will instinctively give the words that immediately follow greater value (in **bold**).

Everything in our store — is on sale this week only at Ponds.
(the event receives natural emphasis)
Everything in our store — is on sale — this week only at Ponds.
(the event and time receive natural emphasis)
Everything in our store is on sale this week — only at Ponds.
(the location receives natural emphasis)
Everything in our store is on sale — this week only — at Ponds.
(the time and location receive natural emphasis)

The only way you'll find the most effective delivery when using the *pause* will be to experiment with the many possibilities in every script.

HOLD THAT THOUGHT — THOUGHT PACING

Interruptions are a way of life. You experience them every day. You might be in the middle of saying something really interesting . . . and then someone breaks in or cuts you off before you finish what you are saying. This also happens in voice-over, especially in dialogue. The challenge for the voice actor is to make the interruption sound real and believable.

In a voice-over script, an interruption is usually indicated by the ellipsis, or 3 dots (. . .). The ellipsis can also indicate a *pause* in the delivery, occasionally replacing a comma or other punctuation.

For example:

Boss: Peterson ... we seem to be having some problems in your division. What do you have to say about that?
Peterson: Well, sir, I ...
Boss: Now, listen up, Peterson. We need this taken care of right away ... Understand?

The trick to making an interruption sound real is to continue the thought beyond the last word to be spoken. Much like a pause, if the line is simply read as written, the performance can easily sound like the words are being read, or the interaction between characters may sound "off" or artificial. However, if the thought is carried beyond the last word, the interruption becomes real and natural.

To continue the thought, all you need to do is make up something your character might say that is appropriate to the context of the script. Write it on the script, if you like, but at the very least, keep the complete thought in your mind as you deliver the line, and be prepared to speak the words. Completing a thought will enable you to create a believable delivery of the words. This concept of *thought pacing* works well in a variety of situations.

In the following script, Peterson continues the thought until interrupted. By completing the thought "Well, sir…" you will set the tone, attitude, and pace for your delivery of the line.

Boss: Peterson ... we seem to be having some problems in your division. What do you have to say about that?

Peterson: Well, sir ... (*I've taken steps to get things back on track.*)

Boss: Now, listen up, Peterson. We need this taken care of right away ... Understand?

When the moment of the interruption occurs, simply hold the thought and let the interruption happen naturally. The continuation of the thought is often more realistic if verbalized, especially in a dialogue performance. If the other actor is a bit late with the interruption, no one will ever know, because you kept the thought going. If you are the actor who is interrupting, you need to make sure you deliver your line with the appropriate energy and attitude, and that you are cutting off the other person in a way that sounds like a real conversation.

Thought pacing is a tool that makes your character real! When you see ellipses in a script, you have an ideal opportunity to reveal the thoughts of your character during your delivery. Not only can you keep the initial thought going until you are interrupted, but you can also make your character more real by vocalizing sounds during the ellipses. For example, in the above script, Peterson might interject unscripted responses during the ellipses, and the Boss might even put in some "umms," or "uhhs" to add believability to the characters .

REVERSE TEXT TO FIND INFLECTION

Occasionally, it can be challenging to find the best way to deliver a line of copy. Usually when this happens, it's because the copy writer wrote the script for the eye and not for the ear. Sentence structure for the written word is often quite different than for the spoken word. A trick I call *text reversal* can often help. The basic idea is to simply reverse the sentence structure to discover a different way of inflecting the words. Once found, put the sentence back as written, and deliver with the newly discovered inflection and energy. It works just about every time! Here's an example:

> Created to bring you the ultimate home theater experience, our showrooms are stocked with the latest high-tech equipment.

By reversing the two parts of the sentence, you may discover a better way to inflect the words.

> Our showrooms are stocked with the latest high-tech equipment, and are created to bring you the ultimate home theater experience.

Once you've found an inflection you like, deliver as written, but keep the new inflection.

RIDE THE ELEVATOR TO TWEAK YOUR TIMING

Commercial scripts are often written with too little, or too much copy. It's just a fact of life. Also, we may discover that the choices we make for our character result in a delivery that is too slow or too fast. We need to be able to adjust our delivery so that we complete the copy within the specified period of time. Sometimes this challenge can only be resolved through script revisions. But, more often than not, we can easily adjust our delivery without affecting the meaning or intentions of our delivery.

The common way to think of this adjustment is to simply speed up or slow down the delivery. But thinking in these terms can have an adverse effect in that the words may sound rushed or unnaturally slow. A better, and much more practical, way to think of adjusting speed is to imagine that you are riding in an elevator. To speed up your delivery, simply imagine that you and the person you are speaking to get on at the same time, and that they are getting off at the next floor. You must tell them what you have to say by the time the elevator doors open. When you need to slow your pace, give yourself an extra floor or two for telling your story.

Changing the way you think about how you speak the words in a script can completely change the believability and effectiveness of your voice-over performance.

IMITATION

It has been said that *imitation* is the sincerest form of flattery. This may be true, but as a voice actor, you want to be unique. You can learn a lot from imitating techniques and performing styles. But be careful that your imitation of other voice-over performers is for the purpose of developing your own unique style. Be yourself, and find the uniqueness of your voice.

That's what will get you work! Only mimic what other voice talent do to learn their techniques. Then adapt what you learn to your personality and style. If you insist on imitating other performers, it could take a long time for you to find your unique voice-acting personality.

Shortcuts that Trick Your Brain — CD/6

THE 2-4 SHORTCUT

When you speak conversationally with a fairly relaxed delivery, the result is that certain words are often pronounced in a manner that is not totally accurate. Regional accents and dialects will reveal a wide variety of how certain words are spoken. For example, the word "tomorrow" is often pronounced as "tahmarrow," or "tamarreh." "Forget" becomes "fergit," "our" becomes "are," and so on.

When you want to speak with the standard non-accented American English to correctly pronounce words that have a "to" or "for" in them, simply replace the "to" or "for" with the numeral "2" or "4." Your brain is trained to say the numbers as "two" and "four," so as you are reading, your brain sees the number and you automatically speak the word more precisely.

RE-SPELL WITH SOUND-ALIKES

The same basic idea as the *2-4 Shortcut* can be used for other words as well. When you find you are mispronouncing a word, or need to speak with clearer diction, you can simply re-spell the word using a different word that has the sound you want. For a word like "our," change the spelling to "hour." One student of mine had difficulty speaking the word "cellular" when used in the context of a script discussing cellular telephones. By simply changing the spelling of the word on his script from "cellular" to "sell-ya-ler," he was almost immediately able to deliver the lines perfectly. This little trick fools the brain and works with most sound-alike words. The possibilities are unlimited, and using this trick can truly be a life saver when working with technical copy.

LINKING

A common problem is the de-articulation, or dropping, of the last letter or sound of a word. This condition is occasionally referred to as *lazy mouth*, and is simply the result of poor diction. Although it may be OK for general conversation, this can present a problem for recorded projects. When the last sound of a word is not spoken, or is spoken too softly, the word can get "lost in the mix" when combined with music or sound effects.

To correct for this, most people will mistakenly adjust their delivery to be overly articulated or over-enunciated. The result is an artificial sound that is not authentic. In some cases, where the character naturally speaks in a "lazy" style, this de-articulation of the ends of words can be completely appropriate. However, for most voice-over copy — especially copy that will eventually be mixed with music or sound effects — the delivery must be spoken with clear diction. Here's a way to do that without resorting to over-articulation.

The technique is called *linking*, and it's a trick that comes from the world of singing. The idea is to take the last letter of a word and attach that letter to the beginning of the next word. For example, the phrase "...and everyone was there" might sound like "an everyone was there," with the "d" not spoken on the word "and." To use the *linking* technique, the "d" on "and" is moved to become the first letter of the word "d-everyone." So the adjusted line will sound like "an deveryone was there."

CHANGE THE CONTEXT TO FIND THE ATTITUDE

Many of the tools in this chapter are intended to help you discover the most effective, or appropriate, choices for delivering a line of copy. Changing *context* is yet another way to look at your script from a different perspective. This simple trick, also known as *substitution*, might make the difference between a flat delivery and one that lands on target.

When you are having problems with a line, completely change the sentence to something that you understand and relate to. It's OK to change the words because this is only a process for you to discover choices. Once you've found a meaningful way to speak the words, go back to the written script and use the same delivery style. For example, this probably won't mean anything to you:

> The GMS fifty-five oh two, and the H-27-R hybrid transducer were successfully tested during a trial period in October of last year.

So, let's change it to something like this:

> The red cherries and the yellow lemon were successfully eaten during a lunch break last week.

The new context doesn't need to make any more sense than the original script. But by using *substitution* to change the context to something you easily understand, you will be able to create a meaningful delivery. Now all you need to do is apply your chosen delivery to the original script.

MAKE THEM THE ONLY WORDS

Occasionally the context of a script or the way a paragraph is written can be troublesome, resulting in difficulty finding an effective interpretation. When you notice that you're throwing away the end of a sentence, or that your inflections are the same for every line of copy, reduce the script to the one line of copy giving you a problem. Make that one line the entire script and deliver the line out loud to hear how it sounds. Experiment with it a few different ways and choose the best way to say the line. Then put the line back into the context of the script to hear how it works with the full text. This trick will usually make a big difference.

Microphone Technique

Microphone technique is a subtle but powerful way of enhancing your character or the emotional impact of your delivery. Mic technique refers to how you use the microphone to your advantage while in the booth.

MICROPHONE BASICS

Before you can use a microphone effectively, it is helpful to first have a basic understanding of how these marvelous instruments work. The basic purpose of a microphone is to convert acoustical energy (sound waves) to electrical energy that can be manipulated and recorded. There are several designs for each of these types of microphones, *dynamic* and *condenser* being the most popular.

- *Dynamic* mics use a moving coil attached to a diaphragm (much like a loudspeaker in reverse) to convert acoustic energy to electrical energy. Dynamic mics are relatively inexpensive and rugged. Sound quality is generally better with the more expensive models. Simply plug it in to the appropriate equipment and start talking.

- *Condenser* mics use two fixed plates very close to each other, but not touching. A constant voltage is placed across the two plates, provided by a power supply (usually from a battery or external power supply). As sound waves strike one plate, a change in the electrical energy is the result. Condenser mics are more expensive, far more sensitive, and more fragile than dynamic mics. The sound quality of a condenser mic is generally cleaner and "crisper" than that of a dynamic mic.

Microphones come in two primary pickup patterns: *omnidirectional* and *cardioid* (*unidirectional*). Of these, the most common type of microphone for recording is the cardioid. Omni and cardioid mics can be either dynamic or condenser.

- *Omnidirectional* mics will pick up sound equally from all directions and are not very common for high-quality voice recording. They are, however, usually the least expensive and most rugged.

- *Cardioid* mics (also called unidirectional mics) come in a wide variety of designs, but virtually all of them pick-up sound best from directly in front of the mic. The sound pick-up reduces or fades as you move off-axis of the front center of the mic. The back of the mic is the point of maximum sound rejection.

- A *bidirectional* mic is a single mic that has the pick-up pattern of two cardioid mics placed back to back. With a bidirectional mic, maximum rejection is from the sides at 90° off-axis.

MICROPHONE PLACEMENT AND COPY STAND POSITION

In a recording studio environment you will generally be standing in front of a music stand (copy stand) with a microphone on a boom at about head level. Adjust the copy stand to eye level so you can see the entire script without having to tilt your head down. Tilting your head can affect your sound by constricting your throat and cause you to move off-mic. Studio microphones are very sensitive and often have a "pop" screen positioned between the mic and your mouth. The pop screen prevents blasts of air from hitting the microphone's diaphragm. Studio microphones are usually *cardioid* (directional), and most engineers position the mic off to the side or perhaps in front of the performer, above the copy stand at about forehead level. The acoustics of the voice booth are *dead*, meaning there are no reflected echoes. The result is a very clean sound.

Microphone placement is simple for a single performer, but becomes more critical when there are several performers in the same studio, each with his or her own mic. In this case, the engineer strives to obtain

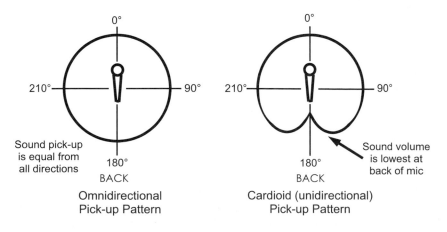

Figure 7-1: Basic microphone pick-up patterns

maximum separation from each performer to minimize how much of each actor's voice is picked up by the other microphones.

As a starting point, you should position yourself so your mouth is about 6 to 8 inches from the mic. You can easily estimate this by extending your thumb and little finger; place your thumb against your chin, and the mic at the tip of your little finger. This is not a critical distance, and your engineer may adjust the mic closer or further from you.

WORKING THE MICROPHONE

Microphones really don't care where they are in relation to your mouth. Six inches off to the left will pick up your voice exactly the same as six inches directly in front of you or six inches above your mouth (at about eye level). You should always position yourself so you are talking across the microphone and never directly into it. Speaking directly into the mic can blast the diaphragm. Although this is rarely harmful to the mic, the resulting "popping" sounds can be a serious problem for the recording and are something that cannot be fixed later on. Over time, moisture from your breath can affect the microphone's diaphragm, dulling it's sound.

As you physically move closer to a studio microphone, your voice increases in lower frequencies (bass) and the overall tone of your voice will be more intimate. This phenomenon is called *proximity effect* and is a common characteristic of all directional microphones. As you move away from a studio mic, the mic picks up more of the natural ambience of the room. This results in a more open sound, which is cooler and less intimate. Don't be afraid to experiment, but do let the engineer know what you are doing because he or she will need to adjust recording levels accordingly.

While performing, keep your head in a constant relationship to the microphone. The rest of your body can move as much as you need, provided you aren't making any noise. But your head must remain relatively stationary. If your position drifts on- and off-mic, your voice will appear to fade in and out. This drives engineers crazy because the overall volume of your performance is constantly changing. Even with the best equipment, moving off-mic is extremely difficult to deal with simply because a change of just a few inches can result in a very noticeable change in the *room tone* or ambience picked up by the mic.

NEVER BLOW INTO OR TAP A MICROPHONE

Studio microphones are delicate and *very* expensive. Blowing into a microphone can cause severe damage. When testing a mic or giving a level to the engineer, always speak in the actual volume of your performance. When the engineer asks you to read for levels, consider it an opportunity to rehearse your performance.

Tapping the mic, although not usually harmful, is annoying to most engineers. It's good to keep engineers on your side; they control how you sound and have complete power in the control room. Remember basic studio etiquette — don't touch the equipment!

LET THE ENGINEER POSITION THE MICROPHONE

Always let the engineer adjust the mic to where you will be standing or sitting. Do not move or adjust the mic yourself. The same goes for the pop stopper. After positioning your mic and returning to the control room, the engineer will ask for your level, and may ask you to physically change your position relative to the mic. You may be asked to *move in* on the mic (move closer to the mic), or *back off* a bit (move an inch or so away from the mic). These physical adjustments should be minor, and are intended to help produce the right sound for your voice. If you are popping, you may be asked to change the angle of your face in relation to the mic, or to turn slightly off-mic to prevent your breath from hitting the mic.

HOLDING THE MICROPHONE

You will rarely need to hold the mic during an actual session. However, it may be necessary for some auditions. If it ever happens to you, you need to know how to properly hold the mic for the best sound.

The correct handheld mic technique is to hold it vertically or at a slight angle, with the top of the mic at chin level, about an inch below the lips and slightly away from the chin, not touching the face. In this position, you will be speaking across the top of the mic rather than directly into it. Talking across the mic minimizes breath pops. You can test for proper mic placement by saying "puh, puh." Slowly raise a finger from below your chin up to your lips and you will know where to position a mic to avoid being hit with your breath.

If you need to hold the mic, do not play with the cord. Just let it hang from the end of the mic. Wriggling the cable can cause noises in the mic that can affect how you are heard. You may not hear anything as you perform, but cable noises can be heard by the producer later on, and may cover up parts of an otherwise good recording.

USING HEADPHONES

Communication during a recording session is extremely important, and a comfortable pair of headphones is the best way to do it. By wearing headphones, you will be able to hear yourself as you are delivering you lines. This auditory or *foldback* of your voice will often allow you to hear subtle mistakes that might go unnoticed if you aren't wearing headphones. It will also allow you to effectively apply certain microphone techniques for achieving warmth or avoiding breath pops.

Another benefit of wearing headphones is that the producer, director, and engineer will be able to communicate with you. Some voice talent feel that headphones are a distraction and prefer to work without them, but the simple fact is that there is often no other option for communication between the control room and booth.

A third benefit of headphones happens when you are performing in sync with, or need to time your performance to a playback. Headphones allow you to hear what you are working with, without the microphone picking up the playback audio.

There is no rule that says you can't take your favorite headphones to a session. It's done all the time. The important thing is that you treat your headphones as another tool for use during your performance of voice-over.

Acting Classes

You can never take enough classes. You've heard it before, and you will hear it again. Acting classes are where you can learn a wealth of techniques for analyzing copy, developing character, delivering lines, discovering motivation, using body language, interacting with other characters and much, much more.

Acting classes are available at most colleges, as well as from local community theater groups and other sources. Many cities have an actor's studio that offers ongoing workshops. Improvisation workshops are another useful class for the voice actor. Improvisation in voice-over is important because it gets your creative juices flowing and helps with your interaction with other characters in multiple-voice scripts. In an improv class, your creative talents will be expanded and you will discover things about yourself you never knew.

Take classes — you won't be sorry. Then take some more!

I used to have voices in my head . . .
Then I got them all jobs.
Wally Wingert, Character Actor and Voice Talent

Here is the proper punctuation for the line on page 84.

That that is, is. That that is not, is not. Is that it? It is.

---

[1] *Flowers for Algernon,* Keyes, Daniel. Harcourt (reissue, April 1995).

8

Voice Acting 101

It's Not about Your Voice . . .
It's about what you can DO with your voice!

As valuable as they are, the Seven Core Elements of Performing in Chapter 6 are just the first steps for creating an effective performance. There are many other things you can do to build on these core elements to improve the effectiveness of your delivery. The techniques you learned in Chapter 7 and the tools in this chapter will help you to develop versatility and expand the range and variety of your vocal performance. As you begin to master these techniques, you will find your delivery becoming increasingly effective. You will also discover that you will become better able to handle a wider range of delivery styles, emotions, and attitudes.

It is important to understand that the techniques you use are *not* your performance. Techniques are there to support and assist you in achieving the objectives of your performance. It's much like building a house: the hammer, saw, nails, and boards are only tools and components that are used to build the house. Acting techniques are the tools and component parts of your performance.

Understanding how to use a technique in and of itself is of only limited value. You also need to know how to apply the techniques you use in the broader scope of your performance. This chapter covers concepts and performing principles that are basic to theatrical acting, and any or all will be of tremendous value to you as a voice-over performer.

Commit to Your Choices . . . and Adjust

All acting is based on initial choices and adjustments made to those choices as a performance develops. As you work with a piece of copy, you will be making lots of decisions and choices about who your audience is, who your character is, what the back story is, and many other aspects of your performance. It is important to commit to these choices in order to be consistent throughout the recording session.

Of course, as new choices are made to enhance your character or performance, you must commit to these also. In some cases, you may find that the choices you have committed to no longer work as well as you or the director might like. You may find it necessary to completely change or revise some of your choices. That's OK! Your choices are not engraved in stone. Learn how to explore a variety of choices and be flexible as a performer so you can make adjustments quickly, without thinking. As new choices are made, commit to them to maintain a consistent performance. As you discover and commit to the best choices that develop the character and strengthen the delivery or emotional impact of the message, you will be creating realism and believability in your performance.

BE IN THE MOMENT

This is basic acting. You must be focused on your performance. You cannot be thinking about what you are doing later that afternoon and expect to give a good performance. You also cannot be in the moment if you are struggling to get the words right or dealing with interpretation. As long as you are focused on the copy, you will sound as though you are reading. To be in the moment, you must become comfortable with the words to the point where they become yours, and you are not thinking about what you are doing. Being *in the moment* is what Core Element #6, *Forget Who You Are*, is all about.

Being in the moment means that you understand on an instinctive level, your character, who your character is speaking to, the message in the script, and innumerable other details. It also means that you speak the words in the script with a truth and honesty that comes from the heart of the character. A good way to be and stay in the moment is to practice the techniques in this chapter. Mastering this skill can take some time, so don't be discouraged if you find yourself drifting out of character or starting to think about what you are doing. Keep working at it and it will come. Some actors will spend many years developing this skill.

Your best and most real performance will be achieved when you are truly "in the moment" of the scene taking place — aware of what you are doing, but not consciously thinking about it.

BE YOUR OWN DIRECTOR — MASTERING SELF-DIRECTION

You need to learn how to look at your performance objectively, as if observing from a distance. This director in your mind will give you the cues to keep your performance on track. *Self-direction* is not only a valuable skill that you can use constantly — even when there is a director on the other side of the glass — but it is a skill that becomes absolutely essential when you record voice tracks from the comfort of your personal home studio.

When you are wearing your "director" hat, you need to be listening for all the little things in your delivery that are, and are <u>not</u> working. Look for the important words in the copy that need to receive importance or value. Look for the parts that need to be softened. Look for places to pause — a half-second of silence can make all the difference. Listen for the rhythm, the pace, and the flow of the copy. As the director, you are your own critic. Your goal is to constructively critique your performance to increase your effectiveness in communicating the message.

The process of looking at your performance objectively is part of Core Element #6, *Forget Who You Are and Focus*. It can be quite difficult if you are working by yourself. The difficulty lies in the fact that if you think about what you do as you are performing, you will break character. Your "director's" listening process needs to be developed to the point where it happens at an unconscious level, yet you still have a conscious awareness of what you are doing as your character. You would be wise to work with a voice coach or take some classes to learn what directors look (or listen) for and how they work with performers to get the delivery they want. Watch and learn as others are directed. Observe how the director focuses the performer on the particular part of the copy that needs improvement.

Record your practice sessions and have a skilled director listen to your recordings to give you suggestions on what you can do on your own. As you gain experience, your performance and self-direction become as one, and you will soon instinctively know how to deliver a piece of copy.

LISTEN AND ANSWER

An actor's job is to respond. And the best way to have a believable response is to listen. Be aware of what is going on in the copy so you have an understanding of the story and can respond appropriately. Don't just read words on the page.

- Listen to your *audience* so that your response is appropriate.
- Listen to your *character*, and to the other performers if you are doing dialogue copy. Interact with what is being said. Be real! Respond to the message emotionally and physically. Remember that acting is reacting. Listen to yourself as you deliver the lines, and observe your internal response to the words you are saying. Then react or respond accordingly. This technique can give life to an otherwise dull script.
- Listen to the director in your mind to stay on track. Learn to think critically to constantly improve your performance.
- Listen to the producer or director to take your performance where it needs to go. Your performance needs to reach the producer's vision.

• Listen to your body to find the physical tension and emotional energy needed for a believable delivery. Without physical energy, there is little more than just words.

It is only by careful listening that you will be able to respond appropriately and ultimately get out of your own way to *forget who you are*.

MAKE IT THE FIRST TIME EVERY TIME

Be spontaneous, every time! Use your acting and imagination skills to keep the copy, and your performance, fresh. Each performance (or take) should be as though the character is experiencing the moment in the script for the first time. You may be on take 24, but your character in the copy needs to be on take 1 — for every take. Use your imagination to create a clear visualization of a scene, character, or situation to help make your performance real and believable take after take.

In the preface to the book *Scenes for Actors and Voices*, Daws Butler is quoted from one of his workshops[1]:

I want you to understand the words. I want you to taste the words. I want you to love the words. Because the words are important. But they're only words. You leave them on the paper and you take the thoughts and put them into your mind and then you as an actor recreate them, as if the thoughts had suddenly occurred to you.

Learn how to be consistently spontaneous! This doesn't necessarily mean that every time you deliver a line of copy it must sound exactly the same — that will depend on your choices and any adjustments you make. What this means is that you need to be able to deliver each line of your performance as though it was the first time your character ever thought of those words.

TELL THE STORY EFFECTIVELY

Don't just read the words on the page. Play the storyteller — no matter what the copy is. Search for an emotional hook in the copy — it's in there someplace — even in a complex technical script. Find a way to close the gap between the performer and the audience. Find a way to connect with that one person you are talking to, on an emotional level.

Your emotional connection may be in the softness of your voice. Or it may be in the way you say certain words. It may be in the way you carry your body as you speak your lines. Or it may be in the smile on your face. Make that connection, and you will be in demand.

Don LaFontaine, one of the top promo and movie trailer voice actors in the US, was once asked what he did as he performed. His answer was, "I create visual images with a twist of a word." It is the little shift of inflection or subtlety in the delivery of a word or phrase that makes the difference between an adequate voice-over performance and an exceptional voice acting performance. Effective storytelling is using the subtleties of performance to reach the audience emotionally and create strong, memorable visual images.

FIND THE RHYTHM IN THE COPY

Consider voice-over copy in terms of a musical composition. Music has a range of notes from high to low, being played by a variety of instruments (the voices). The tempo of the music may be generally fast or slow (the pace), and the tempo may fluctuate throughout the composition. The music also has a range of loud-to-soft (dynamics). These elements combine to create interest and attract and hold the listener's attention. Voice-over copy works the same way.

All copy has a *rhythm*, a *tempo*, and a *flow*. Rhythm in voice-over copy is much the same as rhythm in music. There are many pieces of music that run two minutes, but each has a unique rhythm. Many times, the rhythm changes within the composition. Rhythm in voice-over copy is as varied as it is in music. Some copy has a rhythm that is smooth, classy, and mellow. Other copy has a choppiness that is awkward and uncomfortable.

Some of the factors that affect rhythm in voice-over copy are pacing, pauses, breaths, the subtle emphasis of key words, and even diction and intonation. In dialogue copy, rhythm also includes the timing of the interaction between characters. Find the rhythm in the copy and you will win auditions.

Rhythm is something that can only be found by making the copy your own. You cannot get into a rhythm if you are just reading words off a page. Make the words your own by knowing your character, and you will be on your way to finding the rhythm. You might find it interesting to record yourself in a conversation. You may discover that you have a rhythm in the way you speak, which is quite different from the rhythm of others in the conversation.

A conversation has several things going on at once: There is a rhythm to the words, a tempo or pacing, and the interaction between the people having the conversation. Listen for pauses, people talking at the same time, the energy of the conversation, and the way in which certain words are emphasized. Observe how they move their bodies, especially when expressing an emotion or feeling. All these elements, and more, go into creating the rhythm of a conversation.

An excellent way to study vocal rhythm is to watch classic black and white movies from the 1940s. Many of these films feature some incredible character actors with interesting voices who use rhythm, tempo, phrasing, and vocal texture in powerful ways.

UNDERSTAND THE BIG PICTURE WITH SIX "W'S" AND AN "H"

Look for the basic dramatic elements of a story as you study a script. These are the basic journalism five W's — who, what, when, where, and why; and, of course, the ever popular "how." As an actor, it's very helpful to add a sixth W to define the environment in which the story is taking place — the "weather." The more details you can discover, the more accurately you will be able to portray a believable character in the story.

Here are some examples of what you can ask as you work your way through the six W's and an H:

- Who is your character?
  Who are the other characters in the story?
  Who is your character speaking to?

- What does your character want or need at this moment in time?
  What is your character responding to?
  What is the plot of the story?
  What is the emotional relationship between the characters?
  What is the conflict?
  What complications arise?
  What events brought your character to this situation?

- When does the story take place?
  When does the peak moment happen?

- Where is the story taking place?
  Where, geographically, are other characters or objects in relation to your character?

- Why is your character in the situation he or she is in?
  Why does your character behave the way he or she does?

- Weather: Is the environment cold, hot, steamy, dry, wet, dusty, or cozy? Allow yourself to feel the temperature and other conditions of the environment so you can fully express the feelings and emotions of the story.

- How is the conflict resolved, or not resolved?
  How is the message expressed through the resolution or nonresolution of the conflict?

Ask a lot of questions! By understanding what is taking place, you will discover your role in the story. A dramatic story structure with a definite plot is most often found in dialogue scripts. However, many single voice scripts have a plot structure that evolves through the course of the story.

Unfortunately, many small-market and lower-end scripts are written solely to provide intellectual (or logical) information. Information-based copy, also known as spokesperson copy, rarely has much of a story or plot, and thus there is little or no conflict. With no conflict to be resolved, it can be very challenging to find an emotional hook. Industrial copy often falls into this category. Even with no plot, you still need to determine the audience, back story, and character, and you need to find a way to bridge the gap between performer and audience. Building that bridge can be a much greater challenge than it is with a plot-based story script. However, an emotional connection can still be made with the audience through effective characterization, and a "twist of a word."

ASK "WHAT IF . . ."

While working with a script, you will often find that you deliver the copy in a style that is very comfortable for you, but which may not be the most effective for the script. As you develop your performance, you'll begin to make choices that will affect the many aspects of your delivery and how the words will be perceived. At some point in time, you will settle on your choices, and that's how you will perform the script.

But "what if" you slowed down on part of a line that you hadn't considered before? Or sped up on a different line? Or maybe delivered a line with changing tempo or rhythm? "What if" you lowered your volume to a point just above a whisper? "What if" you gave one word in each sentence a great deal of value and importance? "What if" you chose a different audience? "What if" your character had a different posture? "What if" your character wanted a different outcome? "What if . . ."

Just because you think you've got a "killer" delivery for a script doesn't mean that what you've come up with is what the director is looking for. If you get yourself stuck with one delivery, you may be in trouble when the director asks you for something different. By asking "what if..." throughout your wood shedding process, you'll come up with lots of options which will prepare you for anything the director might throw at you. Ask "what if . . ."

MAKE UP A LEAD-IN LINE (PRE-LIFE) — CD/6

Here's another trick to fool your brain when searching for the proper inflection of a line of copy. A *lead-in line* is simply a short statement of a possible *back story* that will give your character *pre-life* before the first line of copy. Before delivering your first line, you say something that would be a logical introductory statement, or lead-in. You can say it silently, or out loud. If you say the line out loud, leave a beat of silence before your first line of copy so that the editor can remove the unwanted lead-in line.

For example, if you are reading copy for a spokesperson commercial, you might want to have a lead-in line that sets up who you are talking to. Let's say you have determined that your audience is men and women in their thirties and forties, self-employed, and financially well off. You have set your character as someone who is equal to the audience, so you won't be patronizing; however, you will be conveying some important information.

Here's the copy:

> Traffic! Seems like it's getting worse every day. If your
> daily commute feels like being trapped in a parking lot,
> the answer to your problem is just around the corner.
> Take the New Bus. It's not the ride you think it is.

For a *lead-in line*, you might set up the copy by putting yourself in the position of talking to your best friend, John. Rather than starting cold, set a visual image in your mind of a conversation between you and John. Deliver your lines starting with:

> *(Silently: I learned something really interesting today, and you know, John . . .)*
>
> Traffic! Seems like it's getting worse every day. . . .

Your lead-in line (*pre-sentence*) sets up a conversational delivery that helps you to close the gap and communicate your message on an emotional level. This approach works for all types of copy in any situation. The *lead-in line* can be anything from a few short words to an elaborate story leading into the written copy. Generally, the shorter and more specific, the better.

MAKE UP A LEAD-OUT LINE (AFTER LIFE)

Your character lives before the first word of the script and continues to live after the last word of the script. Just as a *lead-in line* will give your character *pre-life* to help you to find the energy, attitude, and proper manner for responding, a *lead-out line* will help you to maintain your character beyond the last word spoken. And, occasionally, a *lead-out line* can help you determine the appropriate mood, attitude, or emotion for a line.

A common problem many beginning voice talent experience is that as they near the end of a script, their delivery begins to fall off, and any character they've created loses believability. There can be several reasons for this, but the most common is simply the way our brains work. Most voice talent will be reading about 6 to 8 words ahead of the words being spoken. As the eye reaches the end of the script (or in some cases a line of copy), the brain sees it's job as being done, so it relaxes and waits for the mouth to catch up. The result is a fade out in energy and delivery.

When you create a *lead-out line*, you are giving extra life to your character. The lead-out line needs to be something that is appropriate for the context of the story. It can be used to set the tone and emotional attitude for a line of copy or the end of a script.

Find an interpretation and deliver the following line of copy, first only by itself . . .

Please don't park the car over there.

Now, using each of the following lead-out lines, deliver the same line of copy again. Just hold the after-sentence in your head — don't verbalize it. Notice how the intention of each lead-out line can completely change your delivery of the copy just by the thought you hold in your mind:

Sweetheart!
You idiot!
I don't want it to get wet!
You'll wake the family!

Use *lead-in* and *lead-out* lines to help maintain your character and lock in the attitude and emotional subtext of your delivery.

BILLBOARDING KEY WORDS AND PHRASES

Generally, if a client or product name appears in a script, you will want to do something in your delivery that will help give it some special impact. There may also be a descriptive phrase or clause that needs some special treatment. Giving a word or phrase that extra punch is often referred to as *billboarding*. Typical methods for *billboarding* a word or phrase include: leaving a slight pause before or after you speak the words, slowing down slightly, changing your body language or facial expression, changing the inflection on the word or phrase, or even reducing the volume of your voice. All of these have the effect of giving more value and importance to the word or phrase you are *billboarding* — but only if you have the appropriate thoughts behind the words.

Emphasis is usually what directors will ask for when requesting extra punch on a word. Most people interpret the word as meaning "to get louder" or "punctuate" in some way. By definition, the word *emphasis* means to change the intensity to add importance or value, specifically in terms of adding vocal weight to specific syllables. If you deliver a word by only making it louder, or "punching" the word, it will sound artificial and unnatural. There must be a thought in your mind in order for an *emphasized* word or phrase to have any meaning. Without the thought, it's just a louder word. When a director asks you to emphasize a word, change the way you think to interpret the request as asking for you to give greater importance and value to the word or phrase.

If you *billboard*, or place extra emphasis, on too many words or phrases, your delivery will sound artificial and forced, losing believability and credibility. Experiment with different ways to give value and importance to names, places, and phrases in a script. You will soon find one that sounds right. As a guide to help with your delivery, underline words you feel are important. As you work on your delivery, you may discover that underlining only the syllable that should receive value, rather than the entire word, can completely change the meaning or create a regional delivery. For example: defense could be spoken as <u>de</u>fense or de<u>fense</u>.

PERSONAL PRONOUNS — THE CONNECTING WORDS

First person personal pronouns — I, me, we, us, our, you, and your — are all words that listeners tune in to. These are *connecting words* that help the voice actor reach the audience on an emotional level. Use these words to your advantage. Take your time with these words and don't rush past them.

In some copy, you will want to give these words a special importance for greater impact. Most of the time, you will want to underplay the personal pronouns and give extra value to words that are the subject of a sentence. For example, the sentence — "It's what you're looking for!" — could have value placed on any of the five words, or a combination of two or more. The contractions — "it's" and "you're" — could even be separated into "it is" and "you are." Each variation gives the sentence a unique meaning. Read the line out loud several different ways to see how the meaning changes. Placing the greatest value on the word "you're" may not be appropriate if the context of the script is all about searching for exactly the right product. In that case, the word "looking" would probably be the best word to receive the greatest importance. Experiment with this phrase by changing the context to discover a delivery that sounds best for you.

It's what you're looking for.

A general rule-of-thumb is that when you emphasize or "punch" personal pronouns, the meaning shifts from the subject of the sentence to the individual being addressed. In the example above, the most important part of the line in the context of the story might be the aspect of finding that special thing everyone is "looking" for. By placing importance on the word "you're," the focus of the intent is shifted to the person and moved away from the action of looking. The result for the listener is that the meaning can be unclear, confused, or in some cases just doesn't make any sense.

There are certainly many situations in which the pronoun is exactly the proper word that needs to receive importance and value. However, this is usually only a valid choice when the individual being addressed is the subject of the intention for that line of copy.

WORK THE CONSONANTS

Bringing life to a script will often mean giving value and importance to certain words and phrases. But you can achieve similar results on a smaller scale when you *work the consonants*. Rather than emphasize an entire word, limit the emphasis to only the primary consonant in the word. This approach will help a word "pop" giving it a crisper edge in the context of a sentence. To do this, simply give the consonants a bit crisper articulation. The trick with using this technique is to find the correct amount of emphasis or articulation. If you hit the consonant too soft, the word can get lost in the mix. If you hit the consonant too hard, it can sound artificial.

This technique works well with copy that is descriptive, or which must be delivered quickly. There may not be enough time to spend with specific words and working the consonants will often achieve the same result. Also, working the consonants may be helpful for discovering a strong delivery for a line of copy. For example, in the following line of copy, the strongest delivery will be one which enables the listener to taste the food.

Crispy duck lumpia, basil scented prawns

Working the consonants in a way that lets you taste the food, will help the listener taste the food. For fast copy, working the consonants can help your delivery "cut through" the mix when music and sound effects are added. Deliver the following line first in a conversational style, then by giving the consonants just a bit more articulation or emphasis at a faster pace, and observe the difference.

The greatest deals of the decade at our grand opening sale.

Notice how *working the consonants* almost forces you into a certain delivery style. If your delivery needs to be conversational, this technique may not be appropriate as it can produce a choppiness or insincere delivery style. Use care when applying this technique. It may not work for every script, but this is definitely a technique worth keeping in your back pocket.

BUILDING TRANSITION BRIDGES

A copy *transition* is a *bridge* between concepts within a line, between subjects within a script, or between characters, and it can take many forms. It may be a transition of a character's mood or attitude. Or it may be a transition in the rhythm or pace of delivery. It might be a transition from a question asked to an answer given. It could even be a transition between concepts or products within a list.

Transitions help "hook" the audience and keep their attention. Look for transitional phrases in the script and decide how you can make the transition interesting. Avoid keeping your delivery the same through all the transitions as you read a script. Give each transition a unique twist. Change your physical attitude, movement, mental picture, or use some other device to let your audience know that something special has happened, or that you have moved on to a new idea.

Sometimes all that is needed is a slight change in your facial expression or body posture. Sometimes a shift in volume, importance, back story, or who you are talking to will create the *transition bridge*. And sometimes, a simple pause in your delivery will do the trick. Experiment with different techniques to find out what will work best for the copy you are performing. In time you will develop a style that sets you apart from other voice talent.

CONTRAST AND COMPARISON

A common writing technique is to present a comparison between two items, or to contrast the positive versus negative aspects of a topic. In almost all cases, a contrast and comparison will be followed by a benefit as to why one or the other is better. When you discover a contrast or comparison in a script, your job is to make the difference very clear to the listener. Here's an example:

> Most digital cameras require expensive, hard to find batteries. The new Sigma Solar camera doesn't use batteries — it uses the power of light. So you'll never have to worry about a dead battery again.

This script contains both a contrast and comparison. The comparison is between regular digital cameras that require batteries and the new solar camera. The contrast is between expensive, hard to find batteries and solar (light) power. The benefit is stated in the last line.

A contrast and comparison is best delivered by understanding the meaning of all aspects of the comparison and the ultimate benefit being discussed. When you understand the benefit you can create an emotional connection to that benefit and an appropriate thought that corresponds to that feeling. Use the feeling and thought as you speak the words for both parts of the contrast and comparison to create a believable delivery. If you don't truly understand the comparison or why the contrast is important, your delivery of the copy will be flat and emotionless.

Physical Attitudes to Help Delivery

M.O.V.E.

Remember Core Element #5 from Chapter 6? That pesky element of *energy* is so important that it deserves some additional discussion here.

Be physical! Body movement is an expression of emotion, and your expression of emotions or feelings is the result of the thoughts you hold in your mind. When you verbalize those thoughts the meaning of the words will communicate through the tone of your voice. Move your body in whatever manner works for you to effectively get to the core emotion of the message. Your **M**ovement **O**rchestrates your **V**ocal **E**xpression! M.O.V.E.

Try the following using this simple phrase: "I don't want to go." Begin by standing straight and stiff, feet together, arms at your sides, head up, looking straight ahead with an expressionless face. Now, say the phrase out loud — without moving your body, arms, or face — and listen to the sound of your voice. Listen to the lack of expression in your voice. Listen to how totally boring you sound.

While keeping the same physical attitude — and still without moving, say the same phrase again and try to put some emotion into your reading. You will find it extremely difficult to put any emotion or drama into those words without moving. When you begin to communicate emotions, your body instinctively wants to move.

Now, relax your body, separate your feet slightly, bring your arms away from your sides, and loosen up. Think of something in your past that you really did not want to do and recall the physical tension or feeling you originally felt. Say the phrase again — this time moving your arms and body appropriately for that original feeling. Listen to how your physical attitude and facial expression change the sound of your voice. Try this with different physical positions and facial expressions and you may be amazed at the range of voices you will find. A big smile will add brightness and happiness to the sound of your voice. A frown or furrowed brow will give your voice a more serious tone. Tension in your face and body will communicate stress through your voice.

It's a mistake to stand in front of the microphone with your hands hanging limp at your sides or stuffed in your pockets — unless that physical attitude is consistent with your character in the copy. Start your hands at about chest level and your elbows bent. This allows you the freedom to move your hands as you speak.

The way you stand can also affect your voice performance. Although body stance primarily communicates information visually, it can also be very important when creating a character. Body language, just as facial expression, translates through the voice. For example, to make a character of a self-conscious person more believable, you might roll your shoulders forward and bring your arms in close to the body, perhaps crossing the arms at certain points in the copy.

Physical changes help to create a believable character who is somewhat self-conscious, a bit defensive, perhaps unsure of the situation and who may even be shy and focused on how she or he is perceived by others. Your body posture assists in framing the attitude and personality of the character. The following are some typical body postures that will help you understand how body stance can affect your performance. If used unconsciously, these postures can have an adverse affect on your performance because they will have a direct impact on your speaking voice. However, when consciously applied to a character or attitude, these and other body postures can be used to enhance any voice performance:

- **Arms behind back ("at-ease" stance)** — This body posture reflects nervousness and implies that the speaker doesn't know what to do with his or her hands or is uncomfortable in the current situation. Clasping the hands in back or in front of the body tends to minimize other body movement and can block the flow of energy through your body. This in turn may result in a "stiffer" sound with a restricted range of inflection and character.

- **Straight, stiff body with hands at the side ("attention" stance)** — Standing straight and tall, with chest out, head held high and shoulders back implies authority, control, and command of a situation. This projection of power and authority can be real or feigned. This stance is sometimes used as a bluff to create an outward image of authority to cover for an inward feeling of insecurity. This body stance can be useful for a character who must project power, authority, or dominance over a situation.

- **Arms crossed in front of the body ("show me" stance)** — Crossed arms often represent an unconscious feeling of self-consciousness and insecurity, creating an attitude of defiance or being defensive. Crossed arms can also imply a certain level of dishonesty.

- **Hands crossed in front of the body ("Adam and Eve" stance)** — As with the at-ease stance, this posture implies that the speaker doesn't know what to do with his or her hands. This stance, with the hands crossed like a fig leaf, is commonly perceived as an indication that the speaker has something to hide. This stance can be useful in helping create a character who projects suspicion.

- **Hands on the hips ("mannequin" stance)** — This posture makes the speaker appear inexperienced or unqualified. Hands on the hips also blocks the flow of energy through the body and limits the performer's ability to inject emotion and drama into a performance. This stance can be used to create an attitude of arrogance.

Don't be afraid to be physical in the studio. Remember, movement orchestrates vocal expression! A simple adjustment of your *physical energy* can make a huge change in your performance. I have seen voice-over performers do some of the strangest things to get into character. The basic rule is "whatever works — do it." I once worked with a voice actor who arrived at the studio wearing a tennis outfit and carrying a tennis racket. Throughout the session, he used that tennis racket as a prop to help with his character and delivery. I've seen other voice actors go through a series of contortions and exercises to set the physical attitude for the character they are playing. A friend of mine was working a dialogue script and her male dialogue partner was having trouble getting into the right delivery. To get into the proper attitude, the two of them actually lay down on the studio floor as they delivered their lines. Your analysis of the copy can give you a starting point for your physical attitude. When you've decided on your physical attitude, commit to it and use your body to express yourself.

Many people are self-conscious when just starting in this business, and that's normal. However, when you are in the "booth," you really need to leave any judgments you may have about your performance outside. If you are concerned about what the people in the control room think about *you* as you are performing (rather than what they think about *your performance*), you will not be able to do your best work. It comes down to taking on an attitude of "I don't care" when walking into the booth or studio. It's not that you don't care about doing your best, or making the character in the copy real and believable. You must care about these things. But you cannot afford to care about what others think of you and what you are doing as you perform to the best of your abilities. And besides, as you'll discover later, it's not you delivering those words anyway — it's really your character who's speaking!

If getting to your best performance means that moving your entire body and waving your arms wildly are appropriate for your character, that's what you need to do. You can't afford to worry that the people in the control room might think you are crazy. The engineer and producer certainly don't care! They are only interested in recording your best performance as quickly as possible, and they have seen it all anyway.

Usually you can perform better if you are standing, but in some cases, being seated may help with your character. If you sit, remember that a straight back will help your breathing and delivery. If possible, use a stool rather than a chair. Sitting in a chair tends to compress the diaphragm, while a stool allows you to sit straight and breathe properly. If a chair is all that's available, sit forward on the seat rather than all the way back. This helps you keep a straight back and control your breath. Most studios are set up for the performers to stand in front of the microphone. Standing allows for more body movement and gives you a wider range of motion without being restricted.

Your physical attitude is expressed through the relaxation and tension of your face and other muscles. All human emotions and feelings can be communicated vocally by simply changing physical attitudes. Often, the copy expresses a specific emotion or attitude. Find a place in your body where you can feel the tension of that emotion or attitude — and hold it there. Holding tension in your body contributes to the realism and believability of your character. Focus on centering your voice at the location of the tension in your body and speak from that center. This helps give your voice a sense of realism and believability.

A tense face and body will communicate as anger, frustration, or hostility. A relaxed face and body result in a softer delivery. Try reading some light copy with a tense body; you will find it very difficult to make the copy believable. You can make your delivery friendlier and more personable simply by delivering your lines with a smile on your face. Turning your head to the side and wrinkling your forehead will help convey an attitude of puzzlement. Wide-open eyes will help create an attitude of surprise. Practice reading with different physical attitudes and you will be amazed at the changes you hear. Your physical attitude comes through in your voice. Remember to M.O.V.E.

Your Clothes Make a Difference

Wear comfortable clothes when recording. Tight or uncomfortable clothing can be restricting or distracting. You do not want to be concerned with shoes that are too tight when you are working in a high-priced recording studio. Stay comfortable. The voice-over business is a casual affair. With the increase in home studios for voice-over work, you can now even record in your jammies and no one will know the difference. I even know of one voice actor who will occasionally record — how shall I say this — in the all-together. He says it's a very freeing way to work.

Another note about clothing: The microphone in the studio is very sensitive and will pick up every little noise you make. Be careful not to wear clothing that rustles or "squeaks." Nylon jackets, leather coats, and many other fabrics can be noisy when worn in a recording studio. Other things to be aware of are: noisy jewelry, loose change in pockets, cell phones, and pagers. If you insist on wearing noisy clothing, it may be necessary for you to restrict your movement while in the studio, which can seriously affect your performance. Maybe my friend who records in the all-together has something!

If you are recording in your home studio, you'll need to not only be aware of clothing noise, but also the many other potential noise sources around your home.

The Magic of Your Mind: If You Believe It, They Will!

Believability is one of the secrets of success in voice acting. One of the objectives of voice acting is to lead the audience to action. The most effective way to do that is to create a *suspension of disbelief* during the time you are delivering your message. You suspend disbelief whenever you go to a movie or to the theater and allow yourself to be drawn into the story. In reality, you are fully aware that the people on the stage or screen are just actors, and that life really isn't that way. However, during the time you are experiencing the performance, you suspend your disbelief and momentarily accept the appearance of the reality of what is happening in the story.

Suspension of disbelief in voice-over is essential for creating a sense of believability in the message. The audience must believe you, and for that to happen, *you* must momentarily believe in what you are saying.

Use your imagination to create a believable visual image in your mind for the message you are delivering. The more visual you can make it, the more believable it will be for you and for your audience. On a subconscious level, your mind does not know the difference between illusion and reality. Just as your physical attitude affects the sound of your voice, if you create a strong enough visual illusion in your mind, your words will be believable.

Creating a visual illusion is a technique used by most great actors and virtually all magicians. For a magician to make the audience believe that a person is really floating in the air, he must momentarily believe it himself. The performer's belief in what is taking place contributes to establishing the suspension of disbelief in the audience. If the magician is focused on the mechanics of his illusion, he will not give a convincing performance.

Any performer focused on the technical aspects of the performance cannot possibly be believable. This is every bit as true for a voice-over performer as it is for a theatrical performer. The technical aspects and techniques of your work must become completely automatic to the point where you are not even aware of them. The words on that script in front of you must come from within you — from the character you create. Only then will you be able to successfully suspend disbelief. This is what's meant by the phrases "making the words your own" and "getting off the page."

Creating visual images is a good technique to use when you are delivering dialogue copy and single-voice or industrial copy that is technical or difficult. If you create the visual mental illusion of being an expert in the area you are talking about, that attitude of authority will communicate through your voice.

Read your script a few times to get an understanding of what you are saying. Then, set your visual image and let your character come in and be the storyteller, the expert, the spokesperson, the salesperson, the eccentric neighbor, the inquisitive customer, and so on. By allowing your character to take over, you automatically shift your focus from the technical aspects of reading the copy to the creative aspects of performing and telling the story.

A visual image helps give life to your character, reason for its existence, an environment for it to live in, and motivation for its words. Visualization helps make your character believable to you. If the character is believable to you, its words become true, and the message becomes believable to the audience. To put it another way: If you believe it, your audience will.

Trends

A considerable amount of voice-over work is in the form of advertising as radio and television commercials. The advertising industry is generally in a constant state of flux simply because its job is to reach today's customers in a way that will motivate them to buy the current "hot item." In order to do that, advertisers must connect on an emotional level with their audience. And, in order to do that, the delivery of a commercial must be in alignment with the attitude and behavior of the target audience. Each new generation seems to have its own unique lifestyle, physical attitude, slang, and style of dress. These constantly shifting *trends* are reflected in the advertising you see and hear on television and radio. You will notice different trends for different market groups, but the most obvious will be for products intended for the younger generation. In other words, what is "in style" today may be "out of style" tomorrow.

As a voice actor, it is important that you keep up with the current trends and develop flexibility and versatility in your performing style. You may develop a performing style that is perfect for a certain attitude or market niche, but if you don't pay attention to the changes going on around you, you may find that you are getting fewer bookings, simply because your style is no longer in demand.

Probably the best way to keep pace with current trends is to simply study radio and television advertising that is on the air today. Listen to what the major national advertising producers are doing in terms of delivery attitude, pace, and rhythm. Observe the energy of the music and how the visuals are edited in commercials and notice how the voice-over works with or against that energy. Look for commonalities among the commercials you study, and you will begin to notice the current trends. One thing you will notice is that most locally produced advertising does not follow the trends presented in national advertising.

You don't really need to do anything about these trends, other than to be aware of what they are and how they might affect your performance. That awareness will prove to be another valuable tool for you to use when you audition or are booked for a session. Use it to your advantage.

*Acting is basically a simple exercise
of living life truthfully under
imaginary circumstances.*
Byran Singer, director of
The Usual Suspects

---

[1] *Scenes for Actors and Voices* by Daws Butler, edited by Ben Ohmart and Joe Bevilacqua, foreword by Cory Burton. Albany, GA, Bear Manor Media, 2003.

9

Woodshedding and Script Analysis

The Director in the Front Row of Your Mind

As you study voice acting you will develop instincts as to how to develop your character, deliver your lines, and create drama in your performance. These instincts are good and necessary for a professional performer. However, if left at the level of instincts, they will limit your ability to find the nuance and subtlety of the performance — those seemingly insignificant things that make the drama powerful, the dialogue interesting, or a comedic script hysterical rather than just humorous.

All voice-over copy is written for the purpose of communicating something — selling a product or service, providing information, education, or expressing an emotion or feeling. No matter how well written, it is not the words in and of themselves that convey the message, it is the *way* in which *the words are spoken* that ultimately moves the audience. It is the details of the performance behind the words — the nuance — that allow a performer to bring a script and a character to life. And behind every performer, there is a director. Somewhere in your mind is a director. You may not have realized it, but that director is there. Allow your director to sit front row, center in your mind so he or she can objectively watch your performance to keep you on track and performing at your best.

Voice-over copy is theatrical truth — not real-life truth — and your internal director is the part of you that gives you silent cues to keep you real. As you work with copy, you will find a little voice in your head that tells you, "Yeah, that was good" or "That line needs to be done differently." The director in the front row of your mind is the result of critical thinking. He or she is the part of you that keeps you on track, helps you stay in the moment, and gives you focus and guidance with your performance. Think of this director as a separate person (or part of you) who is watching your performance from a distance, yet close enough to give you cues.

113

Over time, your internal director and your performance will become as one — a seamless blending of director and performer resulting in a truly professional dramatic artist, without any conscious effort. This mastery of self-direction is the level to strive for. This is what theater is all about. This is what you, as a voice actor, can achieve with any type of copy you are asked to read.

But there is a catch! As with most things in life, you must learn to walk before you can run. When performing voice-over, a mastery of performing skills is only the beginning. You must also learn how to dig deep into a script to uncover the truth that is hidden behind the words. This is a process commonly known as *script analysis*, or *woodshedding*.

"Woodshed" Your Copy

Although this chapter will include some review of concepts covered earlier, everything here is intended to help you discover a process of your own for quickly and effectively uncovering the details in any script so you can practice in a way that will bring the character to life. Once mastered, your personal process for *woodshedding,* or *script analysis,* may happen as quickly as reading through a script.

From the moment you first read any script, you instinctively come up with a way to speak the words. Sometimes your gut instincts will be dead-on accurate. At other times, you may struggle with a script as you try to figure out what it's all about and your character's role in telling the story. The character you create may ultimately be defined as simply an "announcer" or spokesperson doing a hard-sell sales pitch or, perhaps, a "friendly neighbor" telling the story about a great new product he has discovered. In other cases, the character you need to define may have a complex personality with a range of emotions. In almost every case, you'll need to do some sort of script analysis to uncover the information you need for an effective performance.

Let's review some of the key elements of copy that can help determine your character, attitude, emotion, and other aspects of your performance. For a more complete explanation, please refer to chapters 6, 7, and 8.

- **The structure of the copy** (the way it is written) — Is the copy written in a dialect style? Is the wording "flowery" or expressive in one way or another? Is the copy a straight pitch? What is the pace of the copy? What is the mood of the copy? What is the attitude of the character?

- **Know the audience** — Knowing the target audience is a good way to discover your character. Experienced copywriters know that most people fit into one of several clearly defined categories. The words and style they choose for their copy will be carefully chosen to target the specific category of buying public they want to reach. Specific words and phrases will be used to elicit an emotional response from the target audience. Your character may be defined in part by the words spoken to convey a thought, or his or her attitude may be clearly expressed within the context of the copy.

- **What is the back story** (the moment before) — What happened before the first word of copy? The back story is the specific event that brought your character to this moment in time. This may or may not be obvious in the script. All dialogue copy has a back story. There can also be a back story for single-voice copy. If a back story is not defined within the context of the script, make one up.

- **Who are the characters** (in a dialogue script) — Who is your character and how do other characters interrelate with your character and each other? This interaction can give solid clues about your character.

- **What is the conflict** — What happens in the copy to draw the listener into the story? Where is the drama in the story? How is conflict resolved or left unresolved? Is the conflict humorous or serious? How is the product or message presented through the resolution or nonresolution of conflict?

There are many other clues in the copy that will lead you to discovering the character. As the performer, you may have one idea for portraying the character, and the producer may have another. If there is any question about your character, discuss it with the producer.

Creating a Performance Road Map: Analyzing and Marking a Script

One of the first things you should do as you begin working with a script is to quickly analyze it; *woodshed* it, searching for clues to help you create a believable character and effective delivery.

As you begin working with voice-over copy, you may find that it will take you a few minutes to make the choices about your character and other aspects of the copy. However, as you gain experience, you will be able to do a thorough woodshedding in the time it takes you to read the copy a few times.

The Script Analysis Worksheet on pages 116 and 117 can be used when working with any piece of copy. The worksheet is essentially another way of breaking down a script to define the *Seven Core Elements* of a performance. If you find a sequential, linear process beneficial, you may find the worksheet helpful.

Once you've done this process a few times, it will become automatic and you won't need the worksheet any longer. By answering the questions on the worksheet, you can quickly learn everything you need to know about

Script Analysis Worksheet

Answering the following questions, based on the copy, will help you discover the audience you are speaking to, your character, and any special attitude you need to incorporate into your performance.

Who is the advertiser or client? _____

_____

What is the product or service? _____

_____

What is the delivery style?
- ☐ Fast and punchy   ☐ Conversational/friendly   ☐ Relaxed/mellow
- ☐ Single voice   ☐ Dialogue/multiple   ☐ Character/animation
- ☐ Authoritative   ☐ Business-to-business   ☐ Narration

Who is the advertiser/client trying to reach (target AUDIENCE)? Determine the age range, income, gender, buying habits, and any other specific details that become apparent from the way the script is written. Who is the "other person" you are talking to? Visualize this individual as you perform the copy.

_____

_____

_____

Find important key words or catch phrases where the use of dynamics of loudness or emotion will give value and importance. Look for the advertiser's name, product, descriptive adjectives, and an address or phone number. These elements may need special attention during your performance. Underline or highlight the words or phrases you want to make important.

What is the message the advertiser/client wants to communicate to the target audience? What is the story you are telling through your performance? What is the USP (unique selling proposition)?

_____

_____

How does the story (plot) develop? For dialogue copy, find the setup, the conflict, and how the conflict is resolved or not resolved. Discover how the plot flows. Are there any attitude changes with your character or others? Plot development is critical to effective dialogue copy. Determine your role in the plot and how your character develops.

_____

_____

Use arrows ↗ ↘ to indicate copy points for changes in inflection or attitude.

What is your role (CHARACTER in the story) in terms of how the story is being told? Do a basic character analysis to define your character's age, life style, clothing, speaking style, attitude toward the product or situation in the script, etc. What are your character's motivations? What are your character's WANTS and NEEDS (DESIRES) at *this moment in time*? What happened to your character in the moment immediately before the copy (BACK STORY)? Be as detailed as you can in order to discover your character.

_____

_____

How does your character relate to any other characters in the script, or to the audience in general? Is your character an active player in telling the story (as in a dialogue commercial), or is your character that of a narrator imparting information to a captive audience (as in a single-voice "spokesperson" commercial)? What can you do to create a bond between your character, other characters in the script, and the audience?

_____

_____

What can you do to make your character believable? Any special vocal treatments or physical attitudes?

_____

_____

Does your character have any unique or interesting attitudes, body postures, or speaking characteristics (speaks slowly, fast, with an accent, squeaky voice, etc.)? If so, identify these.

_____

_____

Study the copy for pauses that might be used to create tension or drama, and for places to breathe. This is especially important for industrial copy, which frequently contains long, run-on sentences with technical terminology. Mark breaths and pauses with a slash mark (/).

Find the rhythm of the copy. All copy has a rhythm, a beat, and timing. Discover the proper timing for the copy you are reading. Dialogue copy has a separate rhythm for each character as well as an interactive rhythm.

Look for transitions in the script (similar to attitude changes). These may be transitions from asking a question to providing an answer (common in commercial copy), or a transition between the attitudes of your character.

Look for key words you can give importance to, and that will connect you with the audience. Personal pronouns, such as "you," "our," "my," and "I," may be written into the script or simply implied. If connecting words are implied, find a way to make that implied connection through your performance (without actually saying the words).

a script and your character. If an answer is not clear from the copy, then make it up. You won't be graded on your answers, I promise. The answers you come up with are a tool for you to use in developing effective characters and delivery. They are simply a way for you to make practical choices for the script you are performing. For you to maintain a consistent performance, it is important that you stick with the choices you make in your script analysis. If something isn't working for you, of course, you can change your mind. But any new choices or changes should only be made to make your performance and your character more real and believable.

TO MARK OR NOT TO MARK

Through experimentation, you will find a form of script analysis that works for you. You may find that it is very helpful to mark your script with notes, lines, and boxes designed to chart your path through a performance. Or you may find it unnecessary to mark your script, and instead only make minor notations as needed. Whatever works for you is what you should use.

Script notation is very much like musical notation in that the markings are there only for the purpose of guidance. If you find you are paying too much attention to your notations as you read a script, you may be over-analyzing the text. This can result in a delivery that is unfocused and sounds like you are reading. As you develop your personal process for script analysis and notation, and your performing skills improve, you will most likely find you need to mark your script less and less.

Regardless of your individual process, or how much you mark your script, the basic process of *woodshedding* will remain the same. As you analyze a script, you will want to look for key words and phrases that reveal attitude and emotion, and give clues about your character. Notice the context of the copy and how the message is presented. Look for places where you can add variety by using the dynamics of pacing, energy, attitude, tone of voice, and emotion. Look for natural breaks, shifts of attitude or emotion, and transitions in the copy. Look for *catch phrases* that reveal something about your character's attitude, emotion, or feelings.

By the time you read a script through once or twice, you should be able to make some solid choices on how you intend to perform it. You should know who the one person is you are speaking to (the *Audience*), who you are as the speaker (your *Character*) and why you are speaking the words in the script at this moment in time (your *Back Story*).

Marking your script with specific notations can help you create a map of how you will deliver it. These markings are your personal cues to guide you through an effective performance of the copy.

Practice marking magazine or newspaper articles or short stories and you will quickly find a system that works for you. In a short time, you will refine your system to a few key markings which you can use regularly to guide you through almost any script.

Here are a few suggested markings and possible uses. Adapt, modify and add to them as you like:

- Underline (_____) — emphasize a word, phrase, or descriptive adjectives
- Circle (O) — key elements of conflict in the script
- Box (□) — the peak moment in the copy — put a box around the words or phrase at that point in the copy
- Highlight (▓▓▓) or different color underline — resolution or nonresolution of conflict
- Arrow pointing UP (↗) — take inflection on a word up
- Arrow pointing DOWN (↘) — take inflection on a word down
- Wavy line (~~~) — modulate your voice or inflection
- Slash or double slash (//) — indicate a pause

One of the most common markings is to underline a word that needs to be emphasized. This works fine in most cases, but there may be times when you want to make sure you say a word correctly. Try underlining only the syllable of the word that needs emphasis. For example: <u>de</u>fense or de<u>fense</u>.

Another important thing about script marking is that, although you certainly should understand its proper use, it's a good idea to reduce your markings as your performing skills develop. A heavily marked script will require a great deal of thought as you follow your roadmap. The more you must think about what you are doing, the less you are truly in character.

The degree to which you mark your script may vary from project to project, but it will certainly help to have a system in place when you need it.

Woodshed Your Script to Be More Believable

Just as you have a personality, so does the character written into every script. The character for a single-voice script is often simply that of an announcer or spokesperson delivering a sales pitch of some sort, or communicating basic information. But, even this announcer has a personality that is appropriate to the copy. Scripts written for dialogue or comedy have multiple characters that are often more easily defined. For all types of copy, finding the personality of the character allows you to give the character life and helps make your performance believable. Remember, making your performance believable is what voice acting is all about.

The best way to effectively communicate a scripted message is to create a believable character telling a believable story. To be believable, your performance must include variety, tension, and sincerity. It must also be easy to listen to and in a style that the audience can relate to. To be believable, you must know your character and develop a performing style that is conversational and real.

CHARACTER ANALYSIS

The way a script is written may define your character by the manner in which the words are written, or it may be left up to you to create something. Scripts written for specific or stereotyped characters occasionally have some directions written on the script. The directions may be something like: "read with an English accent," "cowboy attitude," or "edgy and nervous." Many times, producers or writers will be able to give you additional insight into their vision of the character. It will then be up to you to create an appropriate attitude and voice for that character.

In theater, this process of defining the attitude and personality of a character is called a *character analysis*. As a voice actor, you need to know as much about the role you are playing as possible. The more details you include in your character analysis, and the more you understand your character, the better you will be able to take an attitude and personality to "become" that character for your performance. Or, to put it another way, the more you understand the character in your copy, the easier it will be for you to find those emotions, attitudes, and personality traits within you that you can use to create your character and bring life to the words in the script.

As you have seen, there are many clues in copy that will help you discover the character and his or her personality. The target audience, the mood or attitude of the copy, the writing style, and any descriptive notes all give you valuable information. The process of analyzing, or discovering, your character is something that will become automatic in time. Once you know what to look for, you will soon be able to define your character after reading through the copy once or twice.

Voice acting does not usually require the same sort of in-depth, detailed character analysis that might be necessary for a theatrical performer. However, to be believable, you do need to have a good idea of the character you are portraying. Here are some things to look for and consider as you read through your copy to discover and define your character:

- Who is this character talking to? (target audience)
- What is the environment for the copy? (mood)
- What is the character's age? (young, old, middle-aged)
- How does the character stand? (straight and tall, hunched over, arms crossed, hands on hips, etc.)
- Where is the character from? (geographic region, country)
- Does the character speak with an accent or in a dialect? (If so, what would be the country of origin? A poorly done dialect or accent can have negative results unless done as a parody or characterization.)
- How would the character dress? (well dressed, business suit, or casual)
- What would you guess to be the character's economic status? (financially well off, struggling, etc.)

- What is the overall mood or attitude of the copy? (fast-paced, slow and relaxed, romantic feel, emotional, aggressive, etc.)
- What is the pace of the copy? (Slow-paced copy often calls for a relaxed type of character while fast-paced copy demands a character with more energy.)
- What is the product or service for which the copy is written? (The subject of the copy often dictates a specific type of character.)
- What is the character's purpose, or role, in the script? (protagonist, antagonist, delivering the message, part of a story script, comedic role, or that of straight-man)
- What life events or actions brought the character to this moment in time?
- What does the character want from telling the story?

Finding answers to questions like these will help you develop a visual image of your character. With a well-formed visual image, you will instinctively know what is needed to deliver the copy effectively and believably. You will know, for example, if the character needs to speak quickly or slowly, with an accent, or with an attitude.

Creating a visual image of your character and the environment she finds herself in will help to develop the necessary tension for drama. The tension here is not between characters, but rather a physical tension located somewhere in your body. It is this tension that will allow you to give life to the character in the copy.

Discovering the character in the copy may appear to be a lengthy process, but, in fact, it happens quickly once you know what to look for.

FIND THE BACK STORY

All copy has a back story, also known as "the moment before." A *back story* is simply the specific event that occurred immediately before the first word of the copy. The back story is the result of the wants and needs of the character that have brought him or her to this moment in time. It is the story that provides the motivation for the words, actions, and reactions to what happens in the environment of the story.

In theater, the back story is frequently unveiled during the course of the performance. With voice-over copy, there is rarely enough time to reveal the back story or provide much character development. A 60-second radio commercial must tell a story with a beginning, middle, and an end — and with fully developed characters from the outset.

In a dialogue script, you will often be able to figure out the back story with ease. A dialogue script back story consists of the life experiences of all the characters in the script and the specific event that brought each to the moment of their story, and more important, the relationship between those characters. The interaction between characters often reveals clues to the back story.

It can be more of a challenge with a single-voice script. A single-voice script back story consists of the life experience of only the speaking character. There may be few, if any, clues that reveal what brought him or her to the point of speaking the words in the copy.

If a back story is not clear from the copy, make one up. After all, you are an actor and you do have permission to pretend. The idea is to create a believable motivation for your character that brings him or her to the particular moment in time that is taking place in the script. The back story will reveal your character's wants and needs at this moment in time, and that information will help guide you in your delivery.

Define the back story and what the character wants in just a few words. Keep it concise, believable, and real.

UNVEIL THE CONFLICT

Conflict is an essential part of dialogue copy, and can also be present in a single-voice script that tells a story. Conflict rarely occurs in information-based copy in which the message is more of a sales pitch or instructional in nature than a story. Conflict creates drama, and drama holds interest.

A dialogue script without conflict will be boring and uninteresting. On the other hand, a dialogue script with a well-defined conflict can be funny, emotional, heartwarming, and informative — all at the same time. Look for the primary conflict in the script. Usually, this will be some difference of opinion, a crisis, an impasse, or some other obstacle. Define this primary conflict in a few concise words.

Once you have defined the primary conflict, look for any complications that support or exaggerate it. These are often secondary or minor conflicts that serve to add meaning and importance to the primary conflict.

Follow the development of the conflict to reveal its peak moment, which is the climax — the key moment in a commercial. It will usually be found immediately prior to the resolution or nonresolution of the conflict.

During the course of developing the conflict, the advertising benefit (*unique selling proposition*) should be revealed. The *peak moment* often is the point in the copy where the advertiser's name is mentioned or the purpose of the commercial is revealed.

DISCOVER THE RESOLUTION OR NONRESOLUTION
OF THE CONFLICT

In commercial copy, it is through the resolution or nonresolution of the conflict that the message is expressed. Sometimes ending a commercial with an unresolved conflict can actually create a memorable impression in the mind of the listener. An unresolved conflict leaves the end of the story up to the listener's imagination, and that can be a very effective motivation for action. For example, a radio commercial we produced for the high-end toy store, Toy Smart, presented a conflict between a mother and her "child." As the story developed, the mother tried to coax her "child" to eat his green beans with less than satisfactory results. This conflict resolved when the "child" turned out to be the husband who said "I'll be happy to eat all the green beans you want, as long as you put them with a T-bone steak!" However, at the very end of the commercial, the husband had one more line, which left the conflict in a state of nonresolution: "What do I get if I eat all my brussels sprouts?" This left the resolution of the conflict to the imagination of the listener and created a memorable impact moment in the commercial.

Look for details in the copy that give clues as to how the message is actually communicated. Are there a series of gags, jokes, or a play on words that lead to expression of the message? Do characters in the copy shift roles (reversals)? Is there a list of information that ends with an unusual twist? Does the story take place in an unusual location? Is there something in the story that appears to be out of context with what is taking place? Is there a personality problem or physical limitation with one or more of the characters? How are these resolved — or not?

MAKE THE COPY YOUR OWN

As you analyze a script, remember that there are no right or wrong answers to the questions you ask. Use your imagination and bring something of yourself into the copy. The idea is to create a believable character and situation for the copy you are reading. Bringing your personal experience into the character you create will aid in making him or her real to the listener.

Use what you learn from the copy and the tools at your disposal to make the copy your own. If you have a naturally dry and sarcastic style of speaking, you may be able to apply that trait to your character to make it unique. If you have a bubbly speaking style, that trait might give a unique twist to a character. Don't be afraid to experiment and play with different approaches to performing a character.

CREATE TENSION

When making copy your own, it is important to be specific when defining a scene or character and to commit to the choices you make. Using specific terms creates a tension in your body that you can use in your voice. Without tension you will be unable to create drama, which is essential for capturing and holding the attention of the listener.

To create tension in your body, begin by observing your feelings and emotions as you read the copy. Allow your senses to be open to experience whatever sensations might appear and make a mental note of where that sensation occurred in your body. As you begin to add life to your character, recall the memory of the sensation you just experienced (*sense memory*). Focus on placing your voice at that place in your body. This technique may be somewhat difficult to master at first, but keep working at it — the result is truly amazing once you get the knack of doing it.

WORK BACKWARDS

To quickly get an idea of the copywriter's intent, the target audience, the client's message, and some solid clues about your character and the story in the copy, try looking at the last line of the script first. The end of a script is where the resolution or nonresolution of conflict occurs and is usually the point where a character's attitude or true motivation is revealed. It is also where the most important part of the client's message usually resides. By working from the bottom of the script to the top, you will be able to learn important information that you can use to quickly create a basic character and attitude. Then use other clues in the copy to more fully develop your character.

FIND EMOTIONAL HOOKS

These are the words or phrases that carry an emotional impact. Call on your past experience to recall a memory of a similar emotion (*sense memory*). Notice that the memory of the emotion creates a certain physical tension someplace in your body. Observe the tension's position in your body and what it feels like. Hold this tension or sensation as you deliver the copy, re-experiencing the emotion or feeling. Now speak from that place in your body, fully expressing the tension. This technique helps to make your performance more believable and your character more real.

LOOK FOR QUESTION MARKS IN THE COPY

Question marks are opportunities for dramatic punctuation. I'm not referring to the punctuation mark — ?. I'm referring to words or phrases in the copy that give you the opportunity to ask a question. If the copy specifically asks a question, you should make that clear with your performance. Question marks that do not ask questions are usually found in sentences that describe or explain something. Someplace in the sentence there will be an opportunity to answer the unasked question.

Find those spots and figure out your own answers to the questions. This woodshedding technique can be incredibly useful to bring your character to life because the answers you come up with are part of the character's knowledge or history, which helps make the character real. Here's a :30 radio script with places noted where question marks present opportunities for discovering information noted in parentheses:

> Have you ever started a relationship (WHAT KIND OF RELATIONSHIP?) – and then discovered the truth? (WHAT TRUTH? AND HOW DOES IT FEEL TO DISCOVER THAT KIND OF TRUTH?) I was thinking about working with an agent to sell my home, (WHAT KIND OF HOME?) but then I found out about their high commissions! (HOW HIGH?) Not my idea of a great relationship. (WHAT IS A GREAT RELATIONSHIP?) Then I discovered MyOpenHouse.com! (HOW DOES IT FEEL TO MAKE A GREAT DISCOVERY?) I can get my home listed with an agent, (WHAT IS THAT LIKE?) and <u>save</u> up to 40% on their commission. (HOW DOES IT FEEL TO SAVE THAT MUCH?) It's like the best of both worlds – professional help, (WHAT DOES "PROFESSIONAL" MEAN TO YOU?) and a really low commission. (HOW DOES THAT FEEL?) MyOpenHouse.com. Now that's a relationship I can live with! (HOW LONG WILL THIS RELATIONSHIP LAST?)

You can take this process as far as you like, even to the point of asking questions about every word in the script. As you choose the answers to the unasked questions, you will be creating the foundation of your character's attitude and personality, and creating a context for your performance. Commit to the answers you come up with and use them as tools for giving your character life. However, be prepared to modify your answers as your character develops and as you receive direction from the producer.

LET GO OF JUDGMENTS AND INHIBITIONS

An important part of the woodshedding process is to experiment with your choices out loud, exactly the way you intend to perform the lines. This means you can't hold back just because you are afraid of what someone nearby might think. Always keep in mind that you are an actor, and as an actor, your job is to perform. And in order to create a great performance, you must rehearse the way you will be performing.

Be careful not to make the mistake of rehearsing and woodshedding silently or at a whisper. Unless you test your woodshedding and script analysis out loud, you can't possibly know exactly what your performance will sound like. Your delivery might sound great in your head, but the minute you start performing on mic, it will almost always come out of your mouth sounding completely different from what you had in mind.

One of the keys to success in voice acting is to let go of any judgments, inhibitions, and concerns you might have about what you are doing. Leave your ego outside. Allow yourself to become the character in your script. If your delivery needs to be loud, go someplace where you can be alone to work on your performance.

The director in the front row of your mind is not there to judge you, but should be considered a coach and an advocate whose sole purpose is to make your performance better. There is an important difference between being critically analytical about your performance and judgmental.

Judgmental thinking would be:

- "The way I delivered that last copy was just horrible! I'll never be able to do these lines right."
- "I just can't get into this character!"
- "I can't do this kind of copy!"
- "I shouldn't feel embarrassed when I do copy like this."

Analytical, or critical, thinking would be:

- "I didn't like the way I delivered the copy — it just didn't seem real."
- "I know I can be more effective than that last read."
- "What can I do to make my character more believable?"

Judgmental thinking usually approaches the subject from a negative point of view, stops you in your tracks, and prevents you from discovering the solutions you need. Critical (analytical) thinking is constructive and helps move you toward solutions that will make your performance more believable. Of the two, judgmental thinking comes naturally to most people, while critical thinking is a learned skill.

When you leave your ego, judgments, and inhibitions in the car, you'll be open to critically analyzing your script to achieve the best possible performance.

TAKE THE "VOICE" OUT OF "VOICE-OVER"

While woodshedding and rehearsing, don't just read your copy. Have a conversation with the listener. Talk *to* your audience, not *at* them, always striving to motivate, persuade, or move the listener to action. Remember that even if you are the only person in the booth, the *other* person is always there. Visualize the perfect person to hear the message, and talk *to* them.

Do whatever you can to draw the listener into your story and expect a response. You are a storyteller! Remember:

- Use drama (*emotional hooks*) to attract and hold the listener's attention.

- Talk in phrases, not word by word.
- Don't read.
- Let the content and subtext of the copy determine your dynamics.
- Have a conversation with the listener.
- Talk out loud to yourself to find hidden treasures in your delivery.
- Experiment with different attitudes, inflections, and emotions.
- Take out the punctuation marks in the script to make the copy flow more naturally and conversationally.
- Have a mental attitude that allows you to create a feeling of reality and believability. If you believe your character is real, your listener will.

Henry and His Friends: A Cold Reading Exercise for Woodshedding

Woodshedding is not just about finding the interpretation of a script or uncovering details about your character. An additional purpose of *woodshedding* is for discovering traps, pitfalls, grammatical errors, phrasing issues, misspellings, and many other details of a script that can affect your performance.

Following is an exercise in cold-reading based on a text written by Guy Buswell.[1] The original script was written as part of a research investigation of adult literacy in 1920. However, a cold-reading of this script reveals the critical nature of proper woodshedding skills.

Do this exercise without reading ahead or stopping to correct mistakes. However, do make a mental note of anything in your delivery that might need an adjustment. After completing the script, go back and note any errors, and how your instinctive choices might change. Perform the script a second time, making any adjustments you may have noted.

> His arrows were nearly gone so he sat down and stopped hunting. He saw Henry making a bow to a little girl who was coming down the road. She had tears in her dress and tears in her eyes. She gave Henry a note which he brought over to the young hunters. Read to the boys it caused great excitement. After a minute but rapid examination of their weapons they ran down the valley. Does were standing at the edge of the lake making a perfect target.

If you have developed skills for reading ahead, you may have instinctively caught most, if not all, of the traps in this script. Reading ahead is a skill that can be developed over time, but it cannot replace proper woodshedding.

The major challenge with this script is that many of the words have two distinctly different meanings. As we read a script, we instinctively interpret the meaning of words based on the most recent context or in the manner in which we most commonly use a word. For example, the first sentence includes a reference to arrows, so our instinctive interpretation when the word "bow" appears is to pronounce the word as in "bow and arrow." However, there is a shift in context with the second sentence that makes the correct pronunciation of "bow" to mean "bow at the waist." The third sentence uses both meanings of the word "tears," and the words must be pronounced correctly for the sentence to make sense. In the sixth sentence the word "minute" appears. Our usual usage of this word is in terms of time, but the meaning of the word as used in this sentence is that of a small quantity. And finally, in the last sentence, the first word is actually referring to female deer.

It is only by woodshedding a script that you will be able to discover the most effective punctuation, phrasing, attitude, character, emotion, subtlety, nuance, and the meaning of words in the context of a story. Remember, just because a script is written with certain punctuation, it doesn't mean you can't change the punctuation to make your delivery more conversational and real.

You can't change the words in a script, but as a voice actor, you have a tremendous amount of flexibility in determining how those words might be spoken. And that's what the process of woodshedding and script analysis is all about.

Tips for Woodshedding

- Develop your woodshedding skills so they become automatic.
- Look under the surface to discover the subtlety and nuance of copy.
- Don't settle on your first choices.
- Always experiment and test different options for delivery of a line.
- Explore emotion, attitude, pacing, rhythm, tempo, etc. to reveal alternative choices.
- Look for key words and catch phrases.
- Mark your script with a pencil. It is inevitable that at least some of your choices will change.
- Be careful not to over-analyze your script. Over-analysis can result in a flat delivery.

---

1 Buswell, Guy (1920). An experimental study of eye-voice span in reading. *Supplementary Education Monographs*. No. 17 — www.nald.ca/fulltext/adlitUS/Page43.htm; www.nald.ca/fulltext/adlitUS/Index.htm.

10

The Character
in the Copy

How Will You Play the Role?

When you are performing a voice-over script, you are playing a role, no different than if you were playing a part in a stage play or movie. That's why this craft is called *voice acting*! Unless you are telling your own personal story, you didn't write the words in the script, and the situations of the story are not yours — they are those of a character who is substantially different from you. If you are merely "being you" when in front of a mic, then the words will sound like you doing the words, and there won't be anything unique or special about your performance.

There are two distinctly different approaches to performing and creating characters. One is where the actor develops a strong and highly identifiable performing style that is at the foundation of every role. The style may be one of a specific voice characteristic, physical appearance, performance rhythm, body movement, or underlying attitude. I refer to actors in this category as *celebrity actors*. When these actors perform, we have no doubt in our mind that we are watching that person perform. We become involved with their performance, in part, because their acting style is completely appropriate for the characters they are playing. In other words, no matter what the role, their characters are believable. Some film actors I would place in this category are Jack Nicholson, Christian Slater, Adam Sandler, Drew Barrymore, Tom Cruise, and Jennifer Lopez. Voice-over talent who fit this category include Don LaFontaine and James Earl Jones.

The other approach to performing is one in which a wide range of skills and abilities are developed which allow the actor to play many different emotions, attitudes, and personalities. Actors who have mastered this approach literally become the character they are playing. As we watch or listen to them, we see the character they have created, not the person they are. I refer to these actors as *character actors*. I consider Jim Carrey, Jodie Foster, Tom Hanks, Dustin Hoffman, Meryl Streep, and Robin Williams all excellent examples of actors who truly become the characters they are playing. In the world of voice-over, many of the best known and highest paid voice talent have developed the ability to create a variety of uniquely different voices and personalities for the characters they play.

Each of these approaches to creating performance characters is equally valid, and both approaches can result in powerful, believable characters. Depending on the area of voice-over work you choose to work in, you may find that one approach or the other may work best for you. For commercial voice-over, it's often the delivery style that gets the work. For animation, it's definitely the ability to create believable voices. Regardless of the path you choose, your job as a voice actor is to bring life to the words in a script, and that requires an ability to understand and define the character who is speaking those words — the character in the copy.

Your Best Tool Is Your Own Personality

The best tool you have to define a character is your own personality. When you know yourself, you can tap into parts of your personality to give life to the character in the copy.

Personality analysis is a subject that has been studied for thousands of years. Hippocrates developed a system of defining personality traits, which placed individuals into four separate personality types with dominant (Sanguine and Choleric) and recessive (Melancholy and Phlegmatic) traits. The Hippocrates system of personality analysis was very restrictive in its definitions of personality types but it did provide a basic structure within which people could be placed.

More recently the psychologists of our world have developed highly refined methods of determining specific personality types. Some of their studies have shown that personality is largely a result of the chemical makeup of the brain. Cultural upbringing and conditioning further contribute to personality development.

There are many excellent books available that will help you discover some fascinating aspects of your personality. Many of these books are written as aids to improving relationships or developing self-awareness. Three excellent personality books are: *Please Understand Me — Character and Temperament Types* by David Keirsey and Marilyn Bates (1984); *Are You My Type, Am I Your Type* by Renee Baron and Elizabeth Wagele (1995); and *Dealing with People You Can't Stand* by Dr. Rick Brinkman and Dr. Rick Kirschner (1994). Another approach to understanding personality types is through the *Enneagram*. There are many books on this subject, among them, *Personality Types: Using the Enneagram for Self-Discovery* by Don Richard Riso. These books look at personality types from different points of view and offer some fascinating reading.

An advertiser's understanding of who buys the company's products is crucial when it comes to a marketing campaign. Your understanding of yourself is equally necessary when it comes to creating a character that will effectively communicate the message in the advertiser's copy. The best way for you to learn more about yourself is to ask questions and find the most appropriate answers. Based on your answers, you will be able to determine some of your dominant and recessive personality traits.

Most studies of personality type start with several basic categories, then divide those into subcategories. Every person has characteristics in several categories, but certain areas are dominant, and others are recessive. The following simple questions will give you an idea of some basic personality differences.

- Do you respond to problems emotionally, or do you think about them before responding?
- Do you have a strong need to express yourself creatively, or do you prefer quiet activities?
- Do you avoid unpleasant emotions (including fear), or are you inclined to take risks?
- Do you rely on your instincts for information, or do you rely on what you see and hear?
- Do you seek approval from authority figures, or do you rebel?
- Do you play the role of a nurturer, or do you treat others in a detached manner?
- Do you express anger readily, are you accommodating and out of touch with your anger, or do you see anger as a character flaw?
- Do you prefer literal writing or a more figurative writing style?
- Are you more realistic or speculative?
- Do emotions impress you more, or do principles?
- Are you attracted to creative, imaginative people, or to more sensible, structured people?
- Do you tend to arrive at events early, or are you generally late?
- Do you do things in the usual way, or in your own way?
- Do you feel better having made a purchase or having the option to purchase?
- Do you operate more from facts or from principles?
- Do you find it easy to speak to strangers, or is this difficult?
- Are you fair-minded or sympathetic?
- Do you prefer planned activities or unplanned activities?

Your answers to these and other questions will only scratch the surface of your personality. When you gain an in-depth understanding of who you are, you will be ahead of the game when it comes to creating a believable character or a marketable performance style. With an understanding of yourself, you will be able to tap into some of the core elements of your own personality as you create a unique character.

THE TWO BOXES

In our *Art of Voice Acting Workshops*, I teach the concept of *The Two Boxes*. You and the character you are playing each live in a box. You are comfortable within the walls of your box. Your box contains all of your life experience, belief system, habits, behaviors, attitudes, emotions, feelings, knowledge, wisdom, and more. The box your character lives in contains all the same stuff you have in your box, only it's those of the character — not yours. The character's box may be larger or smaller than your box, and the character is very comfortable within the walls of his or her box.

You need to understand the real you and how you exist in your box before you can fully understand how your character exists in his or her box.

As an actor, your job is to climb out of your box and into the box of your character. You bring everything from your box with you except the box itself. You separate yourself from the confines of the walls of your box as you enter the box of your character. Everything you bring with you is available as tools that can be used to help bring the character to life.

If your character's box is larger than yours, you need to know that in order to allow yourself to behave believably as the character. Learning how to do this may be uncomfortable at first, but that's only because your comfort levels are relative to existing within your box and you've not yet grown comfortable in a bigger box. The path to becoming comfortable in the character's box is through the use of the many acting and performing techniques you've learned from this and other acting books, acting classes, and improvisation classes.

Once you've climbed into your character's box, you need to let go of the real you and experience how the character lives and behaves. There will always be a part of you there to make your character real. In a very real sense, when you create a character, you are tapping into that part of you where the character lives.

This is the commonality between you and the character. It's the stuff you brought with you from your box that also exists as the same, or very similar, stuff in your character's box. Those things in your character's box that are different from anything in your box must be created through your performance. But in order to achieve this, you must know what they are, and have some way to create them.

A mastery of this process results in a truly believable character that you can create on demand without thinking about what you are doing. This is what Core Element #6, *Forget Who You Are* is all about.

Sociocultural Awareness

You should also know that the corporate business world uses highly refined methods of personality and social analysis to define the demographics (statistical data) of the marketplace for selling products and services. These studies define the buying attitudes and purchasing habits of consumers and aid advertisers in reaching their desired market.

There are several companies whose entire business is based on analyzing the buying trends of different types of people. By understanding what motivates a person to buy, an advertiser can write in specific words and phrases, or a particular style. For TV commercials and print advertising, editing techniques and use of color, font style, and other visual elements are used — all of which are "hot" buttons designed to trigger a buying impulse in the viewer, or reader. In radio commercials, similar hot buttons are triggered through the careful choice of words and phrases, the use of appropriate music and various production techniques. In every case, the desired result is to reach the audience on an emotional level and to motivate the audience to take action.

Today, advertisers are faced with a marketplace of "occasional" consumers who are no longer characterized by predictable buying habits and who no longer exhibit strong brand loyalty. The key objective of marketing sociocultural research is to identify the links between personal motivations and buying behavior in order to understand the consumer and why he or she is attracted by certain propositions and not by others. Simply studying consumer behavior is not adequate, nor is analyzing buying habits in terms of age or class. To understand modern society, it is necessary to look much deeper at the sociocultural diversity of society and find the trends and characteristics that can make the difference between commercial success or failure.[1]

Marshall Marketing & Communications, Inc. (MM&C) is one of the leaders in sociocultural analysis for the purpose of marketing on a local and regional basis. MM&C, in association with the International Research Institute on Social Change (RISC), which has operated nationally in the United States since 1987 and internationally since 1978, uses a program called RISC AmeriScan[2] to help advertisers understand and adjust to purchasing behaviors of present and future consumers. The RISC AmeriScan program is quite extensive and could be the subject of a book of its own, so only those aspects that relate to voice acting are included here.

Through a series of studies, both on national and local levels, a probability sample of people is surveyed with a carefully developed questionnaire. The questions don't ask for opinions, but rather register relevant preferences and facts about the individual. The results of the survey capture the person's sociocultural characteristics.

To more easily view the results, a chart is created that takes on the basic appearance of a compass. The first axis (pointing north and south) is linked to attitudes of change. At the north are people who see change as a positive force in their lives (Exploration). To the south are people who prefer stability, structure, and consistency (Stability). The other axis of the compass (east-to-west) relates to the balance between the individual and society. To the east are those who are more independent and seek immediate pleasure (Individual); to the west are people with strong ethics who are more community oriented (Social).

Respondents are scored on each of approximately 40 sociocultural characteristics. Their scores result in a specific placement on the compass, and can be represented as a "cloud of dots" in multidimensional diagrams (Figures 10-1 and 10-2).[3] The diagram is then divided into ten territories to result in the RISC AmeriScan map (Figures 10-3 and 10-4). Individuals positioned close to each other tend to have shared values and similar preferences, while those at opposite extremes have little in common.[4]

A basic understanding of how advertisers target their message will be beneficial to you as a voice actor. Knowing what the cultural and social norms are for any specific demographic group will give you some much-needed information to aid in the development of a believable character. For example, let's say that, based on the copy you are given, you can determine that your audience is outgoing, youthful, interested in experiencing new things, and likes to live on the edge. You make this determination based on your analysis and interpretation of the words and phrases in the copy. With this information you can now make reliable choices and adapt your character and performance energy to something your audience can relate to, thus creating a sense of believability.

For the audience described here, you would most likely need to perform with considerable energy and excitement in your voice. A slow, relaxed delivery probably would not be an effective way to reach the audience, unless the script was specifically written for that attitude.

The Ten Cultural Territories

Each of the ten segments on the RISC AmeriScan map (Figure 10-4) represents a cultural territory with specific attitudes, beliefs, preferences, motivations, and buying habits. Advertisers use these cultural territories to aid in targeting their advertising and marketing plans. All aspects of a campaign, including words, visuals, colors, music, and sound effects, are carefully chosen to match the targeted territory's characteristics. The closer the match, the more likely it is that the message will reach the target audience.

These ten RISC AmeriScan cultural territories can also be useful in developing a believable character, simply by working the process in reverse. Understanding the motivations, attitudes, and belief system of your audience will enable you to tap into those parts of your own personality and bring them into the character you are creating. When you create a believable character, an emotional connection can be made with the

Exploration

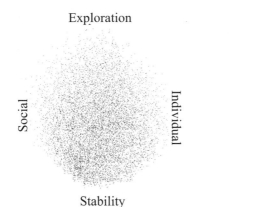

Social

Individual

Stability

Figure 10-1: Respondents' scores create a "cloud of dots."

Exploration

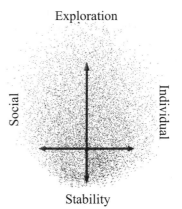

Social

Individual

Stability

Figure 10-2: Respondents are placed on the compass based on sociocultural characteristics.

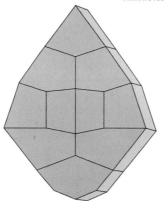

Figure 10-3: The multidimensional diagram is divided into ten territories.

Source: RISC AmeriScan Map, copyright RISC, 1997. Reprinted by permission of RISC International Europe, S.A.

audience, giving the message a stronger impact. Similarly, by understanding your audience and adapting the traits of the RISC cultural territories, you can develop a performing style that will elicit an instinctive response.

The following pages separate the ten cultural territories into their sociocultural profiles, key attributes as defined by RISC, and other useful information to help you understand your audience and create a believable character. As an exercise to develop your acting skills, use the territory charts as a guide to create a variety of characters with different attitudes. Find a paragraph in a book or newspaper and read the same copy from the attitude of a character in each of the ten territories. Allow your mind and body to take on the characteristics, body posture, belief system, and attitudes described for each territory and observe how each character you create can be unique. You'll find more information about RISC AmeriScan on the MM&C website at **www.mm-c.com**. Select the Media Clients area, then click on "sociodynamics" in the first paragraph.

Exploration

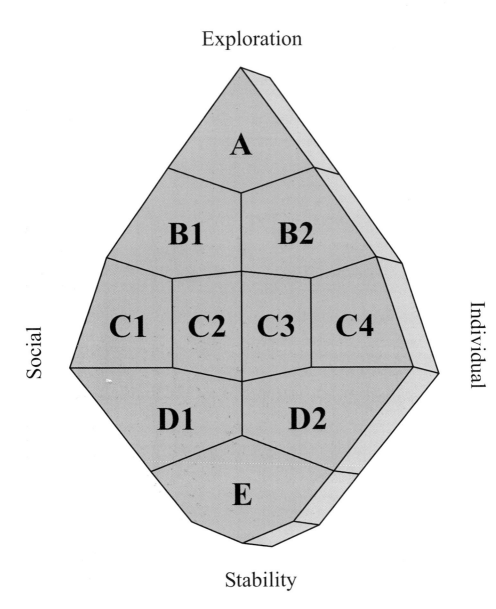

Social

Individual

Stability

Figure 10-4: RISC AmeriScan ten cultural territories map.

TERRITORY A — Personal Growth, Socially Involved, Connected

TONE OF VOICE CONSUMER WILL BEST RESPOND TO: Persuade

Key Attributes	Sociocultural Profile	Motivations
• Exploring human potential • Community ties • Networking • Empathy • Personal growth • Social commitment • Coping with uncertainty • Social flexibility • Well-being	• Integrate society and the self • Combine traditional and modern ideas • Active involvement in the growth and change of society • Social and personal development important	• Belongings, culture, novelty • Rely on own sense of style and instinct • Interest in newness, curiosity, and the unusual • Acceptance of ambiguity and paradox • Interaction, experience, and diversity are important

© RISC, 1997

TERRITORY B1 — Community, Spirituality, Social Responsibility

TONE OF VOICE CONSUMER WILL BEST RESPOND TO: Legitimize

Key Attributes	Sociocultural Profile	Motivations
• Exploring human potential • Community ties • Spirituality • Social commitment • Order and vigilance • Integrity • Global world • Empathy • Well-being	• Comfort and well-being of others is most important • Caregivers and nurturers • Family values • Concern for others • Religious tolerance • Uphold tradition while also creating new rituals for special occasions • Focus daily life on family and social gatherings	• Belongings, culture, novelty • Rely on own sense of style and instinct • Interest in newness, curiosity, and the unusual • Acceptance of ambiguity and paradox • Interaction, experience, and diversity are important

© RISC, 1997

TERRITORY B2 — Independent, Experimental, Interest in New

TONE OF VOICE CONSUMER WILL BEST RESPOND TO: Seduce and Enliven

Key Attributes	Sociocultural Profile	Motivations
• Exploring human potential • Coping with uncertainty • Personal growth • Networking • Pleasure • Risk-taking • Strategic opportunism • Emotions	• Intense and eager to explore • Open and optimistic • Invigorated by diverse, multiple connections • Active and involved • Always push their limits • Strongly individualistic yet open to a broad view of community • Uncertainty equals a challenge	• Culture, novelty, understanding, independence • Fascinated by the avant-garde and unexpected • Will pay more for what they want • Intrigued by the one-of-a-kind and impossible, and the experiences that come with it

© RISC, 1997

TERRITORY C1 — Rituals, Loyalty, Duty, Conventional

TONE OF VOICE CONSUMER WILL BEST RESPOND TO: Build on Trust

Key Attributes	Sociocultural Profile	Motivations
• Order and vigilance • Spirituality • Community ties • Organized life • Well-being • Clear-cut principles	• Defined by duty, morality, family, and community • Lead principled and routine lives • Seek reassurance and stability • Adhere to a firm moral code and a strong sense of values • Observe traditional rituals	• Belongings, understanding, nurturance, stability • Good deeds equal goodwill • React to community involvement • Primary concern is family • Always defined in relation to others • Comforted by the familiar

© RISC, 1997

Source: RISC AmeriScan Sociocultural Territories, copyright RISC, 1997.
Reprinted by permission of Marshall Marketing & Communications, Inc.

TERRITORY C2 — Rules, Principles, Need for Recognition

TONE OF VOICE CONSUMER WILL BEST RESPOND TO: Inform and Position

Key Attributes	Sociocultural Profile	Motivations
• Clear-cut principles • Organized life • Social fairness • Environment • Competitive drive • Integrity • Roots	• Tentative and unsure • Mediate the needs of the family and the individual • Less willing to sacrifice for the common good • Uncertain among those outside of family circle • Unbalanced in desire to explore individuality • Simple and collective enjoyment for well-being	• Recognition, understanding, nurturance, stability • Need positive reassurance from others • Driven by commitment to provide comfort for family • Simple, straightforward messages and symbols are important keys

© RISC, 1997

TERRITORY C3 — Achievement, Exhibition, Trend Setters, Self-Indulgent

TONE OF VOICE CONSUMER WILL BEST RESPOND TO: Inform and Position

Key Attributes	Sociocultural Profile	Motivations
• Strategic opportunism • Risk-taking • Emotions • Pleasure	• Rely on others to promote own achievement • Focus on short-term gains and personal risk-taking • Indulge in pleasures of immediate gratification • Lack a strict moral code • Materialism important • No concern for community • In constant pursuit of being "number one"	• Thrills, accomplishment • Identity reflected in the display of awards, status symbols, and possessions • Need to succeed and to have success recognized • Live life to the fullest • Seek immediate advantages from products and services

© RISC, 1997

Source: RISC AmeriScan Sociocultural Territories, copyright RISC, 1997.
Reprinted by permission of Marshall Marketing & Communications, Inc.

TERRITORY C4 — Materialism, Seek Pleasure, Need for Recognition

TONE OF VOICE CONSUMER WILL BEST RESPOND TO: Stimulate and Flatter

Key Attributes	Sociocultural Profile	Motivations
• Strategic opportunism • Risk-taking • Emotions • Pleasure • Social flexibility • Blurring of the sexes	• Point of view is pleasure • Put themselves first • Willing to take social and personal risks • Tend to be the fashion leaders • Driven by impulse and immediate gratification • Intense and self-centered • Live life in the present, moment by moment	• Thrills, diversion, exhibition, sexuality • Highly attracted to "new" • Want to be entertained • Seek ways to express their uniqueness • Sexual innuendo and overt eroticism hook their interest in being cutting-edge

© RISC, 1997

TERRITORY D1 — Need for Structure, Control, Respect for Authority

TONE OF VOICE CONSUMER WILL BEST RESPOND TO: Demonstrate

Key Attributes	Sociocultural Profile	Motivations
• Organized life • Roots • Security • Clear-cut principles	• Strong beliefs in duty and clearly defined rules • Unquestioning respect given to authority figures • Routine balances the uncertainty of life • Brand loyalty is more habit than conviction • Basic pleasures and familiarity shape their structured lifestyles	• Control, stability, dependence • Abundance is a sign of prosperity • Not particularly selective about purchases • Promotions, gimmicks, price incentives are key • Basic benefits more important than image and style

© RISC, 1997

Source: RISC AmeriScan Sociocultural Territories, copyright RISC, 1997.
Reprinted by permission of Marshall Marketing & Communications, Inc.

TERRITORY D2 — Personal Style, Spontaneous, Concern About Future

TONE OF VOICE CONSUMER WILL BEST RESPOND TO: Gratify

Key Attributes	Sociocultural Profile	Motivations
• Security • Status • Pleasure • Aimlessness • Blurring of the sexes • Risk-taking • Fear of violence	• Pleasure is a feeling of power • Aspire to set themselves apart from the masses • The "wannabe's" of the Rich and Famous • Both whimsical and spontaneous • Fashionably antiestablishment • Resist tradition	• Nonconformity, sexuality, exhibition • Need options that allow them to be different • Resist the persuasions of mass culture • Developed sense of style • Appreciate parodies of conventional values, norms, and status

© RISC, 1997

TERRITORY E — Need for Security, Worriers, Suspicious of Change

TONE OF VOICE CONSUMER WILL BEST RESPOND TO: Reassure

Key Attributes	Sociocultural Profile	Motivations
• Aimlessness • Fear of violence • Security	• Security is the prevailing tendency • Yearning for stability makes them suspicious of change and reluctant to be a part of it • Resist pleasure • Fearful outlook on world • Strong preoccupation with health problems • Possessions equal security	• Security, dependence • Need to feel free of the threat of harm • Want the comfort of knowing that they and loved ones are protected • Expect immediate results from products and services • Long-term or preventive benefits seen as misleading

© RISC, 1997

Source: RISC AmeriScan Sociocultural Territories, copyright RISC, 1997.
Reprinted by permission of Marshall Marketing & Communications, Inc.

Theater of the Mind

Voice acting is *theater of the mind*! You do not have the advantage of props, flashy lighting, or scenery. All you have are the words on a piece of paper, and your individual creativity. From the words alone, you must create an illusion of reality in the mind of your audience. In order for you to create a believable illusion, you need to know what is going on in the mind of the character you are playing. You also need to know your character's role in the story, and his or her relationships to other characters, objects, and the product or service. To learn what is going on in the character's mind, you need to analyze the script. (See *Woodshedding* on page 113).

Analyzing a voice-over script is very much like reducing a play to its essential parts. The more information you can discover in the copy, the easier it will be to create a believable performance. Single-voice spokesperson copy is frequently information-based and may not require much analysis. However, dialogue copy and plot scripts are short theatrical pieces and must be thoroughly understood to be effectively performed.

Although analyzing a script is helpful in understanding its component parts, it is important to realize that *overanalyzing* a script can kill spontaneity and cause the voice actor to place too much focus on technique and thinking about what he or she is doing. Remember, to be effective, technique must become automatic and occur without any conscious effort. Study a script just long enough to discover what you need to know, then put the script down and let your instincts do the rest.

To create effective theater of the mind, your performance must reflect real life, exhibit some sort of tension, contain something the listener can relate to, and have a sense of honesty and a ring of truth. These are all elements of good theater and should be incorporated into any voice-acting performance, regardless of the type of copy or the length of the project.

When creating a character for your performance, keep in mind the following basic elements of good theater:

- Interesting characters with wants and needs "at this moment in time"
- A story or sequence of events that leads to a climax
- Conflict in one or more forms
- Resolution or nonresolution of the conflict, usually in an interesting or unexpected manner
- Closure in which any loose ends are satisfactorily resolved

Uncover these elements in a voice-over script and you will be able to understand your character better.

An Exercise for Creating Real Characters — CD/7

Visualization is a powerful technique that can help bring your characters to life, and this exercise will do just that! The first time I used this exercise in my workshop, the result was amazing. We witnessed a total transformation and the student, who was having difficulty finding the proper voice and attitude, was able to create a completely believable character that she did not know existed within her. As I've mentioned before, for a character in a script to be "real" to a listener, everything about the character must flow through you just as if you were the character.

Once understood, the following visualization process can take as little as only a few seconds to a minute or so. However, as you learn this technique you may want to spend some additional time relaxing your body and mind prior to doing this exercise. Of course, in an actual session you won't have much time for a lengthy visualization, but by then the process should be second nature.

Define your character in as much detail as you possibly can, including physical appearance, clothing, hair, posture, mannerisms, and other features. Begin by thoroughly *woodshedding* your script and making choices for your audience, back story, and character. Visualize this character in your imagination. This character description and image will become important later on, so don't skimp on the details.

You may find it helpful to do this as a guided visualization by listening to track 7 on the CD or recording the script yourself. Take your time with this, and don't rush it. The clearer the visualization, the better the results, and the more believable your character will be.

At first glance, this visualization may seem a bit unusual. However, when you give it a try, you'll be surprised at what you are able to come up with, not only with physical changes, but also with the sound of your voice that results from creating a believable character.

Script for "Creating a Character" Visualization

With your character in mind, close your eyes and take a slow deep breath through your nose. Fill your lungs completely. Exhale slowly through your mouth to relax. Repeat with another long deep breath . . . and slowly exhale. Don't forget to keep breathing.

Imagine yourself standing in front of the microphone, or in the voice-over booth. See yourself in your imagination — it's as though you are observing yourself from across the room. Create the image of yourself as clearly as you possibly can, in whatever manner works for you. When you have a sense of seeing yourself standing in the room, take another long deep breath . . . and slowly exhale.

Now, imagine the character you will be playing coming into the scene in your imagination. See the character walking in. Notice how the character is walking. Observe the posture and physical movement. Notice what the character is wearing: What do the clothes look like? What kind of shoes is your character wearing? Is your character wearing glasses or jewelry?

As you observe this scene, see yourself look at your character's face. Notice any facial details, color of the eyes, appearance of the skin. Does your character appear to present any sort of attitude or have interesting facial expressions? When you have a clear image of the character in your imagination, take a long deep breath . . . and slowly exhale.

Now, as you are observing the two of you in the room, imagine seeing the real you step out of your body and come to the place from where you are observing. As the real you steps out of your body, imagine the character stepping into your body. Everything about the character is now reflected in your body: The character's posture, the way the character stands and moves, the character's physical appearance, facial expressions, and mental attitude. Everything about the character is now expressed through your body, mind, and voice.

Allow yourself to fully experience this transformation. Notice any tension in your body. Be aware of how you feel as this character — physically, mentally, and emotionally. When you have a sense of the transformation, take a slow deep breath; exhale, maintain the physical, emotional, and mental state; open your eyes, and begin speaking the words in your script.

Making Your Characters Believable

FIND THE MUSIC

There is *music* in your daily conversations, and there is a great deal of music in any voice acting performance. Some of the basic elements of music are pitch, tempo, rhythm, volume, quality, and intonation — all of which are present in every sentence you speak.

It is the music of your performance that will convey the subtlety and nuance of the meaning behind the words. Find the music in the way your character speaks and you will create a believable character. Chapter 13, Character Copy, explains in detail how to find and sustain interesting and musical character voices.

STUDY OTHER PERFORMERS

Study film and television actors. Observe how they deliver their lines and interact with other characters. Listen to the dynamics of their voices. Notice that most actors use a lot of variety and inflection — they don't speak in monotone or with limited range (unless those attributes are part of the character). They also move and express emotion physically as well as verbally, just as they would in real life. Mimic what you see other actors do and how they speak so you can get the experience of what they are doing. Study the techniques they use and apply them to your style of performance. You will soon find the boundary of your comfort zone — the point where your stretch becomes uncomfortable. To grow as a performer, you need to find a way to work past that boundary.

STRETCH YOUR BOUNDARIES AND BE WILLING TO RISK

Be willing to experiment and risk moving beyond your comfort zone (Core Element #7, Gamble). Practice the techniques to develop the skills that will make moving outside of your comfort zone easier.

Don't worry about how you will appear or sound to anybody! As a voice actor, your job is to perform the copy and your character in the best manner possible. If you need to make strange faces, or wave your arms wildly to get into the character, then that is what you need to do. Leave your inhibitions and self-conscious attitudes outside the studio door.

Stretch beyond what feels comfortable to you. It is better to stretch too far rather than not far enough. It is easier for a director to pull you back after setting a character that is too far out there than it is to stretch you further. As Nancy Wolfson, a well-known voice-over coach in Los Angeles says, "I can reign you in, but I can't reign you out." Remember, there is no absolute right or wrong way to perform. Each performer is unique and different techniques work better for different performers. Do what works best for you to make your performance real and believable.

As you stretch your abilities, you will probably feel uncomfortable at first. Remember to be nonjudgmental and to not worry about how well you are doing. Each of us has an individual concept of some point at which we feel we would be going too far, or over the edge. Practice taking yourself just a little bit over that line until you begin to feel uncomfortable. Then take yourself a little bit further. The more you move beyond the point of discomfort, the faster you will develop the ability to create any character.

You must be willing to risk total failure. Intend to perform to the best of your abilities. Become the character and do whatever it takes to make the character real. Remember that you are uniquely you, and that you are interesting just as you are. Also remember that the people you are working with have insecurities of their own and may actually know less about the business than you do. Know that you know what you are doing. If you never risk, you can never learn. Use each audition or session as a learning experience. Keep an attitude of always being in training.

MAKE EVERY TIME THE FIRST TIME

Make each and every performance seem as if it is the first time. It is very easy to get sloppy by take 27. Take 28 should sound as fresh and real as take one — only better. Unless the producer or director tells you otherwise, you should maintain the same energy and attitude for each take. Use the director's guidance as a tool to help you focus in on your best performance. Add a little spin to a word, or shift your emphasis here or there with each take, but keep your energy and attitude consistent. This becomes very important to the editor who needs to put the final project together long after you have gone. Variations in your performance energy can stand out very clearly if you are not consistent, and make the editor's job a nightmare.

CHARACTER HAS PRECEDENCE OVER COPY

As you learn how to create believable characters, you will discover that your characters want to say and do things in a certain way. After all, if the characters you create say things exactly the way you do, what would be the purpose of creating the character?

To be real, each character you create must have its own personality, mannerisms, thought processes, and speaking style. Every subtlety and nuance of your character contributes to its believability. Forcing your character to say or do something that is not appropriate will instantly take your performance out of character.

Scripts are often written with a specific attitude, phrasing, or delivery style in mind, yet what the writer had in mind may not be what ends up being recorded. Provided your delivery is *in character*, it is perfectly acceptable, for example, to contract words that are scripted un-contracted, or to un-contract words scripted as contractions. This is closely related to the idea of changing or removing punctuation marks to create a more natural and conversational delivery. Your objective as a voice talent is to bring your character to life, and you should strive to do whatever is necessary to create that reality. You can't change the words in the script, but you can change the way you say the words. The way your character speaks will always have precedence over the way the words are written. This will be true until or unless the director tells you otherwise.

ACT PROFESSIONAL

Play the part! Enter a studio with the attitude of a professional there to do a job and with the confidence that the character you create will be exactly right. Be friendly, cooperative, and ready to work. Making money does not make you a professional. Acting professionally makes you money. When you act like a pro, the people hiring you will believe that you are a pro and they will respect you. Remember that this business is all about creating believability in the mind of the audience. When you enter a studio, your first audience will be the people who hired you. Make them believe you are good at what you do and prove it with your performance.

Become the child you once were! Pretend! Play! Have fun!

Tips for Performing All Types of Copy

Remember, voice acting is theater of the mind, and you are the actor. When you become the character in the copy, you will be believable to the audience, and a suspension of disbelief will be created. When the audience suspends their disbelief in what they hear, they become more open to the message. This all starts when you discover the character in the copy.

- Don't overanalyze your copy. Overanalyzing can cause you to lose spontaneity and cause your delivery to become flat and uninteresting.
- Rely on your instincts, and trust the director in your mind to guide your delivery to keep it on track.
- Tell the story. All scripts tell a story, even dry, technical scripts. Storytelling is always about relationships. To be believable, make the relationships appear real.
- Take the punctuation marks out of your delivery. Be conversational. Add your personal spin to make the copy your own.
- Make your character believable by adding something of yourself. Let your imagination run wild. If you believe in the reality of your performance, the tension of your belief will come through in your words and the audience will believe.
- Don't become so focused on your character that you lose sight of the story, the drama and the relationships between characters and conflict.
- Don't exaggerate your character's attitude, speech patterns, or other characteristics, unless the script calls for an extreme characterization.
- Internalize the wants and needs of your character, both physically and emotionally. Find the place in your body where a tension develops. Hold it there and read your lines. In theater, this is called *setting the character*. Only after running through a script several times will you be able to find the true voice for your character.

- Use your imagination to create a vivid reality of the scene, situation, relationships, and conversation in your mind.
- Be conversational. Don't read! Speak your lines to another person, real or imagined, expecting that they will respond.
- Play it over-the-top on your first time through. Use more attitude, dynamics, or energy in your delivery than you think may be necessary. It's much easier to pull back than to push further out.
- Underplay, rather than overplay. Louder is not necessarily better. Pull back, speak more softly, and be more natural. Remember, "less is more." This may seem like a contradiction to playing it over the top, however if you haven't experimented with a range of delivery, you won't know what works best for a given script.
- Keep your body posture in a stance consistent with the character you have decided on and the choices you have made in regards to how your character stands, moves, and behaves. Maintain this attitude throughout your performance.
- Find the music in the copy. All copy has a tempo, rhythm, dynamics, and other musical qualities.
- Keep it real. Speak as quickly and as quietly as you would if you were talking to someone in a real conversation.
- Ad lib situations or lines to "get into the moment." Give yourself a realistic, specific, and concrete lead-in line to set up your character.
- Stay in the moment. Pick up cues. Interact with other performers. Don't let your lines become separated from those of the other performers. Listen to yourself, the director, and other performers and respond appropriately (*listen and answer*).

I am enough of an artist to draw
freely upon my imagination.
Imagination is more important
than knowledge. Knowledge is limited.
Imagination encircles the world.
Albert Einstein (1879-1955)

---

[1] "Understanding Consumers and Markets," *Why People Buy*, RISC, 1997 (1-2).
[2] RISC AmeriScan compass, map, and other materials copyright RISC, 1997. Used by permission of Marshall Marketing & Communications, Inc.
[3] "Understanding Consumers and Markets," *Why People Buy*, RISC, 1997 (3).
[4] *MM&C RISC AmeriScan Guidebook*, copyright RISC, 1997 (5).

11

Single-Voice Copy

Single-voice copy is written for a solo performer who will deliver the entire message, with the possible exception of a separate tag line which may be voiced by a different performer. There is no interaction between characters, since there is only one, although there may be some implied interaction between the performer and the listener.

All single-voice copy is communicating information, often attempting to reach the listener on an emotional level. All effective communication comprises a four-step process. The first step is to move the listener's attention from what they are currently doing to the message being communicated. This is known in advertising as an *interrupt*. The second step is to *engage* the listener's attention to keep their interest as the message is being delivered. Once the listener is invested in listening to the message, important information can be delivered to *educate* them. Finally, an *offer* can be presented which asks the listener to take some sort of action.

These steps of *interrupt, engage, educate*, and *offer* must be positioned in that order for the communication to be effective. A properly written script will use this structure and may actually repeat it throughout the script. Unfortunately, many advertisers leave out one or more of these elements, or place their offer at the beginning.

Reading or announcing copy will rarely result in an effective communication. Both styles direct the performance inward and imply that the performer is speaking to himself or herself. To properly interrupt, engage, and educate a listener, a voice actor must speak to a one-person audience with the expectation of receiving a response. Only then can the *offer* be made with the expectation that the listener will take action.

The target audience of a single-voice script can usually be determined pretty easily; however, sometimes it can be a challenge to define the character speaking. Well-written copy that clearly tells a story makes the character easy to define. Poorly written copy that contains only information in the form of facts and figures can make this difficult.

Consider single-voice copy as a story you are telling. Find your storyteller and commit to the attitude and style choices you make. Deliver the copy from a set point of view by finding the *subtext* (how you think and feel) behind the words you speak and express it through your voice. Study your script closely to determine if it was written to match a current trend.

One key to effective single-voice delivery is to use the basic dramatic principle of having a conversation with another person. Make the other person the ideal person who needs to hear what you have to say. Another key is to find the appropriate attitude or style. Both of these can be effective interrupts and engagements when done properly. Make your conversation natural, believable, and candid, speaking to only one person at a time. *Shotgunning*, trying to speak to several people at once, tends to make your delivery sound more like a speech than a conversation, although that may be appropriate for some types of copy.

In single-voice scripts, as in others, there can be many different written references to the performer, such as VO, ANNCR, or TALENT — and all may be used interchangeably. You may also see references to music and SFX (sound effects), which are not to be read by the performer. The format may be single or double spaced and may or may not include a separate column for video and other instructions. Read everything on the page in order to fully understand the message and your character's role.

Tips for Performing Single-Voice Copy

- You are a story teller, and stories are always about relationships. Find the relationships in the story you are telling.
- Analyze the copy for character, mood, attitude, conflict, rhythm, etc. (See Chapter 10, The Character in the Copy).
- Look for the message, image, feeling, or unique quality that the advertiser wants to communicate to the listener. What separates this product or service from its competitors?
- Find the subtext, thoughts and feelings behind the words.
- Determine who the one perfect audience is and why she should be listening to what you have to say.
- Speak conversationally, having the expectation of a response. Talk *to* the other person, *not at* him or her.
- Determine the creative strategy that will enable you to build dramatic tension and allow for expression of the message. Use sense-memory techniques to locate tension in your body and speak from that place.
- Find a way to deliver the first line of copy in a way that will interrupt the listener's thoughts and bring them in to listening to your story.
- Be careful not to telegraph the message or send a message of "here comes another commercial."

Single-Voice Scripts

As you work with the following scripts, you might find it interesting to read through the script before reading the Copy Notes. Come up with your interpretation for attitude, pacing, character, and performance, and then read through the notes to see how close you came to what the producers of these projects intended. After working with a script, play the corresponding audio track on the CD that comes with this book to hear the actual commercial.

NO FISH TODAY RESTAURANT — CD/10

Title/Media: "No Fish Today" Local Radio :60
Agency: Direct
USP/Slogan: "Fish or no fish at No Fish Today"
Target Audience: People who like to dine out
Style: Quirky Annoucer
Character: Spokesperson - male or female
VO Talent: Peter Drew - **www.peterdrewvo.com**
Copy Notes: This radio commercial is intended to create an image for the No Fish Today Restaurant as a fun place to dine, with an extensive menu. The delivery needs to be upbeat, fun, and slightly tongue-in-cheek. Notice how the first line of the script immediately gets the listener's attention and how the body of the copy keeps the listener engaged.

And now, a minute of total confusion brought to you by No Fish Today Restaurant on Pratt Street in Hartford. Confusing thought number one: No Fish Today has fish! Confusing thought number three: No Fish Today has daily specials, so you might also want to try No Fish Today tomorrow, or try No Fish Today today! No Fish Today does have some delicious dishes like Chicken Gorgonzola, Penne Primavera, and New York Sirloin, all of which are not fish today or any day. And to shed some more confusion on the subject, the New York Sirloin is served, not in New York, but here on Pratt Street in Hartford at No Fish Today, where it's convenient to the Civic Center before or after a college basketball game in which the mascot is a dog and not a fish. No Fish Today Restaurant also serves people working in Hartford who wish to have fish or no fish for lunch or dinner. Ah, by the way, Maine Lobster, Calamari, Scallops, and Shrimp are not exactly fish, but they are like fish and so they serve these delicious dishes at No Fish Today to people like you who love fish. No Fish Today on Pratt Street in Hartford. Ask for fish or no fish at No Fish Today.

AUCTION CITIES.COM — CD/11

Title/Media: "Only One" Regional TV :30
Agency: The Commercial Clinic — **www.commercialclinic.com**
USP/Slogan: "Buy or sell just about anything"
Target Audience: Adults who use Internet auctioning services
Style: Movie trailer announcer
Character: Spokesperson - strong male
VO Talent: CW Powers
Copy Notes: This is a typical TV script with separate columns for VIDEO and AUDIO. It's a very good idea to read, and thoroughly understand, what will be happening visually as your words are spoken. Many voice talent overlook the visual column and deliver a voice-over performance that is inappropriate. This wastes time in the studio and inevitably requires that the director explain the visuals — something he should not have to do.

This spot was written specifically to attract new visitors to the website **www.AuctionCities.com**. The audio was prerecorded for approval by the client. This was then used as a guide track for timing of the text animation. The completed commercial is at **www.commercialclinic.com/listen**.

VIDEO	AUDIO
FULL SCREEN WHITE TEXT ON BLACK SCREEN	**NO MUSIC:**
The following contains...	**VO: (Male – dramatic – movie trailer style)**
10 FRAME FADE TO BLACK	The following contains information that can change the way you shop . . . Forever!
BLURRED TEXT FADES IN CENTER SCREEN & INTO FOCUS. AC SUN LOGO BEGINS SLOW ZOOM IN.	
There are many auction websites...	**MUSIC—DRAMATIC:**
TEXT FOR "ONLY" DIZ IN, CHANGES TO "ONE"	There are many auction websites . . .
Only one...	But there's only one . . .
"AuctionCities.com" types in lower 3rd	that lets you bid on local auctions.
REPEATS WITH EACH STATEMENT	There's only one . . .
TEXT FLIES OUT FOR "Local" AS "Auctions" & "Shopping FLY IN	that lets you shop from retailers in your neighborhood.
Local Auctions!	Local auctions!
Local Shopping!	Local shopping!
SLOW FLY OUT FOR	With more than 40,000 zip codes!
40,000 Zip Codes!	No matter what city you live in . . .
DISSOLVE TO ANIMATED AC LOGO	Buy or sell just about anything at Auction Cities.com
TAG LINE FLIES IN FROM FRONT TO LAND BELOW LOGO	Copyright © The Commercial Clinic. All rights reserved.

HALLMARK GALLERIES — CD/12

Title/Media: "Lasagna Will Not Be Served" Local Radio :60
Agency: KIFM Radio/Direct
USP/Slogan: "From traditional to contemporary fine art."
Target Audience: Adult men and women
Style: Friendly attitude projecting a sense of fun
Character: Spokesperson - male or female
VO Talent: James R. Alburger, Penny Abshire
Copy Notes: The purpose of this spot was to promote an exhibit of artwork by Jim Davis, creator of the Garfield cartoon strip. Delivery needs to reflect the quirky attitude of the cartoon character, playing off the association of the Garfield character and lasagna. Even though the overall delivery style should be that of a spokesperson, there still needs to be a sense of conversation throughout the spot with a "tongue-in-cheek" attitude. Three different voice talent recorded the original commercial, and all three versions were broadcast in rotation.

May I have your attention, please.

Lasagna will not be served at Hallmark Gallery in La Jolla on December 2nd and 3rd. Jim Davis, creator of Garfield, likes lasagna, and although he will be at Hallmark Gallery, signing his original Garfield art – lasagna will still not be served. This rare event will feature more than 80 never-before-seen pieces – including animation cells, comic strip artwork, oils, airbrush paintings, and more – but no lasagna. Garfield is a cartoon, Jim Davis and lasagna are real . . . but only Jim Davis will be at Hallmark Gallery this weekend. If you love Garfield, and/or lasagna, we encourage you to visit Hallmark Gallery dot com for more information and to reserve your piece of collectible Garfield art. Then meet Jim Davis in person – as he signs your purchased art — this Friday and Saturday at Hallmark Gallery, on Prospect in La Jolla. Please note that lasagna will not be served at any time during this event. Lasagna brought with you must be consumed before entering the Gallery.

LLOYDS PLUMBING, HEATING AND AIR — CD/13

Title/Media: "Clueless" Radio :60
Agency: Direct/Commercial Clinic
USP/Slogan: "You can't stop a Trane"
Target Audience: Adult home owners—focusing on women
Style: Up tempo, slightly frazzled
Character: Woman with a problem - female
VO Talent: Penny Abshire — **www.pennyabshire.com**
Copy Notes: This spot is directed at women, who are the primary decision maker when it comes to home improvements. Women relate to the rapid delivery, while most men find it bothersome. Notice the reference of "four words for you . . ." then the restatement of "OK, FIVE words" as a call-back to the client name. Delivery needs to be upbeat, and fun, with a slight touch of sarcasm.

Sure I love him – but he is so cheap! Like the other day when I said the house felt really cold – he suggested I put on a sweater! I told him my nose was cold and I can't very well put a sweater on my nose!

He says it's southern California — you're being a wimp! But I'm COLD! I know utility costs are high, but I'm sick of dressing like an Eskimo in my own home. It's hard to cook in mittens!

Our old furnace is making noises like a trash compactor and it sure doesn't keep the house warm – I told him what we need is to trash the old furnace and get a new TRANE. You can imagine the look on his face — CLUELESS — Like he's never heard of Lloyds Plumbing Heating and Air. We could get a TRANE furnace, stay warm and save on utility bills.

Anyway, I told him I've got four words for you, buster – Lloyds Plumbing, Heating and Air – Ok, FIVE words! Call them – get a new TRANE furnace TODAY – no more excuses!

And one more thing – another crack about me being a wimp and you're sleeping in the garage – maybe you can wear a sweater!

ANNC: Be comfortable with a new Trane furnace and save up to 70% on utility bills. Lloyds' Plumbing, Heating and Air — your TRANE comfort specialist in Escondido and North County. It's hard to stop a TRANE.

12

Dialogue Copy: Doubles and Multiples

Types of Dialogue Copy

THE CONVERSATION

As with single-voice copy, dialogue copy involves a conversation between two or more characters. The primary difference with dialogue copy is that your one-person audience is present in the script.

Unlike most single-voice copy, dialogue usually involves a story with a specific plotline and interaction between two or more characters. It is important for you to understand the whole story, not just your part in it. If you limit your understanding to just your role, you may miss subtle details that are vital to effectively interacting with the other characters, or for creating the dramatic tension that is so necessary for giving the characters life and making them real to the listener. When two or more characters are having a conversation, I refer to it as *interactive dialogue*.

Another form of dialogue is one in which the characters are not talking to each other, but are instead speaking directly to the audience. A conversation is still taking place, but in this case, it is more one-sided with each actor sharing a portion of the overall delivery. I refer to this type of dialogue as *shared information*. This is very similar to a single-voice delivery, except that in this type of performance each character is interacting primarily with the audience, but must also respond appropriately to the other character sharing information.

Regardless of the structure, all dialogue requires excellent listening and performing skills. Interactions between characters must be believable and timing must be correct for a dialogue performance to be accepted by the listener.

COMEDY

Comedy is a very popular form of dialogue copy. It is not the words on the page that make a script funny; it is the intent behind the words. In part, comedy is based on the unexpected — leading the audience in one direction and then suddenly changing direction and ending up someplace else. Comedy is often based on overstating the obvious or placing a totally serious character in a ludicrous situation. Comedy can also be achieved by creating a sense of discomfort in the mind of the audience.

Think of a comedy script as a slice of life — with a twist. Playing lines for laughs doesn't work. Laughs come only when the audience is surprised.

Rhythm and timing are essential with dialogue. A natural interaction between characters, overlapping lines, or stepping on lines, gives a more real feeling and helps set the rhythm and pace of the story. Pauses (where appropriate), and natural vocal embellishments can add naturalness.

Ask the producer or director before taking too many liberties with any copy; this is especially true with comedy dialogue. If the producer understands comedy, you may be given the freedom to experiment with your character and how you deliver your lines. Ultimately, your character should have precedence over the copy and certain ad-libs or other adaptations may be necessary to create the illusion of reality. Say your lines in a natural, conversational way, appropriate to the situation, and the comedy will happen.

Tips for Performing Dialogue Copy

To be effective, comedy dialogue must have a sense of reality, even if the situation is ludicrous and the characters are exaggerated. The following tips and suggestions will help you perform comedy copy effectively.

- Be real. Keep your character spontaneous and natural. Use a back story or lead-in line to help get into the moment.
- Find the dialogue rhythm. The rhythm for a comedic script will be different from that of a serious script. Be consistent throughout the performance.
- Humanize your character by adding natural sounds, such as "uhh," "yeah," "uh-huh," "mmm," etc. These sounds help give the feeling of a real, natural conversation. Ask before making copy changes.
- Find the *subtext* — what's going on behind the words — this is especially important with dialogue. If your character is that of a normal person in a ludicrous situation, you need to have a subtext of normalcy. If your thoughts anticipate the punch line, it will be communicated through your performance.
- Do not telegraph the punch line.

- Stay in the moment, listen and answer. Respond authentically to the other characters or situations that occur, expecting a response.
- Learn how to use comedic timing for maximum effect.
- Underplay, rather than overplay. Louder is not better. If in doubt, pull back, speak more softly and be more natural.
- Don't read! Be conversational. Be real. Talk *to* the audience or other performer(s), not *at* them. Speak as quickly as you would if you were actually talking to someone in a real-life conversation. Be careful not to overenunciate. In dialogue, less is usually more.

Dialogue and Multiple-Voice Scripts

COASTAL CONDO LIVING — CD/14

Title/Media: "Tell Me What You See." Radio :60
Agency: Media Services
Production: The Commercial Clinic — **www.commercialclinic.com**
USP: "Find your next condo!"
Target Audience: Adult home shoppers
Style: Very conversational, relaxed
Characters: Woman with a problem, Man in authority
VO Talent: Doctor — James R. Alburger, Woman — Penny Abshire
Copy Notes: The purpose of this spot is to drive listeners to the client's website for additional information on Condo living throughout the Carolinas and Florida. The spot begins with a man in control and has a role reversal near the end. The Doctor is serious about his work and expresses concern for his patient. However, he becomes puzzled by his patient's answers and ultimately enthralled with what she is talking about. The woman is fixated on Condo living and sees only what she wants to see. The interaction between characters needs to be spontaneous and real. We need to hear the thoughts taking place in the character's minds as well as the emotional transitions that occur within each character.

Coastal Condo Living:

Doctor:	Okay, take a look at these ink blots and tell me exactly what you see.
Woman:	Okay . . .
Doctor:	Alright, here's the first one.
Woman:	Umm . . . that looks like a condo on the coast – like the one I saw at coastalcondoliving.com. A really nice one!
Doctor:	Um Hum . . . And this next one?

Woman:	Oh! That's a town house with a garage! My husband loves a garage! I saw one like it at coastalcondoliving.com!
Doctor:	I see . . . and this ink blot?
Woman:	That's a villa – with a lake! Oh, will you look at the ducks – they're so cute!
Doctor.	You seem obsessed with condo living!
Woman:	Well sure – we do want a nice place to retire! Haven't you heard of coastalcondoliving.com?
Doctor:	On the Internet?
Woman:	Sure! There are all sorts of resources there for finding a condo – area realtors, MLS listings, maps, golf course locations, interior designers . . .
Doctor:	On the Internet?
Woman:	Yes. Of course. Coastalcondoliving.com will even send you a free magazine to help you find your next condo!
Doctor:	coastalcondoliving.com – right? I'll try it!
Woman:	Great! . . . What are you doing?
Doctor:	Let me see the picture of the condo on the coast again – Looked like it had a great view!
Woman:	What?

GRAND PRIX CAR WASH — CD/15

Title/Media: "Lost" Radio :30
Agency: Ward Advertising
Production: The Commercial Clinic — **www.commercialclinic.com**
USP: "More than just a car wash"
Target Audience: Car owners
Style: Quirky conversational
Characters: Woman: forgetful, short memory, a bit quirky; Car Wash Guy (CWG): proud, trying to help
VO Talent: Penny Abshire, James R. Alburger
Copy Notes: This advertiser is at an ideal location, directly across the parking lot from a Costco Center. The car wash has just been purchased, and the new owners want to establish both their location and an image that they provided more service than any other car wash in the high desert. The characters need to be real, yet somewhat quirky.

Grand Prix Car Wash:

Woman:	Excuse me – I'm a little lost. I saw your sign "Grand Prix Car Wash." What do you do here?
CWG:	We're a car wash. With all the things most car washes have: Sprayers, water, soap, suds…
Woman:	Towels?
CWG:	Yes, and a lot more!
Woman:	So you wash cars at Grand Prix Car Wash?
CWG:	And as a Loyalty Plan member, after 10 car washes, you'll get one for FREE . . .
Woman:	Wait! Do I have to have all 10 in the same day?
CWG:	No . . . and you get a free deluxe car wash on your birthday!
Woman:	Really? For free?
CWG:	That's right!
WOMAN:	That's nice! But where am I?
CWG:	You're at The Grand Prix Car Wash — at the Costco Center on Dinah Shore in Palm Desert.
Woman:	Oh, and what do you do here?

TOWNE CENTER PLAZA — CD/16

Title/Media: "Obscene Phone Call" Radio :60
Agency: Enjoy Development — Commercial Clinic
Production: The Commercial Clinic — **www.commercialclinic.com**
USP: "In the center of things"
Target Audience: Adults
Style: Multi-voice Dialog
Characters: Wife — worried to surprised; Caller — practical joker who loves to play tricks on his wife.
VO Talent: Penny Abshire, James R. Alburger
Copy Notes: The object of this commercial is to increase awareness and visibility of the Towne Center Plaza shopping center. The client wanted every store in the mall to be mentioned in the spot. The food court was having a problem with traffic flow, so special attention was requested to address that issue.

Proper delivery of this copy requires a rapid-fire repartee with tight dialogue and attitude change-ups for each character. The tag announce is a straight read by a third voice to create a localized identity for the shopping center.

Towne Center Plaza:

Caller:	Hello, is this Mrs. Ernest Simpson, that fabulous blonde?
Wife:	Yes, who is this?
Caller:	You've been missin' out on something, baby. Town Center Plaza. It will satisfy your every desire.
Wife:	How did you get this number?
Caller:	Never mind that. This place sells all the stuff you really like – shoes, gardening, crafts, fabrics, even three restaurants to satisfy your . . . appetite.
Wife:	I've heard about these calls and I'm going to report you to the police – now WHO IS THIS?
Hubby:	It's your husband, silly and I just discovered Town Center Plaza. You'll love this place!
Wife:	Oh, Ernie . . .
Hubby:	It's got everything! There's Michael's, E & J Designer Shoes . . .
Wife:	I love shoes!
Hubby:	Garden Fancy, Uncle Don's Hobbies, Joanne's Fabrics, Mikasa, Evans Optometry and Cookies by Design.
Wife:	You love cookies . . .
Hubby:	Oh, and break out a bottle of the bubbly. I'm taking you to dinner at Chez Pierre and if you play your cards right, we'll have breakfast tomorrow at The Sunshine Café and lunch at Fisherman's Market and Grill.
Wife:	Well, you really had me fooled, honey. Honestly, I thought it was Sam.
Hubby:	Sam? Marge, who's Sam?
Tag:	Great Restaurants and Great Stores — In the center of things — Town Center Plaza — at Fred Waring and Town Center Way — just look for Trader Joes.

13

Character Copy

*A good actor can do a thousand voices
because he finds a place in his body for his voice
and centers his performance from that place.*
Charles Nelson Reilly

Vocalizing Characters

Most character and animation voices are an exaggeration of specific vocal characteristics or attitudes, which enable the performer to create an appropriate vocal sound for the character. A forced voice is rarely the most effective, is difficult to sustain, and can actually cause physical damage to your vocal cords. The most effective character voices are those that emphasize or exaggerate the attitudes and emotions of the character you are portraying, or that take a small quirk or idiosyncrasy and blow it out of proportion.

ANIMATION AND CHARACTER VOICES

Character and story analysis are most important with animation voice work. Many factors will affect the voice of the character, so the more you know about your character, the easier it will be to find its true voice.

Consistency is extremely important in character voice work. When you find the character's voice, lock it into your memory and keep the proper attitude and quality of sound throughout your performance, adapting your character's voice when the mood of the script changes. The important thing here is to avoid allowing the sound of your character to *drift*. To make your character believable and real to the audience, the quality of the voice must not change from the beginning of the script to the end.

161

Most animation voice actors have a repertoire of several voices. A typical session may require voicing three characters before lunch, three more after lunch, and then going back for pick-ups on some of the first set of characters. This sort of schedule means character voice actors must be extremely versatile and must be able to accurately repeat and sustain voice characterizations. These demands make animation work a challenging niche to break into, and one of the most creative in voice-over.

In addition to voices and sounds for animation, character voice work can also include dialects, foreign and regional accents, and even celebrity impersonations. Special accents and dialects require an ability to mimic a sound or attitude that is familiar to a portion of the listening audience. Usually, this mimicking is a stylized interpretation and doesn't necessarily have to be 100 percent accurate, unless the character is represented as being authentic to a region or culture. Many times, the best accent is one that reflects what a community "thinks" the accent should sound like, which is often not the real thing. However, when authenticity is required to give the character believability, vocal accuracy is important. Most of the time, however, a slight exaggeration of certain regional vocal traits tends to give the character attitude and personality. Being personally familiar with the culture, region, or dialect is also helpful.

Celebrity voice impersonations are often the most challenging because the celebrities are usually well known. The voice actor's job is to create a voice that offers recognition of the celebrity, yet hints at being just a bit different. Celebrity impersonations are usually done in the context of a humorous commercial in which some aspect of the celebrity's personality or vocal styling is exaggerated or used as a device for communicating the message. In most cases, if a producer wants an extremely accurate celebrity voice, he or she will hire the celebrity. It may cost more to hire the actual person behind the voice, but the increased credibility is often worth it. Also, a disclaimer may be necessary for an impersonation, but is not required if the real person is performing.

There are two critical aspects to character voice work: regardless of the character, the voice must be believable; and it must, in some way, be different from your natural voice. Achieving excellence in this aspect of the craft requires specialized knowledge and a mastery of performing skills.

Pat Fraley is one of the most amazing voice actors I've met. He's not only a consummate performer — in just about every area of voice work — but he's also an excellent, and very generous, teacher and coach. Pat understands character voice work better than most professionals. He's one of the top 10 voice actors for animation, having performed more than 4,000 different cartoon voices. He's narrated dozens of audio books, and voiced thousands of commercials.

Just as I've broken down a performance to its *Seven Core Elements*, Pat breaks down a character voice to its six critical elements.

Pat Fraley's Six Critical Elements of a Character Voice

© Patrick Fraley, 2006
www.patfraley.com

With any artful endeavor, you will find two words that are important to define: Form and Content. What is the FORM of a character voice? The way this applies to character voice is that the FORM is the SOUND of the voice. The CONTENT is the thinking and feeling, the psychology of the character. The Six Elements of a Character Voice are all about the FORM. What makes up the form of a character voice? Like everything else, there's a finite amount of elements.

These are the six elements: *Pitch, Pitch Characteristic, Tempo, Rhythm, Placement,* and *Mouth Work.*

Pitch _____
(Higher or lower than your own?)

Pitch Characteristic _____
(Gravelly? Breathy? Husky? Constricted?)

Tempo _____
(Faster or slower than your own?)

Rhythm _____
(Syncopated? Plodding? Loping?)

Placement _____
(Nasal? Back of Throat? Normal?)

Mouth Work _____
(Accent? Lisp? Tight Lips?)

The first element is **Pitch**. Pitch relates to the musical notes of the character's voice. Is the character's voice higher than your own? Is it lower? Or perhaps the character goes both higher and lower, showing a wider range. Thus far we've dealt with Pitch and it has been assumed that the characteristic of the pitch was clear.

The second element deals with the specific characteristic of the pitch, **Pitch Characteristic**. Pitch Characteristic is the dynamic of the pitch, or coloring. If Pitch were a noun, Pitch Characteristic would be it's adjective, as it describes the nature of the pitch. It is clear? Is it gravelly? Is it hoarse? Is it breathy? Is it constricted? Is it cracking? Velvety?

The third element is **Tempo**. Tempo refers to the character's general rate of delivery. There are three possibilities: (1) Does the character speak faster than you? (2) Slower than you? (3) Or does the character vary or have a wider range of tempo than you?

The fourth element is **Rhythm**. Vivid characters go about getting what they want, and they go about getting it in the same way, over and over. There is a pattern to their behavior. This pattern shows up in the way they speak. Character Rhythm is defined as a repetitive pattern of emphasis in the way the character speaks which emerges from the thinking and feeling of the character. It's kind of a vocal thumb print.

The fifth element is **Placement**. Placement refers to where the voice seems to be coming from or where it's placed. When I think about placing my voice in my nose the sound takes on a whole different dynamic. I feel a lot of air coming through my nose. It sounds a whole lot different than when I place my voice in the back of my mouth. How about if I think of creating the voice in my throat? Distinct sounds? The trick is to learn how to *stay* in the placement all the time for any given character.

Because placement happens in and around the mouth, it has a kind of relationship with our sixth and final element, **Mouth Work**. Mouth Work refers to anything done in and around the mouth to effect the character. The kind of effect that comes to mind is accents. But also, having tight lips effect the way we sound, stretching your mouth to one side and talking, or the way a character pronounces their "S"s.

So that's all the ingredients it takes to bake up the form of a character voice — no less, no more: Pitch, Pitch Characteristic, Tempo, Rhythm, Placement, and Mouth Work.

Finding Your Voice

Begin creating a character's voice by doing a thorough character analysis to discover as much as you can about him or her (or it). Based on the copy, make the decisions and commit to who you are talking to and if your character has any special accent or attitude. Finally, decide where in your body the character's voice will be placed.

Visualize the voice coming from a specific location in your body and work with the copy until the voice feels right, using choices about the character's physical size and shape to help you localize the voice. Use the "sweep" (Exercise #10, page 46) to find a suitable pitch for your character voice. Once you have found a pitch, use placement, pitch characteristics, tempo, rhythm, and mouth work to create a unique sound. Here are some possible placements:

top of head (tiny)	under tongue (sloppy)	nose (nasal)
behind eyes (de-nasal)	diaphragm (strong)	chest (boomy)
top of cheeks (bright)	loose cheeks (mushy)	throat (raspy)
front of mouth (crisp)	back of throat (breathy)	stomach (low)

Practice different voices with different attitudes. Use computer clip art, comic strips and other drawings to get ideas for character voices. You may find that a particular physical characteristic or facial expression is needed in order for you to get the proper sound and attitude. Remember: *Physicalize the moment and the voice will follow.* Record a variety of voices and characters, then listen to what you've recorded. If your character voices all sound the same, you'll need to work on your character voice skills.

The Character Voice Worksheet

In animation, you must be able to recall a voice on demand. The Character Voice Worksheet on the next page is just one of many good ways to document the characteristics of each voice you create. The worksheet is divided into four parts: (1) Accessing/Recalling the character voice, (2) Placement, (3) Physical characteristics, and (4) Other notes.

Accessing and Recalling the character voice:
- Give your character a name for quick recall
- Define age, gender, attitude, physical attributes, and overall energy level
- Create a *Key Phrase* that will allow you to return to the character. You will know the phrase is correct when it sounds natural.

Placement:
- Determine where in your body you are positioning the voice.
- Choose appropriate pitch, pitch characteristics, tempo, rhythm, and mouth work to contribute to the reality of the voice.
- Understand the character's emotions and feelings.

Physical:
- Determine how your character stands and moves in space and time. Experiment with facial expressions, physical gestures, and speaking quirks, including how your character laughs.

Other Notes:
- Include any additional information that will help you recall your voice.

Each voice you document is what Pat Fraley terms a *starter*. This is a core voice from which you can create many more simply by adjusting some of the characteristics. Start with a defined voice, then experiment with changing the pitch and altering pitch characteristics. Change the tempo and rhythm as you work with the voice, or see what happens as you adjust the voice placement or slightly modify the mouth work — and voila! . . . you've got a new character.

MJ Lallo, a top voice-acting coach in Los Angeles, gives you more ideas and exercises for creating character voices on track 17 of the CD.

The Character Voice Worksheet

Sketch or pic of character

Character name: _____

Age _____ Height _____

Gender_____ Body type _____

Character source (where did you get the idea?):

_____

Describe primary energy: _____

Key phrase: _____

Appearance (hair, clothing, etc.): _____

Placement (location of voice in your body):

   Vertical pitch: _____

   _____ Abdomen   _____ Chest   _____ Throat   _____ Eyes

   _____ Adenoid   _____ Nasal   _____ Face   _____ Top of head

   Horizontal placement: _____

   _____ Front of face/body   _____ Centered   _____ Back of head/body

Pitch Characteristics: _____
(raspy, gravely, smooth, clear, smoky, edgy, nasal, de-nasal, nervous, breathy, tight, etc.)

Vocal Dynamics — Phrasing/Pacing (musicality of your character's voice):

   Tempo: _____ Fast   _____ Slow   _____ Moderate   _____ Varying

   Rhythm: _____ Smooth flow   _____ Staccato   _____ Melodic

   Attitude — Tone of Voice: _____

   Emotion: _____

   Volume (loud/soft/varied): _____

Physicalization (how does your character move in time and space?):

   Stance: _____   Walk: _____

   Quirks: _____   Laugh: _____

   Body: _____   Hands/arms: _____

   Mouth work: _____   Dialect/accent: _____

   Associated color, sound, or taste: _____

If your character was real, who or what might it be like?

_____

Other notes: _____

_____

_____

Tips for Character and Animation Copy

Character voice work can be challenging, but lots of fun. Use the following tips and suggestions to help find your character's voice.

- Understand your character and the situation. In animation, you must often use your imagination to make up what you are reacting to.
- Discover who the audience is and understand how the audience will relate to the character.
- Maintain a consistent voice throughout the copy and be careful not to injure your voice by stretching too far. It is better to pull back a little and create a voice that can be maintained rather than push too hard for a voice you can only sustain for one or two pages.
- Be willing to exaggerate attitudes or personality traits for the sake of finding the voice.
- If a drawing, photo, or picture of the character is available, use it as a tool to discover the personality of the character.
- Find the place in your body from which the voice will come.
- Experiment with pitch, pitch characteristics, tempo, rhythm, placement, and mouth work to discover the most appropriate vocal delivery for your character.
- Experiment to take on the physical characteristics of the character.

Character and Animation Scripts

Find a suitable voice and delivery for each of the following characters. Use *Pitch, Pitch Characteristics, Tempo, Rhythm, Placement, and Mouth Work* to create a believable voice. Do a quick "A-B-C" (*Audience, Back Story, Character, Desires*, and *Energy*) for each line of copy to discover clues about your character. Explore any relationships that may exist in the copy or in the drawing. Experiment with different voice possibilities and add layers of *emotion*, *attitude*, and *physical movement*.

Character Name: Wolf E. Lobo
Description: He's a wolf and yes, he eats other animals, but he feels bad about it and would prefer to be a vegetarian.

Copy: "Ever notice how pork always gets stuck in your teeth?"

Copy: "Bubbie! Of course I'd love to hear your movie idea . . . Yea, works for me . . . Have your people call my people!"

Copy: "Ah, at last . . . My basket collection is finally complete!"

Character Name: Norman Winterbottom
Description: President of the Chess Club, the Math Club and Future CEOs of America. IQ is 160.

Copy: "Mark my words, you disbelievers! When global warming occurs, you'll wish the bottom of your pants was as high as mine!"

Copy: "First . . . would you please accompany me to the spring, hedonistic, ritual dance on Saturday? And . . . Second . . . I should not have put my chocolate bar in my pocket."

Character Name: Ivana Richman
Description: She was born "trailer trash" but by working her way through 5 husbands she's now a socialite in polite society.

Copy: "I always say, the bigger the hair, the closer you are to God!"

Copy: "Dahling, of course you want to be me. Everyone does!"

Copy: "Oh, no my dear . . . I'm not smoking . . . it's steam.

Character Name: Marcus Menville
Description: A rascal of a kid who lives for video games, terrorizing his cat with his slingshot and constantly talking his way out of trouble.

Copy: "Yeah, well . . . it's like this . . . The cat was askin' for it! Know what I mean?"

Copy: "Coooooooool. I just broke my own record—24 hrs. straight on my Xbox."

Copy: "There's . . . nuthin' in my pocket . . . what are you talkin' about?"

Character Name: Linda Lee Loo
Description: A sweet young thing who delivers meals on wheels to shut-ins and volunteers at the local animal shelter.

Copy: "There's no such thing as a bad wolf . . . just a misunderstood one!"

Copy: "Every time I see him, that darn wolf tries to eat <u>me</u>! I'm calling the SPCRRH right now!"

14

Industrials: Long-Form and Narrative Copy

Sales presentations, marketing videos, in-house training tapes, point-of-purchase videos, film documentaries, telephone messages, and many other projects all fall into the category of corporate and narrative. Frequently, these scripts are written to be read and not spoken.

Writers of industrials — corporate and narrative — copy are often not experienced writers, or usually write copy for print. There are exceptions to this, but overall you can expect copy in this category to be pretty dry. Corporate and narrative copy is often full of statistics, complex names or phrases and terminology specific to a business or industry. These can be a challenge for even an experienced voice-over performer.

As you perform a corporate or narrative script, you are still performing a character telling a story, just as for any other type of copy. You should know who your character is, who you are talking to, and what you are talking about. You also need to find a way to create an image of knowledge and authority for your character. What is it about your character that gives him the authority to be speaking the words? Is your character the owner of the company, a satisfied customer, the company's top salesperson, or a driver for one of the delivery trucks? To create an image of credibility, figure out an appropriate role for your character and commit to your choice.

A corporate or narrative script for a video project might have several on-camera performers. These are often professional actors, but sometimes include employees of the business. There also may be several voice-over performers for different sections of the script. Many scripts in this category are written for a single voice-over performer, but occasionally two or more performers will alternate lines or voice different sections. There may also be some interactive dialogue sections of the script. The complexity of a corporate script will vary greatly depending on the intended purpose, the content, the length, and the budget for the project.

It is sometimes more challenging to deliver a script of this nature in a conversational manner, but it is possible. Facts, numbers, unusual terms, and complex names all contribute to a presentation more like a lecture than a conversation. However, the information is important, and the audience must be able to relate to the presentation as well as clearly understand what they hear. If the presentation of the information (your performance) is interesting and entertaining, the effectiveness of the communication will be much better.

Tips for Performing Corporate and Narrative Copy

The following tips and suggestions will help you with corporate and narrative copy in general.

- Talk *to* the audience on their level, not *at* them, even though the script might be full of facts, statistics, and unusual names or phrases.
- Take your time delivering the copy. Unlike radio or TV copy, which must be done within a specific time, there is rarely any time limitation for corporate and narrative copy.
- Be clear on the facts and pronunciation of complex words. These are important to the client and need to be correct and accurate.
- Slow your delivery or pace in sections where there is important information; speak more quickly in other parts of the script.
- If you are alternating lines with another performer, and the script is not written for dialogue, be careful to not overlap or step on the other performer's lines. Keep your delivery more open for this type of script, unless the producer specifically requests that you tighten your delivery.

Corporate and Narrative Scripts

As you work with the following scripts, you might find it interesting to read through the script before reading the Copy Notes provided for each one. Come up with your own interpretation for attitude, pacing, character, and performance. Then read through the notes to see how close you came to what the producers of these projects intended. The following scripts are reproduced as accurately as possible, including typos, grammatical errors, and awkward phrasing.

OASIS MOUTHWASH AND DRY MOUTH SPRAY — CD/18

Title: "Oasis Training Module" — audio training program
Agency: GlaxoSmithKlein
USP: "Long lasting moisturization for patients with dry mouth discomfort "
Target Audience: Medical professionals working with patients who experience dry mouth symptoms.
Character: Authority on the use of Oasis product
VO Talent: James R. Alburger
Copy Notes: The Oasis Training Module is intended for use as a website training and marketing tool for physicians and dentists. As such, the voice track narration needs to project a sense of authority and expertise on the subject of dry mouth.

One challenge with this project is that the script is written in 5 modules and each module is approximately 12 pages in length. This means the recording time may be extensive. Pronunciation for the numerous technical, chemical, and medical terms must be consistent and sound as though the words are used daily. The last module must sound as fresh and friendly as the beginning.

An experienced voice talent can narrate a script such as this almost as a cold read after verifying the correct pronunciation for certain words. However, there may still be some sections that require multiple takes.

Oasis mouthwash is a water-based formula optimized for taste and texture through consumer testing.

The water provides the moisture that dry mouth sufferers lack.

To hold onto that water, humectants are added.

Glycerin, also known as glycerol, is a clear, sweet syrupy liquid that is able to draw moisture from the air. Not only is it a humectant that holds onto moisture, but it also is a thickening agent and lubricant.

Like glycerin, sorbitol is a sweet clear liquid, a humectant, thickening agent and lubricant.

Whereas glycerin and sorbitol are relatively small molecules, xanthan gum, copovidone, and carboxymethylcellulose are polymers.

Polymers are long chains of repeating units linked together, like the glucose unit in xanthan gum. When the repeating unit is a sugar, the polymer is a polysaccharide. Xanthan gum (a microbial fermentation product) and carboxymethylcellulose (a derivative of cellulose) are polysaccharides. Copovidone is a synthetic polymer of vinyl-pyrrolidone and vinyl acetate.

These three polymers work together to trap moisture and hold it at the mucosal surface.

The polymers add to the moisturizing properties of the mouthwash as well as to the products persistence of action, or substantivity.

Poloxamer 338 and PEG 60 hydrogenated castor oil are surfactants and stabilizers.

Surfactants, also known as wetting agents, allow for easier spreading at the interface between two substances, such as the spreading of the mouthwash on the surface of the oral mucosa.

Stabilizers keep ingredients in solution.

Poloxamer 338 is a nonionic surfactant. Like copovidone, poloxamer 338 is a co-polymer of two different repeating units. Nonionic means that it doesn't carry an electrical charge.

PEG 60 hydrogenated castor oil is a modified form of castor oil, a plant extract. PEG stands for polyethylene glycol; the 60 refers to its size.

Cetylpyridinium Chloride or CPC may be familiar to you as the active ingredient in Crest Pro-Health rinse.

CPC is an antiseptic agent that inhibits the growth of bacteria.

While the CPC in the Pro-health rinse is promoted for its antibacterial activity, it is added to the Oasis mouthwash as a preservative.

Methylparaben, propylparaben, and sodium benzoate also are added as product preservatives. When used together, these chemicals have both antimicrobial and antifungal activity. This activity extends shelf life and prevents molds and bacteria from growing in the products.

The disodium and monosodium phosphates work together as a buffer. Buffers help solutions resist changes in pH.

Flavor and sodium saccharin, an artificial sweetener which does not promote cavities, provide the product with a flavor profile of slightly sweet with a mild, minty taste.

The flavor profile of Oasis mouthwash was optimized through rounds of consumer evaluations.

The mouthwash is colored with F-D and C blue number 1 to give it a recognizable and pleasing appearance.

THE POWER OF YOUR THOUGHTS — CD/19

Title: "Passion, Profit, and Power" — audio training program
Agency: Mind Power, Inc.
USP: "Reprogram your subconscious mind to create the relationships, wealth, and well-being that you deserve"
Target Audience: Self-motivated people who desire to improve their life
Style: Friendly, professional, expert
Characters: Author/expert
VO Talent: Marshall Sylver — **www.sylver.com**
Copy Notes: Marshall Sylver is a motivational speaker, professional hypnotist, and an expert in the area of subconscious reprogramming. This excerpt from his program "Passion, Profit and Power" is an excellent example of taking the words "off the page." Many professional speakers will produce an audio version of their seminar, or a training program. For studio recordings such as this, the material is scripted in advance and read during the recording session. The challenge for the presenter is to sound as though the words being spoken are coming off the top of the head. They must sound completely natural, very conversational, and be absolutely comfortable with the complexities of their topic — yet it is totally scripted.

With this sort of material, it is very easy to fall into a "read-y" narration style that can sound more like a lecture than a conversation. As an experienced motivational speaker, Marshall delivers his message in an intimate style that presents him as a knowledgeable expert. Notice how effectively he uses many voice-acting techniques like sense memory, pulling lines, pacing, and physicalization just to mention a few. Also notice how you, as a listener, are affected by the way in which Marshall tells the story. He draws you into what he is saying, and keeps you listening by presenting a skillful blend of intellectual and emotional content.

As you listen to the CD, observe the variety in Marshall's delivery; the way he adjusts his pacing to emphasize a point, the way he changes the pitch of his voice, and the way he creates a vivid image in your imagination. Also listen for changes in his delivery that are affected by physical alterations of his body, arms, and face.

As you work with this script, keep in mind that as a voice actor you are both a communicator and a storyteller. Notice that there are several lists in this story, as well as lots of vivid imagery. Use the techniques you've learned in previous chapters to determine your audience, back story, and character so you can create a powerful interpretation. Use sense memory, visualization, and physical movement to create a totally believable experience in the imagination of your audience.

This story is excellent for stretching your performing abilities. Become familiar with the basic story, and then tell it to different groups of friends in different ways — for one group simply tell the story without much emphasis or feeling; for another group, pull out all the stops. Notice how much more effective and real the reaction will be for the second group.

Passion, Profit and Power — script:
The Power of Your Thoughts

Every single thought that you can have possesses the ability to psychosomatically affect you. What this means is that every thought has a response in the physical body. In a moment I'm going to cause your body to respond to something simply by the thought of it.

Recently, I was driving through a citrus orchard near my home, and as I looked around me I saw thousands and thousands of totally ripe lemons. If you've ever driven through a citrus orchard, the first thing you'll notice is the scent . . . it smells like "sweet tarts." As I was driving through the citrus orchard, and looking at these juicy, plump, ripe lemons, I couldn't resist. I pulled my car off to the side of the road and I got out. And I walked up to the nearest tree that was laden full and heavy with the juiciest, plumpest, biggest, sour lemons I'd ever seen in my life.

I couldn't resist. I reached up to the tree . . . and I plucked the biggest, juiciest lemon I could find . . . and when I did, I smelled that scent, popping as the stem burst away from the fruit. That sour, tangy, juicy citrus scent from the lemon. I couldn't resist any more. In that moment, I reached into my pocket. I pulled out my pocket knife, and I pressed the shiny metal blade of the knife against the smooth, juicy flesh of this yellow lemon. And I began to slice through this juicy, tangy, tart, sour lemon . . . and as I did, the pulp and the juices from the lemon ran down the knife blade and across my hand. I put the knife aside, and I took my thumbs and I pressed them between the halves of this juicy, sour, tangy, tart lemon – and I split them apart. It was like sunshine in both hands! I couldn't wait – I tipped my head straight back – and I began squeezing half the lemon into my mouth. The sour juices, dripping, running down my chin, going back into my mouth. I couldn't wait any more . . . I took the other half of the lemon and I bit into it fully . . . tasting the sour, juicy, tangy lemon. And when I did, my jowls tightened, just like yours are tightening now.

Every thought has a psychosomatic response in the body. By virtue of the fact that you think it – you'll telegraph to your body to respond to that thought as if it were true. What you believe is true for you. Nothing else.

15

Other Types
of Voice-over Work

By now you can see that there are many facets to the craft of voice-over. To be successful in this business you need to discover what it is that you do best, and focus on developing those skills and your marketing within that niche.

This chapter covers some of the highly specialized performing areas of voice acting. I've asked some of the top professionals in each area to explain what makes their work unique and their suggestions for breaking in and succeeding.

Audio Books

Audio books are a highly specialized area of voice-over work. This kind of work is not for everyone! To be a successful audio book narrator you must have a passion for reading. Audio books are challenging projects, and the pay is often not as good as other types of voice-over work.

An audio book reader will read a book, on average, three or four times. The first time through is to get a sense of the story. The second time through is for the purpose if identifying and marking the scenes, characters, emotions, and story dynamics; and starting to develop the voice treatments for each character. The third time through is usually the recording session, or perhaps a final read to rehearse the delivery, in which case the fourth time through would be the session.

A typical audio book recording session will last about 4 to 5 hours. Most *readers* recommend taking frequent breaks and speaking continuously for no more than 50 minuets at a time. For the most part, the session goes non-stop, and the same process will repeat for as many days as it takes to complete the project — and that could be one or two days up to several weeks. And even when you think your recording is complete, you may be called back to the studio months later for *pick-ups* to replace some lines or re-track a page or two. When this happens, you need to be able to match the original delivery both in delivery style and vocal quality.

Remember that the microphone hears everything. Even a slight change in position can result in a change in the quality or consistency of your performance. Wear clothing that doesn't make any noise, move silently, and learn to take shallow breaths. Page turns should be done as quietly as possible. If a sentence at the bottom of one page continues to the next, complete the sentence at the bottom of the page, pause, turn the page, then pick up with the next sentence. Don't try to do a page turn in mid-sentence. Changes in your delivery style, vocal placement, or bad edits will all result in your voice becoming a distraction to the listener.

Marketing yourself as an audio book narrator requires some special skills and knowledge. There are some companies that specialize in audio books; they arrange for the recording rights and book the performers. These are companies you can contact regarding work as an audio book narrator. Some will ask that you record at their facility, while others may be open to having you simply provide the completed and edited recordings.

Some audio book voice actors will take on the roles of both talent and producer by finding a book that they think will be marketable, arranging for recording rights from the author or publisher, preparing a production budget, and pitching the book to an audio book publisher with themselves as the performer. Developing an audio book project in this manner can create an income stream from several different areas.

One of the best ways to learn about audio books is to begin by studying acting and other performers who narrate audio books. Then find a voice-over coach who knows the audio book business, and who offers a class in audio book narration. You'll find additional information about the audio book industry at the Audiobook Publishers Association website, **www.audiopub.org**. Audio book work can be tiring and exhausting, but if you enjoy reading and storytelling, it can be very enjoyable and gratifying.

HILLARY HUBER (Hollywood, CA)
www.hillaryhuber.com

Hillary Huber is a successful voice-over talent based in Los Angeles. She has voiced thousands of commercials including national accounts for Toyota, Birdseye, Boeing, Ford, and McDonalds. She is also a critically acclaimed audio book reader for titles including *A Light in the Piazza*, by Elizabeth Spencer, *A Field of Darkness*, by Cornelia Read, *A Map of Glass* by Jane Urquhart, and a six-book series titled *Southern Women*, by Elizabeth Spencer. Hillary is also an accomplished voice-acting coach and will often be found working with Pat Fraley as a co-instructor at his workshops. Here's what she has to say about the field of audio books.

A Bit About Audio Books

Reading audio books is the most rewarding voice-over work I have done. It offers me the opportunity to act, not just announce. I get to be multiple characters, wind a story, do it all on my own time AND I get to line my shelves with my finished work!

This fast-growing market is much easier to break into than other voice-over arenas such as commercial, promo, animation and looping. There are no agents. You forge a relationship with an audio book publisher and they funnel you work. It's that easy.

How does one go about creating that relationship? There are a couple of ways. You might try the gun-for-hire route. In this case you make a demo (generally consisting of three short excerpts from books demonstrating your particular skills. The demo is no more than three minutes total.) Your demo is then sent to small and medium-sized audio publishers with the hope that they need your talents and hire you. The larger audio book publishers are a little harder to get to.

I think a better way is to become your own producer. Most audio book publishers farm out their work. Find a book that has not been previously recorded. Record yourself reading a few excerpts from the book. Then approach the appropriate audio book publisher with an offer. "This is how I can make you money" is more attractive than "How can you make me money."

You can research audio book publishers at **www.audiopub.org**. This is a terrific site loaded with current information about the state of the audio book market.

Reading audio books requires many of the same skills that this book teaches. You must be a good reader. You must be able to interpret themes and wind a story. Acting is critical, unless you want to read nonfiction – medical text, scientific works, self-help, and so on. The ability to change the sound of your voice to differentiate between characters is a big plus. Not all readers do this but I find a little vocal characterization enhances the read and makes the listening easier.

I record for only about four hours at a time. If you work as a gun-for-hire, and record at the audio book publisher's studio, you can expect to read for 6 to 8 hours.

This market is not as lucrative as the commercial world. But it's so much more creative and ultimately, for me, more fulfilling. I produce all of my own work, so I am able to work around my schedule and never have to miss an audition or another job. I record in my home studio (many books are done this way) so I don't have studio and engineer overhead costs. I highly suggest you look into this wonderful, fast-growing world of audio books. It's a blast.

Video Games

Voicing for video games falls within the Character and Animation category, but there are some unique differences for this type of work. For the most part, today's video games have characters that must be presented as real people. Therefore, as a voice actor, you truly need to be able to create a believable and conversational delivery for the characters you create. You'll also need to have a stable of at least several characters who sound completely different from one another — and from you.

When you get a script for a commercial, animation, or narration, the script is complete and you can read what comes before and after your lines. It's in a very linear format, and you will sometimes have a sketch of your character. Video games are nonlinear! Your script will have only your lines, and you may or may not know what your character looks like. Each line will need to be recorded in a variety of ways to express different emotions, attitudes, energy, etc. Also, your delivery for each line will need to be able to be attached before or after one or more other lines. This is because, when a game is played, the exact sequence of your lines will depend on how the player moves through the game. Regardless of the path a player takes, the continuity of the voice-over must be consistent and appropriate for the events taking place in the game.

Video games are usually action-oriented and often include scenes that depict violence or death. When you play a video game character you may find yourself being directed to "die" in a dozen different ways. How would your character sound if he died from being hit by a car? By being stabbed? Shot? Hit on the head? Blown up? Choking? Drowning? Each vocalization of your character's "death" must sound different from the others.

LANI MINELLA
www.audiogodz.com

Lani has been voicing and directing video games since the early 1990s. Her range and versatility have landed her performance and directing jobs with the top game companies in the world.

You Must Be Versatile

Video game voicing requires extreme diversity and range since games are notorious for having tons of small low-paying parts rather than meaty roles that pay well per role. Don't expect to be paid per voice unless it's a union job and those are scarce.

One has to be able to act bigger with your voice because game visuals aren't as elaborate as major studio animation, so the voice has to add all the interest and energy without as much visual enhancement. Speaking of energy, doing deaths, attacks, hits, and pain necessitates thrashing one's voice so anyone afraid of pain, laryngitis for days, sweating and using bigger than life gestures "need not apply." You have to really let loose and give it your all.

An ability to do many believable accents and ages is more useful in games than being able to do a bunch of cartoon characters as "reality" is more in demand. As is often the case, males with deep voices and females with sassy texture or smoky voices seem to get more roles. Being a good stage actor or at least knowing improv skills helps.

I've worked on over 500 titles since 1992 and I still say, the biggest enemy to any voice-over is a badly written script. Feel free to make suggestions if you feel something can be said more naturally and make contractions whenever possible.

Look at current games on the market to get an idea of the kinds of characters that are popular. I see a lot of reality-based natural sounding voices with textures or other distinctive timbres to help differentiate all the characters who may be between 20 and 30 years old.

I notice a lot of producers lean heavily on movie references which may not be applicable to the roles needed in a game. They may ask for a sound alike for an actor who has no distinctive voice or reference an actor for scripted dialogue sounds more like something another actor would say. When auditioning, give them what they ask for and, if they permit it, add something totally different in case they like it better.

When I direct voice actors for games, I sometimes line read them in the way they should try and say it if nothing else seems to be effective. If a person has a problem with that method, I can't afford to keep trying verbal analogies or other time wasting methods, so there has to be a mutual understanding of what works for each actor.

Telephony

This area of voice-over is often combined with Industrials because most of this work is for business. *Telephony* voice-over work includes the broad range of telephone messaging. If you've recorded an out-going message on your home answering machine or cell phone voice mail, you've done the most basic of telephony work. Many businesses will require voice-over for *message-on-hold* (MOH), *voice prompts*, and *concatenation*, among others.

A message-on-hold recording is one or more messages, usually with background music, that are heard when a caller is placed on hold. A good MOH script will contain several short messages that focus on a service, product, or benefit offered by the business. It's a vehicle for self-promotion.

Voice prompts are the automated out-going messages that provide instructions to a caller. One type of voice prompt simply asks the caller to take a specific action, much like the message on your answering machine. Systems using these prompts will require the caller to press a key on their phone in order to proceed, or simply "wait for the tone."

The other type of voice prompt takes the idea of an out-going message to the level of creating a virtual person having a conversation with the caller. This is known as *Interactive Voice Response* (IVR). The caller is greeted by a recorded "person" who engages the caller in a conversation that will ultimately get her where she wants to go. The caller responds by speaking the request, and the computer moves to the next prompt based on what the caller said. It's completely automated, but fully interactive. When properly produced, the voice prompts sound completely natural and may even be mistaken for a real person. Ah, technology.

Voice prompts are increasingly the first contact a customer has with a business.

CONNIE TERWILLIGER — CD/20
www.voice-overtalent.com

Another aspect of voice-over work for telephony requires the voice talent to create a sequence of recorded words or phrases that can be linked together seamlessly in any order without sounding like bad edits. This process of assembling individual recordings is known as *concatenation*. Connie Terwilliger is one of many professional voice talent whose specialty is telephone messaging.

Concatenation

The trick to doing this type of work is to be consistent with each segment and remember what you sounded like when you recorded the part that comes before what you are now recording. Each line of copy must be delivered in context, and with continuity for what is before and what follows. The following script from TeleMinder is typical of this type of work.

Hello, a member of your family has an appointment . . .
at the Eye Clinic.
at the Allergy and Asthma Clinic.
on Wednesday (include Monday through Friday)
April 23rd (include all calendar dates)
in the morning (include afternoon)
at
8:30 (include all times at 1/4 hour intervals)
AM (include PM)
If you need to cancel or change this appointment, please call the office at . . .

Track 20 on the CD, voiced by Connie, demonstrates how this works. The first part of the track is the individual lines. The second part shows how the lines are assembled by the computer system. This is a very simple example. Some complex systems might have hundreds of different short lines that could be assembled into any of dozens of possible sequences that must sound natural when heard over the phone.

As you listen to the CD, you'll notice that the audio quality is considerably lower than what you might expect. Most telephony systems require audio files that are compressed to an 8-bit format. These files are very small, and much easier to use in the telephony computer systems. The lower quality often goes unnoticed when heard over the telephone primarily because most telephones are not designed to reproduce audio much over 8KHz. One of the most popular formats is the mu-law (μ-law) format which starts with a 16-bit .wav file recorded at 44.1KHz. That file is then down-sampled to an 8-bit, 8KHz file during conversion to the mu-law format. Ok . . . That's probably more than you wanted to know.

ADR/Looping

Automated Dialogue Replacement (ADR) and *Looping* are niche areas of voice-over that are have remained hidden secrets for quite some time.

The term looping comes from the early days of film sound when a segment of the film was spliced into a continuous loop. A set of white lines was drawn on the film using a grease-pencil, with the lines converging where dialogue needed to be replaced. The actor, watching the lines converge, would begin speaking on cue, matching his original performance.

In today's complex world of film sound, the process is basically the same, except it is now done with a video playback. Audio beeps have been added to assist with the count-down. Looping has also taken on new meaning in that it not only includes the process of dialogue replacement, but it also includes recording the natural human sound effects of crowd scenes, non-scripted voice-over, and efforts (the sounds of human exertion in fights, etc.)

ADR is the process of replacing dialogue for a feature film. The original dialogue may need replacing for any of several reasons: the original location sound is unusable; the director did not like the way a line was delivered even though the rest of the scene was OK; or, profanity needs to be replaced for television or air travel use. In most cases, the original actor will replace their own dialogue, perfectly matching their original performance. However, occasionally, the actor may not be available, so his or her lines may need to be replaced by a sound-alike voice talent who will perfectly match the actor's lip-sync. Most of the major studio feature films will have 50 percent or more of the dialogue replaced — and some will ADR the entire film, discarding all of the original dialogue.

A typical looping session may include a group of up to 20 "loop group" actors. The ADR session director will assign one or more actors to a specific task, or to replace a line of dialogue, as needed. The actors may perform individually, or as a group, depending on the needs of the film.

Breaking in to ADR/Looping can be a challenge as it is a small niche of voice-over work. Improvisation and acting skills are essential, as is an ability to perfectly match lip-sync. "Loopers" must be excellent researchers in order to create the realism for specific time periods and locations.

The best way to break in to this part of the business is to find a loop group and ask to start sitting in on sessions. As a loop group director gets to know you and learn about your abilities, they may invite you to participate.

TERRI DOUGLAS (Hollywood, CA)
www.looptroop.com

In the world of ADR/Looping for feature films, Terri Douglas is at the top of her game. Through her company, *The Loop Troop*, she handles voice casting and directs ADR/Looping sessions for the major studios, including most Disney feature films. Her television and film credits are a Who's Who of the top Hollywood films, and she's voiced characters in dozens of animated feature films. And if that isn't enough, she also teaches workshops on the craft of ADR and Looping at the top looping stages in Hollywood.

What Makes a Good Looper?

As a voice talent, owner and voice casting director of The Loop Troop in Los Angeles, I am constantly asked how someone can join my roster of actors. As a voice casting director, I'm drawn to talent that knows who they are and exactly what they can do vocally on the ADR stage. I cast talent from age 3 to 80 years old. The most popular working ages are children, young adults and adults with a *vocal* range of 25 to 50 years old. The top loopers who work on most all of the films, television series and animation features, can cover a huge variety of subjects, speak other languages and are excellent at improv and lip-sync. Because 95 percent of loop group is improv, we put many hours into finding the research for the topics being covered on each project in order to sound like we are from a specific period of time or place in the film. Each project provides a wonderful opportunity to learn something new and work with fascinating creative people. Loopers possess a unique skill, have a natural talent for looping and a great dedication to the craft.

Promo/Trailer

This category of voice work is for television and film promotion, which is different from imaging, although there are similarities. While imaging covers station ID's and programming transitions, *promotion* is generally considered to be advertising for the station's programming products. *Promo* voice-over work usually refers to television station promos, although it also applies to radio. *Trailer* voice work refers to the promotion of motion pictures. Although they promote different media, they are lumped into the same category for voice-over because the purpose of both is to promote something that is inherently different from a product or service you might purchase at a local store. They promote programs and entertainment.

As with radio, television stations present a specific image in their market. While radio must rely only on audio, a television station has the advantage of adding pictures and graphics to their broadcast image. If you watch much TV, you'll notice that each station has it's own look and sound. The images and voice-over will be consistent for just about everything the station airs to promote its programming and image. This is true for all television and cable broadcasters, from the local station to the national networks.

Working as a television promo voice talent can often mean the talent is "the voice" of the television station. A promo voice talent will voice station ID's, program introductions, program promos (commercials for the station's programming), program VOC's (voice over credits — the "coming up next" voice-over you'll often hear at the end of a program), public service announcements, news opens, news promos, and possibly even station marketing and sales videos. As the voice of the station, you may be asked to voice anything and everything that serves to promote the station.

Landing a job as a station promo voice can mean a lot of work on a regular basis. You may be required to travel to the station's studios to record your voice tracks, you may record at a local recording studio, or you may be recording at your home studio and send the tracks to the station via ISDN or an FTP website. Promo work is usually recorded on a daily basis, and most promo voice talent are "on call" in the event of a major breaking news story that needs a promo produced quickly.

Promo voice work for a television network is a completely different animal. At one time the networks hired one person as "the voice" of the network. However, today the major networks will use many different voice talent for different aspects of their promotion. Most voice talent who are hired to work on promos at the network level have several years of voice-over experience and understand the performing styles for voicing promos.

Both Promo and Trailer voice work treat almost every word and phrase as the most important and impactful word or phrase ever spoken. The style is often very dramatic with a detached or "announcer-y" delivery. A conversational style used for a commercial will usually not be effective for promo or trailer voice-over.

JOYCE CASTELLANOS (Los Angeles, CA)
www.promoteach.com

Joyce has been an audio producer/director for TV promos for more than 20 years, working at NBC, Disney Channel, Warner Marketing, and The WB Television Network. With a background as a professional voice actor, Joyce has been instructing promo and trailer voiceover for more than seven years. In addition to her coaching, she produces Promo and Trailer demos, as well as provides casting for her clients.

The Essence of Promo and Trailer Work

The essence of both promo and trailer voice-over is to be the storyteller. The difference between the two styles, however, is subtle but significant.

The Promo voice-over is announced to picture with music that indicates the tone, pace, and attitude of the spot. The read is more involved with the story and characters.

The Trailer announce is read wild and needs to be less involved than promo so that it moves the story forward without overpowering the action.

When a director is looking for a voice actor for a promo project, it is often the sound that they listen for first. Each show has a personality so the right sound and attitude that's appropriate for that show or specific spot is what the director is listening for. Also the director is looking for several things: do you understand the copy? Can you make the necessary timing adjustments? And are you good at taking direction?

As with any other type of voice-over work, when you are booked for a promo session, you should always be on time. Arriving a few minutes early is always good to give you a chance to look over the copy while they set up.

Introduce yourself, take your script(s), and ask the appropriate questions:

1) If it's a new show, ask the style and attitude that they're going for.
2) If it's an ongoing show, get familiar with it and ask if there's anything out of the ordinary that they're looking for.
3) Make your decision on how to approach the spot and give your first read.
4) Listen to the director for any changes or suggestions, understand what's asked for, and go again.
5) Should a direction not be clear to you, be sure to ask for clarification.

Radio Imaging, Branding, Signature Voice

The term *imaging* is used to refer to the niche area of voice-over work that specifically promotes a station's sound or marketing image. The best imaging voice talent come from radio station production departments where they learn first-hand what station imaging is all about. An imaging production is usually fast-paced with lots of rapid-fire, short liners, station call letters, station slogan or USP, punchy music cues, catchy sound effects, and processed voice tracks that clearly define a station's "sound" within its format.

An imaging voice talent will be voicing a station's IDs, promos, sweepers, and liners, and in some cases may even be handling the production. If you don't know what those are, imaging may not be for you.

In a large sense, the imaging voice talent becomes the "voice" for the station, thus building its brand in the market. Over time a performer's voice can become the *signature voice* of the station, which is why you won't hear imaging voice talent on commercials for a station's advertisers.

If imaging is something you are interested in, you'll need to know how radio stations promote themselves, and how your voice will be used as an identifiable part of that promotion process. You'll also need to understand the differences between the various radio formats, and you'll most likely need to produce a separate demo for each format. Imaging formats include: Contemporary Hit Radio (CHR), formerly Top Forty; Adult Contemporary (AC); Hot AC; Urban Contemporary; Alternative; Modern; Jazz; Oldies; Classic Rock; Country; and News/Talk. Each format has its unique style.

JENNIFER VAUGHN (Florida) — CD/26
www.jennifervaughn.com

Jennifer Vaughn is one of the most recognized female voices on US radio. Although she also voices a variety of other types of projects, station imaging is one of her specialties. She's the signature voice for dozens of stations and knows this part of the business better than most.

Radio Imaging and Promo

Generally, in Radio Imaging, you really had to get in the business in the mid 90s BEFORE the Internet when there were only one or two production companies that had this niche and there were really only a handful of us. Stations/consultants and veteran PDs and OMs know who the really good people are and those people have their craft specifically for imaging/promo work finely tuned for radio. TV is similar but certainly not the same. Both of the mediums have always relied on word of mouth to get their talent. They've either heard you on another station in another market, have worked with you in the past or are getting a referral from well thought of professionals at other TV and radio stations or at the corporate level.

Voice work on imaging has changed a bit, but it's still steadfast on demanding a voice that can cut through the clutter with a presentation style. The Regular Guy/Actor sound really doesn't work in either medium for Radio Imaging and TV Promo work as it gets lost in the clutter with "the regular guy sound" of commercial voice work and surrounding programming. Imaging/promo work largely continues to be an announcer-dominated style. There are exceptions, but they are short-lived or come in fads. You're golden if you have a "Voice of God/Godess" AND are able to drop out of that personna to do a conversational delivery or characters, but is not really necessary in this specialized line of VO.

Imaging for radio is, for the most part, taking on the personna of station voice. You are really the personality of the entire station and are used to position the station within the market. You will be reading largely liners which go in between songs called sweepers, and other liners like show intros/outros, shotguns, rejoins, IDs, and positioning statements. On the other hand you will be responsible for reading all or most of the station's promotional material which may include station, feature, contest, music, and event promos. And that's just a few of the elements they require.

All of this work is done within a signed contractual agreement between talent and station. Personally, most of my radio stations are on twelve-month contracts that require a monthly retainer and either order weekly or monthly. There's a smaller percentage of my stations that are either bi-monthly, quarterly, or are in one-year licensed buyouts for a term that is not open ended. Those are normally a secondary position to a primary signature voice already on the station where they would only require a "female" to even out the sound of too much testosterone. I should add that those stations that have one-year buyouts are either non-rated, small market, or stations outside the US and Canada.

My advice for talent going into this type of voice work is that you should always be in full control of your material, especially in signature imaging work. It is not wise to work any other way as it is not industry standard and you have no control over your material or how it is used, sold to others, and you'll end up losing hundreds of thousands over the long run. You will lose your marketability in this field if you sell your voice off and have no control over it. You lose marketability and you lose the ability to make money. This field is relatively small, compared to any type of commercial or narrative work. So, if you do sell off your material you just jipped yourself out of a station in the same market or one close to picking you up for more $$$ or regular income through retainers.

Imaging/branding/promo work for television is also a station voice. In news reads, it should be authoritative, informative, and urgent. In feature reads, this read has to do with the subject matter and can be all across the board. You will read elements like sponsor billboards, rejoins, newscast opens, news topicals, feature promos, weather promos, station event promos, id's, bumpers, etc. Again, personally, all of my TV stations are under monthly retainer on twelve-month contracts. The same licensing conditions as just mentioned within radio imaging are also industry standard for TV. Some of my TV stations send scripts daily, some weekly and some monthly. Most are daily.

Marketing for TV promo and radio imaging is largely by word of mouth and reputation. However, I have had limited success with trade magazine ads, trade sites, direct mailers, and a talent manager who has taken a personal interest in all of my dealings. I've also added a personal assistant to my staff to help with follow-up when my manager is working on the bigger deals.

You will need an industry-specific demo for each to start promoting yourself and you will need to contact either ad agencies or production companies who specialize in this field to help you market your demo as they have the contacts and clients already. You can also direct market to these stations, but the chances of a getting a job out of that are slim to none because they get so many demos these days. It is better to contact people who already have these contacts and contracts to get your foot in the door.

Biggest tip! If you are NOT an actor/on-camera talent or if you are an actor/on-camera talent and wish to be more successful in your voice-over craft, try not to include your age or photograph on your bio, website, or any other promotional material.

Question: Why?

Answer: Any person seeking voice talent, whether they are in casting, are a producer, client, agent, and so on, will make up their mind about how you are "supposed" to sound, or carve out an "image" of you right then and there *before* even hearing you. My biggest success is not letting anyone make up his or her mind as to who I am or what I may sound like or be ABLE to sound like based on my appearance. I am largely seen as what I "sound" like rather than what I "look" like and that is to a very large advantage when you are versatile with your voice.

Anime

The term *Anime* refers to a style of animation that originated in Japan, but it has become associated with dialogue replacement voice-over work that requires matching lip-sync and timing to the original foreign-language animation. Anime is among the most challenging types of voice-over work.

DEBBIE MUNRO (Vancouver, Calgary, Edmonton CAN) — CD/24
www.creatingvoices.ca

Debbie's specialty is character voice work for animation and Anime. She has voiced roles in *Dragonball, Dragonball GT, Benjamin Bluemchen, Never Winter's Night*, and *Buddy and Max*, among others. She runs her own production company where she writes, voices, and produces a variety of audio and video projects. Debbie is also one of Canada's top VO coaches.

Inside Anime

Anime is an art in itself. Fans take Anime very seriously. Many watch the original versions (in Japanese or whatever the language) because they get the true intent of the author.

Have you ever watched English dubbed Anime's like *Dragonball* or *Pokeman*? It's often hard to watch because the mouth doesn't always match the words. Let me explain why. Imagine learning all there is to learn about creating characters (which is A LOT) then trying to implement that in your session, not memorize your script, watch TV, and match voice flaps THAT AREN'T EVEN IN YOUR LANGUAGE — all at the same time? It's near impossible!

It truly takes a gifted person to match voice flaps, adlib, and die 5000 different ways. Seriously! Three quarters of a session is sound effects: Falling, dying, running, etc. It all must be done to PERFECT time, matching beeps, mouth work and body actions. Anime is the hardest of all forms of animation voice work.

On top of it all, it pays less. WHY? I asked too. They say that the original voicer is the one who created the character and we are just mimicking it. Although I respect that very much, it's hard to understand, when the Anime dubbing work is far more difficult than any other form of voiceover.

If you want to voice animation, learn to act and how to voice Anime style. There are a few amateur dubbing sites out there to help get you started from the comfort of your own home, but with Anime dubbing, you will more than likely voice in their studios.

Although Anime is more work for less pay, animation in any form is one of the most exciting and fulfilling jobs you'll ever do.

16

Your Voice-over Demo

Your Professional Calling Card

Your voice-over demo is your best first opportunity to present your performing skills and abilities to talent agents, producers, and other talent buyers. Many times, you will be booked for an audition or for a session simply based on something the producer hears in your demo. The purpose of a demo is to get you work!

In the world of voice acting, your demo is your calling card. It is your portfolio. It is your audio résumé. It is your letter of introduction. You don't need headshots, or a printed résumé, but you absolutely do need a high-quality demo. It is the single most important thing you *must* have if you are to compete in the world of professional voice-over.

Demo Rule #1:
Don't Produce Your Demo Until You Are Ready

HOW WILL I KNOW?

OK, you've just completed several weeks of a voice-over workshop and you're excited about getting started on your new career path. You received lots of positive feedback and encouragement during the workshop, and now you're ready to produce your voice-over demo, right? Probably not!

The reality of any performing craft is that unless you already have a strong performing background, you are most likely not ready for your demo after taking a single workshop — or, for that matter, after reading this book. Producing a demo before being ready is one of the biggest mistakes many people make when they are eager to get started in voice-over. Producing your demo too soon may result in a presentation and performance quality that is likely to be much less than is needed to be successful in this business.

Producing your demo too soon is simply a waste of time and money, and can potentially affect your credibility as a performer later on.

Before you even think about having your demo produced, make sure you have acquired the skills and good performing habits necessary to compete in this challenging business. Remember that there are a lot of other people trying to do the same thing as you. Anything you can do to improve your abilities and make your performing style just a bit unique will be to your advantage. Study your craft, learn acting skills, and develop a plan to market yourself before you do your demo. Take lots of classes! Acting and improvisation classes will help you develop your skills and voice-over classes will hone those skills for the unique demands of voice-over work.

So, you're probably asking the question: "How will I know when I'm ready to do my demo?" Good question! In her workshops and E-Book on demos and marketing, my workshop coaching partner, Penny Abshire breaks this question down to four possible answers.

- **The short answer is:** You'll know.
- **The medium answer is:** You'll know when you're ready for your demo after you have the proper training, you've researched and studied other professional voice talent and their demos, know what the marketplace is looking for and feel confident you can deliver at the same level as other professionals doing similar voiceover work.
- **The long answer is:** You'll know you're ready to produce your demo when you can be handed ANY script — cold — and, within 2 or 3 takes, you can perform that script at a level comparable to other professional talent. You also feel confident that you can get work with your demo that is enough to cover the costs of its production.
- **The best answer is:** You'll know you're ready to produce your demo when you can stop asking yourself the question "Am I ready to produce my demo?" Which takes us back to: You'll know!

HOW DO I GET TO BE THAT GOOD?

The craft of performing for voice-over is, for most people, an acquired skill. There are some who are natural born performers, but most of the working professionals in this business started out by mastering their fundamental acting skills and moving on from there.

Of course, you certainly have the option to take some short-cuts and produce your demo after only reading a book or taking a single class. I wouldn't recommend it, but you can do it. And you may get lucky.

Remember this: Your performance, as heard on your demo, will be compared to every other demo a producer listens to — and most producers listen to a LOT of voice-over demos. After a few hundred demos, it's not hard to separate the great talent from the "good," and the "good" from the beginners. Most producers will know within about the first 5 seconds of listening to a demo. You want your demo to present you as one of the great talent and keep them listening a lot longer than that first 5 seconds!

To do that, you must become an expert at communicating with drama and emotion before you have your demo produced. Here are some things that will help you get where you want to be quickly.

- **Study acting.** Acting is the key to an effective performance. Learn how to act and learn how to use your voice and body to express drama and emotional tension.

- **Do your exercises.** Set up a daily regimen for doing your voice exercises. Get into the habit of keeping your voice in top condition. Your voice is the "tool" of your trade — take care of it.

- **Take classes and workshops.** Have an attitude of always learning. You will learn something new from each class and workshop you take or repeat. The voice-over business is constantly adapting and new trends become popular each year. You need to be ready to adapt as new trends develop.

- **Read other books about voice-over.** Every author on this subject presents his or her material in a slightly different manner. You may also learn new techniques or get some fresh ideas from reading a variety of books on the subject. If you learn only one thing from reading a book, it was well worth its purchase price.

- **Practice your skills and techniques.** When you are working on a piece of copy, rehearse your performance with an attitude of continually perfecting it. Have a solid understanding of the techniques you are using and polish your performance in rehearsal.

Demo Rule #2:
Your Demo Must Accurately
Represent Your Abilities

Your voice-over demo must be "great!" It cannot be merely "good." To create a great demo, you must make the effort to develop and hone your performing skills. Since your demo may directly result in bookings, it is extremely important that you be able to match the level of your demo performance when under the pressure of a session. It is quite easy for a studio to create a highly produced, yet misrepresentative, demo that gives the impression of an extremely talented and polished performer. If the performer's actual abilities are less that what is depicted on the demo, the shortcomings will be quickly revealed during a session.

Your demo should be professionally produced by someone who knows what they are doing. Even if you've assembled a top-of-the-line, state-of-the-art home studio, don't think you can put a demo together at home and expect it to sound professional. Even with my many years of experience as an audio producer and sound designer, I still want the assistance of a good director when I'm in the booth. It is extremely difficult for one person to deal with both the engineering and performing aspects of producing a demo at the same time. You need to be focused on your performance and not dealing with any equipment.

You need a director to listen to your performance objectively, help you stay focused, and help get you in touch with the character in the copy. In today's world of voice-over, it is essential that you develop self-directing skills because you may find yourself recording many projects in the privacy of your home studio. However, performing effectively without a director, or by directing yourself, is very challenging and it's the last thing you want to do when producing your demo. Although many professional voice actors believe they don't need a director — and can actually perform quite well without one, all voice actors do, in fact, need a director to bring out their best work. The top professionals will tell you that they perform much better when they have a good director to guide them through their performance.

When you go to the studio to produce your demo, you should consider the session to be just like a real commercial recording session. You need to be able to get to your best performance, in three or four takes. If you need more than six or seven takes to get the right delivery, you may not be ready. Realistically, anything after about the fifth or sixth take should be aimed at fine-tuning your delivery. Be careful that you don't spend a lot of time just getting into the groove of the performance for a script. If you do that, your end result may not be an accurate reflection of your abilities.

I know of one voice actor who was booked through an agent based solely on the demo. The demo sounded great and had logos of major television networks and other advertisers on its cover. The impression was that this performer had done a lot of work and was highly skilled.

The performance was recorded during an ISDN session in San Diego with the performer in a New York studio. A few minutes into the session, it became apparent that the voice actor could not take direction and would not be able to perform to the caliber of the demo. The producer gracefully ended the session and a different voice actor was hired to complete the session the following day. The producer refused to pay the talent agency's commission because she felt the talent agency had misrepresented the voice actor's abilities. The original performer was never told that the session was unsatisfactory and actually sent a nice thank-you note to the producer. The performer did get paid, but the recording was never used.

It turned out that the agent had never worked directly with the performer and, in fact, had not even done a live audition before signing. They had been promoting the person based solely on a highly produced demo. A few days later, it was learned that the performer was actually attempting to memorize the copy due to a problem with dyslexia that made it difficult to perform the lines live, as written.

The agent later apologized to the producer and mentioned that this performer had done some excellent self-marketing, had extensive stage experience, and presented a very professional image during the interview. The only problem was that the performer had created a demo that clearly exceeded his actual abilities. A secondary problem was that the agent signed this performer without first testing his abilities with a cold-reading. Bottom line: You *must* be able to perform to the level of your demo when booked for a real session.

Versatility Is Your Selling Tool

There are two schools of thought for demos. One demonstrates a range of versatility with a variety of examples showing different emotions, attitudes, and characters. The other focuses on the performer being the most real and natural person he or she can be while demonstrating a range of emotion within the natural delivery of their own voice. Good voice actors can do dozens of voices, emotions, attitudes and characters because they are able to find a place in their body from which to center the character and place the voice — even if the character and voice originate from their natural personality. Other good voice actors have developed a highly defined performance style that is at the center of everything they do.

Regardless of which approach works best for you, it is the range and variety of performance in a demo that represent a voice actor's abilities. The essence of who you are needs to be present in every track of your demo. You need to capitalize on your strong points and present them in the best possible manner in your demo. The range of attitudes, emotions, and characters you can express during a voice-over performance is your own, unique, *vocal versatility*. Your strongest, most dynamic, and most marketable voice is called your *money voice*. This is the voice that will get you the work and may eventually become your trademark or signature voice. Your other voices are icing on the cake but are necessary to clearly show your range and versatility as a voice actor.

Demo Basics

DEMO FORMATS

One interesting thing about technology is that it is constantly changing. What was in favor yesterday may be out of favor tomorrow. Although you'll still find some analog cassette recorders around, it's difficult to find a reel-to-reel tape recorder. Reel-to-reel and cassette demos are history! The audio CD, which was the standard for voice-over demos for many years, has now given way to demos that exist as electronic MP3 files, Flash audio files, and other digital audio formats. Electronic audio files of voice-over demos have several major advantages over the audio CD: there is no expense for packaging; the demo can be posted on a website, which makes it immediately available for listening and/or downloading worldwide; the demo can be emailed to a prospect or client as an attachment; and the file can be "burned" to an audio CD as needed. Isn't technology wonderful?

What lies in the future for voice-over demos is anybody's guess. In the early 2000s, however, there are two preferred formats for voice-over demos: electronic files and audio CD.

Electronic files are rapidly becoming the standard with producers and talent agents. MP3 files can easily be copied and cataloged on a computer in folders that identify a performer's style, performance genre, or in whatever way works best for a producer or agent. They can be emailed to clients and prospects; renamed, edited, uploaded, and assembled onto a compilation audio CD. For auditioning purposes, it's very fast and efficient to simply open a folder on a computer and click on successive demo files until the right voice is found.

However, there are still many producers and agents who prefer holding a CD in their hands. Although it may not be as efficient to work with as electronic files, there is something to be said for reading the label of a demo CD and studying the performer's visual marketing image while listening to their demo.

For the purpose of marketing voice-over talent in today's highly technological world, it is an absolute must that your voice-over demo exist as an electronic file stored in an easily accessible location on your computer. From this electronic file, and with the proper computer software, you can create "one-off" audio CDs that can be packaged and mailed to clients and prospects. You should plan to have at least a few CDs on hand for those times when they are requested.

Demo Tips

As you prepare for your demo, keep in mind that you want to feature your best performing abilities. Every script you select should be chosen for the purpose of demonstrating something different. Plan the content of your demo carefully to include copy you can perform well and that is appropriate for the type of market you want to reach. A demo of commercial copy is not appropriate for a producer of corporate projects, and a demo of character and animation voices is not appropriate for a commercial producer.

If you intend to be seeking agent representation with your demo, be prepared to produce a commercial voice-over demo first. A well-produced commercial demo will demonstrate every performing skill that is used in other areas of voice-over such as narration, character, promo, and so on. If you intend to focus your marketing on a niche area of voice-over work, you should consider a second demo designed to focus on only that area.

Producers often listen to a demo tape with their finger poised, ready to move to the next demo. This is somewhat due to time constraints, but is largely due to the fact that dozens of poorly produced demos arrive in email and cross the desks of producers every day. Remember that producers make their decisions about a voice within the first 5 to 10 seconds of listening to a demo — some even quicker than that. If you are going to make it past that crucial first 5 seconds, your demo performance must be well presented and highly skilled.

A good demo keeps the producer listening and it has entertainment value with a new surprise, emotional hook, acting technique, vocal variation, or character twist happening about every 5 to 15 seconds. A good demo does not give the listener an opportunity to turn it off.

Here are some things to keep in mind while preparing for your demo:

- Don't do a demo until you are ready. Make sure you have done your homework and have mastered voice-acting skills.

- Have your marketing plan in place <u>before</u> you spend the money to have your demo produced. You should know in advance who you will be contacting to promote your voice-over talent.

- Your first demo does <u>not</u> need to be a collection of work you have actually done. The purpose of your demo is to demonstrate what you can do with your voice. It's OK to recreate other commercials in your style and mention product names.

- When using magazine ads for demo copy, choose only those products or services that might actually advertise on radio or TV.

- Produce your demo so it features your talent for a specific type of work. Create different demos for different types of VO work.

- Start with just one or two very specific demos. Usually, a commercial demo is the entry demo for voice-over work.

- Include a wide range of variety in style and character, even if your demo is focusing on your voice style, rather than character. Keep the listener guessing as to what will happen next.

- Limit each "clip" to only a single, concise statement or few brief sentences. You only have a short time to catch and hold the listener's attention. The content must be compelling.

- Focus on what you currently do best. Then revise and prepare new demos as your talent grows and you acquire copies of projects you have worked on (usually once or twice a year).

- Keep your demo short. A maximum of 1:30 is the current standard in most major markets, with a cut-down 1-minute version for talent agency compilation CDs and websites. If the producer is going to make his or her decision in 5 seconds or less, you would be wise to have your strongest material in that first 5 seconds.

- Have your demo professionally produced. Don't think you can put a demo together at home and expect it to sound professional. A poor-quality demo — in either performance or audio quality — is a waste of your time and money.

You will be far better off with a solid one-minute and 15 seconds of fast-moving, well-produced, entertaining material than with a slow-moving two-minutes of poorly produced, uninteresting material lacking variety and range. If you have the appropriate performing skills, you can produce demos for virtually every niche area of the business. The actual length may vary depending on the type of demo and your market, so you would best be advised to consult with your local talent agents to find out what they are asking for in your market. As you gain a reputation and become more versatile, you may be able to justify multiple demos, or a compilation of demos on a CD or your website.

Types of Voice-over Demos

Before producing your voice-over demo, it is important that you study current demos of professionals in the area of voice-over you are interested in. As with any business, you need to know what your competition is. One of the best places to study demos is **www.voicebank.net**. On this website you'll find voice-over demos from nearly every major talent agent in the US. Simply click on House Reels, select a category, select an agent, then start clicking on demos. You'll be amazed at what you will learn as you begin listening to some of the top voice-over professionals in the country.

Through your study of the craft and business of voice-over, you will be discovering the delivery style, characters, and performance techniques that work best for you. You will also be making choices as to the types of voice-over work that you are best suited for. Very few voice talent are able to effectively perform in more than a few categories. Animation and character voice actors will rarely work in narration, but many will do commercials. Audio book narrators may not find telephony voice work to be at all satisfying, but they may do industrial narration or documentary voice work. Find the areas of voice-over work you enjoy the best and are most suited for, and focus on mastering your craft in those areas.

There are no hard-and-fast rules for producing a voice-over demo. Your objective is to effectively reach the talent buyers who hire voice talent in the area of your demo. Not too long ago, it was acceptable to produce a single demo that featured multiple talents, such as commercial, narration, and character all wrapped up in a two-minute demo.

Today, producers want to hear a specific demo for a specific type of work. Your demo should feature examples of what you can do for a specific type of voice-over work, and it should be produced in such a way that it meets, or exceeds, the expectations of those who are looking for voice talent in that area. In other words, your commercial demo should consist of only your commercial delivery style, and your character demo should feature your character voices. There may be some cross-over, such as a character voice in a commercial, but you should avoid the temptation to combine multiple demos into one.

Ideally, your demo should be compiled from actual projects you have worked on. However, if you are just starting out, this is not possible. You will need to create your own copy and design a demo that will catch the listener's attention and hold it. Even working professionals sometimes need to make up copy to create a demo that really puts their voice in the spotlight. This can be a challenging task, but it can pay off big.

Voice-over demos are generally produced on a bell curve with the performer's *money voice* at the beginning and end. In between are a variety of performance attitudes and styles that reflect the performer's range and abilities. Having the same voice at the beginning and end provides a reference point for the listener and gives him or her an opportunity to categorize the performer's vocal age and personality type.

There are two basic structures for demos. The first is a *compilation demo* with examples of a variety of performing styles. The second is a *concept demo* that combines the demo clips into a logical sequence or story where each clip leads into the next. As the demo progresses, there will be changes in attitude, pacing, and character development. Concept demos are challenging to write, must be thought out very carefully, and fall into one of two categories: extremely good and unbelievably stupid!

COMMERCIAL DEMOS

Commercial demos are the entry path to the world of voice-over. Even though radio and TV commercials are only about 10 percent of the business, a good commercial demo will demonstrate a performer's abilities for nearly every other type of voice work. Every segment should reveal some aspect of the real you. There is little demand for accents, dialects, and wacky characters in the world of radio and TV commercials. If you are very good, you might include one. Otherwise, save those voices for other demos.

Your demo may contain as many as 12 to 15 segments, each of which demonstrates a different emotion, attitude, level of energy, personality trait, or delivery styles at a variety of tempos. Keep your commercial demo to a maximum of 1:30 to 1:45 unless your research indicates that a longer or shorter length is appropriate for your market and type of demo. Also be prepared to create a one-minute edit of your demo for your talent agent.

CHARACTER AND ANIMATION DEMOS (INCLUDING GAMES)

Character and animation demos are designed to feature your talents primarily for animation and video game work. They also demonstrate your ability to create marketable voices for believable, "real" characters.

Character voice work for animation is probably the single toughest area of voice-over to break into, so both your performing abilities and your character/animation demo must be of extremely high quality.

At its essence, a character or animation demo features voices that are recognized as "real" people, but which are actually voices you create that are different from your real voice. For animation, the characters are often exaggerated or quirky in some way, while video game characters are usually "real people." Each clip features a different attitude, vocal characterization, or personality. Not all voice talent have the ability to create voices that sound completely different from their normal voice. If you don't have this ability, a character voice demo may not be for you.

Producing animation demos is a specialty area of production. Each segment of an animation demo must sound like it came from an actual show and similar voices should be separated from each other. Most studios have extensive music and sound effects libraries, but not all studios have the proper music and sound effects needed for an animation demo. Call around to find a studio that can do this sort of work. There are several in Los Angeles that specialize in animation demos.

A typical animation or character voice demo will be about the same length as a commercial demo, around 1:30 maximum, and may include 10 to 15 individual, fully produced elements. Again, if you have an agent, be sure to ask what length they prefer.

INDUSTRIAL DEMOS

Corporate and industrial demos tend to contain copy that is somewhat longer than the copy in a commercial or character demo. The longer length of copy allows the producer time to more accurately assess your reading and delivery skills. It also gives them an opportunity to hear how you handle complex words, concepts, and sentences. As with the other types of demos, your money voice and strongest material should lead the demo, followed by a variety of styles, range, and versatility. Industrial demos offer a good opportunity to use various microphone techniques, a range of delivery speeds, and storytelling techniques to good advantage.

Where the length of an individual segment for a commercial demo might be 6 to 10 seconds, a segment on an industrial demo might run 15 to 20 seconds, or even slightly longer. You'll need more time to complete the descriptive text for a procedure or technical discussion.

A typical full-length industrial demo will run about 1:45 to 2:00 and will include 5 to 7 segments. As with a commercial demo, your agent will ask for a one-minute edited version for their compilation CD or website.

AUDIO BOOK DEMOS

The format for an audio book demo is far different from all other voice-over demos. An audio book producer wants to hear how you tell a story over an extended period of time.

There are a few important differences between this type of demo and other voice-over demos. Audio book demos are the only type of demo that should include a slate of your name. The slate should be spoken by someone else who simply says your name followed by the word "reader." After this brief introduction, you begin by giving the title of the book and start reading the story. Your choice of material should include a variety of emotions, attitudes, and characters. You'll need to find something unique for each character in the book you are reading for each segment. This can be a challenge for characters of the opposite sex. Usually a shift in energy or attitude will reveal a character far more effectively than a change of pitch. Change-ups of tempo, rhythm, and the use of other techniques can also help to differentiate the characters as you tell the story.

Practice for your audio book demo by recording yourself reading out loud, finding the drama, emotion, and attitudes for each scene and character of the story.

A typical audio book demo will run from 5 to 12 minutes and may consist of as few as 3 to 5 fairly long segments. Ideally, you should be able to perform each segment of your audio book demo as a continuous reading with a minimum of stops and starts. If you find you need to stop frequently, have difficulty reading the text, or need to go back for pick-ups, you may not be ready for audio book work.

VOICE IMAGING, BRANDING, SIGNATURE VOICE DEMOS

Unlike other types of voice-over imaging voice talent need special knowledge of the broadcasting industry. If you don't have a radio background, imaging may not be for you. An imaging demo features a single, specific, often "edgy" delivery style throughout the demo. Most imaging voice talent have a separate demo for each radio format. Also, unlike other types of voice-over work, imaging often presents a detached delivery — more typical of an announcer, rather than the conversational delivery style for commercials and narration.

An imaging demo should be no longer than one minute in length. Although any studio capable of producing a commercial demo should be able to handle an imaging demo, the best production will be from someone who knows and produces imaging work. As with animation demos, imaging requires special music and effects that may not be available at all studios.

PROMO AND TRAILER DEMOS

A *promo & trailer* demo is essentially a commercial demo that focuses on programs or films instead of retail products. A promo/trailer demo can include examples of both TV promos and movie trailers. To properly produce a trailer demo, you'll need to find suitable *sound bites*, or excerpts from a movie that you will use to wrap around your voice work. As with a commercial demo, the length will be about 1:30.

Most movie trailer work is done out of Los Angeles, and there are a handful of voice talent who are consistently hired for this type of work. That doesn't mean you can't break in to trailer VO work, but you'll need to find the companies that produce trailers, you'll need an agent to represent you for trailer work, and you'll need a killer trailer demo.

TELEPHONY DEMOS

Sometimes referred to as a Message-on-Hold demo (MOH), this type of demo is pretty basic. It usually consists of one or two examples of outgoing messages, one or two on-hold messages for different types of businesses, and perhaps even an example or two of a concatenation project. Examples should include appropriate background music. The idea of an MOH demo is to demonstrate what you sound like delivering information over the phone.

One might think, that because a telephone connection has a reduced frequency response (about 8KHz), an MOH demo should be equalized so it sounds as though it is being heard over the phone. Although this is certainly an option, I would not recommend it primarily because the reduced frequency response of your demo will not accurately reveal the subtlety of your performance. Even though the nuance and detail of your delivery may be lost during an actual phone message, you want your demo to show you at your absolute best. I'd recommend producing your MOH demo at the highest possible quality. As with most other demos, this one will also be in the one to one and a half minute range.

Producing Your Demo

PREPARATION IS THE KEY TO A GREAT DEMO

I've said this before, but this is so important that I'll say it again: do not produce your demo until you are ready, and even when you are ready, have your marketing plan in place before you spend the money on producing your demo. Doing your homework will save you time and money.

From this point on, I'll assume you know who you will be marketing to, you've got a marketing plan in place, you've mastered your performing skills, and you've gathered a number of scripts.

Rehearse your copy with a stopwatch — you do have a stopwatch, don't you? An analog 60-second sweep stopwatch is best because it is easy to start, stop, and reset. Digital stopwatches can be cumbersome to use. It may take some searching, but you can find analog stopwatches online starting at about $50. Time yourself with each rehearsal and do a complete analysis for each script. Make notes on your scripts about the character, attitude, and emotional hooks, as well as ideas for music style and sound effects if appropriate. Consider mic placement for each script. Mark off what you believe to be the strongest :10 to :15 of each script and consider a possible sequence for the demo. Be prepared to record the entire script, and be flexible enough to understand that everything you rehearse will probably change. The work you do at this stage will pay off later.

Ideally, you should find a director who can assist you with the production of your demo. Hiring a director is like having a second set of ears. It allows you to focus on your performance so you will not have to worry about the technical details of the session. Many recording studios have engineers experienced in directing voice-over.

Above all, when you are in the studio recording your demo, have fun and enjoy the experience! I encourage you to stay through as much of the process of producing the demo as you possibly can. This is your primary tool for establishing yourself in the business, and you're paying a lot of money for it. Your input will be important for the engineer to create an effective demo. You take a great risk if you simply go in and record your tracks, then leave the production up to the engineer. By observing the production process for your demo, you will learn a lot about what really goes on behind the scenes in a recording studio.

HOW LONG SHOULD MY DEMO BE?

There are two answers to this question. The first answer is: if you have an agent, ask her what length is preferred by their agency. The second answer is: if you don't have an agent, you'll want your demo to conform to the current conventional length for the type of demo you will be producing. As with other trends in voice-over, the length of a voice demo has changed over the years. Preferences in your market may also be a determining factor for the length of your demo. The best way to discover demo length is to listen, and time, other voice-over demos. Visit websites for talent agents in your area or listen to demos at **www.voicebank.net**.

In major markets like Los Angeles, Chicago, and New York, you'll find the average length for a commercial demo to be around 1 minute to 1:30. Other markets may prefer longer demos between 1:30 and 2 minutes. It will be rare to find commercial demos longer than 2:00 in today's voice-over world, although this was the standard length only a few short years ago.

WHAT ABOUT PRODUCT NAMES?

Your demo is an advertisement for you. The clips in your demo do not need to mention any product names, but should demonstrate your ability to communicate emotionally with a variety of styles and attitudes. There are actually two schools of thought on this. Some agents and producers believe that including product names lends credibility to the performer (especially if the spot is one that the performer actually worked on) and that they give a good opportunity for the producer to hear how the performer "sells" the client, or puts a spin on the product name. Other producers feel that the most important aspect of a demo is the performer's talent and ability to communicate the message, and that product names can actually become distracting or that the use of product names may be misrepresentation if you didn't do the original spot. The reality is that most talent buyers, agents, and producers don't really care if you did the spot or not. They want to hear what you can do with the words. They know that most client mentions in demos aren't the real thing — and it doesn't matter. Just don't overdo it. If it concerns you, simply change the client or product name.

If you choose to include product names in your demo, I'd suggest including only one or two and let your delivery and talent shine for the rest of the copy. It may be a good idea to include a product name in your first demo just so you can demonstrate how you can give value and importance to the client or product. As you acquire copies of projects you have worked on, you should include a few product names from actual spots in your updated demos. Unless you have actually worked for the clients you mention, you should never include their logos on your CD cover or in your marketing. That is misrepresentation.

WHERE DO I GET THE COPY FOR MY DEMO?

There are many approaches to obtaining copy for a demo. Be creative!

Some demo studios provide the copy and handle all the production. This is fine if you don't mind taking the chance of other people in your market having the same copy on their demos. The only real advantage of having the studio provide the copy is that your demo session becomes more like a real recording session; that is, you won't have the opportunity to see the copy in advance. The downside is that your session may take considerably longer because you will be working the copy cold and relatively unrehearsed. You might also feel rushed when you are "on the clock" to get through all the copy necessary, which could easily affect the quality of your performance. However, the major problem with the studio providing the copy is that you can easily end up using copy that is not right for your performing style. The purpose of your demo is to present your talent in the best possible manner. Performing copy that is not right for you can only work against you, no matter how well the demo is produced.

A better approach to finding copy for your demo is to listen to radio and TV commercials and browse through magazines. By listening to radio and television commercials, you can find copy that matches your style. Record commercial breaks and transcribe the ads that fit your abilities, putting each script on a separate piece of paper. Transcribe the entire commercial even though you may end up using only a small portion if that script makes it into the demo. Having the entire script in front of you will help you discover the emotional content of the commercial and the target audience.

You can also find copy by re-writing magazine ads, or by searching the Internet for scripts. There are also a variety of resources for copy on the Internet. However, here's an important point to keep in mind: the scripts you'll find on an online script database are there for the purpose of providing rehearsal copy, and may not be the best choice for your demo. The best copy for your demo will be copy that is uniquely yours and presents your performing abilities at their best.

Magazines are a great resource for potential demo copy. Look for ads that include a lot of copy. Technical, news, travel, and women's magazines often have ads that can be easily adapted for voice-over. Most print ads are written for the eye, designed to be read, and include a lot of text that may not be appropriate for voice-over. Look for ads that target specific audiences: men, women, young, older adults, and so on. Look for products or services that will allow you to perform the copy in a variety of styles: serious, humorous, hard-sell, soft-sell, dynamic, emotional, and so on. Look for key phrases and sentences that have emotional content — these will be your keys to an effective performance. Select only those ads that might actually be potential radio or TV commercials. Since print copy is written to be read silently, you will usually need to rewrite the copy so it can be used for voice-over. You don't need to completely rewrite a print ad; just take the strongest sections and rework them so they make sense for voice-over.

If you have some writing experience, you can write customized material for your demo. But be aware that if you write your own copy, it must sound as though it was written by a professional.

Obtain as much copy as you can and narrow the scripts down to about 30 to 40 different ads from radio, TV, magazines, and technical journals. Include a variety of styles that will reveal your full range of capabilities: slow, fast, dynamic, emotional, character, and so on. Also make sure each script you choose is appropriate for the type of demo you will be producing.

Be prepared to perform the entire script at your demo session. The reason for this is that you may actually end up with an extremely effective delivery on a segment of the script that you may not have expected. If you only rehearse portions of your scripts, you might overlook an opportunity for a perfect transitional element, or an especially emotional performance. Your director can help create the best performance for each script and you may end up actually recording only a small portion of the copy.

Take at least three clean copies of each script with you to the studio: one copy for yourself, one for the engineer, and the third for your director.

WHAT ABOUT DIALOGUE, MUSIC, AND SOUND EFFECTS?

The purpose of a demo is to feature *your* voice-acting performance. Including other voice-over performers should be done judiciously. If you include a dialogue spot, make sure that yours is the featured performance and that the other voice is of the opposite gender. This may seem obvious, but you'd be surprised at the number of demos with two voices that are hard to tell apart. Also be certain that the other performer knows how to act. I've heard far too many demos that include a dialogue spot where the second player showed little or no acting ability. And don't be tempted to do both voices yourself. Producers want to hear how you work with other voice talent, not how clever you can be performing multiple voices.

As you prepare your demo copy, make notes about music style or sound effects, but don't worry about finding them. The engineer will handle that at your session. Your job is to focus on finding copy you can perform effectively. You have the luxury of being able to prepare and rehearse. Take advantage of it! You will not have this luxury in a real-life studio session.

Thoroughly woodshed and do a character analysis for each piece of copy, making notes on the scripts. Practice your performance for each script just enough to become familiar with it. Be careful not to get yourself locked into any specific attitude or character. Keep in mind that your session engineer might direct you into a performance completely different from what you had decided on. If that happens, you need to be able to adapt to the direction. If you can't, or if you find yourself getting stuck in the same delivery for each take, then you are not ready to have your demo produced.

WHAT IS THE PRODUCTION PROCESS?

I can't speak for other demo producers, but I follow a nine-step process when producing a voice-over demo.

1. I assign the task of finding copy to the voice talent. I don't provide scripts. This can take from a few days to several weeks. I ask for two to three times the number of scripts that will actually be used.

2. About a week before the session, I'll review all copy with talent to sort out the best scripts and eliminate duplicates. The resulting scripts will still number about twice what will end up in the demo. The voice talent rehearses those scripts, but not too much.

3. On the day of the demo session the first thing we'll do is go through the scripts again. I look for variety, and I'll ask the voice talent to perform a portion of each script. This time, I eliminate scripts until I have what I believe are the strongest scripts for my client. The rest we'll keep handy in case we need them.

4. Next, I'll record the dry voice tracks for each script. Occasionally, I'll determine a script isn't right, so we'll drop that one and move on to the next. Each script will be recorded numerous times, striving for the "perfect" delivery. I handle the session no differently than I would for a commercial session. It's just that we're recording about

a dozen commercials in a fairly short period of time. It may take up to two hours or more to record the 8 to 12 voice tracks for a demo.

5. While I'm recording the voice tracks, I'm thinking of the production value to bring each clip to life. Music and sound effects are critical. I actually start thinking about the "sound" of each clip during the evaluation process, but it's after the recording where we really get down to business. The music and SFX search can be a time-consuming process because for a powerful demo, each clip needs to have music with the proper energy, mood, and dynamics. It takes a skilled audio producer/engineer to do this quickly and efficiently.

6. When all the individual demo clips are produced and mixed, the next step is to sequence them into the most effective order. I'll always start the demo with what I consider to be the talent's strongest voice. The *money voice*! This is the voice I want the talent buyer to remember. From there, I'll place the clips in a sequence that provides variety, interest, and changes in mood. The idea is to create a sequence that will keep the talent buyer listening. If everything on a demo sounds the same, the buyer will stop listening after a few seconds.

7. The master sequencing will result in what I call the full-length demo. For most demos, a talent agent will want a one-minute cut-down version. So, my next step is to edit a one-minute demo from the full-length version. A second or two over or under is OK.

8. The final step is to burn an audio CD and render both versions of the demo out to MP3 files, which are then emailed to the talent and put on a data CD-ROM for future use.

9. I'll send my client home with their demo in hand asking them to call me if they hear any problems or if their agent needs something changed. It doesn't happen often, but since demo production can move fairly quickly, it's possible to miss an edit or for a music or sound effect to need adjusting in the mix. And occasionally an agent will request a different sequence.

This process is the same regardless of the type of demo I'm producing. The amount of time it will take to produce a demo will vary depending on several factors: how quickly the talent is able to get to the best take; how long it takes to find the proper music and SFX; how long it takes to do the post-production for each clip; and how many changes or re-records are needed.

I insist that my demo clients sit in on the entire demo production process. I want their input at each stage of the production, and I want to know that they are happy with each segment. I also want them available in case I need to record a pick-up or if we discover a clip that just isn't working and we decide to replace it with a different script.

HOW MUCH WILL MY DEMO COST?

Production of your first demo will very likely be the single most expensive part of breaking into the business of voice-over. No matter what your level of experience may be, you should seriously consider hiring a demo producer who knows the business and what producers are looking for. The additional ears and professional direction can save you a lot of money.

The cost of producing a voice-acting demo will depend on the type of demo, the market you're in, and your demo producer. It can vary widely from market to market. To a certain extent, it will also depend on your performing abilities. For recording studios, time is money, and the faster you can record a high-quality performance (fewer takes), the sooner your demo will be completed and the less it will cost.

There are two basic ways studios will price out demo production. One is to book the studio on an hourly rate and add on other related costs. The other, and more common approach, is to book the demo production as a package. You can often save some money with a package deal, but if your demo is produced quickly, it may actually cost you more than if you had gone with the hourly rates. It's a choice you'll need to make when the time comes, and if the studio you'll be working with works only one way it won't be a problem.

If you're in a major market (LA, NY, Chicago), you can expect your demo to cost in the neighborhood of anywhere from $1,500 to $4,000. In other markets, you can expect to pay anywhere from $500 to $1,500, or more, for the production of your voice demo. A lot depends on the studio and producer you are working with. Studios that are known for producing excellent demos will give you a great product, but they will cost more.

Although actual session fees vary, and may be somewhat lower or higher, the following gives you an example of how the cost for a typical demo session might break down.

PRODUCTION ELEMENTS	TIME AND FEES	SUBTOTALS
Studio time (voice recording)	2 hours @ $125/hour	$250.00
Postproduction (editing, music)	4 hours @ $125/hour	500.00
Track sequencing and/or dubbing	1.5 hours @ $125/hour	187.50
Music license (for music used)	1 blanket license	350.00
Outside producer/director	1 flat fee	300.00
Materials (CD), including tax		50.00
Total Cost (not including duplication)	7.5 hours in studio	$1,637.50

The actual time it takes to record your copy may vary considerably, and all of these items may not be required, thus affecting the price. The cost of studio time varies greatly from city to city and depends on the complexity of your session. Some studios charge a fee for the music used in your demo while other studios will provide the music at no charge. In most states, the cost of studio time and music license fees are exempt from sales tax, but the materials and recording media are not. Check with your studio to find out what portions of the session or materials will have sales tax applied. If you've set up your voice-over business properly, the entire cost of producing your demo can be deducted as a business expense.

WHAT DO I NEED TO KNOW ABOUT STUDIOS?

As you prepare for your demo, you will be wearing your producer hat. In that role, you will have already prepared your copy and directed yourself in your performance during practice and rehearsals. Some of your other duties as producer will be to make all the arrangements for studio time, hiring a producer, printing, CD duplication, and distribution of your demo.

Most larger cities have at least several recording studios and radio stations. In this age of easily accessible high technology, many small towns have studios capable of recording a high-quality demo. You will find commercial recording studios advertised in the telephone book and on the Internet. However, there may also be many excellent home-based project studios in your community that are not advertised anywhere. Even though recording services and studios may be plentiful in your area, this does not mean that all studios are able to produce a marketable demo.

The majority of commercial recording studios are designed for music sessions. The engineers at these studios are usually very competent at recording music, but may know very little about producing commercials or directing voice-over talent. Home-based project studios are most often designed to handle the recording needs of musicians and composers, but may not be suitable for, or capable of, recording quality voice-over work. Larger recording studios and production houses and even some radio stations are expanding their production capabilities to include a much wider range of services, including voice recording and commercial production. Even if you have a state-of-the-art home studio, you should hire a professional demo producer to produce your demo.

After you have selected your scripts, rehearsed them, and are confident that your performing skills are up to par, it's time to start calling the studios in your area to schedule your session.

When you book a recording studio, you may be assigned an engineer who is not interested in demo production, and may not be skilled at directing voice-over talent. If you are producing the demo on your own, you need to be prepared for this. As the producer of your demo, you need to be ready to guide your engineer through the process and have a good idea of what you want in your demo, including the selection of music and sound effects, and the final sequencing of clips. If your engineer is not capable of directing you, and you haven't hired a demo producer, you'll need to rely on your self-direction skills to get you through. This can be a real challenge because you should be focusing on your performance — not on the details of directing.

HOW DO I BOOK A DEMO STUDIO AND PRODUCER?

The following pages contain some tips and questions to ask as you call around looking for a studio to hire to produce your demo, as well as some important basic information about recording studios.

- **Find a studio that records radio and TV commercials:** If the studio is primarily a music studio, they may not be capable of handling your needs for a voice-over demo. Look for a studio that is experienced in producing commercials or demos.

- **Does the studio have an engineer who knows how to direct voice-over talent?** Unless you have hired a director, you *will need* an engineer who can direct you as you perform your copy. Many studios have engineers who know how to record the human voice, but don't know the first thing about directing talent for an effective voice-acting performance. When you enter the studio, you need to take off your producer hat and become the performer. Even if you hire a director, you need to find a studio that has an engineer who knows how to produce and direct for voice-over.

- **Does the studio have any experience producing voice-over demos?** This should be one of your first questions. You may also have this question answered when you find out if the studio has an engineer who knows how to work with voice-over talent. Even if a studio does a lot of radio commercials, it does not mean that they also produce voice-over demos. Unlike a :60 radio commercial that is a continuous script, your demo will consist of anywhere from 8 to 15 very short clips. The sequencing of these clips will play an important role in how your demo is perceived by the final listener. If the studio has produced demos in the past, ask to hear what they have done for others or for the names of other voice performers for whom they have produced demos.

- **Ask to listen to other demos produced by the studio or producer:** You'll be investing a considerable amount of money in your demo, so it's important that your producer or studio is willing to let you hear previous work they've done and provide you names of other talent you can talk to. If they are reluctant to release any information, find a different studio or producer.

- **Does the studio have session time that will coincide with your availability?** If you can't book the studio at a time when you are available, you need to find another studio. Many recording studios offer evening or weekend studio time, and may either offer a discount or charge an extra fee for those sessions. You may be able to get a reduced fee for late-night sessions, but you may not be able to get an engineer experienced with voice-over.

- **What is the studio's hourly rate for voice recording?** Many studios have a sliding scale of prices depending on the requirements of the project. Other studios book at a flat rate, regardless of the session. Shop the studios in your area to find the best price for your demo production. Find out if there are any price changes between the voice session and the production session. Find a studio that will give you a flat hourly rate for your entire project. Some studios will give a block discount for sessions booking a large amount of time. A demo session probably won't fit this category, but it couldn't hurt to ask. If you're working with a studio that charges a package price for demo production, their hourly rate won't matter.

- **Does the studio use analog or digital equipment?** In today's digital recording age, this question is usually irrelevant. The difference between digital and analog production in a recording studio is in the areas of recording, editing and post-production. Analog quality in a recording studio, although rare these days, is extremely high and should not be a consideration for your demo recording if that is all that's available; however, analog production may take some additional time since it usually involves multitrack recording. Digital workstations reduce the production and editing time considerably because the audio is recorded and edited within a computer. Today, most studios use some form of digital recording equipment as their primary means of recording.

- **Does the studio have access to music and sound effects libraries?** Your demo will need music and possibly sound effects to underscore your performance. If you are producing an animation demo or an imaging demo, you'll need some very specific types of music and sound effects. Many recording studios do not have any CDs of music that can be used in a demo, even though their primary business may be recording music. Find a production studio that has one or more music libraries that can be used to underscore your spots, and that are appropriate for your type of demo. A *music library* is a collection of music created by a company that produces CDs of music specifically designed for use in commercial, TV, and film production. As you were preparing for your session, you made some notes on music and sound effect ideas. Discuss your ideas with your engineer at the beginning of your session.

    It is not a good idea to use music from your personal music collection for your demo. Even though your demo is meant for limited distribution and will not be for public sale, the possibility of copyright infringement for unauthorized use of the music does exist. Also, the use of familiar or popular music may create a distraction if it is not used wisely. If you have a specific sound in mind for some of your demo tracks, you might want to take in some examples from your personal collection, but keep in mind that they should not be used in the final demo.

- **Does the studio have any additional charges for music or sound effects used?** Some studios charge a fee for any music used in your demo, while other studios include the music as part of a package price. If there is a music use fee charged by the studio, make sure it is a *blanket license* rather than a *laser-drop* license. A blanket license covers all music used in a project and is considerably less expensive than several laser-drop licenses. Usually, there is no charge for sound effects. If you provide your own music, there will be no charge, but you take the risk of any copyright infringement issues that might arise from its use.

- **What other fees will the studio charge for materials, including sales tax?** What does the studio charge for CD one-offs, digital media, and any other materials used in the production of your demo? Does the studio have any additional charges for archiving (backing up and storing) your demo project? What portions of the demo production will have sales tax applied, if any? All of these items will affect the total cost of your demo.

- **How much time does the studio estimate it will take to produce your demo?** You should plan on at least six to eight hours for the completion of your demo, although you may be able to have it completed in much less time. The studio's experience in producing demos will be a factor here, as well as your performing abilities. If the studio has experience producing demos, ask for an estimate of production time and an average cost breakdown.

- **What will you take with you when your demo is completed?** In most cases, you can expect to leave the studio with at least least one audio CD of your demo. You should also make sure you receive high quality MP3 files of all versions of your demo. These may be delivered on a data CD-ROM, emailed to you, posted on an FTP website, or transferred to your own digital storage media.

- **How will your demo be backed up?** A backup is different from the master of your session. The *master* is the final version of your demo in a form that will later be presented to an agent or talent buyer. A *backup* is a copy of all the elements of the project, not necessarily in any special order or structure. Even though the backup will contain everything from your session, often including out-takes, it may be in a format that cannot be used anywhere except the recording studio where your demo was produced. It's not necessary for you to keep a copy of your entire project. You most likely would not be able to open the files or know what to do with them even if you could. But you should make sure the studio will keep a back-up copy of your session on file for future reference. If they don't keep archives, you'll definitely want to get your entire session backed up on data CD-ROM.

Your Demo Recording Session

If you have practiced and mastered your voice-acting skills, have your marketing plan in place, and are prepared and ready to work, your demo session can be a lot of fun, and an educational experience. If, on the other hand, you go to your demo session unprepared or without having mastered the necessary skills, your session can be very uncomfortable.

Because you are the executive producer as well as the performer, even if you have hired a producer, you are the one person responsible for making sure your demo is well produced and that it will be a useful tool for marketing your talents. This means you will have the opportunity to supervise the entire process of your demo production. You won't often have this chance when you are doing real-world sessions.

Keep in mind, though, that when you are in front of the mic, you need to be focused on your performance, not on other aspects of your demo. This is where hiring a director or having an engineer who knows how to direct becomes important. Track sequencing, music, sound effects, duplication, packaging, and distribution all can be left for later.

ARRIVE ON TIME AND PREPARED

In recording studios, time is money. If a session is scheduled to start at 10:00 AM and you don't arrive until 10:10, that's at least ten minutes of wasted time and money — probably more, because it takes a certain amount of time for the engineer to prepare the studio. Recording studios usually bill for their time whether you are there at the scheduled time or not. The lesson here is to *be on time* for your session!

If you live your life in a constant mode of running late, you might want to set your clocks ahead, or do whatever is necessary to make sure you arrive at your session on time, or preferably a bit early. Arriving late for real-world sessions will get you a bad reputation in a hurry, and no doubt will cause you to lose work. Arriving late for your demo session will put your performance under unnecessary stress, costing you valuable time and money.

The same goes for being prepared. In real-world sessions, there is little more you need to do than to show up at the studio at the appointed time, ready to perform. However, for your demo session, you are also the producer, and you must be prepared with rehearsed copy and ideas to discuss with the engineer handling your session. If you hire someone to produce or direct your demo, you need to make sure that the two of you take the time to rehearse your copy to find the strongest material and that you both have a good idea of the results you want to achieve from your demo.

Here are some other tips to make your demo session a productive and pleasurable experience:

- Arrive at your session a bit early.
- Eat a light meal or snack before your session.
- Arrive in good voice, fully warmed up and ready to perform.
- Have a bottle of water with you.
- Rehearse your copy <u>before</u> arriving at the studio.
- Make a note of which scripts you think are your strongest.
- Plan in advance for a possible sequence of scripts.
- Plan ahead for music and sound effects.
- Be ready to accept new scripts that the engineer might have available.

WORKING WITH YOUR ENGINEER/PRODUCER

Aside from your producer, if you hire one, your engineer will be one of the most important people you work with during your demo session, possibly even working as your director. In any case, it is important that you and your engineer work together as a team on your project. Remain flexible and open to your engineer's suggestions. If you are careful in booking the studio, you will probably have an engineer who knows much more about voice-over work than you do. You can learn a lot from a good engineer and he or she may even become a good contact for work later on.

KEEPING YOUR DEMO CURRENT

Your demo will be useful for at least six months to a year, although you may actually use your first demo somewhat longer. As you begin doing paid sessions, you will want to get copies of your work and update your demo occasionally, perhaps every six months to a year. Your agent may request an updated demo or a cut-down version for inclusion on their house demo CD or website. Each time you update or change your demo, you will need to book a new session. Fortunately, digital technology makes it easy to update your demo as often as necessary. If you are updating your demo, you will probably not need to spend as much time recording new tracks or in post-production. And you will most likely not incur any additional music license fees, especially if you are simply inserting some of your recent work. If you are adept at editing on your home studio equipment, you may even be able to handle some updates by editing your own demo revisions.

Plan ahead by budgeting for the studio time and have a good idea of the tracks you want to include. Send your updated demo to people you have worked for. A new demo is a good opportunity to stay in touch with past clients and to inquire about upcoming projects.

17

Your Demo Is Done,
Now What?

You've spent a good deal of time studying your craft, and you have made an investment in producing a high-quality, marketable demo. Essentially, you have set yourself up in business. As you begin making contacts for voice work, you will be speaking to and meeting professionals who may have been in this business for many years. These people have seen it all, and have little time to waste on an amateur trying to break into the business. Your first impression needs to be memorable and professional.

Present Yourself as a Professional

From here on, you need to maintain the level of professionalism you have worked so hard to establish with your demo. Presenting yourself as a professional is important when you submit your demo to agents and talent buyers. A professional attitude and visual appearance, with your printed materials and personal contacts, show that you mean business, and take your career seriously.

CREATING YOUR BRAND

One of the best ways to create a professional image is to have a coordinated look in print and on your website, and perhaps even a logo. You might use a special graphic design, a clever application of some computer clip art, or simply a unique font style. Whatever you do, it needs to be clean, clearly legible, and professionally presented.

Creating an identity for your business is not always an easy thing to do, and it is something you might not want to tackle yourself. Fortunately, there are quite a few talented graphic design artists in the business who you can hire to assist you. Even if you hire someone to design your graphic image, you still need to provide some input. You might even want your graphic designer to hear your demo to get a better idea of what you do. Graphic designers can get their inspiration from just about anything, so be as thorough as possible when presenting your ideas.

Your graphic look should reflect your individual personality. It should be consistent in all printed materials and carry through to your website. Your visual image is an important part of your marketing campaign. It can help set you apart from the crowd and ultimately work toward establishing you as a "brand name" in the world of voice-over.

WHAT MAKES YOU UNIQUE?

There are two elements of your marketing that can set you apart from others who do what you do. The first is a *UPS, or unique positioning statement.* This is a short one or two sentence statement that clearly defines what you do, for whom you do it, and your unique solution to an urgent need. Writing your UPS can be a challenge because it requires you to fully understand the value of what you do and the critical needs of your clients. This may require some research on your part and a great deal of thought as you hone and refine your statement. It's not as easy as it looks. There are many excellent books and Internet resources that discuss this aspect of business development, and that can help you create your UPS.

The second element is a *USP*, or *unique selling proposition.* A USP is a refinement of the UPS into a short statement that communicates the specific benefit of a purchase. It says: "use our services and you will get this specific benefit." The essence of the USP can then be crafted into a *slogan* that can be anything from a single word to a short phrase.

Here's the unique positioning statement for my coaching and training services website **www.voiceacting.com**:

> *We teach powerfully effective communication and performing skills that we've developed over more than three decades of stage, television, recording studio, and advertising experience. We work with people who want to break into the business of voice-over and with business professionals who want to improve relationships with their customers, increase sales, improve their advertising, or become better presenters and performers.*

This UPS is intended to give us a clearly defined focus on what we do, who we do it for, and the results that can be expected from using our services. It positions us as expert performance coaches and as a business that understands business communication. An orchestra conductor is our logo, representing the process of combining several core elements of communication to achieve effective results. For marketing this aspect of our business, we refine our UPS to it's essence to arrive at our USP.

We make you sound great!

For our production company, we use a slightly different UPS:

> *We provide highly skilled, professional voice-over talent and award-winning creative production services to business professionals who want to effectively communicate their advertising message, and to marketers and producers who understand the benefits of communication that gets results.*

As a production company we combine the elements of an advertising message — voice, music, sound effects, and so on — to create a product that effectively meets the needs of our clients. Our conductor logo once again provides the visual image for our services, and, because the core of this business — our voice talent and production services — is consistent with the core of the coaching aspect of our business, the essence of our USP remains consistent.

We Make You Sound Great!

You can create your own UPS, USP, and slogan by taking a close, hard look at what you do, who you do it for, and what makes you different. Only by close examination will you be able to discover what makes you unique from other voice talent in your area. When you discover what that is, write it out in a sentence that describes it clearly and concisely. It should describe who your primary customer is and what they gain from using your services. Once that is complete, you'll have a much clearer picture of your role in the world of voice-over. With that understanding in mind, you can begin to explore various ways of refining the essence of your work into a concise USP and slogan. Here are a few examples:

- *She just makes cents!* (Penny Abshire)
- *Orchestrate your message!* (James Alburger)
- *We Make You Sound Great!* (The Commercial Clinic)
- *My Voice Your Way* (Debbie Munro)
- *Will Embarrass Myself Vocally for Food* (Fletcher Kauffman)
- *Voice Imaging* (Jennifer Vaughn)
- *Jump, listen* (Bob Jump)
- *A Friendly Voice* (Clark Anthony)
- *Voiceover America* (Jon Driscoll)

As you work on developing your UPS, USP, and slogan, be creative and let your imagination run wild. Come up with as many ideas as you can and narrow them down to a few that work for you. Pick the best one and use it everywhere. Your slogan and logo, if you use them, should be included in every piece of print material and on your website.

Building your business as a voice talent can be a daunting task that can be made easier when you understand that you don't have to do everything at once. Take things one step at a time. As you complete one aspect of your business development, begin working on the next. Approach your business development from an organized and structured foundation, much like you have done with your performance craft.

There are dozens of excellent books available that can help you develop your USP and business identity. One of my favorites is a small book by Mark Le Blanc titled *Grow Your Business*. This little book gives you the tools and processes to give you the focus to create a powerful defining statement for your business. With that in hand, the world is yours! Mark's website is **www.smallbusinesssuccess.com**.

SETTING UP SHOP

You will probably want to set up some sort of office space in your home, or at the very least keep some records on your computer. Of course, your office can be put together over a period of time, and you may already have much of it in place. Your home office will, most likely, be the same computer that is your home studio.

The purpose of setting up a formal office area is so that you can really keep yourself in a mind-set of handling your talent as a business. The recordkeeping and organizational aspects of a business become increasingly important as you begin doing sessions and generating income. If or when you join a union, you will want to keep track of your session work and your union paperwork. There are also certain tax advantages to setting up a formal business and you would be wise to consult a tax advisor or accountant on this matter.

Some of the items you might want to consider for your office include the following.

- **An answering machine, voicemail box, or service** — This is essential for taking calls when you are not otherwise available. Be sure to check for new messages frequently, especially when you get an agent. There are some interesting messaging services beginning to appear on the Internet for free or for a very small monthly charge. When you sign up for this free service, you get a special local phone number and mailbox extension that gives you access to voicemail, email, and fax — all in one place. This service can even "read" your email to you over the phone, and everything is accessible by both phone and over the Internet.
- **A cell phone** — A cell phone can be one of, if not the, most useful tool you own when you are on the road. It's become an absolute necessity for staying in touch with clients and your agent. Please remember to turn your phone off when you are in the booth. Better yet, don't even take it into the booth.

Figure 14-1: Business card dimensions with sample layout.

- **Business cards, letterhead and envelopes** — You will be making
  many contacts as you develop your voice-acting business. As a
  professional, you should consider each contact as potential work. Your
  first impression leaves a lasting memory. Professionally prepared and
  printed business cards and stationery are essential to creating a
  professional image.

  A business card is an absolute necessity as a voice actor. As part
  of your personal networking, you will want to let everyone you meet
  know what you do. Your business card is the first and best
  introduction to you and your talent, followed closely by your demo.
  Always carry a supply of business cards with you and hand them out
  every chance you get.

  The two most important things on your business card are your
  name and a telephone number where you can be reached. The most
  common problem with business cards is that the telephone number
  is too small to read easily. The second most common problem is too
  much information on the card.

  The purpose of a business card is to be a reminder of who you
  are and how you can be contacted. Include only the most important
  information about yourself on your card. If you are using a slogan or
  logo, those should be on the card as well. Keep the design clean and
  simple for best results (see Figure 14-1).

- **Thank-you notes** — A frequently overlooked, yet very important,
  business practice is the thank-you note. A brief note of thanks is
  often all it takes to leave a good feeling with a producer or client.
  These little notes can easily be prepared in advance, help generate
  positive memories of your work, and provide a gentle reminder that
  you are available.

- **Newsletters and postcards** — Some voice performers send out a brief newsletter on a regular basis to clients and producers. Newsletters can take the form of anything from a simple postcard to a brief letter (mailed in an envelope or simply folded and stapled). Content usually includes a brief description of recent projects and clients and any other interesting information. Of course, your graphic identity should be a part of the newsletter. The purpose of the newsletter or postcard is to keep your name in front of the talent buyer. Keep your copy short, concise, interesting, and to the point. Too much information will result in the mailing being thrown away without even being read. If you have an email address for your contacts, you might compose a brief update on your activities on a monthly basis. The idea is to keep your name in front of the people who book voice-over talent.

Print Materials

There are several marketing items you will want to consider having professionally printed, including business cards, envelopes, and stationery. For best results, take your layout to an experienced printer. However, if you are on an extremely tight budget and posses the necessary computer skills, you can use a laser printer or high-quality, color ink-jet printer to create some of your own print materials.

Consult with a printing service about paper stock and ink colors. These people are in the business of making printed materials look good and may be able to offer some valuable suggestions. If you do your own printing, there are many types of paper stock for letterhead, postcards, and business cards. You can even purchase sheets of preformatted business cards, mailing labels, and CD labels, ready to be loaded into your printer. However, be aware that business cards printed on the perforated paper (available from Avery) tend to present a less-than-professional image.

Avery is considered by many to be the standard for blank, pre-formatted labels. Their website, **www.avery.com**, has a free version of the Avery label printing software that allows for designing and printing on most of their label designs. You can find comparable labels for almost every Avery label design at Label Blank, **www.labelblankcorporation.com**.

If you're printing your own CD labels, you should know that you can save a lot of money by purchasing a box of 100 sheets of Label Blank or Avery labels, rather than the smaller packages of 25 sheets that you'll find at most stationary and computer stores.

PHOTOS

One of the nice things about voice acting is that your physical appearance is far less important than your ability to act. Unless you also intend to market yourself for on-camera work, it is usually not a good idea to include a photo of yourself in your promotion materials. Your job as a voice actor is to market your talents and skills as a vocal performer.

No matter how good your demo might be, a photograph is going to give the talent buyer a face to go with your voice. It is not uncommon for a performer to be pigeon-holed or stereotyped as a result of a photo on their demo. Many agents and producers will associate a face to a name before they associate a voice to a name. Although not intentional, this can be a real disservice for the voice actor. My recommendation for someone just starting in this business is to keep your image clean and simple without photos, and let your voice do the selling.

Of course, there are exceptions to not using photos in your promotion. If you are marketing your talents as a model, an on-camera performer, or if you also do live theater, a photo is a must. As a multifaceted performer, a photo can actually work to your benefit because it will tend to associate your versatility with your name in the mind of the talent buyer.

If you use a photo as part of your packaging, hire a professional photographer who understands performance headshots to take the picture and make sure the photo reflects your money-voice personality. Your photo is an important part of your image and must be of the highest quality.

CD LABELS

CDs will most likely remain an option for voice-over demos for some time to come. If you choose to create audio CD demos, you'll want the cover, label, and tray card designs to reflect your professional image. There are several options for labeling and packaging your CD demo. Perhaps the most common form of CD packaging is the familiar plastic jewel case. Alternative packaging options include a clamshell case, basic paper or cardboard sleeve, a thin-style jewel case, and a DVD case.

Since the purpose of your CD demo is to present your talent in a professional manner so talent buyers will hire you, it is important that they be able to locate your demo quickly when they are in search of the perfect voice. For those producers who use audio CD demos, only the standard jewel case will provide easy storage and access to your demo. The thin-style jewel case has no spine, or edge, labeling, and can disappear when placed on a shelf with other demos. The clamshell case and paper and cardboard sleeves all provide no space for anything other than the CD, and are not recommended. Although an audio CD can be placed in a standard DVD case, this is not recommended for a voice-over demo. Although the case will allow for more information on the cover and provides for an insert inside, it won't fit on the same shelf with other audio CDs.

The standard CD jewel case has two areas that can hold labeling and gives you the best possible presentation of your demo. The label for the front clear door is called an *insert*. The label for the back of the jewel case (which has folded portions for the two edge labels) is called a *tray card*. For the "do-it-yourselfer," there are many computer software programs available that include templates for printing both the insert and tray card as well as the round label for the CD. You can find these programs at most office supply stores and many computer retailers, or download the free Avery label software from **www.avery.com**. For the most professional results you will probably need to find a graphics designer to do the layout for your CD labels for printing by a full-service print shop.

If you are competent with graphics design software, like Adobe Photoshop, you may be able to design your own CD label and packaging. You'll find lots of resources on the Internet for CD label, Insert, and Tray Card design templates to use with your design software. Search for "CD template." If you do create your own designs, keep in mind that they must have the appearance of being professionally designed. It's simply not worth trying to save a few dollars if the final product screams "amateur."

Your jewel case labels should contain the essential information about your demo: your name, a catchy slogan (if you have one), your logo (if you have one), your agent's name, and a contact phone number (yours or your agent's). This information should also be included on both the *insert* and *tray card*. The back should also include the CD contents, especially if there is more than one demo on the CD. You might also include a short bio of yourself or perhaps a brief client list for added credibility. A website and email address might be other items to include, depending on how you are marketing your demo. For example, if you are represented by an agent, it would not be a good idea to put your personal website or email info on the demo CD unless they both direct visitors to your agent. A photo is not recommended, nor is it necessary for a voice-over demo.

Regardless of the outer packaging, the CD itself will need some sort of label. Labeling for the CD comes in two basic forms: a paper label and imprinting on the CD. If you are duplicating your own CDs you will be using paper labels. Some CD duplicators will also use paper labels for short run CD duplication. However, other duplicators will use the more professional-looking process of imprinting your label directly on the CD. Before placing your duplication order, check around for the best pricing and labeling format.

Getting Your Demo Out There:
Duplication and Distribution

You will need to have your demo CD duplicated before sending to your prospects, and there are a few different ways to do this. Burning your own CDs may be cost-effective if you have the time to do it and the talent for designing your labels. Of course, if you're not a graphic designer, you can have your labels professionally designed and printed, ready to insert into the jewel case as you burn each CD. You really want your demo to be of the highest quality possible, so the best approach is to have copies made by a professional duplicator. For CD duplication services, look in your Yellow Pages under Recording Services/Sound and Video or do an Internet search.

CDs can generally be duplicated in any quantity you need and on relatively short notice. Burning a single CD duplicate is called a *one-off,* and is a perfect copy of the original digital information. Multiple one-offs are made during the process of CD duplication. CD replication is an entirely different process for producing hundreds or thousands of perfect copies. You won't need to worry about CD replication until you are doing mass marketing of your talent on a national level. By the way, the term *burning a CD* comes from the fact that during the recording process, the CD laser literally burns tiny holes (or pits) in the CD media.

Because electronic files are so popular as a delivery media for voice-over demos, I wouldn't suggest burning any more than about 25 copies of your demo to start with. These would be reserved for distribution to people you contact who specifically request an audio CD of your demo. When you get an agent, he or she will let you know how many copies the agency needs to keep on hand.

If you've never burned a CD on your computer, it would be to your benefit to learn how to use software designed for that purpose. You'll find a variety of software manufacturers at your local computer store. Most software for creating CDs will also burn DVDs. For your voice-over demo, you'll want to use commonly available media for audio CD or CD-ROM. DVD media won't play in an audio CD player.

Your Home Studio

Home based recording studios have been around since the early days of sound recording. Early recording equipment was bulky, complex, and most of all expensive. Advances in computer and sound recording technology have changed all that. Today, with a decent computer and some relatively inexpensive equipment, you've got the capability to do what used to require a multi-million dollar facility. And it will fit in a corner of a room at home!

A home studio makes for a very short commute to work and provides a perfect opportunity to record auditions and paid projects. With the proper equipment, a home studio can be set up to connect with the telephone system for bi-directional communication, also known as a *phone patch*, and it can even be set up for *ISDN* digital audio. ISDN stands for Integrated Services Digital Network. The service is a method used to connect two or more recording studios to one another in real-time. The quality at each end is identical to the source so, for a producer, it's as though the talent were in their studio. Setting up an ISDN studio can be an expensive proposition and isn't recommended — nor is it necessary — for someone just getting started in voice-over.

With a properly designed home studio, it's possible to record with a quality comparable to many professional studios. For this reason, many producers, especially those with a low production budget, are moving toward having voice-over talent record voice tracks at home studios. By requiring VO talent to record on their own equipment, producers often expect a faster turnaround and the same quality they would get from a professional studio, but for the cost of talent fee only. Unfortunately, most voice-over artists are performers and not recording engineers. For many, the technology of a home studio can be intimidating and overwhelming. Still, in today's world of voice-over it is important to at least know the basics.

HOME STUDIO EQUIPMENT

With today's computer systems, it's a relatively simple matter to put together the equipment for high-quality voice recording. Regardless of the equipment you use, you will have a choice between a primarily analog system or a digital system. As with most things, there's more than one way to configure your home studio recording system, and none is better than another. It comes down to personal preference and ease of use.

There are many excellent books on the subject of building a home studio, most of which are available through **www.voiceacting.com**. If you need a clear and concise explanation of the component parts of a home studio and how everything works together, my *VoiceActing.com Guide to Building Your Home Studio E-Book* will answer most of your questions. This downloadable E-Book is fully cross-linked internally, and loaded with Internet links to websites with more information about every aspect of a home studio. If you're looking for a book that covers the basics of home studio recording and the production process, Harlan Hogan's *The Voice Actor's Guide to Home Recording* is an excellent choice. Focal Press, the publisher of this book, **www.focalpress.com**, also has two excellent books on the subject of home recording: *Practical Recording Techniques* by Bruce Bartlett and *Project Studios* by Philip Newell. The Focal books are intended more for the home music recordist, but they still contain some valuable information that can be applied to voice-over work.

The entire purpose of your home studio is to record and edit audio on your computer. The first thing you need to do is figure out how to get the sound of your voice onto your computer's hard drive. At first glance this may seem a simple task: you purchase a headset mic, plug it into your computer's sound card, open the recording software that came with the computer, and start recording. Although that's the basic process, the reality is that it's not quite that simple.

A computer headset mic is not acceptable for professional voice-over work. These microphones are designed for low-quality recording, and if you use one for voice-over work, you'll be plagued with pops and other noise issues. Although many computer sound cards are very high quality, the fact remains that the sound card is inside the computer — and the inside of a computer is an electrically very noisy place. There is the potential for some of this noise to leak into your recordings, and if that happens, there's nothing you can do to fix it short of replacing the sound card. As for software, the basic audio recorder that comes with Windows is pretty much useless. Mac computers will often come with good audio software, but for a PC, you'll need to look somewhere else.

As I mentioned, there are two ways to configure a home studio, analog and digital. The primary difference between the two is that an analog system uses a microphone or an analog mixer that is connected to the computer's sound card, and converts the audio to a digital signal inside the computer. A digital system converts the audio signal to digital information outside the computer using a USB or Firewire digital interface. The digital interface may be a stand-alone device, a digital mixer, or even a digital USB microphone. USB (universal serial buss) and Firewire both refer to high-speed digital connections between a computer and an outboard device.

Of the two, a simple digital system is the simplest to use and the least expensive. The basic components for a complete digital home studio can cost under $200, not including the computer. A comparable analog studio will cost about the same, or possibly a bit more.

The equipment and software you purchase for your home studio will depend largely on the kind of work you will be doing. If you're only recording voice tracks or practicing your performing skills, you don't need an elaborate digital mixer with all the bells and whistles.

The following are basic components for a home studio, each with some comments as to its role in the studio.

- **Microphone** — You need a microphone that will make your voice sound great. Different mics sound different on different people. It can take some research to find exactly the right mic. To get started, don't buy the most expensive mic you can find. There are many excellent mics available for under $100. The mic will connect to a USB interface, a digital mixer, an analog mixer, or directly to the sound card (not recommended). There are even USB mics that connect directly to your computer. A condenser mic is usually recommended over a dynamic mic, due to its superior performance.

- **Microphone cable** — Professional microphones use a 3-pin XLR type cable that connects the mic to a mixer or USB device. The phantom power for condenser microphones travels through the same wires in the cable that carry the audio signal.

- **USB interface** — The cable from your mic connects to this device, which converts the audio signal to digital. It connects to your computer via a USB cable plugged into a USB port on the computer. A USB device will have a control for adjusting mic recording volume and a volume control for headset monitoring. A good USB interface also provides phantom power for condenser mics.

- **Analog audio mixer** — *You do not need an analog mixer if you are using a USB interface to record only one mic.* An analog mixer may connect to either the computer's sound card or to the line level inputs on a USB interface. The mixer is used to control the volume for several mics or other sources. If connecting directly to the sound card, you'll need some special adaptors, which may be difficult to locate.

- **Recording software** — Virtually all recording software will provide for recording and editing of recorded audio. However, all audio software is not the same. Some are more user friendly than others, and price is not a good indicator. Software prices vary from free to several hundred dollars. Regardless of the software you choose, you should make sure it will easily save or convert your recordings to MP3 compressed files.

- **Microphone Stand** — A floor stand with a boom, or a desk stand. Either way, you'll need something to hold your microphone.

- **Copy Stand** (Music Stand) — You'll need this to hold your copy so your hands are free for performance and operating the equipment.

- **Headphones** — Conventional stereo headphones will work for most voice-over recording. You'll wear your headphones while recording and for other monitoring, if you don't have a set of speakers. You'll want a headset that is comfortable and that reproduces your voice accurately. Some headphones emphasize low frequencies, which will result in a coloration of your voice.

- **Speakers** — Although headphones will serve the purpose for monitoring, and even for editing, they can become uncomfortable if worn for extended periods of time. To start your home studio, a pair of good computer speakers connected to your sound card will do nicely. As you bring in voice-over work, you might want to consider upgrading your speakers to some studio monitors. If you are using a USB device for recording, you may need to adjust your software settings so your computer knows you want to use your sound card speakers for playback monitoring. Basic computer speakers are fairly inexpensive. Studio monitors can run into the hundreds or thousands of dollars for a pair of speakers.

- **Stopwatch** — You'll need some way to time yourself. Digital stopwatches that beep aren't recommended. They're awkward and they make noise. A better choice is an analog 60-second sweep stopwatch. Prices range from about $50 to several hundred dollars. An Internet search for "analog stop-watch" will bring up numerous sources. Look for one that has a separate reset button. Ideally, the button allows the watch to be reset while running. Most of the inexpensive watches require the watch to be stopped first before resetting.

- **Acoustic treatment** — Most home studio areas will need some form of acoustic treatment to reduce echoes and unwanted noise. This subject is too complex to discuss here, and there are many excellent books on this topic. Just be aware that you may need to make some changes to your recording environment for the best recording quality.

That's the basic requirements for any home studio. With the exception of an analog mixer, everything is a necessity. You'll find most, if not all, of it at professional music stores. Computer stores simply don't deal with this type of equipment, and they don't understand home studios.

Your Website

There once was a time when the Internet did not exist, and no one knew what a website was. Hard to believe, but it's true!

For voice-over talent today, a website is an absolute necessity. It's often the first stop a prospect makes to learn who you are and what you can do. A website is your 7/24/365 brochure, available to be visited by anyone, any time, anywhere in the world. If you don't already have a website, I'd suggest you seriously consider learning about the Internet and getting online! A website is an invaluable tool in marketing your voice-over talent.

The Internet is huge, and the mere thought of building your own website can be intimidating. But, it's really not all that difficult if you have some basic computer skills. Many website hosting companies offer website templates as part of their hosting service. With these, you actually design your website online. It can take some time to add all the bells and whistles, but you can often have a simple site ready to go in just a few short hours. There are also several software programs that will allow you to design your own website on your computer. These will offer more options and capabilities than the online templates for your site design, and allow you to keep a backup of your site on your computer. Their ease-of-use, which is generally reflected by price, ranges from pretty simple, to very complex.

Since there are literally hundreds of books and lots of design software for websites, I won't go into all the details here. Chris Wagner, a Denver-based voice actor and web designer, has written some excellent articles on websites for voice talent that you'll find at **www.voiceacting.com**.

WEBSITE ESSENTIALS

There are many important considerations for putting your website online. Here are just a few:

1. **URL** (Universal Resource Locator), also known as the *domain name*: This is the name of your website. You've seen lots of them sprinkled throughout this book. You want yours to be simple, short, and descriptive. Your domain name must be registered before you can set up an account with a website hosting company. Most hosting companies can help you with registering your URL.

2. **Site design:** Your website should be designed to reflect who you are and what you do. If you use a color scheme in your print materials and on CD labels, carry that through to your website to keep your visual image consistent.

3. **Email:** Using an email address such as "you@yourdomain.com" only makes good marketing sense. Most websites allow for email to be viewed through the website's webmail account, or for email to be forwarded to another address. Avoid common .aol, .hotmail, .msn, .yahoo, and similar email addresses that say "amateur."

4. **Tell your story:** Your website is the perfect place to let prospects know who you are, who you've worked for, and what you can do for them. You don't need a complex, multi-page site to do this. A few pages will work nicely. Even a one-page site, if well designed, will present you as a professional. A very good example of a single-page site is **www.pennyabshire.com**. You'll notice that everything you need to know about Penny as a professional voice talent is easily accessible on that one page.

5. **Post your demos:** Your demos are your primary marketing tool, and you should absolutely post them on your website. MP3 is one of the many formats for online audio. This is a compressed audio format that has a file size roughly one 10th the size of raw, uncompressed audio. In other words, a one-minute .wav or .aiff file will be about 10MB in size, while an MP3 file of the same audio will be about 1MB. Smaller file sizes for audio will download faster and can even be sent via email.

    Another way to post your demos is to convert them to streaming audio files. This is a more complex process that is often best handled by your website designer. Real-media and Flash are just two popular methods for streaming audio files from a website. The major difference between MP3 and streaming audio is that MP3 files must first be downloaded before playing, while streaming audio will play almost instantly. The downside of streaming audio is that the files cannot be downloaded for future reference.

Building your own website can be an educational and fun experience — if you have the time and inclination. If you'd rather put your time and energy into developing your performing skills and voice-over business, you might want to consider hiring a web designer to build your site. Ask your friends who they used to build their sites, and if they are happy with their hosting company. Do your research to make sure you are comfortable with the hosting company and designer. You'll want the hosting company to have a good track record and provide excellent customer service for those rare times when you might need it. Your designer should be someone who will listen to your needs as a voice actor and design a website that meets your requirements for communicating your professional image to visitors.

18

How to Work in the Business of Voice-over

Promoting and Marketing Your Voice-over Talent

Getting voice-over work is a numbers game: The more you hustle, the more contacts you will make. The more contacts you have, the more you will work. The more work you do, the better known you will become. The better known you become, the more people who want to hire you, and you get more work. It's not quite that simple, but you get the idea — it truly is a numbers game. This chapter will help get you started on the right track.

If you're just getting started in voice-over, you'll be doing all the work; making the calls, sending the auditions, recording the sessions, handling the billing, and doing the follow-ups. When you are just getting started, this can seem overwhelming, but if you are organized and know what you're doing you can reach whatever level of success you desire.

Before embarking on an all-out promotion campaign for yourself, do your homework and get organized. If you have an agent, they may be able to recommend specific businesses for you to contact, or they may ask that you let the agency handle all your promotion. If you agree to let the agent do all the work, set a time limit. During that time, you can see how many auditions you are called for. Working with your agent is the best way to have an organized and consistent promotion campaign.

If you do not have an agent, and are not planning to get one in the immediate future, you are on your own. If you expect to get any auditions or any work, you must devise your own promotion and marketing campaign and do all the legwork. You'll need to find the names and contact information for your prospects, make the calls, send out the letters, and design your marketing campaign. This can be a time-consuming process, but you can make it go a bit easier if you take it in stages. As you create your promotion campaign, remember why you are doing this, and keep polishing your acting techniques.

There are many good books on marketing and advertising from which you can gain a tremendous amount of information. You can also learn a great deal by taking an adult education or college extension advertising and marketing course. Not only will you learn some excellent ways to promote yourself, but you will also learn what goes into creating the marketing and promotional copy that you work with as a voice-over performer.

When you promote and market yourself, you are acting as your own agent and ad agency. These roles are simply additional aspects of your business and you must become familiar with them if you are to be successful. There are three basic parts to the promotion of your voice-over work: your demo, making contacts, and following-up. Other aspects of your voice-over business will be covered later in this chapter and in the next.

Finding and Working with an Agent

A common question is "Do I need an agent to do voice-over work?" The short answer is "No, you don't need an agent." but this isn't really the right question to be asking. A better question is "Will a talent agent help me in my voiceover career." For most voice-over talent, the answer is "Yes." If you work without an agent, you are limiting yourself to only those voice-over jobs you can find for yourself, and you will be responsible for negotiating your fees and collecting payments. One major advantage of having an agent to represent you is that you will gain access to auditions and clients that you might never have met if you were not represented. Your agent will also handle fee negotiations and collect payments.

Having a talent agent working for you is definitely to your advantage; however, this does not mean that you <u>must</u> have an agent. There are many very successful voice talent who do not have representation. If you do have an agent, it does not mean you can relax and just wait for the work to come in. It is important for you to network constantly and let your talents be known. Networking with other voice-over performers keeps you up on current trends, and, if you are nonunion, you may get a better idea of the fees other performers are earning. Always keep a few demos and business cards with you and be ready to pitch yourself when the opportunity arises. Always present yourself professionally. It's a subtlety, but maintaining an attitude of professionalism communicates credibility and integrity.

You will probably get your first few voice-over jobs through friends, networking, or some other contact you make yourself. As you begin working, your skills will improve, producers will begin to know about you, and your talents will become more valuable. When you reach the point where you are confident with your abilities and are ready for more work, it's time to find an agent. Remember, most working pros have an agent. To present yourself with a professional image, you should too. So, how do you go about finding yourself an agent?

The first thing to understand is that an agent works for you! Some beginners in this business think it's the other way around. Most agents are very selective about who they represent, and even may give the false impression that the performer is working for them. Not true! It is their job to get you work by sending you out on auditions and connecting you with producers who will hire you. Once on the audition, it becomes your job to perform to the best of your ability. Your agent only gets paid when you do. Your agent should also send your demo to casting directors, advertising agencies, and production companies. Once a job is booked, the agent negotiates your fee.

As you begin your search, you will find that no two agents are alike. Some handle the paperwork for the union, while others want the client or performer to handle this task. Talent agents in a large market, like Los Angeles, run their businesses completely different from a talent agent in a smaller market in the Midwest. As with much of the voice-over business, there are no hard-and-fast rules. The most important thing is that you are comfortable with your agent, and that your agent is comfortable with you.

SEARCHING FOR AN AGENT

There are a few things you need to know about talent agents before you start seeking representation: (1) A talent agent is not in the business of nurturing you or grooming you to be a professional voice actor. They expect you to have your performing skills in place and ready to go. (2) A talent agent may not be interested in you unless you have a track record and an existing client list. Agents are in business to get you booked as often as possible, and at the highest fee possible. As mentioned earlier, they only get paid when you work. (3) You may have a great track record, and an incredible demo, but you may be rejected simply because the agency already has other voice talent with the same or similar delivery style as yours. (4) Being rejected for representation is not a personal attack on you or your performing abilities.

One way to find an agent in your area is to contact your local AFTRA office. Even if you are not a union member, they will be able to provide you with a list of all franchised agents in your area. Many agents work exclusively with union talent, although some work with both union and nonunion talent.

Be prepared for rejection. Most agents and producers in Los Angeles will not even open or listen to an unsolicited demo, although this policy is different in other cities. You will have much better success finding an agent and finding work if you spend some time on the phone first. It may take a little research on your part, but the time you spend talking with agents and producers on the phone will pay off later on. Don't expect to get results on the first call. Marketing your talent is an ongoing process and results often come weeks or even years later. You should also know that in major markets like Los Angeles, New York, and Chicago, many talent agents will not even be willing to speak with you unless you are referred by one of the talent they currently represent.

You can start your search for an agent by looking in the Yellow Pages of your local phone book under "Talent Agencies," or do an Internet search for "Talent Agent Your City." Talent agents for major markets in the United States are also posted at **www.voicebank.net**. Yet another way to find an agent is to go to a theatrical bookstore. *Samuel French, Inc.* is among the best. See their website, **www.samuelfrench.com** for store locations in Los Angeles, New York, and Toronto. A keyword search on their site for "the agencies" will bring up several resources with a wealth of other information.

Yet another incredibly valuable resource for locating talent agents in Los Angeles and New York is *The Voice-over Resource Guide*. This is a small booklet — and a website — that includes agents, demo producers, recording studios, union rates, and lots of other information for voice-over talent. It's available at most of the studios in LA and New York, and online at **www.voiceoverresourceguide.com**.

While on your search for an agent, you can also call recording studios, TV stations, and production companies in your area. Ask for the production manager. Let this person know you are available for voice-over work, and that you are looking for an agent. Ask for the names of the talent agencies he or she works with. Let them know your union status. If the company is a union shop (an AFTRA or SAG *signatory*) and you are nonunion, they will not be able to hire you, but may be able to give you some good leads. Don't forget to let companies you contact know that you have a demo you can send to them. Follow up all phone contacts with a thank you letter.

Many talent agents specialize in certain types of performers, such as modeling, on-camera, voice-over, music recording, theatrical, and so on. You can call the agent's office to find out if they represent voice-over talent and if they are accepting new performers. Keep this initial call brief and to the point, but be sure to get the name of someone to send your demo to if the agency expresses any interest.

Proper phone etiquette is important when calling an agent. Agents are busy people and will appreciate your call more if you are prepared and know what you want. Here's an example of an ineffective call to an agent:

AGENT: Hello, Marvelous Talent Agency.
ACTOR: Hi, uh, is there somebody there I could talk to about doing voice-over?
AGENT: Who's calling?
ACTOR: Oh, yeah. My name is David Dumdum, and I'd like to talk to someone about doing voice-overs.
AGENT: This is a talent agency. We don't do voice-overs, we represent talent.
ACTOR: That's what I mean, I want to talk to somebody about representing me.

This kind of call not only takes a long time to get anywhere, but the so-called actor is not at all clear about what he wants to discuss. Even if this performer had a decent demo, the chances of getting representation are poor simply because of a nonbusinesslike presentation. Here's a much better way to approach a call:

AGENT: Hello, Marvelous Talent Agency.
ACTOR: Hi, this is Steven Swell. I'd like to know if your agency
        represents voice-over talent.
AGENT: Yes we do.
ACTOR: Great! I'd like to speak to someone about the possibility of
        representation. Are you taking on any new performers?
AGENT: We are always interested in looking at new voice talent. If
        you'd like to send us a copy of your demo, we'll give it a
        listen let you know.
ACTOR: That's terrific. I'll get a copy to you in today's mail. Who
        should I send it to?

This performer gets to the point of his call quickly and effectively. He is polite, businesslike, and keeps an upbeat, professional attitude throughout the call. Even though he didn't connect with an agent, he did get a name and there is now a clear process for getting his demo into the agency and to the right person.

Narrow down the prospective agents in your area. You can immediately eliminate those who represent only models, print, or on-camera talent. The Los Angeles area has more than 250 franchised agents, and only a handful represent voice-over talent, so in a larger market, you must be very specific in targeting potential agents before sending out your demo and résumé. Smaller markets can have zero to several talent agents, depending on the market size. Representation by a small talent agency in a small market can be an excellent way to break into the business of voice-over. There are also a growing number of talent agents who represent voice talent nationwide, or even worldwide, through the Internet.

Before contacting any agent, prepare a brief and to-the-point cover letter that will accompany your demo. This is not the place to give your life history, and it's not a résumé — keep it to no more than a few short paragraphs. This is a business letter intended to introduce you to the agency. Simply state that you are a voice-over talent and that you are interested in discussing the possibilities of representation by the agency. Depending on the talent agent you are contacting, your cover letter may be sent via postal mail or e-mail.

When sending through the post office, each letter you send out should be an original, and should be addressed to the person whose name you were given during your research. The address on the envelope should be printed by a computer, not by hand. This gives your envelope a professional appearance. If you have relevant performing experience, you should include that in your letter. Any reputable agent will require a demo from any talent they are considering, although a résumé is not generally used or necessary when marketing for voice-over work.

Here's an example of a good cover letter that is short, to the point, gives a professional appearance while providing some important information, and suggests the performer's potential value to the agency. Notice that the following letter concludes by requesting action from the agency to arrange an interview.

Dear Mr. Agent:

Thank you for your interest in my demo. As I mentioned on the phone, I am a voice actor seeking representation. I have been booking myself as a freelance performer for the past year or so and have had several successful commercials on the air.

My background, training, and additional information are on the enclosed résumé. A copy of my current demo is also enclosed. You can also learn more about me at www.alburger.com.

I believe I can be a valuable asset to your agency, and I look forward to hearing from you so that we can arrange for a meeting to further discuss representation by your agency.

Sincerely,

Once you've been asked to send your introductory letter and demo, do not call to see if your demo was received. It will often do you no good, and may even irritate some agencies. It will also do you no good to call to get a reaction to your demo — and don't expect to get your demo back. Talent agents know you send out demos to other agents in the area. If they hear something they like, they will call you. If you are good, they will call quickly, simply because they don't want to miss out on representing an excellent performer by not getting back to you in time.

Don't be surprised if you don't get a call. There may be many reasons for an agent not accepting you. Don't expect or ask for a critique of your demo. If an agent is kind enough to critique it for you, use that information to learn how to improve your skills and create a better demo. It is not uncommon to produce two, three, or more demos before landing that first agent.

Sooner or later you will find a talent agent who is interested in talking to you. But be aware, the agent's interest does not mean you have representation. It only means that he or she is interested in learning more about you and your talent, and to determine if you will be a good fit with their talent agency. When you are selected for representation, expect your agent to request changes in your demo. Your agent knows their clients and what they need to market you to them.

INTERVIEWING AN AGENT

When you get a positive response, you will be asked to set up an appointment to meet with the agent. This can be quite exciting. What will you wear? How should you act? What will you say?

Remember that although it may appear as though the agent is interviewing you, the reality is that you are interviewing the agent. Handle this interview just as you would an interview for a new job. Dress nicely, and present yourself in a businesslike manner. Be careful to wear clothes that do not make noise. A good agent will probably ask you to read a script as part of the interview. Enter the office with confidence. Play the part of the successful performer. Create your character for the interview just as you would for a script, and act as if you are a seasoned pro and already represented. Your chances of signing with an agent will be much better if your first impression is one of a skilled and professional performer.

Interview all your prospective agents as thoroughly as possible. Don't be afraid to ask questions at any time. What types of work have they booked in the last month? What is the average scale they get for their performers? What is their commission? Is their commission added to the performer's fee, or taken out? How many voice-over performers do they represent? How long have they been in business? You can even ask whom they represent and for a list of some performers you can contact.

During your meetings with agents, you may talk about everything except your voice-over work. They will want you to be comfortable so that they can get a sense of you as a person, and you will want to get to know them a bit. You need to decide if you like them and have confidence that the agency will be able to get you work. They need to determine if you can work with them as a team.

Take your time. Don't rush to sign up with the first agent who offers to represent you. Also, if any agent gives you the impression that you are working for him or her, you might want to consider eliminating that person from your list. The agent works for you — not the other way around. If an agent requires a fee of any amount before they will represent you, they may be operating illegally and you should end the conversation and leave. By law a talent agent is only entitled to a commission based on the work they obtain for you. When an agent directly charges you a fee to be posted on their website, or for headshots, or for anything else, they may be *double-dipping,* and that's illegal, or at the very least potentially unethical.

When you sign with a talent agency, it will normally be a contract for one year. Some agencies request a multi-year agreement, but this can cause problems if your agent doesn't promote you, and you don't get work. It is generally a good idea to renegotiate with your talent agent every year.

A large agency may have many people in the office and represent a large talent pool. A small agency may have only one or two people handling the entire business. It is easy to become a small fish in a big pond if you sign with a large agency. On the other hand, most large talent agencies sign only voice-over performers with years of experience and a solid track record. Your first agent most likely will work for a smaller agency that can give you more attention and help guide your career.

WORKING WITH YOUR AGENT

Once signed, you should keep your agent up to date on your work. Let him or her know how your auditions and sessions go, and keep the agent current with an updated demo as needed. Calling your talent agent once a week should be adequate, unless he or she requests you call more or less frequently. Your agent can also be a very good indicator of the areas you are weak in, and may recommend classes and training if necessary. The key to working with an agent is to stay in touch and ask for advice. They generally know the business far better than you.

One good question to ask your agent is how you should handle work you obtain on your own. Some agents will allow you to handle your own personal bookings without paying a commission. However, it may be advisable when someone directly approaches you for work, that you refer the company or person to your agent, especially if you are a union member. As a professional performer, your job is to perform. Your agent's job is to represent you and negotiate for the highest fee. Although it is generally wise to let your agent handle the negotiations, there may be some situations where it might be best for you to handle the money talk yourself. If you have a good relationship with your agent, and the situation warrants, you may have a better chance of landing the job.

I know one voice actor who auditioned for a CD-ROM game and noticed that the other voice actors who said they had an agent were being passed over for callbacks. With this in mind, he called his agent to discuss the situation. Their mutual decision was that the voice actor would avoid any mention of representation until after he was booked. He handled the negotiations himself and actually managed to get a higher fee than most of the other voice actors booked for the project. Even if you are an accomplished negotiator, your agent is your representative. Generally, it is not a good idea to take things into your own hands until you have discussed the situation with your agent.

As a career grows, it is common for performers to change agents several times. A word of warning, however: Changing agents can be traumatic. You are likely to have a case of the "guilts" when leaving an agent, especially if the person has done a lot to help promote you and develop your career. When this time comes, it is important to remember the reasons why you must change agents. You may have reached a level of skill that is beyond your agent's ability to market effectively, or you may simply be moving to a new part of the country. On the other hand, you might be changing agents because your current agent is simply not getting you the kinds of jobs you need.

A Business Plan for Voice Actor You, Inc.

You have probably heard the phrase: "If you fail to plan, you plan to fail." This is as true in voice-over as it is for any other business. You need to have a vision of where you want to be and have some sort of plan as to how you will get there. If either of these is missing, chances are you will not be as successful as you hope to be as quickly as you would like to be. Things will get in your way from time to time, and you will be distracted by just living your life. However, if you have a plan, you will be prepared to work through those obstacles when they jump in front of you.

As an independent professional, you need to look at what you do as a business. With that in mind, my coaching and business partner, Penny Abshire, has adapted a simple business plan that you can use to develop focus on the business side of voice acting. You will wear many "hats" as you operate your business. You are the CEO, CFO, Sales Manager, Marketing Director, Director of Education, and finally, a performer. It is critical to your success that you understand what you are doing for each of your duties and that you have a direction in which you are moving. The "Business Plan for Voice Actor You, Inc." on the following pages is something to which you should really give some serious attention. Don't just skim through this and forget about it. Copy these pages and read through the questions. Set it aside for a few hours to think about how you will plan your career, market yourself, sell your services, learn new skills, and protect your future. Some of the questions will be fairly easy to answer, while others may take a great deal of time and thought.

The time you spend preparing your plan will be time well spent. Refer to your plan on a regular basis and review it about every six months, or at least once a year. Things do change, and your goals and objectives may change. Your business plan is intended to be a guide to keep you on track for your career.

Should you want to take your business plan further, there are many good computer programs on the market that will help you prepare the ultimate business plan for "Voice Actor You, Inc."

YOUR DEMO

This is your audio brochure and your product (at least at this point in time). Your demo is what your potential employers (your customers) will use to judge your talent as it applies to their projects. Your demo is your primary marketing tool. You will need a high-quality demo to market your talent and sell your services. Chapter 16, Your Voice-over Demo, covers this subject in detail.

Business Plan for *Voice Actor You, Inc.*

This simple business plan is designed to help you focus on your business and propel you in the direction you want to go. Give each question some serious thought before answering and review what you've written at least once or twice a year.

1. As **Chief Executive Officer**, what is your vision or plan for a career as a voice actor; it should be specifically designed to ensure your growth, profitability, and financial gain?

    _____

    _____

    _____

    What change(s) must take place to bring this plan to fruition?

    _____

    _____

2. What strategic alliances are you forming to ensure the achievement of the vision or plan of **VOICE ACTOR YOU, INC.?**

    a) With whom are you aligning?

    _____

    b) How will this be beneficial?

    _____

3. As **V.P. of Quality Control**, what are you *specifically* doing to ensure and/or improve the quality of the service provided by **VOICE ACTOR YOU, INC.?**

    _____

    _____

    _____

4. As **Chief Financial Officer**, what plans must be made to accommodate the financial and marketing continuity of **VOICE ACTOR YOU, INC.?**
    Current Strategy: Anticipated Cost:

    _____

    _____

    _____

    a) Alternative sources of revenue?

    _____

    _____

    b) Probability of primary revenue continuation over next 5 years?
       Excellent____   Very Good _____   Fair____   Poor____

c) Back-up strategy:

_____

_____

5. As **V.P. of Marketing**, what steps are you taking to seek new or additional target markets for your services?

_____

_____

_____

a) Local markets?

_____

_____

b) Other markets?

_____

_____

6. As **V.P. of Promotions**, what steps are you taking to complete the following:
   a)   Seek representation?

_____

_____

   b)   Collect materials and prepare for demo?

_____

_____

   c)   Demo production?

_____

_____

   d)   Graphic design (logo, U.S.P., business cards, stationery/thank-you cards, etc.)?
        Design _____
        Printing _____

7. As **V.P. of Sales**, what is the projected revenue for year end?
        $_____
   a)   Is that enough to cover company expenses? ____yes ____no
   b)   What about expected revenue growth for next year?
        $_____

238 The Art of Voice Acting

8. As **V.P. of Education**, what is the training plan *specifically designed* to ensure the services offered by **VOICE ACTOR YOU, INC.** are equal to, or exceed, industry standards?

_____

_____

_____

_____

What is the time line for implementation of the training program?

By _____ I will be enrolled in _____ Completion Date: _____
By _____ I will be enrolled in _____ Completion Date: _____
By _____ I will be enrolled in _____ Completion Date: _____

By _____ I will read _____ Completion Date: _____
By _____ I will read _____ Completion Date: _____
By _____ I will read _____ Completion Date: _____

By _____ I will study and/or research _____
_____ Completion Date: _____
By _____ I will study and/or research _____
_____ Completion Date: _____
By _____ I will study and/or research _____
_____ Completion Date: _____

9. As **V.P. of Human Resources**, what needs to be done to protect the mental, physical, and spiritual health of the primary employee (*you*)?

_____

_____

a) Vacation allotment, family leave, and general mental health maintenance?

_____

_____

b) Maintaining connection with corporate stockholders? (*family*)

_____

_____

c) Your spiritual health?

_____

_____

10. As *Director of Maintenance*, what adjustments should be made to improve the visual appearance and physical health of the primary employee (*you*), the product, or service?

a) What do you plan to do?

_____

_____

_____

_____

b) When will you get started - *specifically*?

_____

11. As *Chief Benefits Officer*, what financial planning is in place to ensure your future financial security (*i.e., retirement*)?

a) What do you plan to do?

_____

_____

_____

b) When will you get started?

_____

_____

_____

12. As *Accounting Department Head*, what steps are you taking to maintain accurate invoicing, recordkeeping, and IRS accountability?

_____

_____

_____

_____

_____

_____

_____

MAKING CONTACTS WITH PROSPECTIVE CLIENTS

Sales calls are an art form all their own. This primer will give you some basic ideas, but you should also consider some additional study on the subject of sales and marketing.

You will need to spend a fair amount of time on the phone, contacting potential clients. Before making any calls you must be prepared and know what you want to discuss. Know what you do best, and be specific about the type or types of voice-over work you are promoting. If you are trying to get into animation voice-over, it's not appropriate to call ad agencies or discuss your expertise with telephone messaging.

Before calling, do some research on your prospects to learn how they use voice talent. When you call, let your professionalism speak for itself and show your prospect that you understand their needs and how your voice work can be of benefit to them. Be careful not to be in a rush to sell your services. You'll be much more successful if you engage your prospect in a conversation to let them get to know you, and for you to gather additional information about how you can help them. Have some prepared notes to look at so that you don't forget anything important during your call, and be prepared to answer any questions that might arise during the conversation.

Needless to say, your stationery should be printed, your demo should be produced and ready to mail before you begin making calls, and you should have a system in place for cataloging prospects and following up.

Remember, you need to talk to someone who is directly responsible for hiring voice-over performers. If you do not have a contact name already, tell the receptionist the purpose of your call. She will most likely direct you to the person you need to speak to, or refer you to someone who might know to whom you should speak. If you can't get connected right away, get a name to ask for when you call back. If you get voice-mail, leave a clear and concise message that includes your phone number at the beginning and end. It's a very good idea to write out your message so you know what to say when you are forwarded to voice-mail. Keep it conversational so you don't ramble or sound like you are reading as you leave your message.

It may take a few follow-up calls before you connect with someone. If you already know how the company you are calling uses voice-over, your conversation should be of an introductory nature. If you don't know, your call should focus on how voice-over work might be used to benefit their business. Either way, the call should be more about them than you. You probably will find some companies that have not even considered hiring an outside professional for their voice-over needs. Undoubtedly, you will also find many that are not interested in what you have to offer. Remember, this is a numbers game, so don't let yourself get discouraged.

Offer to send a copy of your demo to those who are interested. Follow up by mailing your demo with a letter of introduction. It is amazing how many people never follow up a lead by sending out their promo kit. You will never get any work if you don't follow up.

FOLLOW-UP

You will need the following basic items for follow-up:

- A cover letter on a professional-looking letterhead
- Business cards
- Labels or envelopes capable of holding your print materials and demo
- A voice-over client list detailing any session work you have done
- A website you can refer prospects to for additional information about you and your services, and where they can listen to your demo
- Your demo as an audio CD for mailing and as an MP3 file for posting on your website and e-mailing.

First impressions are important, and the more professional you look in print, and sound on the phone, the more your prospect is likely to consider you for work. If you use color in your logo or graphics design, you should consider using special paper designed for color ink-jet or color laser printing. With appropriate computer software and a good printer, you can design a simple form letter that can be adapted to your needs. A little research will reveal many resources to assist with design and printing.

You will need several different versions of your letter of introduction, depending on whether you are following up from a phone call, or if the follow-up is from a personal meeting.

Keep your letter to no more than three or four short paragraphs in a formal business style. Personalize the heading as you would for any business letter. Thank the person you spoke to for his or her interest, and for the time spent talking to you. Remind them of who you are and what you spoke about. Let the company know how you can help them and how they can contact you. Also, mention in the letter that you are enclosing your demo. Be sure to include your website and e-mail address in your letter. The following is an example of a typical follow-up letter:

Dear Mr. Client:

Thank you for taking the time to speak with me yesterday, and for your interest in my voice-over work.

As I mentioned during our conversation, I am available to help your company as a voice-over performer for in-house training tapes, marketing presentations, and radio or television commercial advertising. I am enclosing a list of some recent projects I have voiced and a copy of my demo, which runs approximately two minutes. You can learn more about me and listen to more of my work at www.voiceacting.com. This will give you a good idea of the types of voice-over work I do that can be of benefit to you.

Should you be in need of my services, please feel free to call me anytime at the phone number above or send an email to info@voiceacting.com. I look forward to working with you soon.

Sincerely,

You might include a copy of your voice-over résumé, provided you have some experience. If you have an agent, include the agent's name and phone number in the letter. In larger markets your agent's number should be the only contact reference. In smaller markets you may want to include your own number as well as your agent's. (NOTE: Your agent's name and phone number should be on your demo, but mention it in the letter as well.)

Two things you *do not* need to mention in your follow-up letter are your union status and fees. Your union status should have been established during your phone call, if that was an issue, and it should be noted on your demo label. Your fees are something to be negotiated either by your agent, or by you, at the time you are booked. If it comes up in a conversation, just tell the person that your agent handles that, or that you cannot quote a rate until you know what you will be doing. If they insist, quote the current AFTRA scale for the type of work they are asking about. At least that way you will be quoting a rate that will be close to any union talent interviewed later on. If you are booking yourself as nonunion, freelance talent, you might want to let your contact know that your fees are negotiable.

After sending your follow-up letter and demo, wait about a week, then call your contact again to confirm that the package was received. This helps to maintain your professional image and serves to keep your name on their mind. Don't ask if the person has listened to your demo. That's not the purpose of your call. If they bring it up, fine, but you should not mention it.

Before completing your follow-up call, ask if there are any projects coming up in the near future that might take advantage of your talents. If so, and if the company is considering other voice-over talent, be sure to make yourself available for an audition. Phrase your conversation in such a way that it seems like you are offering to help them. This puts you in a position of offering something of greater value to your potential employer, rather than just being someone asking for work.

Once you have established a list of possible employers, you will want to stay in touch with them. Consider sending out a brief note or postcard every six months or so and on holidays. The purpose here is to keep your name in front of the people who book talent. You can even include a list of recent projects, and enclose a reply card, or offer to send a current demo.

Perhaps the only rule for follow-up is to be consistent and persistent. Maintain a professional image, keep your name in front of your prospects, and you will get more work. Here are some ideas for follow-up reminders:

- Thank-you card (after session, meeting, or conversation)
- Holiday and seasonal cards
- Birthdays and anniversaries (if you know them)
- Current projects you have done
- Generic reminder postcard
- Semi-annual one-page newsletter updating your activities
- Special announcement about upcoming projects

REACHING THE PEOPLE WHO BOOK TALENT

Many large companies have in-house production units, while others hire outside production houses and work with agents. There usually will be someone who is in charge of coordinating promotion and advertising that may require the use of voice-over performers.

One problem in reaching people who use voice talent is figuring out which companies are likely to need your services. Some possibilities are:

- **Watch local TV and listen to the radio.** Look for local advertisers who are doing commercials with voice-over talent.

- **Call advertisers and ask who coordinates their radio and TV advertising.** Radio stations frequently use station staff for local commercials, and will not charge their advertisers any talent fees. You need to convince these advertisers why they should pay you to do voice-over work when the radio station does it for free. When talking directly to radio advertisers, you need to put yourself in a class above the radio DJ. Some advertisers like the tie-in by using station talent. Other advertisers may simply prefer to spend as little as possible on advertising. You *can* get work from these people, but it will be an educational process to get them to understand the value of using you instead of doing it themselves or using a DJ for their commercials. You may find that they have other uses for voice-over talent for which you would be far more qualified than a DJ.

- **Contact the local chamber of commerce.** Get a list of the largest companies in your area. Many of them will use voice-over performers and some will do in-house production.

- **Check the local newspapers.** Call advertisers that you think might be likely prospects.

- **Use resource directories.** Many cities have a resource directory or a service bureau that can provide you with specific information about businesses in the area. Or, your chamber of commerce may be able to provide this information.

When you contact a nonbroadcast business that has a production unit, start by asking to talk to the creative, promotion, or marketing department. You should talk to a producer or director. Don't ask for advertising or sales, or you may be connected to a sales rep. If you ask for the production department, you may end up talking to someone running an assembly line.

Television stations can be a good source for bookings. They use voice-over for all sorts of projects, many of which are never aired. At a TV station, the production department handles most audio and video production. Some TV stations may even have separate production units for commercials, station promotion, and sales and marketing projects. Start by asking to talk to the production manager, an executive producer, or someone in creative services. You may end up talking to someone in the promotion department, because a promotion producer frequently uses more voice-over talent than anyone else at the station.

Recording studios usually will not be a good source for work, simply because most recording studios specialize in music recording. Usually, those that produce a lot of commercials work with performers hired by an ad agency or client. Some studios do a limited amount of producing and writing, and may book their voice-over talent from a pool of performers they work with regularly. In most cities, there are at least one or two studios that specialize in producing radio commercials. Use good judgment when sending your demo to recording studios. You might be wasting your time, but then, you never know from where your next job might appear. Some studios will recommend voice talent when asked.

Of course, contacting advertising agencies directly is another good way to reach the person who books talent. At an ad agency, the person you want to reach is the in-house agency producer (AP). Some ad agencies may have several in-house producers, and some agencies have account executives (AE) who work double duty as producers. If there is any doubt, ask to speak to the person who books or approves voice-over talent.

There are no hard-and-fast rules here. As you call around, you just need to try to find the correct contact person. Once you connect, use the basic marketing techniques described in this chapter to promote yourself.

KEEPING RECORDS

As an independent businessperson, whether you have an agent or not, you need to keep complete and accurate records of income and business-related expenses. This is not just for your tax records, but also so you have a way of tracking your career as a professional voice-over performer. Consult a tax advisor as to the best way to set up your recordkeeping or refer to some of the many books or computer software on the subject.

You will want to keep records of clients you have worked for, what you did for them, and when you did it. When you get called by a producer you worked for last year, you can avoid undercharging by checking your files to see what your fee was last time. You can also use these records for future promotion and reminder mailings. A simple scheduling book can serve the purpose nicely, or you can even set up a database on your computer. Personal money management computer programs are another excellent way to keep records. Prices range from under $50 to several hundred dollars.

Under the current tax code, just about any expense you have that directly relates to your business can be deducted as a business expense. Even if you work another full-time job, you can still deduct expenses that directly relate to your voice-over business. Depending on your situation, you may want to obtain a business license in your city, and eventually may want to incorporate. Setting up a legitimate business entity may have certain tax advantages. A tax advisor can help you with these decisions.

Voice-Acting Expense Report

Use this expense report on a weekly basis to track round-trip mileage for classes, sessions, errands, and other business-related expenses.

WEEK OF: _____

DATE	DESCRIPTION	START MILEAGE	END MILEAGE	MEALS	OTHER	TOTAL
TOTALS						

ENTERTAINMENT:

DATE	PERSON(S) ENTERTAINED	BUSINESS PURPOSE	PLACE	TOTAL

NOTE: Attach all receipts to this expense report.

The following are some of the things you should keep records of:

- **Income** — Keep separate account categories for income from all sources of income received.
- **Expenses** — The costs of doing business.

  Taxes and deductions: Document anything deducted from your pay, including income taxes, social security taxes, Medicare taxes, state disability taxes, union fees, and any other deductions from a paycheck.

  Demo production: Keep track of payments for studio time, costs and materials, duplication, printing, letterhead, business cards, envelopes, postcards, résumés, and CD labels.

  Telephone: Keep track of phone calls made to prospects or your agent, especially any long-distance charges. You might consider a separate phone line to use exclusively for your business. If you have a cell phone or pager, these costs may be deductible as well.

  Website: The costs of registering your URL (domain name), website hosting, and website design are all deductible expenses.

  Internet access: The portion of your telephone bill, cable bill, or DSL bill that applies to Internet usage may be a deductible expense.

  Transportation: Keep a log book in your car and note the mileage for all travel to and from auditions, sessions, and client meetings. Include parking fees.

  Other business expenses: Keep track of postage, office supplies, office equipment, computer equipment, and other supplies. The IRS tends to view computers as personal equipment, rather than business equipment, unless the use is well documented. Identifying your computer as an "audio workstation" may be a more accurate business description of how your computer is used.

  Classes, workshops, and books: Classes, workshops, and books may be deductible as expenses for continued education and training in your chosen field.

  In-home office: Deducting a portion of your mortgage or rent, and utilities for an in-home office, although legal, may trigger an audit by the IRS. Consult a tax advisor before taking this deduction.

You may want to set up a separate checking account for your voice-over business and perhaps use accounting or money management software on your computer. This can help to keep all the financial aspects of your business in one place. The bottom line is that, as a professional voice actor, you are in business for yourself whether you work another job or not. As a business person it is important that you keep accurate records of your business-related income and expenses.

19

Setting and
Managing Your Fees

Setting Your Talent Fee

The first, and most important thing you need to know about setting and negotiating your fee is that you have value. You can do something your client cannot. You have something to offer that is of value to your client, and your client needs what you have to offer. There is something about *you* that the producer believes is right for his or her project. It could be the way you interpret the copy; it could be a quality in your voice; it could be anything. You are the chosen one! Congratulations! If your client didn't want what you have to offer, they would be talking to someone else. You've got the job! All that's necessary now is to work out the details.

Because you have value, you should be fairly compensated for your work. At first glance you may think that a client's proposed budget for voice talent is very reasonable. But be careful not to rush into accepting voice-over work simply based on what the client is offering without first doing a little research. When the script arrives, you may be unpleasantly surprised by the amount of work you really need to do, and as a result, how low your compensation really is. The details of your work need to be clearly defined before you agree to the job.

The second thing you need to know about setting or negotiating your talent fee is that your time is valuable. You've made a considerable investment of time and energy to get to a place where you are ready to market yourself as a professional voice actor. You've invested in training and workshops, purchased books, and probably spent more than a few dollars to build a home studio. You've built a business that is intended to produce an income that will recover your investment and result in a profit. For many, the goal is to eventually move into voice-over as a full-time career. If you expect to ever see a return on your investment, you need to

247

give some serious consideration to how you will set your talent fees and how you will work with clients. You need to think like a business person.

If you plan to get paid for your voice-over work (and you should), you'll need to learn some negotiating skills. As a voice actor, you are in business for yourself, and fee negotiation is part of doing business. Even if you have representation, you should still work on your negotiating skills if for no other reason than you will be able to discuss your fees and marketing strategies intelligently with your agent. Since part of an agent's job is to handle fee negotiations, the next few sections of this chapter will address setting fees and negotiating techniques for independent voice talent who do not have agent representation.

YOUR HOME STUDIO INVESTMENT

Although the advantages of working from a home studio for voice talent are many, there are a few things many voice artists fail to take into consideration. During training, most voice talent learned their technique through a process of being directed by the instructor or coach. For most home studio sessions, you will be your own director. Therefore, it is imperative that you develop, and master, skills for *self-direction*. You must be able to listen to what you are doing as you perform, and then make immediate adjustments based on your choices and observations.

The primary job of a voice actor is to deliver an effective and believable performance. This can be a challenging task when you are placed in a position where you must multi-task by running the computer software, making sure your recording quality is up to standards, finding the proper character and attitude, and delivering a performance that meets the client's needs. With a home studio, you're a one-person-shop, and you do it all!

Another often over-looked consideration is the investment of time and money in getting started in the business of voice-over. The cost of books, workshops, and demo production can easily add up to several thousand dollars. Add to that the cost of your home office furnishings; business software; office equip; supplies; business development and marketing; the cost of your computer; your audio equipment; Internet connection; website hosting; website design services; graphics design; printing; and telephone lines. It doesn't take much effort to discover the true financial investment you've made in your voice-over business.

EVALUATE THE JOB REQUIREMENTS

Many experienced producers have a very good understanding of what it takes to record a quality voice track, or produce a complete production. They have been through the production process many times and know what it is like to work with voice talent of all levels of experience. There are many others, however, who have no experience working with voice talent, and have absolutely no idea of what is involved in voice recording and audio production. For a voice talent just getting started, the unfortunate reality is that many first-time clients will be inexperienced and uneducated in the world of audio production, voice recording, and voice-over work in general. As a voice actor, it's not your job to educate your client, but that may be something you'll need to do as part of your negotiations.

Another aspect of voice-over reality is that other producers eager to maximize their profits may be willing to take advantage of beginning voice talent. If you don't know your personal worth, and how to negotiate your fee, it could be a very long time before you begin to see any financial success as a voice actor.

Keep in mind, as you talk to prospective clients, that the fee they offer is not necessarily the fee you will actually receive for professional work. Your potential client may have a price in mind, which is based on completely uneducated and unrealistic expectations. You, on the other hand, may have a fee in mind that is considerably different, based on your knowledge of your investment, your understanding of what it will take to complete their job, and your level of skill. The purpose of a negotiation is to arrive at a level of compensation that is mutually agreeable to both parties. The bottom line in this business is "everything is negotiable." If a prospective client is unwilling to negotiate with you regarding your compensation, you may be wise to reconsider working with that individual.

It is not uncommon for clients booking through Internet audition sites to offer a fee that, at first glance, may appear reasonable, but upon closer examination is little more than minimum wage for a considerable amount of specialized work. Here are two examples of how you can evaluate a potential booking to determine if it will be worth your time and energy:

Example #1: The Trial Transcript

> We have a trial transcript of 2,000 pages double spaced that we need read for an audio book. Contains male and female characters - you would read all parts. Pay is $1,000 +

One thousand dollars — not bad for a few hours of recording time, right? But take a closer look: the project is two thousand pages long. A quick calculation will reveal that this producer is offering only $0.50 per page to record this project! Still, $1,000 is a lot of money! Or is it?

Let's say you estimate that an average completed double-spaced page will take about 1 minute to read. Now triple that because you'll need to edit your recordings and it will take at least an additional 2 minutes of editing time for every minute of completed voice track.

We're now up to 6,000 minutes for recording and editing. Divide 6,000 by 60 minutes and you get 100 hours of work to complete this project. And that's assuming everything goes extremely smoothly.

But wait a minute! You take a look at the script, and you discover the trial had something to do with the BioTech Industry and there are lots of technical terms sprinkled throughout the script. Better be safe and add another minute for each page to allow for mistakes and re-takes.

Let's be conservative and estimate that it will take about 5 minutes of recording and production time for every minute of completed voice track. We're now at 10,000 minutes — or roughly 166 hours — or about 4 weeks! At their offering fee of $1,000 you'll be making a total income of about $6.00 per hour. The reality is that it will probably take 6 or 7 minutes for each completed minute, so your actual work may be more and your compensation considerably lower. Even if this client is willing to negotiate a higher talent fee, it will most likely not come even close to anything reasonable for the amount of your effort involved. And don't forget that you won't be able to work on anything else while you're recording this epic project. Although 50 cents per page may be a reasonable price for the client, after factoring in your time, it really isn't a very good deal for you. Is your time — and are you — really worth that little?

This example, based on an actual audition request, shows that you need to have a very clear understanding of what your involvement will be in a project before you can realistically discuss price. Unfortunately, there are some voice talent who only look at the offered fee and don't take the time to properly evaluate projects like this.

Before you can provide a realistic estimate, or discuss your talent fee with a prospective client, you need to know as much as possible about what you will be doing. You need to know the going market rate for comparable work, and you need to place a value on your time and performing abilities.

Example #2: The Short Session

Consider this: You've auditioned for, and landed a voice-over job for a 60-second radio commercial for a mid-sized market. The audition took you 10 minutes to record, edit, and send out. The job will pay $150, and based on the script, you expect it will take you about a half hour to record, edit, and deliver the final project. That works out to $150 for about a half-hour's work, or $300 per hour. Pretty good pay, right? Wrong!

That $150 gig may be the only job that came in that week — or that month. Let's say you spent 10 hours recording and sending out auditions before you got this job, plus another 5 hours on the phone and sending out email. Now, consider what you've spent on phone calls, postage, your website, marketing, training, and everything else that led up to this job.

Just taking into consideration the 15 hours you spent that week, you're looking at a gross income of about $10/hour for that $150 job. But don't forget that the IRS will want part of that income, so you'll actually net something in the neighborhood of $5-$7 dollars/hour for that $150 job.

The point here is that before you can negotiate a reasonable fee for your voice-over work, you must know the value of your time and talent.

THINK LIKE AN ENTREPRENEUR

If you haven't already, start right now thinking of your voice-over work as a business. Your objective as a business owner is to make a profit, and to do that you have to be smart about how you use your time and energy, and how you price your services.

As voice talent, we may never be able to change the way producers think. However, we can control the way we think about what we do, and we can control what we charge for our services. We need to factor in every aspect of our investment in the business before we can arrive at a realistic fee for our services.

When one of my students asks about what they should charge, I suggest they first do some homework. Find out what the best Union voice talent would be paid for the same work. You've spent a lot of time, money, and energy getting yourself to the point where you can market yourself as a professional voice talent who can compete with the best talent out there. You deserve to be fairly compensated for your work. Even if you're booking your first job, that is no reason for you to undercut your worth. If you have the talent and ability to provide the same quality of work as a veteran voice actor, you should be compensated accordingly.

If you establish yourself as "working for cheap," you may get yourself into a rut that could be difficult to get out of later on. At the very least, it will be extremely difficult raising your fee for a client you've already worked for at a "bargain basement rate." In voice-over work, it's always easier to pull you back than to push you out. The same is true with your fees. You can always lower your fees, but it can be extremely difficult to raise them.

SETTING YOUR FEE

If you are a member of AFTRA, SAG, or another performing artists union, your talent fees are set by your union. Through a process of collective bargaining, AFTRA has determined what are considered to be reasonable performance fees for different types of work. These *scale* fees are posted on their website at **www.aftra.com**. These posted talent fees are not negotiable and are considered as the lowest level of compensation. Signatory producers have agreed to pay the posted minimum fees, or a higher fee that might be negotiated by an agent. This is one advantage of being a union member — you know in advance what your base talent fee will be for any given type of work.

If you are nonunion, you will need to negotiate your talent fee with your client at the time you are booked. But before you can begin any sort of realistic negotiation, you need to establish a *fee schedule* that outlines your specific fees for specific types of work.

Only you can determine your personal value as a freelance voice-over performer. The process begins by identifying the type or types of voice-over work you are best suited for. Once you've figured out what you do best, the next step is to identify the market price for comparable voice-over work in those areas. It used to be that you could simply make some phone calls in your city to gauge the current talent fees, but no more. The Internet has changed all that, and your market is now the world. When you submit an audition, you may have no idea what city the producer is in or how your recording will be used, so you may have no real information upon which to base your fee — yet most producers want you to provide a quote for the job you are auditioning. This is why it is important to establish your personal value as a voice talent.

You have made a major investment in developing your business and performing skills to get where you are. If your performing skills are at a level where you can effectively compete with other professional voice talent — and the fact that you are getting calls for work proves that you are — then why would you consider yourself any less professional than they are? Why should you accept a talent fee of anything less than other professional voice talent? *Low-balling*, or under-pricing, your talent fees may get you the job, but does a disservice not only to the voice talent accepting the fee, but to everyone else in the business as well. It tends to lower the bar, which can only result in lower quality work at cheaper prices. To get, and keep, the best clients, you need to provide excellent work at fair and competitive prices — not the "cheapest" price. You may be better off starting with a higher fee and negotiating to an acceptable middle-ground.

One way to set your personal talent fees is to use union scale as a starting point. When negotiating with clients you can, of course, mention that you are nonunion and therefore can be somewhat flexible with your talent fee. By starting at union scale, you are telling your client that you are a professional and there is an industry wide value for your work that needs to be appreciated. Where you go from there is up to you, and it's what the rest of the negotiation process is about. But you've got to start someplace. Here are some considerations as you set your personal talent fees:

- **Your experience and abilities:** How good are you at setting character quickly, finding the right interpretation, seeing the big picture, working as a team player, taking direction, etc? The more skilled you are as a performer, the more likely you will be able to demand a higher fee — especially once you have established a name for yourself and are confident with the work you do.

- **Prior experience and clients:** Have you already done some work for a few satisfied clients? If so, their names may help to establish credibility and thus help to justify a higher fee. Be sure to consider any recent work for inclusion in your demo, but make sure it's good enough in both recording quality and in performance quality.

- **The client's budget:** If you're nonunion freelance voice talent, you'll need to be flexible and decide if you want to work for a minimal fee (which is all that many small or independent producers are willing to pay). Keep in mind that local radio stations will often give away production and voice talent for free just to get an advertiser to buy time on their station, and many independent producers will offer to do the voice work themselves in an effort to save a few bucks. Your challenge as a voice artist is to offer a service that is superior and more effective for the client than what they can get anywhere else.

- **Can you justify your fee?:** This gets back to your abilities. If you market yourself with professional print materials, a dynamite demo, and an awesome website, you had better be able to meet the level of expectations of your client when they book you for a session. If you give the appearance of an experienced pro, but can't deliver, word will spread fast and it may be a long time before you can overcome a negative image. The challenge in setting your fee is to match the fee to your abilities and the market, and still be within the range of other freelance talent, without creating an impression that you will "work cheap" or that you are "overpriced."

- **Consider your market:** Nonunion talent fees vary greatly from market to market. In order to set an appropriate fee for your talent, you'll need to find out what other voice actors are getting paid in your area. In your own city you can call the production department of local radio and TV stations, and advertising agencies to ask what they usually pay for nonunion work. However, if the work is out of your city, you may have no other option than to simply decide if the fee offered by a producer is worth your time and energy.

Your training is of less importance than your abilities as an actor. Of course, you must have a great sounding demo, but you need to have the abilities to match. Don't ever think you know all there is to know about working with voice-over copy. Continue taking classes and workshops, read books, and practice your craft daily.

WHAT ABOUT ALL THAT EQUIPMENT?

You do realize, don't you, that if you are recording professional voice tracks on your computer at home, you have a *home studio*? The operative word here is "studio." OK, so your investment in a computer, a microphone, audio equipment, and acoustical improvements may not amount to the hundreds of thousands of dollars a full-blown recording studio would spend — but the simple fact is this: you've got your own studio!

From a business standpoint, it makes no sense to set a talent fee that does not at least take into consideration the costs of your studio equipment, office supplies, marketing expenses, training, demo production, and so on. Unless you're performing strictly as a hobby, you'll eventually want to recover all those expenses. One way to do this is to create a separate rate for studio time that you charge in addition to your performance fee. If you have production skills and can offer additional production services, this can be a good way to create an additional revenue stream. Separating out your studio rate and talent fee also gives you some additional negotiating leverage because you can always discount one or the other if needed and still have enough income to make some profit.

However, if you are only voice talent with limited production and editing skills, you may not want to take this approach. For you, the best way to factor your investment into your talent fee is to simply keep your fee a bit higher. As nonunion talent, you'll still have room to adjust your fee if necessary. Of course, your performing skills will need to be at a level where you can justify the higher fee. The important thing to remember is that just because you may be new in this business, it doesn't mean you need to charge unrealistically low talent fees.

BUYOUTS

Projects which are, by nature, limited in their distribution and use, such as industrial training programs, marketing videos, documentaries, and audio books can reasonably justify a *buyout* agreement, meaning that the producer pays you a one-time flat fee for your work, and then has the right to do whatever he wants with that recording for as long as he wants — without ever having to pay you another cent.

Take a look at the way AFTRA handles its talent fees and you'll notice that most categories have a time limit for the use of a performance. If a client wants to reuse a performer's work, they pay the talent a new fee called a *residual*.

As a nonunion voice talent, you do <u>not</u> need to (and should not) accept a buyout talent fee for any commercial voice-over work. If you agree to a buyout fee for a radio commercial, there's a very good chance you may be hearing that commercial for years to come. Or a portion of the radio voice track may be used for a television commercial, an in-store message, a telephone message, on a website, or any number of other uses — and you'll never get paid a dime beyond your original buyout talent fee.

If you negotiate a time frame for use of your work, you'll need the terms clearly stated in your agreement, and you'll want to create a follow-up system to remind your client of the agreement. Enforcing a reuse clause may be difficult as a nonunion voice talent, but if you don't include it in your original contract, potentially, you'll be leaving money on the table; and you'll have no legal recourse if or when your client reuses your work.

THE AGREEMENT

Depending on the type of project and it's ultimate use, you may want to negotiate for certain conditions. For example, if the project is to be sold, you might negotiate a clause that includes a residual payment when sales exceed a certain number of units. You may want limitations on how long your voice track can be used for a commercial, or for which kinds of media it can be used. Everything is negotiable!

The manner in which your performance can be used, and the duration of its use, are most definitely negotiable points that you should consider and discuss with your client. There are no hard and fast rules here, nor are there any specifically worded contracts available. The goal is to reach an agreement that is mutually acceptable. Every agreement is unique and you'll need to come up with the appropriate wording to describe the terms and conditions for the use of your recorded material. You'll also want to make sure you include adequate controls for tracking any restrictions, and possible remedies for any violations of the agreement.

Your agreement is a contract, and if the project justifies it, you may want to seek legal advice to make sure you are protected and receive the compensation you deserve.

Negotiating and Getting Paid

The best way to learn how to negotiate is to do it! If you've never done it, the best way to learn how is to study some of the many excellent books on the subject. A search for "negotiating" on **www.amazon.com** will bring up hundreds of books on this subject. Find one that looks good to you, buy it, study it, and begin practicing.

The ultimate purpose of any negotiation is to create an agreement that is acceptable for all parties. For voice talent, this agreement is ideally in the form of a written contract that is signed by both parties prior to the start of any work. It is a written description of the work to be done, the time frame within which it will be done, who is doing it, the conditions for it's use, the agreed-upon compensation, and the terms of payment, among other details.

Unfortunately, a great deal of voice-over work is booked on only a *verbal agreement*, which is only as good as the paper it's written on. When you begin work with only a verbal agreement, you take the chance of not getting paid, or of having serious problems of miscommunication, or worse. Always get your agreement in writing before you begin work.

Ideally, an agreement should be received in the mail, but with tight schedules and deadlines, this often isn't practical. A faxed document will work to get things started and in today's electronic age, most courts of law will accept an email agreement as a legal document provided it contains the sender's email address and name.

There are literally dozens of effective negotiating techniques that can be used to maintain high standards and fees for voice-over work. Here are just a few, with only a very brief explanation of how they might be used:

- **Talk about the project:** No matter what you know about a job when you get the call, it isn't enough. One of the first things you should do in any negotiation is to get more information. Ask as many questions as you can, while avoiding any discussion of your fee. When the subject of your fee comes up, divert the discussion by asking more appropriate questions. This requires extremely good listening skills.

- **Get the client to mention the first number:** This can take some skill, but it can often be achieved by simply engaging the client in a conversation and guiding that conversation to a discussion of what they have paid for voice talent for prior work. If your client is comfortable with you, they will often feel safe in talking about what they have paid in the past. At an appropriate point in your conversation you may ask what their budget is for this project and wait for them to answer.

- **Echo . . . Pause:** This is a technique for maintaining your fee, or perhaps even increasing it. If your client says he does not have a budget, it may be necessary for you to provide some education as to what will be involved for you to do the job. In this way you will be creating a perceived value for your work. The idea is to get your client to tell you how much he is willing to pay for the job in question. Whether he says so, or not, he has a number in mind. It's your job to coax it out of him. Let's say he mentions the number $200. You, in a very thoughtful voice, simply repeat the number as though asking a question to verify that you heard it correctly — then stop talking. Be absolutely silent. It may get uncomfortable, but don't speak. At some point the discomfort will be too great and your client will likely come back with something like ". . . well, we might be able to go to $300." At that point, you repeat the Echo and Pause. Usually by about the third time, your client will say something like ". . . $325 — that's really all we can afford for this project." You can then use your best acting skills as you say ". . . $325! I can do that for $325."

- **Discount this fee for future work at full fee:** During your conversation, you may find that your client is reluctant to discuss any numbers, or that he truly has only a very limited budget for this project. If that is the case, you can tell him that you base your fees on union scale, but that as nonunion talent, you can be flexible with your rates. If the project appears to be something that might result in future work, you might even offer to discount your talent fee with the understanding that you will be paid your regular fee for future work. When you deliver an outstanding product, your chances of having a new long-term client will be very good. This technique can be a bit risky, so make sure you have your agreement in writing.

The desired outcome of any negotiation is to get paid for your work based on the terms of your negotiation. The challenge today is that the Internet has created an international marketplace. It is common to never meet, or even speak to, your client with everything handled through email. Even with a solid agreement in place, you still have no guarantee that you will be paid when you deliver your voice tracks.

GETTING PAID FOR YOUR WORK

As a freelance voice-over performer, you need to protect yourself from unscrupulous producers (yes, they are out there). The best way to protect yourself is to use a simple agreement known as a *deal memo*. Even if you are a union member, having a written agreement is a good idea. It protects you and outlines the details of your work. The format for this can be as simple as a brief letter or an invoice, to something more formal, such as a contract for services. Keep it as simple as possible. A complicated, legal-sounding document might scare off a potentially valuable employer.

Preparing your deal memo should be the first thing you do when you book a session. A written agreement is your only proof in the event you need to take legal action to collect any money owed to you, or if your performance is used in a manner that you did not agree to. It's a common practice and should be used whenever possible. Make sure you have a signed agreement in hand before you begin any work.

Getting paperwork out of the way before the work begins is a good way to make sure that the terms of your performance are understood by all parties and that the producer doesn't try to change the agreement after you have done the work. If you are booked early enough, you might want to fax a copy of the agreement to the producer in advance. But you should still plan on having two copies with you when you arrive for the session — the producer is probably not going to bring his copy. Leave one copy for the producer and make sure you have a signed copy before you leave the studio. If you're recording at your home studio, you can do everything via email and fax. Although an email confirming the details of your work may be considered a legal contract by some courts, it is still a good idea to use your own document and get a written signature.

Most voice-over work is due and payable upon delivery, but that usually doesn't mean you walk out of the studio with cash in hand. For many clients, you'll need to send an invoice that states "payable on receipt." Even with that, you may still end up waiting 30 to 90 days before you receive payment. That's just the way some businesses work.

If you don't want to wait to be paid, there are other options available:

- Insist on clients sending a deposit for talent fee and studio time to be paid in advance with the balance to be paid on delivery. If your client doesn't pay as agreed, at least you'll receive a partial payment.

- Ask your client to make payment through an online payment service like **www.paypal.com** or **www.worldpay.com**. You'll need to set up your own account with these services to make it easy for your clients to send their payments.
- Set up a *merchant account* for your business that will allow you to accept credit cards. Most small businesses can have a merchant account, including individuals operating as a sole proprietor.
- Deliver a partial project (75-80%) or deliver a *watermarked* project for approval, and only send a complete, clean copy upon receipt of payment. A *watermark* is a tone, or sound embedded in your audio that effectively makes the recording unusable, but will allow the client to determine if it otherwise meets their needs.

The specific payment arrangements may be different with each client. If you've never worked with a client before, there is no track record upon which to build trust, so it is reasonable to request a deposit or use one of the above techniques for getting paid. It a client is repeat business, it might be reasonable to invoice them with the payment due net 15 days.

Here's how I work with my clients to make sure I get paid: I have a Merchant Account, and I have a stated policy on my website that says I require a valid credit card number at the time of booking to guarantee a session. When booking a session, I take my client's credit card information and run a verification to make sure the card is valid for the amount we've agreed upon. I tell my client that their credit card will <u>not</u> be charged until they have approved my work. When I deliver my watermarked voice tracks, I call my client to verify that they received the recordings, and to ask how they would like to make payment.

Since I already have their credit card number, most clients simply ask me to charge their credit card. As soon as the transaction is processed, their payment is electronically transferred to my bank account. If, for some reason their credit card is rejected (after it was originally verified), or the payment bounces, I have legal recourse and a contract. I have some additional protection in that I don't deliver a clean copy of the work until their payment clears. I have never had a client question this policy, nor have I ever had a problem with a credit card transaction for payment of services. The peace of mind I have in knowing I will be paid for my work makes the discount fees and other minimal charges for maintaining a Merchant Account well worth the price.

Some clients, however, prefer to pay by company check. If they do, I request a *purchase order* number. A PO number is a record of transactions that is kept by the company. I use their PO number as a reference number on my invoice, and my invoice will state "payable upon receipt." If I don't receive payment within a reasonable period of time, I'll call my client to follow-up on the payment. If it appears that they are delaying payment, I can still charge their credit card, since I don't destroy that information until after I have the money in the bank.

My payment policy is clearly stated in the deal memo I send to my client. I've developed a form that includes a lot of information about the client, the work I'll be doing, the delivery method, my talent fee, my studio charges, and anything else that applies to the project. I'll fill out the form during the booking conversation and either fax or email a copy of our agreement for them to sign and return. A faxed or emailed copy is good to confirm the session, but I'll also ask that they mail an original to me. The signed agreement and either their credit card information or a deposit constitutes a confirmation of the booking. With that in hand, I'll start recording and complete my part of the agreement.

The following is an example of a simple deal memo letter. This deal memo includes all the necessary information to confirm the agreement, yet it is presented in a nonthreatening and informal manner. With minor modifications, this letter could be used for either a studio location session or one that you record in your home studio.

Dear Mr. Producer:

Thank you for booking me to be the voice for The Big Store's new radio commercials. As we discussed on the phone today, I will be doing four (4) radio commercials (including tags) for $150 per spot as a limited run 90-day buyout for radio only. If you later decide to rerun the commercials, or use my voice for television spots or other purposes, please call me to arrange for a new session or to modify our agreement.

You have also agreed to provide me with a recording of the final commercials. I'll call you next week to arrange to pick up a CD or you can send an MP3 file to my email address.

As we discussed, I will keep your credit card information on file to guarantee the session.

I will arrive at Great Sound Recording Studios, 7356 Hillard Ave. on Tuesday the 5th for a 10:00 AM session.

For your records, my Social Security Number is 123-45-6789. Please make your check in the amount of $600.00 payable to My Name so that I can pick it up after the session. Should you prefer that I charge your credit card, please let me know so I can bring the proper paperwork with me to the session.

I look forward to working with you on the 5th.

Sincerely,

Some larger companies, such as major radio and TV stations, will not accept or sign a performer's deal memo or contract. These, and other reputable businesses, often have their own procedures for paying talent. You will be asked to provide your social security number and sign their document before you can be paid. If you are not offered a copy, you should request one for your own records in case payment is delayed. You usually will not be paid immediately after your session, but will receive a check in the mail within four to six weeks. If you have representation, this detail will be handled by your agent. However, if you are working freelance, some producers and large companies can take advantage of a 30-day payment agreement by basing the payment terms on 30 working days rather than 30 calendar days. This can result in your payment arriving long after you expected it. If you have not received your payment by the agreed upon time, it is up to you to call your client and gently remind them.

Another common problem with working freelance is that you can do a session today and be called back for changes tomorrow, but unless you are redoing the entire spot, the producer may expect you to do the pick-up session for free. If you don't like working for free, you should consider including this contingency in your deal memo.

When you are called back to fix a problem, the callback session is technically a new recording session. As a union performer, the producer must pay you an additional fee to return to the studio. As a freelance voice actor, it is up to you to negotiate your fee for the second session or provide for this contingency in your original agreement. Unless the problem was your fault, you should be paid for the follow-up session. The producer must be made to understand that you are a professional and that your time is valuable. You are taking time away from other activities to help fix their problem and you are entitled to fair compensation. A good producer knows this and expects to pay you for the additional work.

If you didn't include pick-up sessions in your original agreement, try to find out what needs to be fixed before you begin talking about how much you should be paid for the new session. If you are redoing most of the copy, you might want to ask for a fee equal to what you charged the first time. If the fix is simple, you might ask for one-half the original session fee. If you are exceptionally generous, and expect to get a lot of work from the client, you might offer to do the new session for free. If you do negotiate a fee for the follow-up session, make sure you get it in writing in the form of an invoice, a new deal memo, or a copy of their paperwork.

UNION COMPENSATION

By joining AFTRA and working union jobs, you will be assured of reasonable compensation for your talents and protection from unscrupulous producers and advertisers. Your union-sanctioned agent will normally handle negotiations for your work and will sometimes negotiate a fee above scale. Regardless of what you are paid, the agent will only receive 10%, and that amount is usually over and above your fee. With AFTRA the "plus-10" (plus 10%) is automatic. With SAG it must be negotiated, or the 10% agent commission will be taken out of your fee. A performer just starting in the business may make less than scale, but the agent's commission will still be added on top of the performer's fee. The client also contributes to the union's Health and Retirement (AFTRA) and Pension Welfare Fund (SAG). For many voice-over performers, the health and retirement benefits are the primary advantage of being an AFTRA or SAG member.

Residuals were implemented to guarantee that performers are paid for their work as commercials are broadcast. Each airing is considered a separate performance and talent are compensated based on the period of time a commercial is aired. Commercials produced by an AFTRA or SAG signatory have a life span of 8 or 13 weeks. After the original run, if the advertiser reuses the commercial, a new life span begins and the performer's fees, agent commission, and union contributions must be paid again. This happens for every period in which the commercial is used. In radio, residuals begin on the date of the first airing. In television, residuals begin on the date of the recording session, or the "use" date.

If an advertiser is not sure whether the company wants to reuse an existing radio or television commercial, a *holding fee* can be paid. This fee, which is the equivalent of the residual fee, will keep your talents exclusive to that advertiser, and is paid for as long as the spot is held. Once the commercial is reused, residual payments are made just as for the original run. If the advertiser decides the spot has lived its life, your residuals end. At that point, you are free to work for a competing advertiser.

Union recording sessions are divided into several fee categories and specific types of work within each category. For radio and television work, the performer's pay varies depending on the type of work and the market size where the product will be aired. The following is a description of the basic AFTRA performance fee categories. Although some of the details may change from time to time, this will give you an idea of the broad range of work available in the world of voice acting.

- **Session Fee.** The session fee applies to all types of union voice-over work and will vary depending on the type of work you are doing. A session fee is paid for each commercial you record. For radio and TV commercials, an equal amount is paid for each 13-week renewal cycle while in *use* (being rebroadcast) or if the spot is on *hold* (not aired).

  Session fees for dubbing, ADR, and looping are based on a performance of five lines or more, and residuals are paid based on each airing of the TV program.

  Animation voice work is paid for individual programs or segments over ten minutes in length. Up to three voices may be used per program under one session fee. An additional session fee applies for each additional group of three voices, plus an additional 10% is paid for the third voice in each group of three voices performed.

  For off-camera multimedia, CD-ROM, CDI, and 3DO, a session fee is paid for up to three voices during a 4-hour day for any single interactive platform. Additional voices are paid on a sliding scale and there is a one hour/one voice session fee and an 8-hour day for seven or more voices. Voices used online or as a lift to another program are paid 100% of the original session fee.

  Industrial, educational, and other nonbroadcast narrative session fees are based on the time spent in the studio. A day rate applies for sessions that go beyond one day.

- **Wild Spot Fee.** Paid for unlimited use of a spot in as many cities, for any number of airings, and on as many stations as the client desires. The Wild Spot *use rate* is paid based on the number and size of the cities where the spot is airing.

- **Tags.** A *tag* is defined by AFTRA as an incomplete thought or sentence, which signifies a change of name, date, or time. A tag can occur in the body of a radio or television commercial, but is usually found at the end. For radio, each tag is paid a separate fee.

- **Demos.** "Copy tests" for nonair use, paid slightly less than a spot fee. An advertiser might produce a demo for a commercial to be used in market research or for testing an advertising concept. If upgraded for use on radio or TV, the appropriate *use fee* applies.

- **Use Fee.** This fee begins when a commercial airs. Voice-over performers for national TV spots earn an additional fee every time the commercial airs. A standard of 13 weeks is considered a normal *time-buy* that dictates residual payments.

PRODUCT IDENTIFICATION

Radio and television commercials are unique in that they both create an association between the performer and the product. This is most common when an advertiser uses a celebrity spokesperson to promote their product. The viewing audience associates the performer with the product, and the advertiser gains a tremendous amount of credibility.

Product identification can, however, result in some serious conflicts, usually for spots airing in the same market. For example, if you performed the voice-over on a national television commercial for a major furniture store, you may not be able to do voice-over work for a local radio commercial for a competing furniture store. You will need to make sure both spots are not airing in the same market, even though one is for radio and the other is for TV. Conflicts are not a common problem, but they do occur from time to time and usually with union talent. As usual, if you have any questions, the best thing to do is to call your union office.

LIMITED RELEASE PRODUCTIONS

Many projects are never broadcast, such as in-house sales presentations, training tapes, programs intended for commercial sale, and point-of-purchase playback. For most of these projects, performers are paid a one-time-only session *buyout* fee with no residuals. These projects usually have no identification of the performer with the product or service in the mind of the audience, and therefore present little possibility of creating any conflict.

20

Auditions

Auditions may seem frustrating and nerve-wracking, but they are an essential part of the voice-over business. Without auditions, it would be very difficult for performers to get exposure to producers and ad agency talent buyers.

If you are a union performer, there are specific rules regarding compensation for auditions and callbacks. I know of some high-priced voice performers who demand $1,000 for an unsupervised and undirected audition. This is an extreme case, but it makes the point that if you are very good and in demand, you will be paid what you are worth.

The Audition Process

Over the past several years, the audition process has changed from one where the voice talent would go to a studio or other site for a live audition, to one where, more and more often, the talent will now audition via the Internet or email by recording their audition in their home studio.

No matter how it's done, the audition process is still the most efficient way a producer or advertiser has of choosing the best performer for a project. The process actually begins when the copy for a project is first written. Quite often a script is written with a particular attitude in mind, and sometimes even with a specific performer in mind.

Once a script is written, copies are sent out to talent agents, casting directors, and online audition services. Specific performers or character types may be requested for an audition, and in some cases voice-over talent are cast directly from a demo or prior work.

Talent agents and casting directors will select performers from their talent pool who they feel will work best for the project being submitted. If a specific voice actor is requested, the talent agent will attempt to book that performer. You, the *talent*, are then called and scheduled for an audition.

If you are just starting out, you probably don't have an agent. So, chances are you will get the audition call from one of your contacts, through classes, recommendations, friends, networking, or sending out your demo. You may receive the call several days in advance, the day before, or even the day of an audition.

ON-SITE LIVE AUDITIONS

On-site live auditions can be held anywhere. Some ad agencies have a recording booth for handling voice auditions. Sometimes auditions are held at a recording studio, the client's office, a radio or TV station, or even at a hotel conference room. In Los Angeles, many of the talent agents ask their talent to record auditions at the agency. In this way the agent has some degree of control over the quality of the audition for the talent they are representing.

You will be given a time and location for your audition, but usually you will not be asked when you are available, although you often can arrange a mutually agreeable time. Auditions are generally scheduled over one or two days, every 10 to 20 minutes and, depending on the scope of the project, there may be dozens of performers auditioning for the same roles.

You may or may not be told something about the project, and you may or may not receive the copy ahead of time. I've actually done auditions while on my cell phone after the casting person dictated the copy.

Once scheduled for an audition it is your responsibility to arrive at, or prior to, your scheduled time, prepared to perform. Only if you absolutely cannot make the scheduled appointment should you call the casting agent to let him or her know. The agent may, or may not, be able to reschedule you.

In this day of electronic communication, a variety of other types of auditions are becoming popular. You might receive a script by email or fax with instructions to call a phone number to leave your audition. Or, if you have your own recording equipment, you might be asked to record your audition and email it as an MP3 file.

ONLINE AUDITIONS

The Internet has spawned a number of specialized websites that exist for the sole purpose of providing talent buyers the opportunity to reach hundreds of voice talent for auditions, and talent the opportunity to audition for hundreds of talent buyers.

There are three types of websites where voice talent can post their information and demos in the search for voice-over work. The first is a website operated by an Internet talent agent. To be listed on these sites, a voice actor must be accepted by the talent agency for representation. The submission process here is the same as for any other talent agent. Online talent agents do not charge a fee to be listed, but they will take a commission for any work they obtain for the talent they represent. In other words, they operate as any other talent agent — it's just that their talent pool is spread across the country (or around the world.)

The second is a free listing site that will usually offer to post the talent's name, a brief description of the talent's services, and a link to the talent's own website. As with most things in life, you get what you pay for, so these free listing sites are often not very well promoted and don't result in much work — if any. The real benefit of listing on these free sites is not in the listing, because there simply won't be that may people visiting the site. The benefit is the fact that Internet search engines are constantly scanning websites to catalog names and links. The more frequently your name is found by these search engines, the easier it will be for someone to find you.

The third type of listing website is one where voice talent can receive requests to submit auditions for a fee. These sites are very clear in stating that they do not act as a talent agent, but instead, serve as an intermediary between the voice-over talent and those seeking voice-over performers. They do not take a commission for work obtained by the talent, but they do charge a membership fee to gain access to audition requests. As long as they do not take a commission, they are operating within the law. However, occasionally one of these sites will pop up that will charge a membership fee to be listed, and will also claim to work as an agent, thus taking a commission from any work obtained for a member. This method of charging the talent twice is known as *double-dipping*, and is illegal in most states. Owners of these sites will argue that the membership fee they charge is in reality a marketing fee to offset costs of operating the website. However, marketing their talent is a cost of doing business for an agent, and the fact remains that if they take a commission, they may be seen as charging a fee for representation, and that is illegal in the US. Legitimate Internet talent agents do not charge a fee for representation or to be posted on their website.

The vast majority of membership audition websites are legitimate, do not act as a talent agent, and truly do their keep their promise to market and promote the website (and thus the talent) to producers, ad agencies, and other talent buyers. One of the largest, and most successful voice-over membership sites is **www.voice123.com**. One of the reasons Voice123.com has become so successful is their ability to adjust their business model to meet the needs of their members by upgrading their standards, educating both their members and producers seeking voice talent, and by developing systems for providing qualified auditions in a variety of ways.

There are more than 25 membership sites that provide voice-over auditions. A comprehensive list is maintained at **www.voiceacting.com**. On most of these sites a voice actor can, as part of their membership, receive a personalized web page with their bio, performing styles, and several demos ready to be heard. Members also receive a continuous stream of audition requests. The web page is a huge benefit for a beginner who doesn't have a site of their own. A website is a powerful marketing tool, and this feature alone may make a membership worth the price. Established professionals, however, will almost always have their own website, so this feature is not of much value to them.

Another benefit for beginning voice talent is the constant stream of audition requests. Each audition is an opportunity to practice performing skills and experiment with voice-over technique with real-world copy without risking anything. For this reason alone, it can be well worth the membership fee just to get access to a wide variety of scripts. Experienced voice-over performers don't need the practice, and dealing with the vast number of unqualified auditions that come in can be very time consuming.

Although most online audition sites truly have the best interests of their members in mind, there are some that seem to cater to the talent buyers who do not pay for the service, rather than to their voice talent members who pay a fee to receive audition requests. This has created a great deal of controversy in the voice-over community primarily because of the low-end, entry-level quality of the producers, copy, and talent fees.

Some audition requests are submitted by experienced producers who know what it takes to be a qualified voice actor; and who appreciate the time, energy, and money that a serious voice talent has spent developing their skills and business. Their audition requests are clear, specific, and informative. They know what the work will entail, what it is worth, and they offer a reasonable fee, expecting professional work.

Then there are the talent buyers who don't know what they're doing, or who simply want the most work for the lowest price. These producers do not appear to have even the slightest comprehension of what it takes to create a voice-over performance that will actually get the desired results. Their auditions are often fragmented, incomplete, or excessively demanding and unrealistic. Here's an example of a typical "low-ball" audition request:

> I need this VO done ASAP. My script is only about a page, so it shouldn't take longer than about 10 or 15 minutes. What you send should be finished with the VO, music, and sound effects tracks. If this works out, I'll have a lot more work for you. I would prefer if you do the spot spec. I will pay on completion, just prior to delivery. I have a budget in mind for this, but I'd like you to send me your prices so I know who will work within my budget range.

One of the major problems with audition requests like this is that the talent buyer is obviously looking for the lowest price he can get for a lot of work. This places the auditioning voice actor in a position of trying to come up with the lowest bid for the best performance, which can only serve to lower the voice actor's credibility. This producer is probably inexperienced and knows very little, if anything, about what it takes to record a high-quality voice-over performance, let alone one that has music and sound effects. Another aspect of these sites is that there may be several thousand members, many of whom are receiving the same audition request. This means that a producer could receive hundreds of auditions from voice talent at every level of experience.

One of my students submitted an audition through one of these member sites and was awarded a job to provide the voice-over work for a radio commercial. It was only after she was hired, and had committed to a fee, that the producer told her they also needed music and sound effects for a completely produced commercial. She was not prepared for this, she is not a production engineer, and she did not have access to the music and sound effects libraries she needed. Yet, she was under contract to provide her services, and because she was eager to please her new client, she was placed in the very uncomfortable position of having to deliver a complex job for a minimal fee. Had she only recorded and delivered the voice track that she had originally agreed to provide, she considered her compensation would have been adequate, because this was one of her first jobs. However, by the time she completed the production, she had put in many hours more than necessary and had to spend her own money for production elements, all of which resulted in her actual compensation equaling far less than minimum wage. Her mistake was that she agreed to the additional demands of the client, and did not have a clear agreement about what she would provide. At her choice, she will never work with that client again.

Many experienced voice talent have commented that it appears as though some of these website operators do not screen the audition requests, and that they provide no education or training to those seeking voice-over talent or to their voice talent members. Although the site operators may truly be attempting to serve their paid members, the outward appearance is that they really don't care — or worse, that they care more about the producers than those paying for the audition service.

Some membership audition sites actually put auditioning members in a bidding war by requiring the members to state what they would charge for their work, often without having enough information from which to make an intelligent estimate. The result of this is that the experienced voice talent will not submit auditions, and the beginning voice talent end up low-balling their talent fees to unrealistically low levels. This does a disservice to everyone concerned. The talent are not fairly compensated for their work, and the client ends up receiving a voice track that, although it might fit his budget, is less than ideal or effective.

Internet audition websites can, however, be a useful resource and a valuable tool for obtaining work for both beginners and professionals. It may take some time, but it is quite possible to land a single job that could pay for several years of membership. If you're performing skills are good enough; if your recording quality meets the standards of the producer; if your talent fee is comfortable for both you and the producer; and if you don't mind submitting at least 40 auditions before you get a good lead, joining a membership audition website may be a good choice for developing your skills and marketing your talent.

Auditioning From Your Home Studio

The advent of home studios for recording voice-over has made it easy to provide high-quality auditions on a moment's notice. The key to a great sounding audition from your home studio is in two parts: 1) your studio design and equipment, and 2) your performing skills.

If your studio isn't designed properly, your audition recordings may contain excessive room reverberation or unwanted outside noise. These must be addressed because there is always the possibility that you maybe expected to deliver a high-quality voice track if you get the job. Many voice talent believe that the sound quality of an audition recording is not important because producers are using the audition only to hear how you interpret their script.

I disagree. You have only one chance to make a good first impression. Most auditions will be the first time a producer will experience what you sound like and your performing abilities. If your audition is full of room echo or there's a lawnmower or baby crying in the background, their first impression of you may be considerably less than desirable. If you have given so little care to the quality of your audition, should a producer reasonably expect anything more from your work if they hire you? Think of each audition as a customized demo.

To submit auditions that stand a chance of getting you work, you must know how to properly use your equipment, you must know how to work the microphone (mic technique), you must know how to deal with adverse noise conditions, and you must know what you are doing as a performer. In short, you must know how to produce a "killer" audition.

Let's assume you've designed your home studio so the room is quiet and functional. And let's assume you know your equipment, microphone technique, how to operate your computer, and your performing skills are at a level where you feel you can effectively compete with other professional voice talent. With all that in place you've just recorded what you consider to be a great audition for a script that fits you perfectly. Now what?

The first thing you need to know is that just because you think a script is a perfect match for you, it doesn't mean your performance is what the producer is looking for. All you can do for any audition is to perform to the best of your abilities, using what you consider to be the best choices for your performance. Then, let it go.

Most talent buyers request auditions be sent as MP3 files without any production, music, or effects. In other words, they want to hear only your *dry voice* at the best possible quality. For most auditions, you don't have enough information and simply don't know what the producer is looking for. You are effectively second-guessing the producer in an attempt to come up with a performance that you think will meet their needs. Sometimes, they don't really know what they're listening for, so it may be worth sending two, or at most three, different interpretations of their script.

One of the most important things to keep in mind when sending out an audition from your home studio is to follow the audition instructions to the letter, especially if the audition request came from a talent agent. If you are asked to *slate*, or identify, your audition in a certain way, do it! If you are asked to name your MP3 file a certain way, name it that way. If you are asked to send only one track, don't send two. If you are asked to send your MP3 file at a specific sample rate, you had better know how to do it. If you are asked to upload your audition to an FTP website, don't email it. Producers want to know that you have the ability to follow their instructions and take their direction. There may be a specific reason for some of their requests, they may simply be a very controlling producer, or they may be testing you. Read audition instructions carefully, and follow them. If you don't, there's an excellent chance your audition will be never be heard.

So, you've followed all the instructions and you've sent out a very good dry voice track recording as your audition. At this point, you don't really know who you're sending your audition to, and you certainly don't have any sort of agreement for compensation should you be chosen for the job. If you've sent out a clean recording, the only thing preventing a producer from using your work without telling you is their personal morals and ethics. The vast majority of producers maintain ethical standards and will not use a performer's work without compensation. But there are those unscrupulous producers who will take advantage of a situation. How can you protect yourself so your work will not be used without compensation?

There are several ways to do this. One is to simply send only a partial performance as your audition, leaving out a few critical lines. This makes your recording effectively useless for a production, but still provides a good representation of what you can do and the quality of your work. Another approach is to use a *watermark* or drop out the audio at certain key words, again for the purpose of making your audition unusable.

When auditioning from your home studio, you must be prepared and ready to do the work should it come your way.

Preparing for Your Live Audition

You most likely will feel a rush of excitement when you get the call for an audition or you get that email audition that is a perfect fit for your skills. That excitement could quickly turn to panic if you let it. Don't let yourself get caught up in the excitement. Whether you're going out for a live audition, or you're recording in your home studio, focus on the job before you and keep breathing. Approach the audition with a professional commitment to do your best.

If you're auditioning from your home studio, you can take your time and keep recording until you have recorded something you feel comfortable in sending out.

Live on-site auditions are a completely different experience.

WHERE DID THOSE BUTTERFLIES COME FROM?

As soon as you get the call for a live audition, you will probably begin to feel butterflies in your stomach. This is a good time for you to practice some relaxation exercises. You need to prepare yourself mentally and physically for the audition. Just the fact that you were called to audition is a good sign, so keep a positive mental attitude. After all, you have been invited to be there, and the client wants you to succeed.

THE DAY HAS ARRIVED

On the day of the audition, loosen up with some stretches and voice exercises. Dress comfortably, yet professionally. Be careful not to wear clothing or jewelry that will make noise when you are on-mic. If your audition is close to a meal, eat lightly and avoid foods that you know cause problems with your performance.

Plan to arrive at your audition about 15 to 20 minutes before your scheduled time. Make sure you leave enough time to allow for any traffic problems and for parking. If you are not on time, you may arrive too late to read for your part, especially for multiple-voice auditions. When in your car, continue with some warm-up exercises and listen to music that will put you in a positive frame of mind. Sing *loudly* to songs on the radio to loosen up your voice and relax your inhibitions, but don't overdo it. Use your cork.

Always bring several sharpened pencils for making copy notes and changes, and a bottle of water. A briefcase containing your supplies, business cards, and several copies of your demo can add that extra touch of professionalism to your image. Don't plan on giving your demo or business cards to the people you are auditioning for, unless they request them — they already know who you are. These are for other people you might meet whom you did not expect to be there.

Act as if you know what you are doing, even if this is your first audition. Watch others, follow their lead, and keep a positive attitude.

KEEP TRACK OF THINGS

Under current tax laws, any expenses you incur that directly relate to earning income are deductible, including travel expenses to and from auditions and parking fees, whether or not you get the job. It's a good idea to keep a journal with you so that you can itemize your mileage and expenses. You also may want to keep a record of auditions you are sent on, who the casting people are, where the audition was held, and how you felt about it. You might include names, addresses, and phone numbers to add to your follow-up mailing list.

What to Expect at a Live Audition

When you arrive at the audition, you may find several other performers already there. Also, you may find that several auditions are being conducted at the same time, with different copy for a variety of projects. Find the correct audition and pick up your copy. If the audition is for a large account, someone may be "checking-in" the scheduled performers. In most cases, there will simply be a sign-in sheet at the door and a pile of scripts. Once signed in, you are considered available to audition and may be called at any time. If you are early and want to take some time to study the copy, wait a few minutes before signing in.

In many cases, you can expect to see the copy for the first time only after you have arrived at the audition site. However with email, fax, and online casting services, it is becoming more and more common for audition scripts to be delivered to the talent ahead of time. On some occasions, for reasons only the producer can understand, you will have to wait until you are *in* the booth before you know what you are doing. I've even heard of auditions where there is no formal script and the performers are simply asked to improvise on lines or props provided by the producer. Fortunately, this is rare, but it does happen.

BE PREPARED TO WAIT

Even if the audition starts on schedule, chances are that within a short time, the producers will be running late. Have something to read or do while you wait for your turn at the mic. Stay relaxed and calm, and keep breathing. This is a good opportunity to get to know some of the other performers who are there, if they are willing to talk to you. Many performers prefer to keep to themselves at an audition in order to stay focused or prepare themselves. Always respect the other people who are auditioning. You may end up working with them some day. If the opportunity arises to get to know someone new, it might be in your best interest to take advantage of it.

Remember, networking can be a valuable tool — it's often not what you know, but who you know that gets you work. Even though these people may be your direct competition, you may make a connection for future jobs that would have otherwise passed you by.

If the copy is for a dialogue spot, you may find another performer willing to *run lines*, or practice the copy with you. This can be an advantage for both of you, even if you do not do the audition together. However, be aware that many performers prefer to keep to themselves before an audition and sometimes interaction with the competition can be distracting.

EXPECT TO BE NERVOUS

When you first enter a studio, you will probably be nervous. This is only natural, but it is something you need to control. You must be able to convert your nervous energy into productive energy for your performance. Focus on your acting rather than on the words in the script. Allow a loving and long breath deep down through your body to center yourself and focus your vocal awareness. Chapter 5, Using Your Instrument, explains how to do this.

You know you are nervous and so do the casting people. Don't waste time trying to suppress or conceal your nervousness. Breathe through it and focus on converting the nervous energy into positive energy.

EXPECT TO BE TREATED LIKE JUST ANOTHER VOICE

At most auditions, the people there really want you to be the right person for the job. However, if the audition is for a major account in a major city, expect the possibility of being treated rudely by people who just don't care and are trying to rush as many performers through the audition as possible in a limited amount of time. If anything other than this happens, consider yourself lucky.

PREPARE YOURSELF

Once you get your copy, use your waiting time for woodshedding: to study it for your character, key words, target audience, and for anything that is unclear — especially words you don't understand or don't know how to pronounce. Try to get a feel for what they are looking for. What attitude? What sort of delivery? Most of the time, your choices will be clear. Sometimes, there will be a character description on the copy, or some notes as to what the producers are after. Note the important words or phrases, the advertiser and product name, where to add drama or emotion, where to pull back. Mark your copy in advance so that you will know what you need to do to achieve the delivery you want. Read the copy out loud and time yourself. Don't rehearse the copy silently by merely reading and saying the words in your mind. In order to get an accurate timing and delivery, you must vocalize the copy. Make sure you know how you will deliver the copy in the allotted time.

Be careful not to overanalyze. Read the copy enough times to become familiar with it and know what you are doing, and then put it aside. Overanalyzing can cause you to lose your spontaneity. Decide on the initial choices for your performance, and commit to them. But be prepared to give several different variations. Also, be prepared for the director to ask for something completely opposite of what you came up with.

Auditions for a TV spot may or may not have a storyboard available. This may be attached to the script, or posted on a wall. It may be legible or it may be a poor copy. A *storyboard* is a series of drawings, similar to a cartoon strip, that describes the visual elements of a TV commercial or film that correspond to the copy. If there is a storyboard for your audition, study it thoroughly. Instead of a storyboard, many TV-commercial scripts have a description of the visuals on the left side of the page with the voice-over copy on the right side. The storyboard or visual description is the best tool you have to gain an understanding of a video or film project. If you only focus on the words in the script, you will be overlooking valuable information that could give you the inspiration you need to create the performance that gets you the job.

MAKE A GOOD FIRST IMPRESSION

Greet the producer or host, introduce yourself, shake hands, be spontaneous, be sincere, and be friendly. If you are auditioning near the end of a long day, the people in the room may not be in the best of moods. You still need to be friendly and professional as long as you are in that room. Remember, first impressions are important. Your first impression of them might not be very good, but you need to make sure that their first impression of you is as good as possible. Your personality and willingness to meet their needs will go a long way.

Answer any questions the casting producer, agency rep, or engineer ask of you. They will show you where the mic is and let you know when they are ready for you to begin. Do not touch any equipment — especially the mic. Let the engineer or someone from the audition staff handle the equipment, unless you are specifically asked to make an adjustment.

There will probably be a music stand near the microphone. Put your copy here. If there is no stand, you will have to hold the copy, which may restrict your performance if you need to move your arms or body. If headphones are available, put them on — this may be the only way you will hear cues and direction from the control room. In some cases, you may be asked to read along with a *scratch track* for timing purposes and you will need the headphones to hear it.

A *scratch track* is a preliminary version of the commercial that is usually produced as a guide for video editing or as a sample for the client. Sometimes, you might be lucky enough to actually have a music track to listen to as you perform. This can be very helpful, because music is often used to help set the mood for a commercial and can provide clues about the target audience. If you don't have anything to work against, you might ask the producer or director to give you an idea of the rhythm and pacing for the project.

Before you start, the engineer or producer will ask you for a *level*. This is so the proper record volume can be set on the equipment. When giving a level, read your copy exactly the way you plan to when you perform the audition. Many people make the mistake of just saying their name or counting 1, 2, 3, . . , or speaking in a softer voice than when they read for the audition. It is important to give the engineer an accurate level, or your recording may be distorted. Use this as an opportunity to rehearse your performance.

MAKE THE COPY YOUR OWN

Your best bet for getting a job from an audition is to discover the character in the copy and allow that character to be revealed through your performance. Play with the words that are written! Have fun with it! Put your personal spin on the copy! Do not change words, but rather add your own unique twist to the delivery. Don't focus on technique or over-analyze the script. Use the skills of voice acting you have mastered to make the copy your own. If they want something else, they will tell you.

Making the copy your own is an acquired acting skill. It may take you a while to find your unique personality traits, but the search will be worthwhile. Chapter 10, The Character in the Copy, discusses this aspect of voice-over work.

INTRODUCE YOURSELF WITH A SLATE AND DO YOUR BEST

You will have only a few moments to deliver your best performance. Remember, you are auditioning as a professional, and those holding the audition expect a certain level of competency. When asked to begin, start by slating your name, then perform as you have planned.

To *slate*, clearly give both your first and last name, your agent (or contact info), and the title of your audition. You may be asked to give your slate in a specific order or to add additional information. The following is a typical audition slate:

> "Hi, my name is Reina Bolles. My agent is Cameron Ross and I'm reading for Toasty Magic Squares."

There are two schools of thought on slates: One is to slate with your natural voice. The other is to slate in character. In most cases, slating in your natural voice will be like a second audition by giving the casting person a taste of who you really are and what your voice is like. This may actually result in a future booking based only on your slate.

After your slate, wait a few beats as you prepare yourself mentally with a visualization of the scene, and physically with a good diaphragmatic breath, then begin your performance. Don't just jump in and start reading.

You may, or may not, receive direction or coaching from the casting person. If you are given direction, it may be completely different from your interpretation of the copy. You may be asked to give several different reads, and you need to be flexible enough to give the producer what he or she wants, regardless of whether you think it is the right way. You may, or may not, be able to ask questions. It depends entirely on the producer.

Don't let yourself get distracted by the people in the room. There may be one, two, or three up to several people in attendance. Focus on your performance and don't worry about the people in the room.

Many auditions are simply intended to narrow down possible voices and the performance is secondary. The copy used in some auditions may be an early draft, while other auditions may provide a final script. Either way, you are expected to perform to the best of your abilities. Do your best interpretation first, and let the producer ask for changes after that. It may be that your interpretation gives the producer an idea he or she had not thought of, which could be the detail that gets you the job.

Offering your opinions is usually not a good idea at an audition, but it is something you can do if it feels appropriate. Some producers may be open to suggestions or a different interpretation, while others are totally set in their ways. If the producer is not open to it, he or she will tell you. These are not shy people. At other times, the audition producer will be doing little more than simply giving slate instructions and recording your performance.

The casting person will let you know when they have what they want. Two or three reads of the copy may be all the opportunity you have to do your best work. They may, or may not, play back your audition before you leave — usually not. If you do get a playback, this is a good opportunity for you to study your performance. Do not ask if you can do another take unless you honestly believe you can do a much better performance, or unless the producer asks if you can do something different. When you are done, thank them, and then leave. Your audition is over. If you like, take the script with you, unless you are asked to return it.

After the Audition

After an audition, and if this is something you have already discussed with your agent, you can call and let him or her know how it went. Most of the time, though, you will simply wait for a call from your agent. If you do not hear anything within 72 hours, you can safely assume that you did not get the job. As a general rule, agents call only if you get the booking or are requested for a callback.

While you are waiting for that call from your agent, don't allow yourself to become worried about whether or not you will get the job. Write your follow-up letter and continue doing what you usually do. Remember that voice acting is a numbers game, and that if you don't get this job, there is another opportunity coming just down the road.

WHEN THE ACTORS ARE GONE

At the end of the day, the audition staff takes all the auditions and returns to their office. There, they listen to the recordings and narrow down the candidates. They may choose the voice they want right away, or they may decide to do a second audition — called a *callback* — to further narrow the candidates. The audition producer will contact the appropriate talent agents to book talent for a session or callback, or may call independent performers directly. Voice-over audition callbacks are fairly rare, but when they occur, they are usually for a major regional or national account.

If you are scheduled for a callback, you may find there is less pressure and the attitude of the people involved may have changed a bit. At a callback, the producer may say that they really liked what you did on take 3 of the first audition. Chances are, unless they have a recording of that audition to play for you, or unless you have an exceptionally good memory, you will not remember what you did on take 3, or any of the takes for that matter. When this happens, all you can do is go for your best interpretation of the copy (which probably changed since the original audition), and use any direction from the producer to guide you.

The simple fact that you are called back for a second audition shows that there is something about your performance that the producer likes. Try to find out what it was that got you the callback. Do whatever you can to stay on the producer's good side and make friends. If for some reason you do not get this job, the producer may remember you next week or next month when another voice-over performer is needed for another project.

After the callback, the audition staff once again takes their collection of auditions (much smaller this time), and returns to their office. This cycle may be repeated several times until the producer or client is satisfied that the right voice is chosen.

BE GOOD TO YOURSELF

You've done a good job! You have survived your audition. Now you deserve a treat. Take yourself out to lunch, buy that hot new DVD you've been wanting, or simply do something nice for yourself. It doesn't really matter what you do — just do something special.

When you left the audition, you probably came up with dozens of things you could have done differently. You might even feel like going to your car, winding up the windows, and screaming real loud. Second-guessing yourself is self-defeating and counterproductive. Instead of beating yourself up with negatives, do something positive and be good to yourself.

Demos

Not all auditions are held for the purpose of casting a final project. In some cases, you will be auditioning for a demo. *Demos* (or spec spots) are produced by ad agencies as potential commercials to sell an idea to their client. Often, the entire concept of an advertising campaign is changed between the time a demo is produced and production of the final spot.

You may be told that the audition is for a demo at audition, or at some time later. Either way, the recording from your audition normally will not be the recording used for the demo spot. If it is to be used for the demo, you will be compensated for your time at the audition.

AFTRA has a separate rate for demo sessions, which is different from their commercial scale. Demos are usually paid for on a one-time-only fee basis. However, a demo can be upgraded to a commercial if the client decides to use it. In this case, your fee would also be upgraded to the commercial rate. Independent voice actors need to negotiate their own fee for a demo, or let their agent handle it.

Audition Dos, Don'ts, and Common Courtesies

The following are some tips for making your audition an enjoyable and productive experience:

- Do arrange your schedule so that you that you can attend the audition
- Do arrive early — at least 15 to 20 minutes before your audition time
- Do call if you absolutely can't make the audition
- Do be prepared to do your best
- Do be spontaneous, sincere, friendly, and willing to adapt
- Do redirect your nervous energy into constructive performance energy. Keep breathing and focus on performing, not on the words in the script
- Do stay relaxed and confident of your abilities — remember, you were invited to be there
- Do act as if you know what you are doing — don't let on if this is your first audition
- Do make the copy your own — add your personality and individual "spin" to the copy
- Do keep track of your expenses — the IRS requires detailed records
- Do thank the casting agent or producer when you leave
- Do leave a current demo if appropriate — ask the casting person first if it would be appropriate for you to leave a current demo

- Do make a note of names and addresses and add them to your mailing list for holiday cards, reminders, and follow-up
- Do leave quickly and quietly — when your job is done, make a professional exit
- Do treat yourself to something special — it's a gift from you to you for a job well done — whether you get the job or not
- Do your best — remember that the casting person wants you to succeed and wants you to be the person they are looking for
- Don't touch any equipment (anything on the copy stand is OK); let the engineer make adjustments to the microphone
- Don't let them know how nervous you are. Act like the pro you are.
- Don't ever argue with the casting people about their direction or doing the performance the way they want
- Don't apologize if you make a mistake — just ask to start over
- Don't ask the casting agent when they will know who is hired — they won't be able to tell you anyway
- Don't ask if you can call later — they will call you or your agent if they want you for the job or a callback
- Don't ask for advice or a critique of your work — this is not the time or place
- Don't ask if you can audition again — this is your only chance

The Voice-over Survival Kit

As you begin to work voice-over sessions you will find there are certain things you will want to always have with you. Here's a list of some of the items to keep in your "survival kit." Feel free to add more.

- Water
- Pencil (at least one; mechanical pencils are always sharp)
- White-out pen (the bottles can be messy or spill)
- Small photos (of just one person; to help with conversational delivery)
- A small travel pack of tissue
- Throat lozenges
- Dry mouth spray
- Chap stick or lip balm (to treat dry lips)
- A green apple or dry mouth spray (to reduce mouth noise)
- A wine bottle cork (for the articulation warm-up cork exercise)
- Business cards
- Demo CD
- Blank invoice or agreement
- Other items you'll think of later

21

You're Hired!
The Session

Congratulations, you've got the job! Your audition was the first step — and on average, you'll have submitted about 40 auditions for every job you land. The client likes your audition better than anyone else's. You already know the details about the project and they've agreed to hire you at a fee you or your agent has negotiated.

Now, you need to know the details of the session: When does the session start (your *call time)*? Where will the session be recorded, or are you are expected to provide the recordings from your own equipment? If you're going to be recording in your home studio, you may or may not get direction from your client. For the purpose of this chapter, your session will be at a local recording studio in your city. Either way, the process will be basically the same. It's just that if you're recording voice tracks in your own studio, you'll be wearing many hats.

A Journey Through the Creative Process

The recording session is where your voice is recorded and all the pieces of the puzzle are put together to create a final commercial or soundtrack. Besides your voice, the project may include music, sound effects, other voices, recordings of interviews, or other *sound bites*, and digitally processed audio. It is the job of the recording engineer to assemble these various puzzle pieces to form the picture originally created in the mind of the producer or writer. It can be a challenging and time-consuming process.

If you are recording from your personal home studio, you are your own engineer, producer, and director. You may have your client on the phone or on a *phone patch* connection to your audio mixer, but you are ultimately in control of both the recording process and your performance. Doing both can be a challenge, and although the purpose of this book is not about audio production, it is important that you at least have a basic idea of what's happening on the other side of the glass.

Much of the creative process involves a lot of technology and a high level of creativity from the engineer. As a voice-over performer, only a small portion of the recording process involves you. To give you a better idea of how your performance fits within the whole process, the rest of this chapter will be devoted to walking you through a typical production.

THE PRODUCTION PROCESS

It all begins with an idea! That idea is put into words on a script, which may go through many revisions and changes. At some point during the script's development, thoughts turn to casting the roles in the script. In some cases, a role may be written with a specific performer in mind, but this is usually the exception to the rule. To cast the various roles, the producers listen to demos and hold auditions. The audition process (Chapter 20) narrows the playing field to select the most appropriate voice talent for the project at hand. If your voice is right for the part, and your demo or audition was heard by the right person, you could be hired for a role.

Be absolutely certain you arrive *before* your scheduled session time. It is much better to be early and have to wait a few minutes than for you to be late and hold up the session. Recording studios book by the hour, and they are not cheap. Basic voice-over session time can be in the range of $100 an hour or more, depending on the studio. Some Hollywood and New York studios book out for $300 to $500 per hour. You do not want to be the person responsible for costing the client more money than necessary.

Time is also of the essence when you are in the studio. Things can happen very fast once you are on-mic and recording begins. You need to be able to deliver your best performance within a few takes. If the producer or director gives you instructions, you need to understand them quickly and adapt your delivery as needed.

If you are working a dialogue script with a performer you have never met before, you both need to be able to give a performance that creates the illusion that your separate characters are spontaneous and natural. This is where your character analysis and acting skills really come into play.

SESSION DELAYS

Studio time is a valuable commodity. The producer will want your best performance as quickly as possible. In reality, it may take a while to get it. A voice-over session for a :60 radio commercial can take as little as 5 minutes to as much as an hour or longer. A long session for a seemingly simple spot can be the result of one or more of the following factors:

- There may be several voices speaking (dialogue or multiple-voice copy), and it may take some time to get the characters right.
- Microphone placement may need to be adjusted or the mic may need to be changed.
- The copy may require major changes or rewrites during the session.
- A session being done to a video playback may require numerous takes to get the timing right.
- There may be technical problems with the equipment.
- The voice tracks may need to be inserted into a rough spot for client approval before the performers can be released.
- The session may be a *phone patch* and he or she may request changes that need to be relayed through the producer or engineer.
- Your client may not know what he or she really wants.
- There may be several would-be directors trying to offer their ideas, creating unnecessary delays.
- The voice-over performer may lack experience, and may not be able to give the producer the desired reading without extensive directing.
- An earlier session may have run overtime, causing all subsequent sessions to start late.

Regardless of how long you are in the studio, you are an employee of the ad agency, producer, or client. Present yourself professionally and remain calm. Above all, do your best to enjoy the experience. Keep breathing, stay relaxed, and keep a positive attitude.

WORKING WITH PRODUCERS, DIRECTORS, WRITERS, AND CLIENTS

A voice-actor friend of mine once described a producer/director as "headphones with an attitude." Regardless of the producer's attitude, you need to be able to perform effectively. You must be able to adapt your character and delivery to give the producer what he or she asks for. And you need to be able to do this quickly with an attitude of cooperation.

It is common for a producer, after doing many takes, to decide to go back to the kind of read you did at the beginning. You need to be able to do it. It is also common for a producer to focus on getting exactly the right inflection for a single word in the copy. You might do 15 or 20 takes on just one sentence or a single word, and then a producer will change his mind and you will have to start all over.

Every producer has a unique technique for directing talent. You must not let a producer frustrate you. Occasionally, you will work for a producer or writer who is incredibly demanding, or simply does not know what he or she wants. When working for this type of person, just do your best and when you are done, leave quietly and politely. When you are alone in your car, with the windows rolled up, you can scream as loud as you like.

There are some producers who operate on a principle of never accepting anything the first time — no matter how good it might be. Your first take might be wonderful — hitting all the key words, getting just the right inflection. Yet, the producer may have you do another 10 takes, looking for something better, all the while drifting off target. When all is said and done, that first good take may be the one that's used.

WHO ARE THOSE PEOPLE?

Some sessions may be crowded with many people deeply involved with the project you are working on. Of course, the studio engineer will be present, and there will usually be someone who is the obvious producer/ director. But the client or storeowner may also be there, as well as his wife, their best friend, the agency rep from their ad agency, the person who wrote the copy, and maybe even an account executive from a radio or TV station. All these people have an opinion about what you are doing, and may want to offer suggestions about what you can do to improve your performance. It's a nice thought, but too many directors will make you crazy.

You may actually find yourself getting direction from more than one person. One of the obvious problems with this is conflicting direction. As a performer, you must choose one person in the control room to whom you will listen for direction and coaching. Most of the time this should be the producer handling the session. However, if it is obvious that the producer cannot control the session, you might choose someone else, if you feel the person is a better director. That will often be the engineer.

Once you have made your choice, you must stick with that person for the duration of the session. Changing directors in mid-session will only make your performance more difficult. Simply focus your attention on the person you picked and direct your questions and thoughts to only that person, mentioning him or her by name when necessary. There's a way of doing this that won't offend anyone.

When someone else presses the talkback button and gives you some direction, you need to bring control back to the person you chose. Allow the interruption to happen, and then refer to your chosen director for confirmation or further comment. After this happens a few times, the would-be director will usually get the hint and let the person in charge handle the session. Future comments will then be routed to you via your chosen producer or director — as they should be.

Types of Sessions, Setups, and Script Formats

There are many different types of voice-over projects, and recording sessions come in all shapes and sizes, with a variety of format styles.

DEMOS

A demo session is for a project that has not yet been sold to the client. It will be a demonstration of what the ad agency is recommending. The client may or may not like it. The ad agency may or may not get the account. A demo is a commercial on spec (speculation).

Mel Blanc, one of the great animation character voices of the 1950s and 1960s, once gave the following definition of working on spec:

> *Working on spec is doing something now for free, on the promise you will be paid more than you are worth later on. Spec is also a small piece of dirt!* (Mel Blanc, from *Visual Radio,* 1972, Southern California Broadcasters Association)

Ad agencies, television stations, and radio stations often do projects on spec when they are attempting to get an advertiser's business. The potential profit from a successful advertising campaign far outweighs the cost of producing a spec commercial — provided the agency lands the account.

Demos will not air (unless they are upgraded by the client), and are paid at a lower scale than regular commercials. In some cases, the demo serves as an audition for the ad agency. They may have several different voice-over performers booked to do the demo session. It is not technically an audition, since completed spots will be produced. Instead, demos are intended to give the advertiser a choice of performers for the final commercial. If the demo is simply upgraded, your agent will be contacted and you will be paid an additional fee. If a separate session is booked, you will be contacted, scheduled, and paid an additional fee.

SCRATCH TRACKS

A *scratch track* is similar to a demo in the sense that it is the preliminary form of a commercial. The major difference is that a scratch track is used as a reference for a commercial that is already in the process of being produced. Scratch tracks are most often used for TV commercials and serve as a reference track for the video editor before the final voice track is recorded. A scratch track will often be voiced by the producer, director, or sometimes the editor or audio engineer, and the music, sound effects, and other elements of the spot may or may not be in their final placement.

As a voice-over performer, you may be providing the original voice for a scratch track, or you may be providing the final voice that replaces an earlier recorded voice used on an already-assembled scratch track. Either way, your job will be to perform as accurately as possible to the existing timing. The process is similar to ADR (Automated Dialogue Replacement) used in the film industry, except that you are working to an audio track instead of lip-syncing to a picture.

Just as for a demo session, your performance for a scratch track may be good enough for use in the final spot. You or your agent will know if the scratch track session is for a demo or a final commercial, and you will be paid accordingly.

REGULAR SESSION

This is a session for production of a final commercial. Many engineers refer to *regular sessions,* to differentiate them from demos, tags, scratch tracks and so on. The only difference between this type of session and all the others is that it is for a complete production.

SESSION SETUPS

There are two basic session setups: *single session* and *group session*. At a *single session*, you are the only person in the studio, but this does not mean you are the only voice that will appear in the final project. Other performers, to be recorded at another time, may be scheduled for different sections of the project, or for the tag. There will be only one microphone, a music stand, a stool, and a pair of headsets. Many recording studios also have monitor speakers in the studio, so you can choose to wear the headset or not. Let the engineer make all adjustments to the mic. You can adjust the stool and music stand to your comfort.

Multiple-voice, or *group sessions*, are often the most fun of all types of sessions simply because of the ensemble. Each performer normally has his or her own mic, music stand, and headset. Depending on the studio, two performers may be set up facing each other, working off the same mic, or on separate mics in different areas of the studio. A group session is like a small play, only without sets. Looping is almost always done as a group session with from a few to a few dozen voice actors in the studio.

SCRIPT FORMATS

There are a variety of script formats used in the business of voice-over. Radio, television, film, multimedia, video game, and corporate scripts all have slight differences. Regardless of the format, all scripts include the words you will be delivering and important clues you can use to uncover the building blocks of any effective performance.

The Session: Step-by-Step

Let's walk through a session from the moment you enter the studio, until you walk out the door. Much of this is review from other parts of this book; however, this will give you a complete picture of a studio session. After reading this section, you will know what to expect and should be able to act as if you have done it all before. Although the studio session process is very consistent, there are many variables that may result in variations on the following scenario. Just "go with the flow" and you will be fine.

Once you enter the studio lobby, your first contact will be the receptionist. Introduce yourself, and tell her which session you are attending. If the studio is in an office building and you paid to park in the building's parking structure, don't forget to ask if the studio validates.

The receptionist will let the producer know you are there. If you don't already have the script, you might be given your copy at this time, or you might have to wait until the producer comes out of the control room. Depending on how the session is going, you may have to wait awhile.

The producer or engineer will come out to get you when they are ready, or the receptionist will let you know that you can go back to the control room. Or, someone might come out to let you know that the session is running late. There are many things that can put a session behind schedule. Remember, this is a hurry-up-and-wait kind of business.

When you enter the control room, introduce yourself to the producer, the engineer, and anyone else you have not yet met. You can be certain that anyone in the control room is important, so be friendly and polite.

If you did not receive the copy earlier, it will be given to you here. This is your last, and sometimes only, opportunity to do a quick "woodshed," or script analysis, set your character and ask any questions you might have about the copy. Get as much information as you need now, because once you are in the studio, you will be expected to perform. Get a good idea of the target audience and correct pronunciation of the product's and client's names. Make notes as to attitude, mood, and key words. Mark your script to map your performance so that you will know what you are doing when you are in the studio. The producer or engineer may want you to read through the copy while in the control room for timing or to go over key points. When the engineer is ready, you will be escorted to the studio.

In the studio, you will usually find a music stand, a stool, and the microphone. Practice good studio etiquette and let the engineer handle any adjustments to the mic. Feel free to adjust the music stand to your comfort. If a stool is there, it is for your convenience, and you may choose not to use it if you feel more comfortable standing. Some studios will give you the option of performing without having to wear headphones, but for most you will need to wear them to hear the director. Find out where the volume control is before you put on your headphones.

Make sure your cell phone is turned off, or better yet, leave it in the control room.

The microphone may have a *pop stopper* in front of it, or it may be covered with a foam *wind screen*. The purpose of both of these devices is to minimize popping sounds caused by your breath hitting the microphone. Popping can be a problem with words containing plosives such as "P," "B," "K," "Q," and "T." If the wind screen needs to be adjusted, let the engineer know. If the mic is properly positioned, the pop screen may not be needed.

When the engineer is ready to record, you will be asked for a *level* or to *read for levels*. He needs to set his audio controls for your voice. Consider this a rehearsal, so perform your lines exactly the way you intend to once recording begins. You may do several reads for levels, none of which will likely be recorded. However, the producer or engineer may give you some direction to get you on the right track once recording begins. Some engineers will record your rehearsals, which occasionally are the best takes.

The engineer will *slate* each take as you go. You will hear all direction and slates in your headphones. This is not the same as slating your name for an audition. The engineer may use an audio slate or identify the project or section you are working on, followed by "take 1," "take 2," and so on. Or he may simply use flag markers inserted into the digital project. Before or after an audio slate, you may receive some additional direction.

Do not begin reading until the engineer has finished his slate and all direction is finished. You will know when you can start by listening for the sound of the control room mic being turned off. If you speak too soon, your first few words might be unusable. Wait a second or two after the slate, get a good supporting breath of air, begin moving, then begin speaking.

As you are reading your lines, the engineer will be watching your levels and listening to the sound of your voice. He will also be keeping a log sheet and will time each take with a stopwatch. He may also be discussing your delivery or possible copy changes with the producer or client.

Common Direction Terms

After each take, expect to receive some direction from the producer. Do not change your attitude or character, unless requested by the producer. Do not comment about things you feel you are doing wrong, or ask how you are doing. Let the producer guide you into the read he or she is after.

Marc Cashman (**www.cashmancommercials.com**) has compiled a list of common direction terms from some of the top voice-over resources available, including prior editions of this book. Here's his list:[1]

Accent it: Emphasize or stress a syllable, word or phrase.

Add life to it: Your reading is flat. One expert advises: *"Give it C.P.R.: Concentration, Punch, Revive it!"*

Add some smile: Simply put, smile when you're reading. It makes you sound friendly and adds more energy to your read.

Be authoritative: Make it sound like you know what you're talking about. Be informative.

Be real: Add sincerity to your read. Similar to *"make it conversational."* Be genuine and true-to-life in your delivery.

Billboard it: Emphasize a word or phrase, most always done with the name of the product or service.

Bring it up / down: Increase or decrease the intensity or volume of your read. This may refer to a specific section or the overall script.

Button it: Put an adlib at the end of a spot.

Color it: Give a script various shades of meaning. Look at a script as a black and white outline of a picture that you have to color, with shading and texture.

Don't sell me: Throw out the "announcer" voice, relax; the read is sounding too hard-sell.

Fade in / fade out: Turning your head toward or away from the microphone as you are speaking, or actually turning your entire body and walking away. This is done to simulate the "approach" or "exit" of the character in the spot.

False start: You begin and make a mistake. You stop, the engineer refers to this as a *false start* and either goes over the first slate or begins a new slate.

Fix it in the mix: What is done in post-production, usually after the talent leaves. This involves fixing levels, editing mouth noises, etc.

Good read: You're getting closer to what they want, but it's not there yet.

Hit the copy points: Emphasize the product/service benefits more.

In the can: All recorded takes. The engineer and producer refer to this as having accomplished all the takes they need to put the spot together.

In the clear: Delivering your line without *stepping* on other actors' lines.

In the pocket: You've given the producer exactly what they want.

Intimate read: Close in on the mic more, speak with more breath, and make believe you're talking into someone's ear.

Keep it fresh: Giving the energy of your first take, even though you may be on your twentieth.

Let's lay one down: Let's start recording.

Less sell / More sell: De-emphasizing/stressing the client name/ benefits.

Let's do a take: The recording of a piece of copy. Each take starts with #1 and ascends until the director has the one(s) they like. Also heard: *Let's lay it/one down.*

Let's get a level: The director or engineer is asking you to speak in the volume you're going to use for the session. Take advantage of this time to rehearse the copy. Any shouts or yelling will require you to turn your head 45-90 degrees away from the mic. If the mic needs to be adjusted, the engineer will come into the booth. Do not move the mic unless instructed to do so.

Make it conversational. Just like it sounds, make your read more natural. Throw out the "announcer" in your read, and take the "read" out of your delivery. If it sounds like you're reading, you won't be believable. Pretend you're telling a story, talking to one person. Believe in what you're saying.

Make it flow: Also heard as: **Smooth it out.** Avoid choppy, staccato reads, unless the character calls for it.

More / less energy: Add more or less excitement to your read. Use your body to either pump yourself up or calm yourself down. Check with the engineer (i.e., do a level) to make sure you are not too loud or soft.

Mouth noise: The pops and clicks made by your mouth, tongue, teeth, saliva and more. Most mouth noises can be digitally excised, but make sure that you don't have excess mouth noise, because too much is an editing nightmare and will affect your work. Water with lemon or pieces of green apple can help reduce or eliminate most mouth noise.

One more time for protection: The director wants you to do exactly what you just did on the previous take. This is similar to "that was perfect, do it again." This gives the director and engineer a bit more selections to play with, should they need them in post-production.

Over the top: Pushing the character into caricature.

Pick it up: Start at a specific place in the copy where you made a mistake, as in: *Pick it up from the top of paragraph two, or Let's do a pick-up at the top of the second block.*

Pick up your cue: Come in faster on a particular line.

Pick up the pace: Pace is the speed at which you read the copy. Read faster, but keep the same character and attitude.

Play with it: Have fun with the copy, change your pace and delivery a bit, try different inflections.

Popping: Noise resulting from hard consonants spoken into the mic. Plosives, which sound like short bursts from a gun, are most evident in consonants like B, K, P, Q and T.

Punch-in: The process of recording your copy at an edit point in real time. In a punch-in, as opposed to a "pick-up," the engineer will play back part of the copy you recorded and expect you to continue reading your copy at a certain point. The director will give you explicit directions as to where in the script you will be "punched in," and you will read along with your pre-recorded track until your punch-in point. From there, you'll continue recording at the same level and tone you originally laid down.

Read against the text: Reading a line with an emotion opposite of what it would normally be read.

Romance it: Also "Warm up the copy." Make it more intimate.

Run it down: Read the entire script for level, time, and one more rehearsal before you start recording.

Shave it by…: Take a specific amount of time off your read. Also heard as "shave a hair." If your read times out at :61, the director might ask you to "shave it by 1.5 seconds."

Skoche more / less: A little bit, just a touch more or less. This can refer to volume, emphasis, inflection, timing, etc.

Split the difference: Do a take that's "between" the last two you just did. For example, if your first take comes out at :58, and your second take comes out at :60, and the director asks you to "split the difference," adjust your pacing so the third take should be in at :59. Or, if your first take is monotone-ish and your second one is very "smiley," and the director asks you to "split the difference," adjust your read so that the third take will be somewhat in between the first two.

Stay in character: Your performance is inconsistent. Whatever character and voice you commit to, you have to maintain from beginning to end, take after take after take. Focus. Be consistent with your character and voice.

Stepping on lines: Starting your line before another actor finishes theirs. Sometimes the director wants actors to "overlap" their lines, or interrupt. Others want each line "in the clear," where there is no overlapping or stepping.

Stretch it / Tighten it: Make it longer/shorter.

Take a beat: Pause for about a second. You may be asked to do this during a specific part of the script, like in between paragraphs, or inside of a sentence or in a music bed. A good sense of comic timing is particularly helpful.

Take it from the top: Recording from the beginning of a script.

That's a buy/keeper: The take that everyone loves—at least the director loves. If the client loves it, then it's accepted.

That was perfect—do it again: An inside joke, but a compliment. Usually the producer wants you to reprise your take "for safety" (i.e., to have another great alternate take).

This is a :15 /:30 /:60: Refers to the exact length of the spot in seconds, also known as a read or take.

Three in a row: Reading the same word, phrase, sentence or tag three times, with variations. Each read should have a slightly different approach, but all should be read in the same amount of time. The engineer will slate three in a row "a, b, and c."

Throw it away: Don't put any emphasis or stress on a certain phrase, or possibly the whole script.

Too much air: Noise resulting from soft consonants spoken into the mic. Most evident in consonants like F, G, H, and W, and word beginnings and endings like CH, PH, SH, & WH.

Under/over: Less or more than the time amount needed. If you were *"under or over"* you need to either shorten or lengthen your delivery and *"bring it in"* to the exact time.

Warm it up a little: Make your delivery more friendly and personal. Whatever makes you feel warm and fuzzy is the feeling you should inject into your delivery.

Woodshed: To practice or rehearse a script, reading out loud. From the old days of theater where actors would rehearse in a wood shed before going on stage.

Wrap: The end — as in "that's a wrap!"

You will hear many other directions. Do your best to perform as the director requests. There is a reason why he or she is asking you to make adjustments, although that reason will sometimes not be clear to you.

One of my favorite directing stories is one that Harlan Hogan tells about a session he once voiced. He had just completed a delivery that the producer said was extremely good, but wasn't quite where he wanted it. In the producer's words, "...that last take was a bit burgundy, I'm looking for something a little more mauve." With direction like that, what could Harlan do? So he delivered the script exactly the way he had just done, and the producer's response was "...now that's what I'm looking for!" Go figure.

Producers usually have an idea of what they want, and may or may not be receptive to your suggestions. Find out what the producer is looking for when you first read the script. Once in the studio, you should be pretty much on track for the entire session. If you get a great idea, or if it appears that the producer is having a hard time making a copy change, by all means speak up. You are part of a team, and part of your job is to help build an effective product. If your idea is not welcome, the producer will tell you.

Recording studio equipment sometimes has a mind of its own. There are times when the engineer may stop you in the middle of a take because of a technical problem, and you may have to wait awhile until it is corrected. Once corrected, you need to be ready to pick up where you left off, with the same character and delivery.

If you left your water in the control room, let the engineer know and it will be brought in for you. If you need to visit the restroom, let them know. If you need a pencil, let them know. If you need *anything*, let them know. Once your position is set in front of the microphone (on-mic), the engineer will prefer that you not leave the studio, or change your position. If your mic position changes, you can sound very different on different takes, which can be a problem for the engineer if he needs to assemble several takes to build the final commercial. This can be a problem when doing long scripts or lots of takes. If you must move off-mic, try to keep your original mic position in mind when you return to the mic.

Keep your volume consistent throughout your session. Changes in dynamics may be useful for certain dramatic effects, but, generally, you will want to keep your voice at a constant volume or in a range that is consistent with your character. If your performance does call for sudden changes in volume, try to make sure they occur at the same place in the copy for each take. This becomes important later on, when the engineer edits different takes together. If your levels are erratic, the changes in volume may become noticeable in the final edit.

You know what the producer wants. You stay in character. Your timing and pacing are perfect. Your enunciation and inflection are on track. Your performance is wonderful. The producer is happy. The engineer is happy. And, most important, the client is happy. That's it! You're done, right?

Not quite.

Wrap It Up

Before leaving the studio, make sure you sign the contract for your services. If you are a union member, the producer will probably have a contract already filled out for you. Read the parts of the contract that apply to your session before signing. If you were booked for one commercial (spot announcement), and the producer had you do three spots plus tags, make sure the changes are made on the contract. Also make sure you call your agent and let her know about the changes. If you are unsure of anything on the contract, call your agent *before* signing the contract.

For union work, send your AFTRA form to the union within 48 hours of the session to avoid any penalties. The union form is the only way AFTRA has of tracking your work, and making sure you are paid in a timely manner. If you are working freelance, make sure you are paid before you leave the studio, or that you have a signed invoice or deal memo — and make certain you have the contact address and phone number of your client. If you have a Merchant Account, you can take a credit card number to be processed, or to hold as a guarantee until your check arrives. You've completed your part of the agreement, and you are entitled to be paid. It's up to you if you agree to have your payment sent to you, but keep in mind that you take a risk of delays or not being paid if you do this.

It's good form to thank the producer, engineer, client, and anyone else involved in the session before you leave. Keep the script for your files, if you like. If you think your performance was especially good, you can ask the producer for a copy of the spot when it is finished. You can ask for a CD but don't be surprised if you only get an MP3 file emailed to you. If the project is a TV commercial, there may be a charge for you to receive a copy. In this digital age, finished commercials are increasingly being distributed to stations via ISDN networks directly from the studio's computer, emailed as MP3 files, uploaded to a website, or sometimes mailed as a one-off CD. One way to ensure that you get a copy is to include a clause to that effect in your agreement. However, even with that, you may find yourself waiting several weeks, or even months, before you get it.

Once your session is over and the paperwork is done, you are free to leave. Your job is done, so don't stick around for the rest of the session or to talk. The producer and engineer have lots of work to do and your presence can cause delays, costing time and money. After you are gone, the process of assembling all the pieces of the puzzle begins. It may take from several hours to several days before the final audio track is complete.

If your session is for a TV commercial, the completed audio will often be sent to a video post-production house where the video will be edited to your track to create a final TV spot. In some cases, just the opposite occurs — the video may have been edited to a scratch track, and the purpose of your session would have been to place your voice-over against the preproduced video. Once mastered, a number of copies are made and distributed to the radio and TV stations scheduled to air the spot.

Follow up your session with a thank-you note to the producer. Thank him or her for good directing or mention something you talked about at the session. Be honest and sincere, but don't overdo it. A simple note or postcard is often all that's necessary to keep you in the mind of the producer or director and get you hired again. If you haven't already, be sure to add their names to your mailing list for future promotions you send out.

---

1 Adapted and compiled by Marc Cashman from the following sources:
  James Alburger—*The Art of Voice-Acting,* Focal Press (1998, 2002).
  Susan Blu and Molly Ann Mullin, *Word of Mouth*, Revised Edition, Pomegranate Press (1996).
  Terri Apple, *Making Money in Voice-Overs,* Lone Eagle Publishing Company (1999).
  Alice Whitfield, *Take It From the Top,* Ring-U-Turkey Press (1992).
  Sandy Thomas, *So You Want to Be a Voice-over Star,* Clubhouse Publishing (1999).
  Terry Berland and Deborah Ouellette, *Breaking into Commercials,* Plume Publishing (1997).
  Chris Douthitt/Tom Wiecks, *Putting Your Mouth Where the Money Is,* Grey Heron Books (1996).
  Chuck Jones, *Making Your Voice Heard,* Back Stage Books (1996).
  Elaine A. Clark, *There's Money Where Your Mouth Is,* Back Stage Books (2000).

22

Tips, Tricks,
and Studio Stories

The world of voice-over is not only a unique area of show-business as a performing craft, but it is also unique in that the people who are professionals in this business are, for the most part, far more supportive and generous than those working in many other areas of show-biz. As with any business, professionals tend to develop their own unique insights as to what works for them and how to become successful. This chapter is a gift from some of the many professionals around the world whom I've come to know over the past few years. Please join me in thanking them for sharing their knowledge, and use this chapter to learn from their experience.

DON LAFONTAINE (Hollywood, CA)
www.donlafontaine.com

Don LaFontaine has perhaps one of the most recognizable voices in the United States. In a career spanning more than 40 years, he has voiced well over 4,000 major motion picture trailers, and he is one of thirteen voice artists who can be heard as the signature voice for national television networks around the world. Don is often credited as being the originator of the "trailer voice sound" and has been called "The King of Voice-overs," and "The Voice of God."

"The" Talent

Many times in my career, I have heard myself referred to as "The Talent." It's a phrase that is commonly used to describe the Voice-over artist, and while it's extremely flattering, it can lead to a very bad place. A place where the VO artists actually believes that they are "The Talent." Don't get me wrong, it's fine to consider yourself "*A*" Talent — if you're working, you undoubtedly are. But so are the other people who worked on the material — the writer, the editor, the producer — these are all talented people also. Remember this — you are simply a *part* of the project. An integral part, undeniably, but to consider your contribution to be greater than anybody else's — even if in reality it is — can be deadly.

You may have heard one of many recordings that exist of (usually high-profile) actors attacking their directors for daring to try to direct them. They have allowed their egos to obscure one basic fact — they are hired to please their *clients*, not *themselves*.

While the vast majority of directors are very capable individuals, without a doubt, as a VO artist, you will, on occasion, be subjected to the wild caprices of some bone-headed, misguided, pompous, untalented hacks who will presume to know more about your business than you do. You will be treated to clichéd line readings that you will be expected to parrot. You will, from time to time, be lead further and further astray from the best interpretation of the copy, and you will, I can guarantee you, become angry and frustrated because of it. My advice is not to react in a negative manner. It is (one of the very few) occupational hazards. Just do the best you can. Feel free to make suggestions, but couch them in terms that make it seem like you're trying to clarify *their* direction. Remember this: Directors come and go, but clients are forever. If you antagonize a director, regardless of how much he or she may deserve your wrath, you could blow an entire account out of the water because of it. All the director has to do is report that you are "difficult to work with," and you could lose any possibility of future work for that client.

Look at it this way; If you were a painter, and you disagreed with the color your client wanted, you'd *suggest*, not *demand* an alternative. If your client disagreed, you'd go ahead and use the color they wanted. The only difference between being a painter and doing voice-overs is, nobody blames the *painter* for the color choice, but *you* can be blamed for a bad read reaching the air, even if it is the result of misdirection. Well, if you have any kind of a career, it's going to happen from time to time. All you can do is try and gently guide your mis-director back to the proper path.

If you can't, suck it up and move on. Your righteous indignation isn't worth losing an account over. If it can be enough for you to know that you've done the best you could, *that's* a real Talent.

BOB JUMP (Norfolk, VA) — CD/27
www.cowboyvoice.com, www.jumpworldwide.com

From the moment I met Bob Jump, I knew there was something very special, unique, and unusual about him. Bob impressed me as a brilliant voice talent with "great pipes," but that was just the start. From his demo I could tell there was a lot of acting experience behind the voice, and a whole lot of creativity and thought that went into each performance. If you've listened to the radio, you've heard Bob at one time or another. He's a national level voice talent with a knack for brilliant marketing.

Be Yourself . . . (or not!)

I had a famous, highly-regarded voice-coach in L.A. tell me to find that one voice — that voice *print* — that was, well, me. I couldn't. Seems I don't know the real me. Maybe, because the real me is a *bunch* of people; each one with his own way of reading a script, his own attitude, his very own way of delivering a "call to action." It could be a deep cowboy voice pitching car products for Armor All; a fifties "Classic Big Voice" selling Subway sandwiches; or perhaps the trusted soft spoken voice of State Farm Insurance.

Holy smoke! Now I know what Sally Field felt like when she filmed Sybill!!

As a voice actor, I don't feel like limiting myself to just that one voice. And why should I? Why would any voice actor not try something so different, so new that not even his own talent agent would recognize him or her?

Can you say Dustin Hoffman in "Tootsie"?

Every day, I challenge myself to a little game of who do I want to be today. And the best way to play is through auditions. Here you have the freedom of not having to worry about always getting it right . . . I mean, after all, *they're auditions!*

Anyway, back to the voice coach who went on to say: "With so many different voices on your demo, you'll confuse the person who is listening to it. He won't get a clear picture of who you are." I disagree; I think people are smarter than that. I believe people come away from my demo thinking I'm going to bring a lot more than just one voice to their campaign. And *that* is what gets you invited *back* to the mic over and over again.

Now here's the proof:

One of the most successful characters I developed a few years ago was a voice and a character called Cowboy Bob. This voice was so different and so distinct I felt it needed to be on its own. From the beginning I realized I had to separate Cowboy Bob as far from Bob Jump as I could. In order to do that, I decided a new and separate website with its own web address was needed. Also, a new and separate demo with its own CD label as well as a new and separate letterhead with stationery and rate sheet would fill the bill. And, most importantly, all of it would be written in easy-going Cowboy Bob lingo.

Here's how this helps:

Rates can be a sensitive issue for many clients. But Cowboy Bob can proudly state on his rate card "Rates lower than a dang snake's belly in the middle of June." Now I honestly don't know what that means, but I can tell you that clients got a chuckle out of that and figured that this Cowboy Bob was a real character with wry, Western charm. And maybe, ol' Cowboy Bob was a little easier to deal with than just some voice-over doing a knockoff of Sam Elliott.

Then, I took the cowboy persona even deeper.

Why not *look* the part? I figured why not dress in cowboy duds and let the clients get a sneak peak. On the website, the stationery, and the CD label, Cowboy Bob poses wearing a cattlemen's coat and ten gallon hat. He's holding his shotgun, sporting a scruffy mustache, and wearing a six-shooter while looking down at a table of whiskey and cards. When it came to the actual presentation (hard product) to be sent via mail or FedEx, however, I needed one more gimmick - something that would really make this presentation memorable and stand out. Then, it hit me — like a shot. Bullet holes . . . right through the letter of greeting and the rate card. The slight smell of gun powder and the shape of a bullet hole was duplicated by using a small cigar the size of a 45-caliber bullet and burned into the parchment in three different areas of the paper. When clients got my demo package with the letter full of bullet holes, the comment was usually "You've got to be kidding — *how* the heck did you do that?" They were intrigued, amused, engaged and most of all, VERY enthusiastic.

The marketing of Cowboy Bob didn't happen overnight — it took a good five years of experimenting and tinkering — not to mention a lot of smokin' those cheap little cigars to create those bullet holes in the parchment. Today, I'm happy to say that that high-priced voice coach was wrong — about me at least. Cowboy Bob, a separate and distinct voice, was just sitting there in a saloon, waiting to be brought to life. Cowboy Bob's overwhelming success showed me that sometimes, just sometimes, you have to throw the dang rule book out the window. (It helps to have a back-up plan though!)

Just punch in number 27 on that new-fangled CD player of yers, or skidaddle over to **www.cowboyvoice.com** to hear Cowboy Bob pitchin' everythin' from blazers to banks.

SUSAN BERKLEY (Englewood Cliffs, NJ)
www.susanberkley.com, www.greatvoice.com

If you've even slightly explored the world of voice-over you've come across Susan Berkley's name. Susan is truly one of the most listened-to voices in America. Why? Because she is one of the voices who says "Thank you for using AT&T" and "Welcome to Citiphone banking." She is the author of *Speak to Influence*, and since 1987 she has trained thousands of people around the world in voice-over and public speaking techniques. Her company, Greatvoice.com specializes in telephone messaging.

Find Your Niche

I got into voice-over via radio. I was on the air for 15 years, and that career culminated with a two year stint on *The Howard Stern Show*. I was his traffic reporter. He called me Susan Bezerkowitz, teased me mercilessly and I never got to do the traffic. But I did become a celebrity. It was fun, but I was broke and exhausted from getting up at 4 AM to do the morning show. Radio pays terribly, there's no job security and the hours stink.

I decided I'd had enough and quit to pursue a full-time voice-over career. Because I was getting into a freelance career, I also started teaching to provide myself a little more financial security. I took classes with everyone I could find in New York, including speech and diction training, so I could perfect my instrument. But unlike many actors, I also became a serious student of marketing and sales. It paid off. Within several months, I had more than doubled what I was making in radio and I had both a thriving voice-over school and a successful voice-over business.

One of the weirdest auditions I ever had was at one of the big Madison Avenue ad agencies for a candy bar. All they wanted me to say was "OOOO. AHHHHH." Competition was fierce. They called in about 20 actresses. I didn't get the job.

Another time I auditioned for the voice of a Mom at a New York City production company. When I got there they said: "No script. We're just looking for voice quality." They pulled a book off the shelf and said "Here. Just read something from this book." The book was Truman Capote's *In Cold Blood*. So in my warmest, friendliest Mom voice I told the story of how a pair of depraved killers committed a brutal murder. I didn't get the job.

I soon discovered that the market wanted me not for the glamorous world of commercial voice-overs, but for the exciting world of . . . phone systems! While I love my customers and am grateful for their support, doing this type of voice-over can be pretty boring and can take lots of patience and stamina. But hey, who cares? I have a wonderful life because of it.

I once did a monster job for IBM. In this application, the engineers were using my voice to create natural sounding computer speech. They needed all the phonemes in the English language in all different inflections. To do this, I had to read tens of thousands of speech snippets. It meant 60 hours in the studio over several months. This was probably one of the most difficult sessions I have ever done. To meet IBM's exacting technical standards, I had to remain motionless while speaking in front of a mic and also wear a larynx mic strapped around my neck.

I've also read all the minutes in the day (1,444) for the time on AT&T, and all the roads and every conceivable traffic condition for the Tampa Bay telephone traffic network.

If you find yourself in one of these marathon sessions, here are some tips: Your voice needs to sound the same from the first prompt to the last. You need a healthy instrument. Take frequent breaks. Try not to read for more than 50 minutes out of every hour. Stay hydrated, of course. But make sure you avoid drinking black or green tea during sessions. These teas can dry out your voice. Warm up your voice before sessions.

For a healthy, strong, beautiful voice, you need to take care of your body and soul. You can't abuse your body and expect not to sound like it. You can't abuse your soul with unloving thoughts and not expect it to come through in the sound of your voice.

Biggest piece of advice? Find a niche and own it. For me it was phone systems. You can't be all things to all people. Most beginners try to go too broad on their demos. Scrap versatility and showcase what you do best.

Best of luck! This is a wonderful way to make a living and I hope you excel.

MARC CASHMAN (Los Angeles, CA)
www.cashmancommercials.com

If you're in Los Angeles, and you want to learn about voice-over for commercials, Marc Cashman is one of the top coaches you will want to work with. He understands both the performance and production sides of voice-over, and has a unique talent for teaching how to find the subtlety and nuance of a performance.

There's Music in Copy

We're all musical, whether or not we sing or play an instrument. Music is all around us. We hum tunes to ourselves all the time. At one time or another most of us have pounded drums, tickled the ivories, sung in a choir, strummed, plucked, blown or wailed. We sing in the shower, we sing in the car. We've sung on Saturday or Sunday morning services, and have followed the notation in the hymnal. It's a rare person with a "tin ear." Even someone who can't carry a tune or dance can understand rhythm. Most of us can tell whether a note is sharp or flat, whether it extends or stops abruptly.

Copy or text is musical. It has a cadence and one or more keys. It has sharps, flats, rests, words that are held, chopped off, high or low, soft or loud, all the same emphases or wild ups and downs, with dynamics and crescendos. Copy usually reads or plays like a story/song, with a beginning, middle and end. Directors sometimes use musical terms to direct voice actors. *Take a beat* means waiting a moment. *Up a key* means raising your pitch a bit. *Staccato* means hitting words crisply and quickly.

But there's one thing that copy doesn't have—a steady beat. Music has a time signature—copy doesn't. We don't talk in a steady beat. In our conversations, we talk fast, then slow; we stammer and stutter. Sometimes our speech is a bit jerky. But that's how we talk! Our job as voice actors is to take written words, lift them off the page and turn them into the cadence of everyday conversation.

Try taking a musical approach to copy and you'll have a better understanding of the music hidden in scripts. Listen to the sound of your voice in playbacks and hear the variation of notes and volume. Most voice actors tend to stay within a middle range of notes, with slight inflections, up or down a note, and maintain a consistent volume. The more breath control you have (from the diaphragm, and with proper posture), the more you'll be able to hit certain notes as you deliver your copy. If you're not delivering a specific phrase the way the director wants, ask them to give you a *line read*. This is how the director hears the phrase to be spoken. Consider this a gift, not an insult. You can't expect to read the director's mind. If you have a good ear, you'll be able to perform the phrase exactly, note for note.

WALLY WINGERT (Hollywood, CA)
www.wallyontheweb.com

Wally has got to be one of the busiest actors in Hollywood! If he's not voicing a commercial, he's on TV shows like *Just Shoot Me*, *Saved by the Bell: The New Class*, and *The Martin Short Show*. Or he's creating any of his dozens of zany character voices for animated films and shows like *Family Guy*, *Invader Zim*, and many others. He's also voiced at least a few hundred video games, sings, and performs in major theatrical productions. Wally is much more than just your average voice-over guy! He may not be a "big name," but he's working . . . a lot! When it comes to succeeding in this business Wally knows what he's talking about.

The Ing's

I realized early in my career that the only rule in voice-over is . . . there are no rules — at all. I was told my demo should only be one and a half minutes. Mine was three minutes. I was told I shouldn't have my photo on my demo. I had my photo on my demo. I unwittingly made my own set of rules. Not necessarily because I was knowingly rebelling against the system. I just listened to what my instincts were telling me and I obeyed them. Nancy Wolfson, who at the time was an agent at Abrams-Rubaloff and Lawrence, appreciated my "unique" approach and we've enjoyed a wonderful working relationship ever since.

One of the first things I knew had to occur in order to cultivate a successful career, was what I call "The Ing's." This includes (but is not limited to) smiling, listening, networking, promoting, branding, and marketing.

SMILING: Always go into the audition with a smile, an effusive attitude, and a kind word. A producer loves nothing more than an enthusiastic talent. Though you may not be right for that particular role, the producer will always remember what a delight you were, and how eager you were to please. I always tell producers "thanks for having me" because I truly am appreciative for their confidence in me and the employment. Oftentimes, I've heard of actors getting work over other actors simply because "they're easy to work with." And as talented as some actors are, sometimes it's just not worth the trouble.

LISTENING: Isn't it funny that all our lives we train ourselves to speak, but never really train ourselves to listen? Learning to take direction well . . . to LISTEN . . . is an important element. Being able to take what the director is telling you and translate that into results is very important. If you don't understand their direction, ask questions. They'll be happy to clarify it for you in order to achieve the desired read.

NETWORKING: Always ALWAYS have business cards and demos within your reach no matter where you go. You never know when you're going to meet someone who works with someone who knows someone who is looking for someone with your abilities. It gives you the edge. As you're networking, it's a good idea not to be too over-the-top with the "Hi. I'm a voice-over actor" schpiel. But learn to craft your conversation abilities in such a way that you drop little hints along the way. Then if the subject turns toward that subject, be prepared to talk about your skills and talents in a concise and humble manner.

PROMOTING: You never know when you're going to have the chance to promote yourself to others, so have your schpiel prepared and ready to go. Nothing's worse than telling someone you're a voice artist, getting them interested in hearing more, and then fumbling with words to tell your story. Memorize the bullet points that best illustrate your talents and promote, promote, promote.

BRANDING: It's important to figure out how you fit into the scheme of things in the industry. Listen to the radio, watch TV, research cartoons, videogames and promos. Try and lock into "your voice" (or in some people's cases "voices"). Are you a man/woman of 1000 voices? Do you have a single, distinctive voice? Do you hear yourself as being more of a character voice? Determine what your strengths are and exploit them. Many of your better voice-over coaches will be able to help you with this.

MARKETING: Next to smiling, this is my favorite "ing." The old adage "you've gotta spend money to make money" is definitely true! There's no guarantee it will work in every instance, but if it's done cleverly and creatively it will definitely make a positive impact on your career. It could be as simple as mailing out postcards to casting directors and agents to notify them of your appearances and abilities (which you should do), or creating a website that has easily accessible information about you and your demos (which you should REALLY do). Once you've developed your brand, branch that off into marketing ideas. Once I decided I was going to be a "man of 1000 voices" I created the slogan "I used to have voices in my head, but then I got 'em all jobs." It appears on my demos, website, and promotional items. I took out a loan and had 1000 bobbleheads of myself made up bearing that slogan. I wanted to create a unique "leave-behind" to hand out to casting people, engineers, agents, etc. I still see them to this day in various studios and offices. Apparently it was a promo item that many considered just too cool to throw away.

When I sang a song for a CD which was included on Boo Berry cereal boxes, I bought a case of the cereal boxes and handed out boxes of cereal. I would bring them to sessions and hand them out to the producers. I was elated to see the production staff breaking open the boxes and eating the cereal right out of the box during the session! If there are toys released featuring characters that I've voiced, I'll buy a quantity of those and hand them out. I usually put a little sticker on the outside announcing that the character was voiced by me and where the cartoon can be seen.

One of the artists at *Family Guy* drew a cartoon of me "family guy" style for my most recent business card. I had them printed on high gloss paper, and with super vivid colors. The card has a very unique look and almost resembles a miniature animation cel. I haven't whipped out the card yet and not had the recipient say "WOW!" Again, it's about creating a unique marketing piece that is not going to be quickly thrown away, but instead will be kept around for a long time because of its attractive and interesting design. Unless you're giving out cereal, then you should eat it as soon as possible. There's a shelf life for that stuff for cryin' out loud!

Think about other "ing's" that you can apply to your own career aspirations. I'm sure you'll find many others that I didn't cover here.

JOE CIPRIANO (Hollywood, CA)
www.joecipriano.com

If you've watched any TV in the United States, you've heard Joe Cipriano! He's been the signature voice of NBC, The Fox Television Network, and The Food Network, and the comedy voice of the CBS television network. He has introduced dozens of network awards shows and provides the imaging voice for radio and TV stations around the world. He's one of only 13 voices in the world heard as Imaging voices for the major US television networks.

Finding Your Niche: Promo and Trailers

I guess by the time you reach this portion of the book you are very familiar with the notion that the voice-over business is one which is very competitive. Take heart in the fact that there are many, many facets of voice-over as pointed out in this book and no one is successful in all genres. There is an area that fits your talents and sensibilities, I'm sure.

At this point in my career I have found that I'm not in demand in the commercial or retail genre, I don't do much in the narration field nor do I do animation. My strengths lie in promos for television, TV networks, syndication and other forms of promotion. It's just one niche in the wide wonderful world of voice-over. And it's interesting how close in style or at least perceived style many of these genres are.

One would think, if you do well in promos you would probably do well in movie trailers. The intent of the product seems the same, promoting an entertainment show to a wide audience. You would think both genres utilize the same general talent pool. Surprisingly, this is not necessarily true. TV network promos require a proactive, aggressive style that reaches out and demands attention. There is a lot going on in a living room while that TV is on, especially during a commercial break. So, a TV promo not only must tell the story of the show it is promoting, it must also grab the attention of the viewer whose attention is already spread thin and in various directions perhaps by the kids, the phone, the dog, the refrigerator and who knows what else.

A movie trailer is a whole other story. First of all, the audience is in a dark and quiet theater. Phones are hopefully off, kids are hopefully quiet, the popcorn, lightly salted, is already in your hands and there is only one focus for that viewer; the big screen in front of them. There is no need to grab the attention of the viewer, they are sitting "eyes front" and ready to be entertained. So now, the art is in the story telling. A different skill, a different stage.

I often compare a TV network promo voice to a one-man-band standing on top of your television set jumping up and down if need be, working hard to get your attention so they can then tell a story about a great TV show. While the style of a movie trailer voice is much like having your seatmate lean into your ear and softly tell you a wonderful story about a land far away. A very intimate experience.

The point being in all of this . . . here are two styles of voice-over: Promos and Trailers, which are seemingly so close in general terms but are in reality widely different in performance. And the difference in styles between all genres of voice-over is so vast it's almost impossible to label it all under one name, "voice-overs." But for all of us pursuing the business, we can embrace the chasm spanning the genres because it allows all sorts of talented people to find their niche and in turn, find success.

Water is very important. I remember seeing my voice-over friend George DelHoyo carrying a bottle of Smart Water with him to sessions. Smart Water — it's a brand name but I wondered if it gave him a physiological edge over mere mortal voice-over artists. I'm kidding, it's his talent of course that gives him the edge . . . and he's tall, that helps. I always have bottled water with me during the day, from session to session, in the car in the VO booths. Liquid lubrication is good. Some folks say that coffee is bad for the voice but I don't know, I kinda like a coffee or a cappuccino at the right time, it can give you a nice dry edge in your voice when you need it for a drama read, at least for me.

Different foods and liquids affect people in different ways. I'm big into moderation and it's best to find what does and doesn't work for you specifically. And it can change too through the years, I used to find that having a cigar from time to time added a little gruffness to my voice. At some point it became more of a hoarse sound than a gruff sound. No more cigars before sessions. So, you should find what is good and what is bad for you.

RODNEY SAULSBERRY (Los Angeles, CA)
www.rodneysaulsberry.com

What do Zatarain's, ALPO, Honda Accord, Lincoln LS, Verizon, Toyota, White Castle, 7UP, Burger King, SBC, and Nestle Crunch all have in common? Rodney Saulsberry has voiced radio and TV commercials for these and dozens of other products. He is one of the top movie trailer voices in the United States and can also be heard reading Books on Tape, as a documentary narrator, as animation character voices, and as a background singer. And if that isn't enough for you, Rodney is also the author of *You Can Bank on Your Voice*.

Succeeding in Voice-over

I work in a number of areas in the voice-over industry. Therefore, I'm lucky in that I have several opportunities to get employment. My genres include Commercial, Animation, Promo, and Trailer.

Because I have success in all of these areas, I am going to talk briefly about what I believe it takes to be successful in each one of them. Let's start with commercials. This is the foundation of all the other types of voice-over work. If you are successful in this area you will definitely have a career that will sustain you.

The key to success is in keeping up with the current trends. For a long time the trend has been the ability to sound like "everyman and everywoman." This in fact is very hard to do. Because we are trained to project our voices, articulate clearly and perform. The thought of simply "saying something" seems very awkward to our technique-based backgrounds. The ability to get in touch with your natural voice and produce it at the whim of a director is what will make you an employable actor in today's climate.

Animation requires the ability to come up with a number of character voices that you can put in various situations. Do you have a great old man or woman character voice in your repertoire? Then you'd better be able to put accents and dialects on that voice. You should know how to laugh and cry in that voice. How does this character sing? How does this character voice lie or tell the truth? Be prepared to do at least two other voices that are nothing like the character you were hired to perform in a given animation session. Producers will learn in quick time that you are very valuable because of your versatility and ability to make their lives much easier.

Promo work requires the ability to present copy in a fashion that is very presentational. There are hard sell and soft sell promos that require finesse and technique that is unique to the genre. It is your job to convince the listening audience to tune in to the production you are advertising. The difference between this genre and the commercial genre is that for the most part, unless you are directed to do otherwise, you are always performing. You are putting that extra presentational pizzazz into your delivery. The ability to read copy fast and at the same time hit all of the intended beats and interpretations in the time allotted is the key to staying busy in this area of the industry. Opportunities have increased lately with the advent of pay channels and satellite radio.

Trailer work is a very exclusive field. However, there has been a move toward a more casual trailer read. In fact, the everyman and everywoman commercial read has become a trend in the trailer world. Don't get me wrong, the traditional read is still alive and well for both dramatic and comedy movies but the playing field has definitely opened up for new talent that can deliver that easy going, laid back, natural read. No longer do those of you who lack low bass voices, have to relinquish your dreams of doing major motion picture movie trailers. The fact is you can.

Some of the techniques I use when I work are analogous to a song. In other words, the script is a melody that I make up based on how I interpret the copy. Vocal ups and downs, highs and lows are a rollercoaster method that I use to color my delivery. A song has a verse, a bridge and a chorus. Scripts tend to follow that same pattern. Remember, it's not how you sound that wins the job; it's how you interpret the copy. If you think about it, there have been many versions of some of your favorite songs and yet your favorite rendition is the interpretation you like best. When you audition for a job, how right you are for the role is in the ear of the beholder, the director. Ultimately, you will be judged by your interpretation.

So forge ahead and pursue all that you are truly capable of doing. As far as demos go? If you don't have one, let your first one be a commercial demo. Any producer worth his or her salt will hear your potential for all of the aforementioned genres in your commercial demo. If you show true promise in the other areas, make a demo in those areas too.

My secret to success is simple. I practice, practice, practice which in turn makes me confident and confidence breeds success.

BOB BERGEN (Hollywood, CA)
www.bobbergen.com

The opening line of Bob Bergen's one-man show, "Not Just Another Pretty Voice," is *When I was 5 years old I told my parents "when I grow up I want to be Porky Pig." My Mother told me, "Honey you can't be Porky Pig, you're Jewish."* Today, Bob is the official Warner Bros. voice of Porky Pig and he's considered one of the most versatile character voice actors in Hollywood. If you've seen just about <u>any</u> major animation feature film over the past several years, you've heard Bob Bergen's work.

Bob has been a professional voice actor since the age of 18, working in every aspect of the business. If anyone in Hollywood knows voice-over, it's Bob Bergen.

Voice-over Demos

The biggest mistake I see new voice-over actors make is to record a demo before they are ready. Everyone wants to start their voice-over career yesterday! But one bad demo can ruin an entire career. If you send out a demo that isn't outstanding it will be close to impossible to get a second listen to a better demo down the road. People, especially agents, rarely give you a second chance. So make sure you are as good or better than what you hear on the air before producing your first demo.

Make sure your demo represents WHO you are, not just your sound. No one needs another "voice" in this business. Agents have all the "voices" they need. What they need is YOUR personality. Personality is the one thing missing from most beginner's demos. And you shouldn't try to be all things voice-over! You need to do what YOU do well. Don't attempt styles that aren't you. Your voice doesn't lie. Listen to demo reels on Voicebank.net. Check out the voice talent from the top LA agencies, such as CESD, ICM, and SBV. You'll recognize personalities behind the voices you hear. In one minute you'll know who the person is, not just the sound of their voice.

I hear students say all the time, "People always tell me what a great voice I have!" Well, there's no such thing as a bad voice! There are only good and bad actors. Your acting skills need to be honed before taking voice-over classes. A voice-over class isn't an acting class. Voice-over classes teach you how to use your acting skills to properly interpret commercial, promo, and animation copy. You'll be spinning your wheels in a voice-over class without a good solid acting foundation. Also, improvisation is great training for all performers!! If your demo doesn't represent who you are, your personality, your sense of humor, etc., in one minute, then you aren't ready to make a demo!!

LANI MINELLA (San Diego, CA)
www.audiogodz.com

Lani has been voicing and directing video games since 1992, and was a professional actor and voice talent long before then. Her voice-over credits are a Who's Who of the video game industry.

Celebrity Voices, Producers, and Impersonations

It's unfortunate for us voice talents who are not Hollywood name stars to have to continually compete with the marquis value that marketing puts on hiring Cameron Diaz to be in *Shrek* or Ben Stiller in *Madagascar*. What makes these on-camera actors able to get away with passable voice acting is the level of animation that brings their voices to life. If you close your eyes when watching a Disney movie, chances are great the voices won't seem as lively or interesting.

Instead of hiring unique new creative character voices, many producers rely on remembering who they liked in some movie or TV show and we end up doing a sound-alike of some nondescript voice of a famous actor or actress. On the plus side, this means you have more of a chance to get hired sometimes if you do impersonations, but whatever you do, don't say, "This is my Arnold Schwartzenegger impersonation," and do a mediocre one. Instead, file that impersonation under "Arnold" in your own brain and then create a new character from that basis. There's nothing worse than being labeled as a weak impersonation.

In voice acting you don't get the benefit of the Groucho glasses or make up artists to sound like a real celebrity. It's all in the voice. The real talent is when the impersonator can hold a total conversation in the celebrity voice and pull off the entire persona for a conversation with totally new words in a script.

Voice actors have to be chameleons, able to stay in character, switch to a different character or version of that character if the producer decides to change what you auditioned with. As far as whom I prefer working with, it's talent who has no trumped up attitude, who can take direction, who can cold read well and who can act or at least maintain their voice and delivery without losing energy, focus, or natural conversationality.

My best advice to anyone who wants to excel in voice acting is to practice cold reading, experiment with body and facial gestures which will alter your voice inherently and start making your own mental library of voices you find yourself coming up with, either by imitation or messing around. The more voice control you have, the easier it is for you to be that chameleon and find more opportunities in the voice-over business.

MICHAEL MINETREE (Fairfax, VA)
www.minewurx.com

Michael's been coaching voice-over talent for well over a decade and performing a lot longer than that. His approach to coaching is factual, honest, and direct. Michael tells is like it is and gives his students training designed to teach them what they need to know to work in this business.

The difference between men and women when it comes to training . . . At least when they train with me!

Not that this is a rubber stamp on the sexes saying "this is or isn't how they are." It is more an observation that I have made over the years of training voice talent. That observation is: Though everyone is nervous to some degree when they start sessions at the studio, there is something that men do much more often than women, and I wish they wouldn't . . . because there is just no need for it.

For those of you who have never met me in person, I'm kind of a man's man. I work on cars, love football, do my own construction. I'm rather handy with tools and power equipment. I'm a big guy. I'm known to show up in the studio in a football jersey and ball cap on Saturdays.

Anyway, given that description I can see how when other guys come to the studio for lessons they are occasionally struck with that uncontrollable urge to be a "guy's guy" too — and harumph-harumph their way around the studio and through the lesson and not be anything but a guy's guy for a while. I kind of expect it at first and I hope that it will fade after or during the evaluation. That way when it comes time for lessons, I'm not trying to fight through it. You see, here is the problem:

When a guy is preoccupied with being a guy rather than focusing on being a voice talent, very little actually gets done in the studio. They're afraid to make a mistake while reading the copy (making mistakes is not something a guy's guy likes to own up to, I should know). So they dance their way through the read with that John Wayne-esque "Howdy, I'm readin' copy partner, so just you sit back and listen ya' hear!" which usually sounds like anything other than the way the copy is supposed to sound.

Now we all know that this is not proprietary of voice talent, it's proprietary of guys. What that culture dictates in the voice-over studio is that guys sometimes have a hard time settling down and being OK with making mistakes in front of anyone, let alone me. I think it is also that no one wants to look silly in front of a coach. Trust me, no matter how hard you try, when you are doing something for the first time in front of anyone who has been doing it for a while, you are going to look a little silly. My job as a coach is to look beyond that silliness and get down to the core quickly, allowing a talent to find their way out of the silly phase as fast and as painlessly as possible.

When a guy is preoccupied with being a guy and not making mistakes, he is making it near impossible to direct him, and is missing the true point of voice-over coaching. I am not here to teach a person how to read every piece of copy as a guy's guy. I am here to teach them how to read the copy the way it was intended to be read and with the right attitude, inflection, pace and emotion. If the only emotion the talent is capable of demonstrating is that of a tough guy's guy, it makes it kind of hard to deliver a piece of Pampers copy.

Guys need to realize when they get into this, that no one out there is going to pay them to sound cool, or smooth, or tough unless they can demonstrate the ability to sound any of those three ways and more. Learning how to convey those three emotions or states will forever elude the voice talent who only wants to be a guy's guy. That can be a tough nut to crack when the "guy's guy" is the guy they've been listening to in their head all their lives.

Guys . . . You need to settle down, and even if it takes a lot of practice, be OK with the fact that when you begin to pursue voice over, you don't know how to do it. You can't do it without looking at the directions. You can't do it by opening the hood and looking under it pretending to know what you are looking at. You can't do it by picking it up and jumping on it and riding it until you learn how to keep it upright. You have to be shown by someone, and that's OK. You at least need to get to a point where that is OK, or you're in for a bumpy ride.

I have noticed over the years that the older, more mature men who come by the studio are much better at letting it be OK to not know how to do it. But sometimes we guy's guys just refuse to grow up.

By comparison, I have found that most if not all women who come to the studio are much more inquisitive. They want to know. They want to be instructed, if not why else would they be there? Though they demonstrate the same behavior as anyone else when they come across something they don't understand, they are much more likely to stop and ask before proceeding.

When a talent, whether they be male or female, is capable of following my instructions I can accomplish so much more in the short time we have together. I am a perfectionist in many respects and will repeatedly go over something again and again until the talent gets it right. It is part of my job to continually repeat things until they sink in because the talent may have not heard me clearly the first time, but if I am forced to do it because someone is refusing to listen to me, it is another story entirely.

Many of the women I have coached are just more willing to make mistakes in front of me sooner than men are. It is most likely because they don't have the whole machismo issue going on when they walk in the door. Women's lack of that issue expedites their learning process and sets them up to learn and retain the information I am providing faster, which in turn gives them the opportunity to soak in more.

My suggestion to men looking into this business is: When you venture out onto the path of learning voice over, be sure to select a path that you know has a guide along it somewhere. But don't worry about looking at the directions first, just wander out onto the path and start walking. (That you should be able to handle.) At some point you are going to come across that guide — and this is where I want you to make the right decision. Sit down on a log next to the guide and listen to them. Listen to everything that they say and take it all in and trust it. After all, they are the guide. They are the one with the knowledge of the pathways. Let what is in their head slowly become yours. Once they have taught you all you are capable of learning from them, get up, dust yourself off and return to your journey along the path. For then you will know it much better than you did before. You may find yourself still interested in the trees and rock formations that the guide didn't bother to mention to you, but you will know in the back of your mind that your feet continue to fall where they should.

Remember the guide and all that they taught you; their teachings may come to benefit you when one day as you are walking the path, you stop to rest and some other lost wanderer who ventured onto the path without looking at the directions comes walking up and sits down next to you. By the time they have made it that far, they will be willing to listen . . . and will be OK with letting you be right.

CONNIE TERWILLIGER (San Diego, CA)
www.voiceover-talent.com

Connie is a consummate professional and college-level voice-over instructor with more than 3 decades of experience teaching, voicing and writing commercials, working on-camera for industrials, and recording a lot of phone messaging. As a professional voice talent, working from her home studio, much of the time without a director, Connie has found it necessary to develop some techniques to break out of the ruts that can easily develop when doing the same thing repeatedly, which is typical of the Telephony work she does. Here's one of her tricks-of-the-trade.

Defrosting Your Brain . . . or How to Dig Yourself Out of a Rut

One of the biggest challenges a voice talent faces is getting a great read when there is no director around. Oh, every working talent has a few areas where they slip into what I call Voice-over Zen, where the "right" read just emerges from your mouth without much thought. But most of us still have to do some creative "self-directing" to bring out the best read. You will face this every day when you are practicing scripts — recording copy and trying your flat out best to bring it to life.

You break down the script. You figure out the key messages and copy points. Your figure out who you are and who you are talking to. You're relaxed. You mark the material. Your body begins to move as you start the recorder and you read the script — again and again and again. Five times, ten times, fifteen times — and darn if it all doesn't start to sound the same.

You have just dug yourself into a deep rut and it will be very hard to climb out of it. This is where a director comes in handy. Someone who has a fresh look at the copy. Another brain with a different set of life experiences. And the last time you looked around the room, there was no director handy.

Ah, but there probably is. And that person is — YOU. Just a different side of you. What you need to do is have another set of eyes and ears look at the copy from a new point of view. I use a few "tricks" in my voice-over classes to try to get students to find another way to read the words.

Try reading the copy as s l o w l y   a s   y o u   p o s s i b l y   c a n. I mean slooooowly... to the point where it doesn't make any sense at all. Or try reading it as if you were standing outside in a cold rain storm in your undies. Try crying your way through the entire piece of copy — with racking sobs and deep sighs. Or how about a strong accent of some sort — one you do well, without thinking about it. Do you have a really goofy character that you slip into to crack up your friends? Or someone who just escapes from you unbidden. Have that person read the copy — ad libbing around the actual words a bit — using that person's slang and speech patterns.

Do it through once with that other person or accent or completely WRONG approach. Then quickly start back at the top and read it again in the RIGHT voice and approach for the material. You should hear a dramatic difference. It should have subtle nuances and shadings that it didn't have before.

What's happening is that your brain is learning in the background. By letting your brain listen to that other person talking, it will learn more about the material. In effect, you are directing yourself into a different read.

One of the keys is to not spend any time thinking about what you did in the WRONG read. Over intellectualizing at this point will put you right back down in that rut. You've already done the analyzing when you did the copy breakdown. Just finish up the WRONG, but probably very funny, read and immediately switch gears and read the copy again using the RIGHT approach. Don't overthink at this stage.

Another quick brain unfreezer (if you do it right) is to simply say a line three times (give or take) —- digging deeper and deeper into the underlying meaning of the words and then — after the third time — continue on with the script. Your brain should be in the background giving you the high sign to continue when it finally "sounds" like a good delivery.

KATHY GARVER (San Francisco, CA)
www.kathygarver.com

Kathy Garver is perhaps best known for her portrayal of Cissy in the CBS television series *Family Affair*. She has a long list of credits including many television series and programs, theater, and numerous feature film appearances. More recently, Kathy has been working in voice-over as an actor and director for audio books.

In the Studio with Audio Books

Although I am engaged in all facets of the voice over world — one area that I enjoy most is that of Audio Books. I have both narrated and directed books for Brilliance Audio, Timberwolf Press, Listen and Live, among many others,

I recently shared an Audie Award (given by *Audio File Magazine* for excellence in audio book recording) with Amy Tan, the author of and reader for *Opposite of Fate*. Some months after the award, I was directing Amy again in another one of her books, *Saving Fish from Drowning*. Before a session, I said to her, "Isn't it great, Amy, that we won the Audie Award?" She said. "Yes. When they first called me and told me I had won an Audie, I said 'Great — a Car!'"

It is a wonderful experience recording an audio book — you are in control of all the characters, playing all the parts. When taping, numerous times narrators get "on a roll" reading merrily along — many readers do not like to be interrupted and they will continue to read no matter what.

There is an urban legend — I call it a legend because I wasn't actually there when it happened but the directors and producers at Brilliance Audio have verified its occurrence —

about Dick Hill, an excellent narrator. He is able to read numerous pages with nary a mistake and hates to stop. One day the director and the engineer decided to play a trick on him. They started dimming the light in his recording booth, but he kept on reading; they dimmed it lower, but he kept on reading. Finally when the light was almost out, they stuck in their heads to see how he could still be reading without light. They saw Dick voicing his copy — he had flicked his lighter and was victoriously reading by that tiny flame. True dedication! And a true studio story!

BETTYE PIERCE ZOLLER (Dallas, TX)
www.voicesvoices.com

Bettye Zoller is an international voice-over talent with an impressive collection of Golden Radios, ADDYS, and CLIOS. She's also an audio engineer/producer/director and recording studio owner in Dallas, Texas. For more than 30 years, Bettye has been performing and coaching voice-over talent, including some who have gone on to the Fox Channel, MSNBC, Broadway, Las Vegas, New York, and LA. She's served on several college faculties, including the University of Texas and Southern Methodist University. Bettye knows this business from both sides of the microphone. As with most pros in this business, she is eager to share her vast experience with her students so they will avoid making the same mistakes she made.

Never Count Your Chickens (make that, "Residuals") Before They're Hatched!

I was thrilled to discover, arriving at a recording session one day about fifteen years ago, that I had been chosen to announce a major, national television account. This one was "guaranteed" to pay handsome amounts of money periodically to me (as residuals). (Residuals are paid every thirteen weeks or once each year at a producer's discretion to union performers voicing spots that keep airing on radio or TV.) At the session's end, I signed the union contract presented to me by the advertising agency producer. Yes, this was a "blanket national." This was a dream job!

Happily, I hopped in my car and drove straight to a large department store and skipped up the escalator to the "house wares" department where, some weeks before, I had fallen in love with a very expensive set of bone china that I could not afford to buy. I immediately purchased the entire place service for twelve! Granted, I didn't even know twelve people to invite to a formal dinner at that time. In fact, I didn't even have money to buy *food for twelve*, but I bought it anyway! The saleswoman now was as happy as I was! She instructed me to drive to the loading dock where the precious dishes would be placed in my car.

Arriving home, as I entered my front door, the phone was ringing (this was prior to "cell phone days.") It was—guess who—my agent. She said that I was being replaced by another female voice talent on the spot I had just recorded.

"Why?" I responded in anguish. Because, according to the producer's brand new wife, my voice sounded just like his ex-wife! The producer fired me immediately!

The china was still in my car. I drove immediately back to the store and returned it. Ever since that day, I've never counted on a penny earned from my voice work until I see the money, can hold it, and can deposit it in a bank!

And some advice: Leave your "ego" at home whenever you record a voice-over spot. You're "just a piece of meat," I'm fond of saying. You're "a commodity like milk or cheese." Put things in the correct perspective. You may be talented, but you're ALWAYS replaceable! There are dozens of voices just like yours out there. It's personal service and being "liked" that counts most!

STEFAN KINELL (Sweden) — CD/28
www.artecon.se

Stefan is one of those voice-over performers you might refer to as a professional's professional. Based in Sweden, he works in every medium from commercials to industrials to web learning for some of Europe's biggest companies. The voice-over business is pretty much the same no matter what country you are in. We all face the same basic business issues when dealing with clients. Your success as a voice actor will partly be the result of how you think of yourself as a voice talent. As you listen to Stefan's demo on the CD, notice that even though you may not understand the language, you can very clearly understand the emotion and attitude of the message.

Getting Paid

You are doing voice-overs just for fun, right? The powerful feeling of hearing your voice on the radio, impressing friends, boosting your sex appeal and increasing your value on the mating market . . . if I may put it that way. When it comes to boosting your ego, riding in your car with your friends when suddenly your commercial comes on the radio is perhaps the next best thing to having a hit record in the charts or a major part in a movie.

No, seriously. When the initial flash has worn off, this is a job in an industry and basically you deliver a product. But there is one problem: you are considered an artist, and artists are expected to live on air, right? You would never dream of questioning a plumber or carpenter charging for his work, although you might groan over the bill. So stop being just an artist and start being a professional craftsman.

From time to time I get the honor of being asked how to get started in the voice-over business and how to go about doing it. My advice is to look upon it and handle it just like you would handle any other industrial production. You are a business person working in an industry, delivering a quality product.

So what are the essentials of getting paid? First, business practices may of course vary from country to country, so the opinions I express here are just from my viewpoint.

First: make sure you consider yourself and act and work as a professional in all aspects. This includes everything from handling the client and assignment to delivering the product. Remember, you are as much an "artist" as a business entrepreneur, working in an industry. What I want to say by this is that if you act and work and deliver professionally, you can also demand that the client acts the same way from his side.

Of course you also need to keep your payment routines professional, including professional-looking invoices with standard bank transfer information, etc. On the international arena, two things are essential: SWIFT information and a PayPal account. SWIFT is the name of an international bank system in which every bank has a code name, and by supplying that along with your account information, payments can (usually) be made easily from any bank account in the world to any other bank account in the world. (In the European Union, we also have the IBAN system, which is an even more automated system, allowing you to make international transfers directly via your online Internet bank at a mere cost of about a dollar and a half.)

So you do the job, deliver the product and send your invoice, or whatever input your client's payment system demands. Incidentally, US clients seem to have each their own payment routines, while in Europe it is usually sufficient with just a standard international invoice.

Now, provided you have all this ready and working, then what do you do if some client does not want to pay? One method that I have used a couple of times is to contact the end user directly, asking whether they have paid the production company that you have delivered your recording to. This is however a method that requires a certain finesse and "fingertip feel," or you will risk being considered a traitor. So be careful, do your ground work well, be correct and above all, very polite.

Always send at least one written reminder, stating what the agreement was and the reason why you should get paid: you have fulfilled your part of the deal, now you expect your counterpart to do the same. Be friendly but correct with the facts and be polite but not begging.

At one time, I called up a producer in Denmark that was a "slow payer" to ask him (politely!) when payment was to be expected. He then accidentally said that he was going to Florida for windsurfing next week . . . Hmmm . . . so he could afford that but not to pay me, I thought . . . ? On that particular occasion I called up the end user (a German company) and chatted with the general manager, mentioning the conversation with the producer. The German company manager obviously then called the producer. And two days later, payment arrived. And, of course, a really angry email from the producer where he was calling me things you would not say in church.

But, as to conclude this moralizing story, I had previously guarded myself in advance by sending at least two payment requests to the producer, so there was good and documented reason for taking action. After the incident, I let sufficient time pass to cool things off and now we are doing business again and have done so successfully for over two years. And nowadays he pays on time.

There are of course some other simple tricks. If you are just doing a short 30-second VO, first send the file with protection beeps mixed in, and after payment, send the original. Another (if a larger material) is to send 80% of the material and the rest after payment. Or simply demand prepayment. However, the last is not really recommended.

In my mind, the most reliable in the long run is to build trusting professional relationships. Handle your voice-over business just like you would handle any other industrial business operation in all aspects.

DON BARRETT (Los Angeles, CA) — CD/25
www.laradio.com

Don Barratt is an authority on Los Angeles radio. The following is excerpted from an article he wrote in February 2003 about the challenges radio DJs face when moving into the voice-over arena. If you're currently in radio, and thinking of making the move to voice-over, these two major market DJs — "Shotgun Tom" Kelly (**www.tomkellyvoiceover.com**) and Don Elliott — have some advice that is well worth reading — and heeding. You'll find Tom's trailer demo on the CD. You'll also find more than eight years of archived articles about LA radio on at **www.laradio.com**.

Making the Move from Radio to Voice-over

"I didn't want to go! I didn't want to go! I didn't want to go!" That was "Shotgun Tom" Kelly's reaction when it was suggested that he go to a voice-over workshop or an acting voice coach. After all, Tom had been pitching product during thirty years of radio and TV gigs, mostly in San Diego and for the past four years in LA while working afternoons at KRTH. "For four years, I tried to get a voice-over agent and nothing," said Shotgun.

Vanessa Gilbert, one of the veteran voice-over agents in Hollywood, can "smell a radio person a mile away." She confessed that a red flag goes up when she is approached by a radio person for representation. "Radio people don't invest in acting, they are more worried about time," said Vanessa. "Most radio people are announcers. They have no heart and no acting skills."

"Shotgun" was incensed. He didn't get it. He was working afternoons at an important Infinity station in Los Angeles and didn't like what he was hearing. "Shotgun" wanted to make the transition to voice work and reluctantly signed up for a voice-over workshop conducted by Marice Tobias. He joined ten others for a full weekend in a recording studio. "We were assigned copy and read it in front of the group. We were taught how to read what LA casting directors were looking for. We were learning a way to be a V/O actor."

Shocked at all that he was learning, "Shotgun" stepped up a level and invested in one-on-one study with Marice for six months. Every week he met with her to fine tune his voice acting skills. "It wasn't cheap, $500 for the seminar and $175 an hour for the individual training," said Shotgun.

At some stage you need a demo. "Shotgun" felt that Marice knew what should go on the demo. "When she feels you're ready, she does the demo by selecting the copy, and directing the read."

Taking direction seems to be the key. Radio people are used to doing their own spots without direction. There seems to be reluctance to take direction. "Reading what the program director wants from liner cards about the format and ad-lib on occasion doesn't prepare one to enter the competitive world of VO," said Don Elliot. "Of 40,000 registered AFTRA and SAG members here, only about 400 of us really make a living at it. Isn't that around one percent? To compete in that takes commitment, not an attitude of, 'Oh well, I'm on the radio already so they kind of owe it to me.' Yeah, right."

"For four years I knocked on doors," "Shotgun" reflected.

"Rejection after rejection. In fact, I was rejected by virtually every VO agency in town." But the "new" demo from "Shotgun" so impressed the Tisherman agency that he was signed immediately. On his fifteenth audition, he got a Yamaha national spot. "I thought I was doing horrible, but Vanessa told me that it usually takes about 30 auditions to get that first national spot." He's gone on to do an Anheiser-Busch campaign.

"Shotgun" is not stopping there. "I'm still in training," he enthused. Two weeks ago "Shotgun" graduated from the Working Pro Workshop put on by Kalmenson and Kalmenson. "I learned that voice quality means nothing. It's all about realism and attitude. We were taught to not announce the words. We have to make people believe it's real." Shotgun said this latest workshop taught him another level of expression.

"If you don't believe the resistance that agents have against radio people, ask yourself when the last time was that you ever heard a DJ on a legit national commercial?" asked Elliot. "A few of us did make the break. Casey Kasem is an exception. Ernie Anderson was an exception. Dan Ingram in New York is another."

Elliot explained that times have changed. There was a time when the phone would ring at the radio station with clients calling to do freelance, because you were exposed and if they liked your act, you'd get a direct call without an agent! "The last time that happened to me was in the 80s. It's a different world now. The reality is that you have to keep learning and honing your skills."

Don suggests that you join groups for workouts if you aren't reading every single day. Take direction as well as criticism. And persevere. "A lot of it is like a numbers game, or throwing a dart. If you lose an audition, it doesn't mean you did a bad job, someone just didn't like your read for that situation. No audition is ever wasted. You made a connection. Nurse it. Keep the networking going. Stay in touch. Go read for the blind. Lector in church. Take an improv class!"

Elliot knows of a creatively thinking general manager in LA who tried to get a morning team to stay in an improv class he paid for to hone their skills. "I think it was the Groundlings. The team walked on the arrangement. Too smart for them. Uh, they're still not doing any spots! It's actually hard to convince or tell a radio person that they have to unlearn bad habits. After all, they've been on the radio for years and are making money at it, right? So when they meet a little resistance, ego gets in the way of logic and reason. Once you can get over that hurdle, you are on your way to making your mark in the voice-over world . . . and that's one you can really take to the bank!" encouraged Don.

PETER DREW (Hartford, CT) — CD/10
www.peterdrewvo.com

Peter Drew has developed a wide variety of styles over the years. From precisely spoken medical narration . . . to mumbling (with a Western cowboy accent nonetheless!) . . . and everything in between. He has done it all to bring a script to life. Peter has voiced thousands of radio spots; TV spots; TV and radio images; narrations; infomercials; and messages-on-hold for local, regional, national, and international clients. I'll just say Peter knows what he's doing! Listen to track 10 on the CD and hear for yourself.

Trick-of-the-Trade: "Pick-ups" and "Gibberish"

I find that many producers, engineers, and talents are surprised when I do a pick up from the line before the line I fluffed. By voicing at least the last few words of the line before the line I'm picking up, the flow from the previous line into the picked up line is very smooth and natural. Don't know how original that is, but I find many people don't do it that way, they just pick up with the line they fluffed and very often you can hear that the line was edited in because it doesn't match up with the natural intensity or inflection from the previous line.

I remember getting paid quite well for not speaking well on purpose at a session I did many years ago in Cincinnati, Ohio. They needed someone to mumble with a Texas accent. I got paid for standing in front of a microphone and nattering gibberish in a bogus Texas accent. People look at me incredulously when I tell them this story . . . then they ask how they can get in on such easy money!

PENNY ABSHIRE (San Diego, CA) — CD/23
www.pennyabshire.com

Penny is one of those people who found her passion fairly late in life. Although she had been performing since childhood, she didn't discover voice-over until her late forties. Life and family had taken her in other directions — a common situation for many with a passion for performing. Her discovery of voice acting literally changed her life. After several years of training and study, she was ready to leave her job as a paralegal and move into a new career as a full-time voice talent, copy writer, and producer for commercials and other projects. Penny's creativity, stage experience, acting talent, and ability to quickly learn and apply voice acting techniques, combined with her natural teaching ability, resulted in her becoming co-instructor of The Art of Voice Acting workshops and seminars. Her teaching style and personal message are inspirational.

> **"Those who dance are considered insane**
> **by those who cannot hear the music"**
> *George Carlin, Comedian/Actor*

Ever wonder why it is that no one seems to really understand your passion for performing? That it *drives* you — that it's almost as important as air and food? At times, has it been a source of frustration for you? At its worst, has it kept you from performing?

I've always known my family thinks I am "off my nut." I'm sure I'm the one they refer to as a little *odd*. They love me, but they don't necessarily understand me. For the longest time I resented it. Couldn't they understand I wasn't crazy just because I liked to pretend? Just because I orchestrated full three-act plays in my backyard at the age of eight? Just because I liked to make up stories and characters and speak in silly voices? Something had to be wrong with them! Didn't they understand this is just what I <u>do</u>?

When I first saw Mr. Carlin's quote, it finally began to make sense to me . . . it wasn't my family's fault they thought I was strange! They just couldn't <u>hear</u> my music — the music I heard every day of my life — the music that made me a performer! Of course they thought me slightly crazy! And *viola* . . . it was suddenly very clear — I didn't understand why they were different from me because I couldn't hear <u>their</u> music!

It's just part of being human beings that makes us overly concerned with the opinions of others and it can often stop us from following our dreams. In fact, it can stop us <u>dead in our tracks</u>! If this has been the case with you, and you desperately want to perform, you have to find a way to get over it! While it's true we often perform to entertain others, the greatest drive to perform comes from inside us. We would do it even if we never got paid. It's who we are – it's what we do!

You know it's true, don't you?

One of the best ways to follow your dreams is to hang out with those who are dancing to the same music you are. Don't ask your family or friends (who are not performers) for validation or acceptance. You won't get it and it's unfair to them. They can't understand. Find a group of voice actors and talk to them, ask them questions, brainstorm! You'll have much better success, and ultimately be a much happier actor.

If you have allowed the melody of others to drown out your own, it's time to walk out onto the dance floor, lift your head high and dance to the music your heart is singing. You've been given these talents and abilities for a <u>reason</u>. What a terrible shame it will be if you don't let them shine!

How big would you dream if you knew you couldn't fail? Dream BIG! Good luck to you!

Index

LIMITED WARRANTY AND DISCLAIMER OF LIABILITY